BLACK-BROWN SOLIDARITY

BLACK-BROWN SOLIDARITY

Racial Politics in the New Gulf South

JOHN D. MÁRQUEZ

UNIVERSITY OF TEXAS PRESS ⟁ *Austin*

First edition, 2013
First paperback edition, 2014

Requests for permission to reproduce material from this work should be sent to:
    Permissions
    University of Texas Press
    P.O. Box 7819
    Austin, TX 78713–7819
    http://utpress.utexas.edu/index.php/rp-form

∞ The paper used in this book meets the minimum requirements of
ANSI/NISO Z39.48–1992 (R1997) (Permanence of Paper).

LIBRARY OF CONGRESS CATALOGING-IN-PUBLICATION DATA
Márquez, John D.
Black-brown solidarity : racial politics in the new Gulf South / John D. Márquez.
p. cm
Includes bibliographical references and index.
ISBN 978-0-292-75387-7 (cloth : alk. paper)
ISBN 978-1-4773-0216-3 (paperback)
1. Gulf Coast (U.S.)—Ethnic relations—History—20th century. 2. African
Americans—Gulf Coast (U.S.)—History—20th century. 3. Mexican Americans—Gulf
Coast (U.S.)—History—20th century. 4. Gulf Coast (U.S.)—Social conditions—20th
century. 5. Intercultural communication—Gulf Coast (U.S.)—History—20th century.
I. Title.
F296.M114 2014
305.80097609′04—dc23

                                                                2013016696

doi:10.7560/753877

IN LOVING MEMORY OF RICHARD ITON.
REST IN POWER, BIG BREDDA.

CONTENTS

ACKNOWLEDGMENTS

One never accomplishes anything in this world alone. My commitment in this book to honoring the efforts of grassroots activists for social justice originated in Baytown, Texas, long before I knew much about the life of scholars or ethnic studies and via the inspiration of former friends and neighbors. I met Gary Eagleton, Michael Wilson, and Janet Stansbury when I was still a bit of a knucklehead, and they helped steer me toward the path of social justice work in my home community, a path that exposed me to the complexities of racial politics and a process that stirred my intellectual curiosity. Ruben De Hoyos, Hilda Martinez, Arthur Martinez, Fred "Kiko" Aguilar, Laura Razo, Eva Benavides, Esther Andrade, Mercedes Renteria, Quanell X, Marga Hernandez, Rosa Rodriguez, Travis Morales, Charles Mixon, Carmen Torres, Henry Carr, Ray Wilson, Trixie Washington, Don and Wendy Messerschmidt, and Jesse Shead provided inspiration through their volunteerism and civic engagement in my hometown, making sacrifices in their daily lives to aid and defend the disadvantaged. Dennis Robbins, Dee Ann Navarre, Janie Gray, and Terry Pressley have all been helpful in Baytown during different stages of my research, as have been institutions like the Baytown History Museum, Lee College, the *Baytown Sun*, the Houston Metropolitan Research Center, the Houston Public Library, the University of Texas at Austin Library, and Sterling Municipal Library in Baytown.

The following educators and mentors have been instrumental in my journey: Mike Carraway, Karen Swart, Jim Stroud, John Britt, Mike Bass, Maceo C. Dailey, Leonard Villareal, Michael Topp, Mike Riojas, Steve Best, Ernesto Chavez, Pablo Vila, Emma Pérez, Jorge Mariscal, David Gutierrez, David Pellow, Rosaura Sanchez, and Quincy Troupe. I owe an extra-special thanks to Denise Ferreira da Silva and Yen Le Espiritu for their love, support, and patience with me and for helping me trust my voice and subjectivity. Denise has been particularly inspirational in her boldness as a thinker and writer and for the support she has shown for me as a friend and *comadre*. She has been a valued role model and inspiration.

A very special thanks to José "Cha-Cha" Jiménez and Rodolfo "Corky" Gonzáles for their inspiration and mentorship. Cha-Cha has been a political *padrino* for me, and I am eternally grateful for the time and energy he has offered in support of my evolution. He is correct in that the only people who can free us "is us." I don't think Cha-Cha realizes how important he is to many of us younger cats. I can only hope he does.

Emma Pérez, David Pellow, and Rosaura Sánchez have given me great feedback at different stages of this project, as have George Sanchez, Albert Camarillo, Laura Pulido, Kevin Johnson, Alexander Dunst, Caroline Edwards, and Martha Menchaca. Emma has demonstrated how to be fierce in thought and word regardless of who or what the gatekeepers are. Laura's and Martha's close readings and critiques of the project have been particularly instrumental. Laura's support has been especially encouraging. Theresa May of the University of Texas Press has been a superb editor. I am eternally grateful for her vision for this book and trust in me as its author. Tana Silva's copyediting has helped me make sense to myself, which is not an easy task. Thanks also to Molly O'Halloran for her fabulous maps.

My colleagues at Northwestern University have been incredibly supportive and inspirational and are a major reason for the effort I have put into making the book significant within conceptual and political debates beyond the Gulf South. Barnor Hesse and Darlene Clark Hine have been terrific mentors and have helped me find my place in this profession. Each has reminded me of the difficulty and yet importance of original thought and intellectual vision within critical ethnic studies. Darlene has inspired me in her desire to expand the significance of African American studies beyond national, ethnic, racial, and disciplinary boundaries. She keeps it real and is an exemplary coalition builder. Barnor's humor, sophisticated theoretical analyses, and capacity to link the plights of subaltern peoples across centuries and continents has been a profound inspiration. He is opening a critical space for theoretical innovation within a field that is often too urgent in its empiricism. I hope he can read his influence in the following pages, and I am very grateful for his close reading and critique of this project at various stages.

Richard Iton and Alex Weheliye have been great role models and friends, demonstrating kindness and care for my work and showing me how to navigate the relationship between political commitments and intellectual voice. Richard has been especially kind and generous to my family and me, helping us ease anxieties along the way. Martha Biondi, Sandra Richards, Dwight McBride, Ana Aparicio, Nitasha Sharma, Frances Aparicio, Mary Pattillo, Ramon Rivera Servera, E. Patrick Johnson, Aldon Morris, Sherwin Bryant, Celeste Watkins Hayes, Jinah Kim, Monica Russell y Rodriguez, Jennifer Brody, Ji-Yeon Yuh, Charles Mills, Aron Kamugisha, Merida Rua, Sharon Holland, and Lisa Calvente have all been wonderful allies and colleagues, each in his or her own way. Lisa, Merida, Sherwin, Nitasha, Martha, and Jinah have all given me excellent feedback on this project, each highlighting a different area of needed revision and consideration. Lisa has always opened a space for real talk in academe.

The support of former classmates, students, teaching assistants, and research assistants has been vital. These include Bibiano Maldonado, Ricardo Sanchez, Mark Alvarado, Shaun Ossei-Owusu, Jeff "Wonder" Yarbrough, Selfa Chew-Smithart, Cindy Fang, Desmond Taylor, Laura Manzo, Reid Spitzer, Courtney Patterson, Adam Mendel, Ethan Caldwell, Joe Jordan, Martha Gonzales, Ruth Hayes, Antonio López, Sobeida Peralta, Assata Koyayi, Pablo López de Oro, Ernesto Martínez, Denise Pacheco, Lauren Alexander, Katie Bemis, Sonia Hart, Boone Nguyen, Marisa Ybarra, Lauren Mesa, Victor Viesca, Ofelia Cuevas, Cecilia Boyd, Jean Pierre Brutus, Alexandria Gutierrez, Rafiki Jenkins, Grace Kim, Sandra Angeleri, May Fu, Tony Tiongson, and Ruby Tapia. Cindy, Sonia, Shaun, Ricardo, Joe, Antonio, and Alexandria have lent a hand to different components of this project over the years, and I am grateful for their aid. For anyone I forgot—my bad. I love y'all.

Beyond academe, the love and support of dear friends has often helped sustain me during this journey. Bo "Ski Money" Aguilar, Frankie Hildenbrand, Quino McWhinney, and Paul "Groove Galore" Kastick have been the best compadres a guy can ask for, standing with me through triumph and tragedy. Quino's moral witnessing as an artist has had a strong influence on how I detect and critique power in our world. Paul has taught me the importance of not being a wagonist regardless of the context or situation. We march to the beat of our own drums. Frankie and Bo have been in my corner since we were boys and continue to be so as men—and so, I also got ya back, homies. A special shout-out to Donald "Binky" Abraham, Manuel Molina, Kerwin McKenzie, Bubba Stark, and Joey Castillo. May you each RIP.

A special thanks to Don Martín, Don Sabas, Don Ricardo, Don Antonio, Alexis, Gio, Ronald, Machete, Chino, Sam, Big Perm, Rafa, Jacinto, Pony, Pollo, Güero, Tito, and Manuelito for teaching me the game of *futbol* at Chase Park. Nothing has been more therapeutic after a long day of writing than smashing around with you guys and running around like locos in the Chicago night.

Without a doubt, those deserving of the most of my gratitude are my family. Making my father and namesake proud and trying to fulfill his goals for the both of us has been a major motivation for this book—RIP Pops. Being a role model to Ben, my *carnalito*, has grounded me and has been a steadying force in my life—RIP BAM. My mother, Mary Lozoya Juarez, has been a tremendous inspiration for her strength, resilience, and faith. More than anyone I know, she has demonstrated the power of reconciliation and of love for humanity, qualities that have had a profound influence on how I see and explain the world around me. I want to thank my grandpa Chencho for telling me that there is no room for a clown on the rancho and for describing himself to me as a "man with no country." Dolores Corral has offered significant support, love, and encouragement. Ida's love, companionship, and patience have been my bedrock, a source of all empowerment and from which I imagine anything as possible, even amidst chaos. No human beings have ever given me more hope in humanity, happiness, good health, and strength than have my lil' bumpers, Nahuel and Necalli. Now that I am done with this project, I will have more time to hoop and play lions, birds, and Hot Wheels with you, I promise. There are so many rivers that we shall cross, and we'll never stop roaring at villains. I love you both soooo baaad.

BLACK-BROWN SOLIDARITY

HYBRID SUBJECTIVITIES

MY PARENTS ARE A CHICANO AND A CHICANA. One was born in the United States and one in Mexico. Both were raised in El Paso, Texas, a town that predates the United States and was established by Spanish missionaries and conquistadors and their Tigua-Pueblo allies who fled the Pueblo Revolt of 1680. Both my parents graduated from Ysleta High School in El Paso and were employed at a textile mill near their home that in the early 1970s was in the midst of a tense labor strike. As their economic standing became increasingly destabilized by that struggle, they decided to move with their infant daughter, my sister, a thousand miles away from the desert Southwest to the upper Texas Gulf Coast. Their destination was Baytown, a blue-collar town of roughly 50,000 residents twenty-five miles east of downtown Houston and around eighty miles from the Louisiana state line.

My parents were part of a wave of migrants to Baytown all seeking economic opportunities in its booming oil-refining industry and contributing to Houston's growth into the nation's fourth-largest metropolitan region. That wave included Latinos/as from across the U.S. Southwest as well as from Mexico and Central America, African Americans and whites from across the U.S. South, and black immigrants from Caribbean islands such as Trinidad and Tobago, Saint Lucia, and Saint Croix.

I was the first of my parents' three children to be born in Baytown. The first fifteen years of my life, my formative years, were spent in a large apartment community on Baytown's eastside built to accommodate the town's booming working-class population. African American families were the predominant residents in that community, along with a handful of Latino/a families like mine, a few black families from the Caribbean, and a few white families. The demographic makeup of my childhood community was far different from the place my parents came from, a place where the vast majority of the population was Mexican, Mexican American, or Native American.

The social climate was also quite distinct. Baytown is a quintessential southern and Gulf Coast town, established originally by European settlement and the removal or elimination of the indigenous Karankawa. It is steeped in a history of stark black-white tensions originating in the mid-nineteenth century when it was inhabited only by white slave owners and black slaves on cotton and rice plantations. My childhood apartment community was just a stone's throw from where the region's largest slave plantation once operated and near the spot where one of the region's and nation's first and largest freedmen's settlements thrived after the emancipation of slaves in Texas on June 19, 1865, still commemorated as Juneteenth.

This particular setting of black history, culture, and politics bore a strong influence on how I experienced and understood the social significance of race in ways that made me different from my parents. Like many Latinos/as, a genetic link to the black diaspora was already a part of my family's ancestry prior to Baytown, a product of slavery in Latin America. It was, however, the symbolic or discursive blackness of the South, derived from African American history—from the experiences, survival tactics, and cultural adaptations of the descendants of that region's slave population—that most strongly influenced how I have envisioned and navigated my place in the world as a boy and man of color.

The experience has made me marginally Chicano. It is also a reason that as a darker-hued Chicano I have commonly been confused by whites, African Americans, Asian Americans, and especially Latinos/as as a lighter-hued African American. The confusion, however, was more the product of performed rather than embodied signifiers of difference. My southern origins, evident in my accent, language, and other regional traits, have never been easy to conceal, even when I have attempted to do so.

I moved from the South to the Southwest in the early 1990s and later to Southern California at the dawn of the new millennium, and I now live in the Midwest, in Chicago. My *latinidad* has been scrutinized by Latinos/as in these other regions as peculiar if not inauthentic. When I was a graduate student and activist on the West Coast in the early twenty-first century, these traits were commonly a source of suspicion for Chicano/a activists. I was never Chicano enough for them, always too black to be trusted as representative of La Raza, and commonly ridiculed by Chicano friends and by family members as *negrito*, *moro*, or, in the worst case, *mayate*. I did my part to attempt to reconcile this tension by supporting Chicano/a political causes, embracing and promoting Chicano/a culture, and mimicking the speech and accents of my father and uncles, old-school Chicanos. But these attempts invariably felt like a performance, more rehearsed than natural.

A friend exposed my fraudulent Chicanismo in 2004. Trey was reared in Beaumont, Texas, another blue-collar oil boomtown in the Gulf South just up Interstate 10 from Baytown and nearer the Louisiana border. Our friendship was based largely on our similarities. Trey and I share the same phenotype and build. I am a darker-brown Latino with a Hispanic surname. He is a lighter-hued African American, a self-described French-speaking Creole with a French surname. I am not Spanish and he is not French. Our racial and ethnic categorizations are the product of overlapping Spanish, French, and U.S. colonialisms that have structured the region of our birth and upbringing. Our phenotypes are the product of intermixing Native American, African, and European genetic traits. Trey and I look so similar that we have been commonly mistaken for twin brothers, a mistake we have often manipulated for amusement. Despite this corporeal similarity, we have been assigned to separate racial categories in the United States and within its racial hierarchy, a kind of taxonomy that has been particularly significant to and in our lives. Besides those corporeal and historical similarities, what bonds Trey and me most strongly are our similar subjectivities.

This bond was manifest in a unique way in 2005, in a moment when Trey felt that I was dismissing its significance by reinventing myself as a different kind of political subject and for selfish reasons. He happened to overhear a conversation I had with a white colleague of mine in which I had described myself as a "proud Chicano." Trey interjected by asking the question, "A what?! Da hell is that?" I explained to him that despite our similar origins, I became a "Chicano" when I lived in the Southwest and California and largely through my experiences as a student and activist. In response Trey commented, "Boy please . . . you ain't nothing but a swamp nigga just like me." He was problematizing my Chicanismo.

The term "swamp nigga" contains a word that is polemical within debates regarding black politics. I am not validating it and I try not to use it. I do, however, understand its meaning, and it is a term that I commonly used among peers when I was a kid in the South. Trey's description of me as a "swamp nigga" in that peculiar moment to counter the term "Chicano" is an intriguing intervention. I knew precisely what Trey was talking about and why he communicated to me in that way in that moment, and it actually brought me a degree of relief. For one, he was bringing me home, away from the geographic settings of the U.S. Southwest and West Coast to the swampy soils of our home region. On the other hand, he was disassociating me from Chicano/a history and culture. This disassociation is not as easy as Trey perceived it to be, as my parents and extended family are indeed Chicanos/as, and hence, Chicano/a history and culture are a part of me if I choose to emphasize that particular kind of identity. Trey, however, was correct in that I was also distinct from my parents and more like him in many ways, our bond the product of shared experiences, memories, and knowledge derived from life in the southern Gulf Coast during the late twentieth and early twenty-first centuries.

In retrospect, Trey's intervention reflected the tension between traditional and organic intellectuals that Antonio Gramsci made famous in his theory of cultural hegemony—only in this case, the tension was inside me. I gained most of my knowledge about the historical and political significance of Chicanismo through Chicano/a studies courses in college. That education helped me better understand my indigenous connection to North America, my parents, and their generation in addition to conquest, genocides, borders, Manifest Destiny, and the plight of the "undocumented," all conditions that are significant to the Southwest and to those territories that Chicano/a activists call Aztlán, the ancestral homeland of Chicanos/as.

By the time I learned about this history, I had already gained a sharp understanding of white supremacy and the social meaning and significance of race. That understanding came before college, before my introduction to Aztlán, and arose from simply being a youth of color in the South, that is, from being the social type that Trey was describing me as. Baytown was the place where my parents migrated in order to fulfill their American dream. It was where they chose to start their family. Twentieth-century industrial towns and cities in the United States have often served that role for the historically disadvantaged. People migrate to those places from across the world. They are places of hope and of new beginnings.

Baytown made some things better for my parents. Jobs within the local oil- and chemical-refining industries provided them with opportunities and resources they were denied as children. My siblings and I ate better and dressed better than my parents did when they were kids, and we had access to schools with better resources. These were all signs of progress in their eyes. When I air any bitterness about conditions of inequality in my hometown, my mother, always the optimist, often reminds me, "Yes, but we have much to thank Baytown for."

I understand her perspective. She lived her entire childhood as an undocumented immigrant and as part of the peasantry of the borderlands, on both sides of the border. Both of my parents came of age during the post–World War II and civil rights era and at the start of the Cold War. They were American patriots and fully invested in its capitalist ethics. My mother recalls being inspired by President John F. Kennedy while in high school and was a youth member of the League of United Latin American Citizens in El Paso. My father was also a big JFK fan. Both were deeply saddened by his assassination when they were teenagers, sensing that it signified a lost opportunity for inclusion. My father's patriotism was always associated with a critique of communism. "A real American," my father often told me, "is willing to work hard to earn a buck."

His patriotism was very much influenced by his father, a soldier in the U.S. Army who participated in and survived the infamous D-Day invasion at Normandy Beach during World War II. My grandfather was living in Mexico in 1944 when he received a letter informing him to report for military service. He rented an apartment in El Paso just so he could enlist. Weeks later he was in France in battle against fascism and was wounded while defending his troop from a German tank attack. He died just years after returning home to his family in El Paso. My father was four years old, thus never getting to know his father very well. My widowed grandmother raised my father and his three brothers as a migrant farmworker in West Texas on a cotton picker's wages and her deceased husband's military pension.

Like so many Latino/a and African American World War II war veterans, my grandfather also had his heroism suspended. When he died in 1948 he was denied a military burial due to segregationist policies in the U.S. military during the late 1940s, a segregation that was a major impetus for civil rights activism across the South and Southwest. In December 2012, sixty-nine years after he was wounded by Nazis in France, the military posthumously awarded Private Juan C. Márquez the Purple Heart and Bronze Star medals. The medal ceremony took place at Fort Bliss in El Paso and made news headlines across the nation. A U.S. Army representative told the Associated Press, "Juan C. Marquez exemplifies the citizens our nation sent to liberate the world from tyranny."[1]

Although I never met my grandfather, his presence has loomed large in my life due to his significance to my father. My father's primary memory of his father was that he was an American hero, a man who paid his dues so his family could access the American dream. In my father's eyes, Baytown's industries provided a context for the fulfillment of that dream. He took pride in being a provider, a staunch supporter of the Democratic Party, and a blue-collar worker. He insisted on American flag decals as the only adornments on his hardhat and lunch pail. I've never met a person more patriotic.

There were things about life in Baytown, however, that were nightmarish. Baytown provided ample work opportunities but was also rife with racial tensions that originated in slavery and were normalized during the town's industrialization in the Jim Crow era. Those tensions were transposed over generations as part of the town's status quo, its social order.

The spatial and temporal lines of racial segregation were clearly drawn when my parents arrived in Baytown in the 1970s. Those tensions were pronounced in the industrial workplace, where men of color like my father had to cope with routine insult and marginalization. My parents were a Latino and Latina from the Southwest whose lives were being strongly influenced by African American history in the South.

My parents were certainly not naïve about race. They just migrated to Baytown from a place with different racial dynamics, ones that generally played out in tensions among Latinos/as and associated with the politics of citizenship and nationality, the kind of borderlands community that Gloria Anzaldúa has described as a wound that could not and would not heal, a place that will always be a grating edge of U.S. imperialism.[2] The South, their newer hometown, signified a different kind of wound, one inflicted primarily by slavery and what Saidiya Hartman describes as "its afterlife."[3] Despite how hard my parents worked, how much they contributed to the economy, and how patriotic they were, and despite the sacrifices made by people like my father's father, the South's history and social climate routinely exposed them to a kind of indignation that ultimately drove my father mad.

We all saw it coming. My father was not the kind of person who could suffer indignation in silence. He was as much the warrior as his father. His patriotism prevented him from admitting that capitalism was flawed, that the years of hard labor were not fulfilling to him in the ways that as a younger man he imagined they would be. By the time he was of late middle age, the cruelty of capitalism, its unfulfilled promises, and the multitude of hours he spent at the refinery and not with his wife and kids were wearing him down. He was depressed, angry, bitter, and impatient.

Much of his hostility was vented against persons he commonly referred to as "rednecks," stereotypical southern white men who remained explicitly dedicated to the racial segregation of old, the kind of men who flew the Confederate flag with pride and enjoyed acting like frontiersmen on their days off from work. Those men symbolized the grandest obstacle to his happiness. In his eyes, they were the primary obstacle to his American dream.

The rebellion stirred slowly, culminating in routine tensions with local law enforcement authorities that on one occasion nearly cost him his life, leaving him and us badly wounded. The rebellion ended where they so often do, in a cage alongside so many other men of color within the Texas penal system.

I was named after my father and he after his father. They were both Juan, and I am John, the name change a reflection of a common immigrant story. When I was a child my nickname was "John John," which my parents appropriated from JFK's oldest son, also a John Jr. yet another slice of Americana.

The names of my grandfather, my father, and me vary only by dialect. Our experiences have not varied by much.

Each of us has been wounded at or by wars motivated by racist ideology. I was coming of age during my father's rebellion. It all began to unfold during my late teen years. The destabilization of my family in my father's absence allowed for his anger to slowly become mine. I did not blame him for our situation. I blamed capitalism and white supremacy, two trademark characteristics of my blue-collar hometown in the South.

This was in the early 1990s, a time when local industry was in peril and jobs were less available, thus making it easier for me to disinvest in my father's blue-collar American ethos and seek an alternative way of being and knowing. I was not the only one in rebellion. The sons and daughters of those black and Latino/a men and women who came to Baytown in the 1970s to fulfill the American dream faced an unsettling horizon. They/we were full of rebellion and angst, sentiments we mistakenly too often exercised against one another in street violence.

The local police department responded with full force by declaring a "war on gangs," using our displaced anger, our inter- and intra-tribal warfare, to legitimate a kind of violent segregation that many in our town always longed for—to preserve a kind of racial status quo in the South that Clyde Woods has described as the postbellum "plantation bloc."[4] Regardless of whether one was a gang member, we were a criminalized generation of black and Latino/a youth. One need not be victimized by violence in a literal sense to have been traumatized by it. Our friends were dying, we witnessed gun violence, and some of us participated in it.

I fled Baytown in the early 1990s, scarred psychologically and physically by its street and police violence, exhausted by the routine of death, mourning, and hopelessness, and not wanting to submit to life at the refinery or in a prison cell. I ended up at a university in my parents' original hometown thanks in part to the sport of football and to a group of educators and social workers who were desperately trying to interrupt the school-to-prison or -refinery pipeline. I fled in search of answers, leaving behind my family and burdened with a load of guilt that remains. I was introduced to the paradigm of Chicano/a studies at that university.

As a result of higher education I found myself negotiating two understandings of race, one visceral and the other more academic, each more relevant to a certain space and set of circumstances. This book is the result of that negotiation, my attempt to redefine a tension as an emergent site of political possibility, a kind of complexity and diversity that is likely within all of us despite the ethnic and racial compartments to which we are assigned.

Prior to college, blackness was very much the frame through which I understood race and its effects, a frame that was particularly influenced by African American history. My firsthand exposure to black nationalism was especially significant. In the late 1980s I recall running into representatives of the Nation of Islam (the Fruit of Islam, or FOI) at various social events across Houston. On one occasion FOI members came to our apartment complex and other neighboring "hoods" in Baytown to recruit working-class black and Latino/a youths to their cause. I remember being incredibly inspired by them and yet not quite knowing what to do or if I should join them. I was too young to decide. It was my first exposure to men of color wearing sharp suits and speaking with a sophisticated intelligence about things that I felt deeply—a fear of police officers, neglect by the public school system, the trauma of rampant drug and alcohol abuse in our community, the horrors of gang violence, the shame of poverty and of being dark.

Soon thereafter I read *The Autobiography of Malcolm X*, a book my father, an avid reader, bought for a dime and brought home from his monthly trip to a bookstore in Baytown. I remember him telling me, "Mijo, this guy's story is interesting. It gives you a different point of view of life in this country." It did indeed. I vividly understood the kinds of psychosocial obstacles Malcolm described in his journey from being a boy to a man of color in the United States. Perhaps my father anticipated this and used Malcolm's narrative as a method to help him open my eyes to race and racism in this country. I was of darker hue than he, and my understanding of such matters might vary from his, a variation enhanced by my being reared in the South, where anti-black racism was particularly prominent and to an extent carried over to harm us as Latinos/as as well. Pops is no longer around for me to ask him more about his intentions. *Que en paz descanse.* I more than appreciate his efforts, all the subtle ways he guided me as a young man in this world.

The inspiring presence of the FOI and Malcolm X's influence were reinforced by Rastafarian men in my neighborhood. Their families had migrated to Baytown from the Caribbean during the 1970s in search of oil-refinery jobs. I recall that my sister and I were awestruck by the presence of rastas. On some long, hot summer days we would sit, often for hours, in our second-story bedroom staring out our window and anticipating when the rastas would walk by. Their linguistic patois, long dreadlocks, and vivid critiques of Eurocentrism made them seem like black superheroes in a world that reduced youths of color like us to social problems and offered little sense of empowerment beyond jobs at the local refinery, gang life, or athletics.

There was plenty of *latinidad* or Chicanismo within our home, evident in the food we ate, in the *pachuco*-tinged borderlands Spanish (Caló) that my parents spoke to one another, in our Mexican Catholicism, and in other ethnic customs. That private *latinidad* was not generally reflected in the public domain. Most of my peers at school were either black or white, and all my classmates from our apartment community were either African American or the children of black Caribbean immigrants, people we called "island folk." There was certainly no attention paid to Latino/a history or culture in the public schools I attended, schools named after white men who were the original slave and plantation owners in Baytown, heroes from the Texas war for independence, or Confederate war heroes. The most famous Latino/a civil rights leader, César Chávez, was an unknown figure to me until I enrolled in those aforementioned Chicano/a studies courses in college. When I first heard of him I thought one of my favorite professional boxers, Julio César Chávez, had retired from the sport and was now working as an activist on behalf of immigrant rights. My maternal grandfather would tell me stories in Spanish about Pancho Villa and later when my grandfather worked on a ranch, but my deficiency in the Spanish language caused me to misjudge or discount Villa's significance. I often assumed that Villa was just another colorfully criminal friend of the family who might spontaneously show up at the next wedding or funeral.

Che Guevara was the closest to a Latino/a political hero I knew about during my childhood in Baytown, and even then, I assumed he was black. Initially I believed he and Bob Marley were the same person: the first image of Che that I came across was a cartoon interpretation on a T-shirt sold at a local record store. The shirt was displayed near the "world music" section at Evolution Tapes and Records where images and albums of Marley proliferated. Even after I learned that Che and Bob were not the same person, I still thought the former was a reggae music singer due to my general ignorance of Latin American history. I didn't know what tune Che sang, but Bob's tunes pulsated through the thin walls of the apartment community where I lived, the deep and melodic bass lines of Aston "Family Man" Barrett, Marley's bassist, often rattling our pictures on the wall. Marley's songs about mental and spiritual emancipation appeared to inspire residents of our community in profound ways.

My pre-college knowledge of Latino/a history was thin. I, however, was well versed in the significance and biographies of persons such as Fredrick Douglass, Dr. Martin Luther King Jr., Marcus Garvey, Malcolm X, Louis Farrakhan, and Thurgood Marshall. I learned as well about influential elected officials like Barbara Jordan and Mickey Leland who had participated in Houston's considerable African American civil rights activism. Much of my knowledge of black history and politics came from curricula of the local public schools. Most of it, however, I learned from just living in the South in a poor and predominantly African American neighborhood. I knew more about local freedmen's colonies established in the 1860s and 1870s than I did about any historic barrio or pueblo in the Southwest, even the one my parents were from.

Artists like Bob Marley, Marvin Gaye, James Brown, Parliament-Funkadelic, Public Enemy, N.W.A., Ice Cube, X Clan, and the Geto Boys provided the images and words I would appropriate in learning how to cope with racial injustices. I was very much of the hip-hop generation, an avid participant in this culture when it was based on improvisation, turning scraps into art pieces, blurring gender lines with our fashion and hairstyles, using our bodies as musical instruments that called truth to power—the language and domain of poor or working-class youths of color prior to its acquiring the name "hip-hop" and prior to its commercialization, prior to the Beastie Boys and its evolution into pop culture. The gangsta-rap group N.W.A. was particularly influential to me in the 1980s, my formative years, as a result of growing tensions between my community and the Baytown Police Department, namely in its "war on gangs." In addition to Malcolm X's autobiography, N.W.A.'s song "Fuck the Police" captured everything I knew and felt about being racially profiled by law enforcement agents, educators, and other authority figures, about feeling susceptible to marginalization and state-sanctioned violence simply because of how I looked or where I lived. When N.W.A. member Ice Cube rapped "young nigga got it bad 'cuz I'm brown," I knew exactly what he meant. The "brown" signified an experience that was not unique to blacks or Latinos/as but reflected a certain kind of unsettling and anxiety-ridden vulnerability, an expendability derived from the production of brownness as a signifier of deficiency and criminality. The signification originated from a set of historical and contemporary circumstances associated with the settler-colonial society and the moment we were born into, an experience that made Trey and me feel like brothers, that made me feel like a younger brother to Ice Cube, even though we had different parents, ancestries, and ethnicities. We indeed had had it bad because we were darker and lighter shades of brown, and that badness and brownness bonded us all—at least in my imagination.

BLURRING BLACKNESS, BROWNNESS

Building on Trey's intervention, his blurring of the border between black and Latino/a subjectivities, and the inspiration of gangsta rappers like Ice Cube, in this book I examine the historic and contemporary circumstances that have produced recent fusions of black and Latino/a subjectivities in the Houston metropolitan area. Some of those fusions have resulted in expressions of political solidarity or collective resistance of the two groups, a counterhegemonic assemblage. In this interdisciplinary study I analyze expressive cultures, ethnographic data, popular media, historical archives, oral histories, legal documents, and theories about racial power to argue that Houston's location on the southern Gulf Coast and its history as a region shaped by racial dynamics of the Old South have created a condition through which blacks and Latinos/as have shared a common experience as targets for state-sanctioned racial violence and numerous other forms of discrimination.

That shared struggle has produced a wariness of racial power—or a subjectivity—that often bonds the two groups together politically. These bonds are evident across a diverse discursive terrain including recent grassroots, activist, and antiracist movements in Houston-area communities like Baytown, in youth gangs, and within expressive cultures such as hip-hop. Blackness—in this case, as more a symbolic than embodied difference—has served as an important adhesive in that bond because of what I argue to be its function as a universal signifier of opposition to whiteness from which Latinos/as often draw strength.[5] Blackness, however, also attains this influence due to the role popular culture has played in advancing black politics and due to misconceptions about the origins of Latino/a, Asian American, Arab American, and Native American histories.

Before exploring the ways black and Latino/a subjectivities have been in dialogue, the importance of race in their constitution needs to be scrutinized. Critical race theorists Barnor Hesse and Denise Ferreira da Silva have shown that race has been a central characteristic of European modernity, a language and knowledge form produced to undermine the promise of universal rights of modern, liberal nation-states and to enable white privilege.[6] This certainly has been the case in the United States despite its being commonly mythologized as a flagship for egalitarianism in the world. The definition and self-definition of U.S. political groups as racial or ethnic draw attention to these contradictions and the lingering effects of slavery, imperialism, and settler colonialism. Such conditions deserve recognition in any discussion regarding subjectivities within the United States and especially as they pertain to the phenomenon of racial politics.

The concept of "subjectivity" here varies from that of "identity": the latter is a more common term used to describe how oppressed groups relate to oppression. Identity is a static concept suggesting a fixed and homogeneous social consciousness unable to maneuver through time, circumstance, and discursive schema. The concept of subjectivity complicates this description and the presuppositions that structure its political significance or meaning. "Subjectivity" is a term that was introduced by Michel Foucault as a critique of neo-Marxist conceptualizations of the relationship between the state and ideology by Antonio Gramsci and Louis Althusser.[7] While the term "identity" is used to fix a gaze upon the oppressed in order to understand relations of power, Foucault developed the term "subjectivity" to call critical attention to oppression itself and to a wariness of power within the psyches of individuals in society. This wariness is irreducible to a "modes of production narrative" and instead reflects an array of oppressive or controlling conditions, disciplinary processes based on the meanings ascribed to bodies, spaces, and behaviors and the normative discourses and social categories in which they are situated. Foucault describes these processes as "subjectification," also commonly referred to as "subjection," a condition or modality of power that is also a component of what he has called "governmentality" and that, more importantly, generates subjectivity in discrete ways according to time and space.

Although race was never central to Foucault's conceptualizations, they are still useful for understanding the effects of subjectification on the domain of racial politics in modern nation-states. Kelly Oliver has effectively argued the importance of scrutinizing subjectivities in debates regarding oppression within colonial or postcolonial formations.[8] Likewise, subject positions cannot be delinked from subjectivities if one is truly interested in unveiling the ways any form of oppression, and more specifically those forms that qualify as violently traumatic, shape the agency and imagination of the oppressed and ultimately influence the multiple ways they produce and perform racial politics in the public realm. An analysis of subject position without critical scrutiny of how the psyche interprets and shapes behavioral responses to injustice results in a depiction of the other or subaltern as a mere artifact of victimization and not as an active agent who participates in and often restructures the domain of politics. Oliver explains that subjectivity "is experienced as the sense of agency and response-ability constituted in the infinite encounter with otherness—the realm of ethics. And although subjectivity is logically prior to any possible subject position, in our experience, the two are always interconnected."[9]

Considering such an interconnection, my primary goal in writing this book is to demonstrate how collective memories of similar forms of subjection have functioned as an imaginative adhesive that often bonds the subjectivities of two racial subject positions, black and Latino/a, resulting in a compound subjectivity as well as a transracial and transethnic subject position from which blacks and Latinos/as can and often do collectively engage in new forms of resistance. These compounds have become more frequent due to demographic shifts caused by the global political-economic demands of neo-liberalism often referred to as "globalization" and the broader assortment of time and space compressions neoliberalism has produced. Neoliberalism has intensified the rate at which information is exchanged and the transnational immigration patterns from the global South to the global North. It has initiated new patterns of residential segregation in cities in the urban North within which many immigrants from the global South have taken up residence as neighbors of existing minority groups.

It is estimated that up to a third of the human population is currently in motion or engaged in the process of migration across national borders. The current massive flow of people across borders—despite the militarization of borders in the global North to prevent it—represents the largest and most intense migration of human beings in world history.[10] It is, moreover, a condition that has been produced by an assortment of displacements associated with neoliberal and global capitalism, or what David Harvey has described as a post-1970s "regime of flexible accumulation."[11] People are leaving Latin America, the Caribbean, Africa, Asia, and the Middle East in record numbers, and their arrival in cities across the United States, Canada, and Europe is reconfiguring the social and political climates of their new home spaces.[12] These structural changes have been enhanced by advancements in information technologies during the late twentieth and early twenty-first centuries that have amplified transnational, intraminority, and interminority conversations if not understandings.

In the Houston area the Latino/a population has grown fast since the late 1970s due in large part to increased immigration from Latin America.[13] Working-class Latinos/as have often linked themselves to U.S. black oppositional cultures, and to memories of anti-black racism in the U.S. South in particular, to cope with having their own civil and human rights suspended within that region. My scrutiny is conducted within the context of the rapid growth of the Houston area's Latino/a population in the late twentieth and early twenty-first centuries, and I also pay special attention to deeper historical patterns and processes that pertain to the region's black and Latino/a communities.

In this book I examine how, concurrent with the more recent growth of the Latino/a population, working- and middle-class blacks have often incorporated Latino/a causes, persons, communities, and acts of anti-Latino/a injustice into their critiques of racial inequality. There is evidence that blacks have envisioned the increased presence of Latino/a immigrants and Latino/a population growth at large as an opportunity to destabilize the hegemonic influence of whiteness to unprecedented levels in communities within which they have been struggling against racial injustices for significantly longer than have their newer Latino/a neighbors. Rather than being seen as a condition that weakens or dilutes black politics, Latino/a growth is often seen as a condition that strengthens and expands it. As Latinos/as have increasingly fallen victim to conditions that have long been defining characteristics of the black experience, blacks have taken these instances, along with the increased size of the region's nonwhite population at large, as offering more compelling evidence of the moral and ethical crises that have been imposed and sustained by the normative discourse of white supremacy.

Within those visions and political strategies lie fusions of subjectivity and overlappings of subject positions that call attention to the similar space that blacks and Latinos/as have occupied in the racial hierarchy, or what Michael Omi and Howard Winant might describe as the "racial formation," of the Houston area.[14] These fusions illuminate the influence of black history and culture on the subjectivities of nonblack yet also nonwhite peoples. This influence is important considering that African Americans now comprise a shrinking percentage of the U.S. polity, while the Latino/a population continues to increase through immigration and birth rates. It is important to note that immigration from the Caribbean, mainly Jamaica and Haiti, and from Africa, primarily Ethiopia and Nigeria, has been the major impetus behind black population growth in the United States over the past two decades.[15] These more recent transnational realities tied to late global capitalism necessitate that we, now more than ever, look beyond the black-white binary when assessing the social meaning of race in the United States, as that binary often limits our focus to relationships between African Americans and whites in singular locales. I map out a new terrain here, underscoring the expanded political significance of African American history beyond African Americans and providing a serious theoretical scrutiny of the conditions that have made that history so influential in debates about race, an influence that has often resulted in the histories of Latinos/as, Asian Americans, and Native Americans being neglected.

Lastly, I focus on the fusions of black and Latino/a subjectivities that complicate how the subjectivities of those two groups tend to be analyzed and politicized. Both in scholarly and media discourse, these subjectivities are generally viewed as a product of "majority-minority" and "intraminority" relationships, while relationships between minority groups and those relationships forged by dynamics that transcend and travel across national borders are given less attention. This limited scale of inquiry frequently discounts what Avery Gordon has described as the "complex personhood" of the oppressed.[16] With that term Gordon seeks to complicate the popular perception of the oppressed as mere artifacts of victimization by accentuating how the oppressed fabricate complex narratives of coping, survival, and resistance that reflect the social agency they retain despite their aggrieved conditions and reflect spatial and chronological specificities. In sum, the oppressed or historically disadvantaged retain the ability to shape how they see and are seen by the rest of the social world despite how others may perceive them to be. This happens through the multiform narratives and political imaginaries they enact to respond to multiform experiences of oppression.

Gordon's term "complex personhood," then, represents a contrast to the condition that Homi Bhabha has referred to as "imaginative fixity."[17] "Complex personhood" calls attention to an array of effects produced by oppressive conditions. Bhabha, on the other hand, defines "imaginative fixity" as a debilitating representation and controlling image of the subaltern similar to the concept of "identity" that is "dependent on the concept of fixity in the ideological construction of otherness."[18] As it applies to my analysis of black and Latino/a subjectivity, an imaginative fixity discounts or even disregards the ways the multiform cultural performance of blackness and the unification of black and Latino/a politics become the dominant catalysts for a subjectivity that transforms blackness from a marker of racial oppression into an inclusive formation that decisively transcends the racial boundaries of its original denotation.

This position regarding the relationship between Gordon's "complex personhood" and the dynamism of racial subjectivity is inspired by and reminiscent of arguments advanced by Bhabha, Stuart Hall, Paul Gilroy, Nestor Garcia-Canclini, Gloria Anzaldúa, and Walter Mignolo regarding the notion of hybridity, the symbolic blurriness and structural rigidity of borders, both literal and figurative, or "hybrid cultures" within debates about multiculturalism and postcolonialism across the global North. In the work of these scholars, the abilities of individuals assigned to subaltern groups to draw from an array of knowledges, experiences, and epistemologies in the constitution of their subjectivities make the individuals less manageable by colonial powers. Similar to interventions in the field of queer theory, hybridity thus creates new visions of and for social change and even an alternative ethics that resists the normative discourses controlled and manipulated by the state and enables the oppressed to cope with and often resist oppression. Hall, for example, describes these fusions as "new ethnicities" that are reshaping our understanding of racial and ethnic politics across the global North in particular and within the context of the conditions associated with neoliberalism.[19] "In late modern times," he explains, "identities . . . are increasingly fragmented and fractured; never singular but multiply constructed across different, often intersecting and antagonistic, discourses, practices and positions."[20] As a result, Hall argues, monolithic or static representations of identity (or presumably even of subjectivity) should be avoided in favor of representations that reflect chronological, discursive, and geopolitical specificities.

This hybridity is not to be confused with conditions of racial blending, the *mestizaje* or *mestiçagem* that is commonly cited as a condition of embodied racial complexity in Latin America. Within that representation, a sense of political solidarity or resistance across racial lines is routinely presupposed as inherent to political subjects because they derive from a genetic mixture of Native American, European, and African progenitors. The kind of hybridity I examine here is not a corporeal or genetic one; in fact, it conflicts with the popular idea that a recent increase in biracial births is destabilizing the stress on rigid racial uniformity that has characterized U.S. racial order from the outset. By contrast, the hybridity that I privilege is one that springs from shared forms of subjection and that is manifest in subjectivities. This hybridity reflects how shared memories, wariness, experiences, and desires often bond subaltern groups across those racial, ethnic, and even national boundaries that the state and its legal apparatuses have erected to exert control over how race is politicized. Those bonds among subaltern groups or blends of their subjectivities do not represent resistance in and of themselves. However, these bonds often result in a type of collective consciousness or hybrid subjectivity that is capable of unsettling the racial/colonial architecture that remains fundamental to or foundational within modern states across the global North and despite postcolonial or postracial proclamations. Edward Said explains that Europe discovered itself through colonial encounters. The sovereignty of modern social formations or nation-states required the creation, categorization, and policing of difference.

Hybridity theory, put simply, suggests a kind of complex personhood that retains the potential to disrupt such categorization and/or colonial assemblage. It refers to a politics of self-determination that conflicts with the political recognition sanctioned by colonial authorities, meaning it grates against a kind of representation that is designed primarily to remind the subaltern of his or her perpetual deficiency and political inefficacy. As Said contends:

> No one today is purely one thing. Labels like Indian, or woman, or Muslim, or American are not more than starting points, which if followed into actual experience for only a moment are quickly left behind. Imperialism consolidated the mixture of cultures and identities on a global scale. But its worst and most paradoxical gift was to allow people to believe that they were only, mainly, exclusively, white, or Black, or Western, or Oriental.[21]

This hybridity is not to be confused with what is often described as "multi-culturalism" or the normative management of "unity" that characterizes much of the post–civil rights discourse regarding racial or ethnic diversity in Europe and the United States. Liberal multiculturalism is a mere discursive reconfiguration that has had little or no effect on the structural force of race. Rather, it reproduces the existing hierarchy under a discursive guise and maintains a sense of ethnic (Eurocentric and Anglo American) if not racial (white) uniformity as the foundation to which effects of "difference" are merely added as afterthoughts. As Manuela Ribeiro Sanches explains, "Unity defines itself against hybrid spaces. The concept of hybridity is significantly absent from Eurocentric discourses, which tend to promote an idea of diversity understood as the addition of new cultures rather than innovative ways of thinking about and living with difference."[22] Applying this critique to my focus on black-Latino/a hybridity in the United States, I am not making a case that Latino/a causes have been merely added onto political debates and civil rights discourse regarding racial inequality that are generally limited to black-white tensions and are popularly perceived as more central and significant to the U.S. political culture. To regard Latino/a causes as merely an addendum, an appendage to racial politics, belatedly and only recently added onto more important ongoing conversations, would be to discredit the dynamism and complexity of Latino/a history in the Houston area and more generally.

To be sure, Latinos/as did not arrive in the Houston area only recently, and many of them are not immigrants from Latin America. They have an extensive history there beginning in the early twentieth century, and they have developed their own methods of survival and resistance to racial injustices over time. But it is also true that throughout most of the nineteenth and twentieth centuries, Latinos/as were a much smaller group than were blacks, and anti-black racism was the most rampant and influential condition structuring the climate of racial politics in the region. This arrangement was true up until around the late twentieth century, when a surge in immigration from Latin America and consequently a rapid growth of the Houston area's Latino/a population stirred an increase in anti-Latino/a racism by those who were dedicated to maintaining a status quo of white privilege. Much of this increase was made visible through a rise in anti-Latino/a police brutality, a specific condition of oppression that is privileged in this book's analysis. The Houston area's urban development can be narrated as having originated in stark black-white tensions but then extending into tensions of black and Latino/a versus white, a proliferation that has placed black and Latino/a subjectivities in closer proximity to one another.

As a result of this history and symbolic compression of subjectivity, the area has produced its own hybrid subjectivities that destabilize, disrupt, and complicate much of the conventions through which subaltern lives are analyzed, understood, and even politicized and that tend to destabilize the existing racial hierarchy. Similar to what Bhabha, Emma Pérez, Walter Mignolo, and Nelson Maldonado Torres have argued regarding decolonial knowledge, the hybridity that I privilege in this book calls attention to new political possibilities, emergent political cultures and languages, changing interpretations of existing terms and categories, and fresh engagements of racial politics for both groups.[23]

Decolonial knowledge is a system of representation or counterhegemonic discourse in emergence. It is dynamic, improvisational, and produced by detecting, exposing, and subsequently naming the sustained horrors of white supremacy in the United States. Decolonial knowledge represents a space of emergence and untapped potential. It represents a response to Fanon's driving question of "In reality, who am I?"—a question that derives from the alienating effects of settler-colonial formations, that is, from the ways such formations depend upon condemning subjections and concurrent imaginative fixities that dislocate the subaltern from himself or herself. Self-determination, the capacity to define who we are, how our subjectivities spill over the compartments designed by the state to harbor or segregate them, how we envision and speak about relations of power based upon our own sets of complex memories and experiences, does not represent resistance per se. But it does call attention to conditions from which new forms of resistance can and will emerge. Hybrid subjectivities are a component of decolonization in how they unsettle and destabilize the protocols through which social truths, categories, and processes are sanctioned and thus through which settler-colonial formations are disciplined and controlled.

This book is then a narrative of decolonization that highlights how shared and often traumatic memories of discrimination have provided the impetus for black and Latino/a imaginations and subjectivities to amalgamate and mutate in the production of decolonial critiques of racism. Hip-hop culture, grassroots activism, and even youth gang culture have often provided the space for such mutations, resulting in new expressions of racial knowledge and politics that complicate conventional conceptual models for assessing the social meaning of race.

There are specific types of oppression that I feel are particularly generative of these mutations. While they may not fit neatly within debates about colonialism or postcolonialism, the examples of hybrid black and Latino/a subjectivity that I accentuate are the product of an interdependent cultural, political, and economic oppression that Foucault famously has described as the productive capacity of contemporary biopower.[24] However, the lived experience and cultural-political expressions of these positionings that I describe as a fusion of black and Latino/a subjectivities speak to a transindividual subjectification that constantly overruns the grasp of such biopower. Their fusion should be understood, in Michael Hardt's more pronounced contemporary distinction, as the product of "biopolitical militancy."[25] The term critiques a normalized and deeply entrenched regime of institutionalized and disciplinary mechanisms of oppression, a determined and comprehensive surveillance of deviance from sovereign authority within modern liberal states across the global North. Such a regime has been buttressed by an omnipresent threat of combined police and military violence since the 1980s that should be considered part of the broader reconfiguration of the global and neoliberal political economy.[26]

The 9/11 tragedy has played a significant role in exacerbating biopolitical militancy to the extent that theorists including Giorgio Agamben, Henry Giroux, Jacques Derrida, and Foucault, in newly published lectures, have called attention to a shift toward a new form of global authoritarianism or even the advent of protofascism characterized by new suspensions of civil liberties, the further blurring of the lines distinguishing military control from law enforcement, and the deployment of hypersurveillance by the neoliberal state that is directed primarily at subaltern populations.[27] Claudio Colaguori has referred to this as the origination of the "hypersecurity state," and Gilroy has more recently referred to it as "securitocracy."[28]

In the United States this protofascist turn has only exacerbated the disparaging meanings ascribed to the bodies and behaviors of blacks and Latinos/as as a method to segregate them within the settler colonial architecture. The most evident result has been the mass incarceration of people in these two groups in particular and their frequent obliteration as a consequence of "zero tolerance" wars on gangs, immigration, and urban crime since the late 1980s.

Most of the persons described in this book are either Mexican American or African American. And yet the forces that I find to be influential on hybrid black and Latino/a subjectivities have also structured the experiences, memories, and subjectivities of black and Latino/a persons from the Americas and Africa who reside in the Houston area and beyond. Consequently, I generally opt for the terms "black" and "Latino/a" in this book to accentuate an oppressive articulation of racial power, a kind of subjection, a modern knowledge form that functions without much regard to ethnicity, nationality, or even class. As mentioned and for added clarity, the definition of "race" that I use in this book is most influenced by Denise Ferreira da Silva and Barnor Hesse, who consider race to be a defining attribute of European modernity that produces and is produced by a collective desire to identify difference in bodies, spaces, and behaviors.[29] Race, in this conceptualization, is irreducible to a mere social construction that is produced to justify conditions of economic exclusion or political marginalization. It is also irreducible to a mere corporeal or primordial category of human difference. Instead, race is modern social knowledge itself produced to generate conditions of inequality primarily in its capacity to inflict and justify death, in union with other categories of difference that attain a disciplinary power.

ETHNIC COMPARTMENTALIZATION

One condition I specifically seek to complicate in this book is the general tendency of scholars and media analysts to perceive black and Latino/a subjectivities or even identities as inherently separate and subject only to majority-minority or intraminority influences. I describe this limitation as "ethnic compartmentalization." I use this term to specify how much of our knowledge about race in the United States has been fragmented into a series of parallel, vertical, and seldom intersecting binaries between whites and certain nonwhites whose experiences are generally encapsulated by an ethnic signifier that is harbored by national borders: African American, Mexican American, Hispanic, Puerto Rican, or Latino/a.

Compartmentalization largely results from the racial power movements of the 1960s when group histories and causes were essentialized through the language of cultural nationalism to gain visibility amid a diverse assortment of minority-rights initiatives in the United States. African American studies and Latino/a studies are themselves academic interdisciplines born from this activism, and activism has in turn significantly influenced the ways subjectivity is analyzed in these studies. In sum, African American and Latino/a studies originated with the responsibility of recouping lost racial histories and representing the subjectivities of subaltern populations that had long been neglected in critical media and scholarly discourse.

The political purpose and design of these fields, therefore, has something akin to a built-in propensity toward statism and ethnic uniformity and a somewhat limited capacity for analyzing and theorizing of race across national borders and racialized groups. The existence and purpose of each relies upon accentuating the uniqueness of the designated ethnic group, upon a politics of recognition, with less attention to forces that make them less than exceptional. Conditions like hybridity, the result of amalgamated subjectivities catalyzed by a shared susceptibility to racial oppression, are then routinely discounted or even ignored in expert analysts' discussion of the social meaning of race. The emphasis has been on single-group representation.

One can read this influence across the literature produced within each field. For most of the 1970s and 1980s, for example, black and Latino/a subjectivity was generally represented by academics via the image and perspective of a nonwhite, working-class, heterosexual, male activist or victim who represented a clear antithesis to white slave drivers, colonizers, conquerors, or statesmen. Much of the "movement" historiography—books published from the late 1960s into the 1980s on the civil rights and racial power activism of the mid- to late twentieth century—can be characterized as such. The literature tends to reflect worlds within which only African Americans and whites or Latinos/as and whites reside and privileging the perspectives of heterosexual men.[30] Certainly a history of rigid segregation helped to implant and standardize these analytic frameworks, resulting in real demographic binaries.

The lives of the subaltern, however, have always been far more complex and dynamic, and their communities generally have been far more diverse. Neoliberalism has only intensified this dynamism and complexity. In the late 1980s scholars working within African American and Latino/a studies began to break up that uniformity by means of intraminority foci as they paid more critical attention to class, gender, and sexual divisions within minority groups.[31] They also began to highlight transnational dynamics that challenged the boundaries of ethnic nomenclature.[32]

However, the critical edge of these fields seems to have paused there. In the field of African American studies, black subjectivity continues to be generally assessed on how it is shaped by relationships among African Americans and whites, African Americans and other African Americans, African Americans and Africa, and African Americans and a black diaspora that spans centuries and continents. While these perspectives continue to raise critical awareness about black history and politics and about black people the world over, not much attention is given to how relationships of blacks (be they African American or not) and their Latino/a neighbors, classmates, and co-workers affect their subjectivities and hence the ways they engage in racial politics on a local level.[33] This limited perspective undermines the dynamism and complexity of black subjectivity and curtails an understanding of black politics. Additionally, knowledge about racial phenomena, abilities to heal traumas wrought by white supremacy and settler colonialism through the production of new knowledge and political visions, and an ability to draw attention to the grounds for more progressive interminority alliances are all limited by what Sharon Holland describes as "subconscious machinations to disremember a shared past," which she cites as a characteristic of the "American political imaginary."[34]

More recently, the field of critical ethnic studies has been developed as a challenge to this and other limitations of "ethnic compartmentalization." This new paradigm focused attention on the existence of hybridity by looking across and beyond ethnic and national boundaries to gauge the social meaning of race in modern social formations and by comparatively linking histories of violent oppression in particular as a comprehensive critique of European modernity. The critical ethnic studies paradigm made racial subjection and subsequent oppression, rather than any particular racialized and ethnic minority group or human subject, a central object of inquiry and paid better attention to regional and chronological specificities in addition to structural and symbolic shifts associated with neoliberalism in the late twentieth and early twenty-first centuries.[35] This turn reflected Hall's suggestion that racial dynamics are best understood as producing a "politics of representation" rather than as evident in "relations of representation" between minority and majority populations.[36] Hall's intervention asks us to envision identity or subjectivity as produced within historically and geographically specific configurations of representation and discourse rather than as something that in itself produces those phenomena.

This point of conceptual departure is reflected within the critical ethnic studies paradigm in that it looks less at who a race or racial group is, what its "identity" is and/or its particular interests, and more at what race does to the social world, how it fragments one's subjectivity internally, how it produces categories of being and differential experiences with what are designated as "rights," how it produces space, how it allocates people to categories and spaces, how people inhabit those categories and spaces, and what they do to manipulate their meanings in performances of racial politics. While it is more common, for example, to examine how Latinos/as produce or engage in politics, it is also vital to understand how racial politics produce Latinos/as and their subjectivities within a much more expansive matrix of power and epistemologies. The critical ethnic studies approach, in its gaze away from the racialized human subject (the victim of racism) and toward the productive and disciplinary power of race and its consequences, allows us to better understand how race works in union with other discursive practices to structure hierarchies, systems of dominance, categories, identities, and subjectivities that can be unique according to time and space. Considering this, as the goal of previous generations of African American studies or Latino/a studies scholars has been to delink race from biology, the goal of new and future gen-

erations of scholars working within these fields has been and must be to further delink race from ethnic categories, from a corporeal gaze, and from geopolitical boundaries such as nations in order to more critically comprehend its
salience, that is, the ways race structures social life.[37]

In the United States this type of transethnic and transnational scrutiny has
helped to decolonize ethnic studies and its compartmental configurations and
shed a more critical light on the origins and nature of racial injustices, often
resulting in a better awareness of how to address and combat them for the
betterment of society at large. While practices like racial profiling are commonly represented in the media and in scholarship as victimizing African
Americans, and for good reason, the critical ethnic studies approach allows
us to see how such practices similarly victimize Latinos/as and—since 9/11—
South Asian Americans and Arab Americans.[38] Comparably, while the civil
or human rights of immigrants are commonly debated only as they pertain to
Latinos/as, the plights of millions of African and black Caribbean immigrants
tends to be ignored.[39]

BEYOND BLACK VERSUS BROWN

The critical ethnic studies paradigm has encouraged comparative and/or interminority analyses as a method to accentuate the diversity of geographical locations where most minorities live and to show how hybrid subjectivities prob-
lematize the politicization of conditions like multiculturalism and contribute
to a decolonial turn. The comparative approach deepens understanding of
certain kinds of racial injustice by illuminating how those conditions are not
and never have been exclusive to any "minority" group's experience. Analyses of black-Latino/a relationships have become increasingly important in
this regard due to the growth rate of the Latino/a population since the 1980s.
There are now more people in the United States who speak Spanish as their
primary language than there are in Spain.[40] The post-1980s Latino/a population surge is the foremost reason that at the turn of the twenty-first century
Latinos/as surpassed African Americans as the largest racial/ethnic minority
group in the United States for the first time. They have also done so in many
cities, including Chicago, New York, and Houston, where blacks and more
specifically African Americans have traditionally been the largest and most
politically influential minority group. Most scholarly and journalistic analyses
of these historic demographic shifts contend that they have pitted blacks and
Latinos/as in a fierce struggle over scarce jobs, housing, social services, electoral seats, and even criminal markets.[41] These claims are generally produced

GAY MARRIAGE   CAMPAIGN FINANCE   AIDS IN SOUTH AFRICA

CRISIS

BLACK-LATINO RELATIONS

Strength in Numbers

Latino population growth has outpaced Blacks. Should the communities join forces?

PLUS

Washington Insiders Maria Echaveste and Christopher Edley on the politics of race

Cover of *The Crisis Magazine*, January/
February 2004. Courtesy of the NAACP.

by the logic of resource competition, a sociological model contending that the subjectivities of political groups stem exclusively from group competition over material resources.[42]

The January–February 2004 issue of the NAACP periodical *The Crisis Magazine* focuses on black and Latino/a relations and explores the social and political shifts. Its cover depicts two young and apparently angry men, one black and one Latino, in what might be an advertisement for an upcoming boxing match. Beyond the logic of resource competition, this imagery seems to follow a tendency to view black and Latino/a politics through the limiting perspective of working-class and heterosexual men as well as stereotypes that often depict those actors as savage warriors.

While *The Crisis Magazine* offered some attention to black-Latino/a coalitions, the selection of that image for its cover reveals a deeper dilemma. It sheds light on the tropes of pathology and chaos that have influenced academic discourse regarding poor people of color in the United States. The profound emphasis on black-Latino/a conflict reflects a media model that presumes that a fight is more exciting to watch than a friendship, especially when the fight involves two subjects who have been demonized as the scourge of white America to the extent that blacks and Latinos/as have and who, if united, could have a transformative effect on U.S. politics. The statistics regarding each group's "quality" of life are quite alarming. Blacks and Latinos/as represent not only the two largest racial minority groups but also the two most impoverished, politically underrepresented, undereducated, environmentally sickened, police-brutalized, and incarcerated groups in the United

States.[43] They tend to share space in neighborhoods, jobs, and schools of most U.S. cities, a proximity that continues to intensify. There is a vast array of phenomena to consider when debating the origins or causes of these conditions. It seems safe to presuppose, however, that they are some of the many by-products of an enduring history of institutionalized anti-black and anti-Latino/a racism. The logic for political coalitions of blacks and Latinos/as is quite compelling inasmuch as members of the two groups recognize the sources of much of their deprived livelihoods, and this recognition registers as an essential component of their subjectivity. I presume that this recognition is not rare even if or when it is not acted upon politically.

Media and academic discourse on black-Latino/a conflict suggests that the two groups generally lack this recognition or the capacity to achieve it. These stereotypical depictions reveal a deep-seated characterization of racial others in the United States as problems, as W. E. B. Du Bois asserted more than a century ago.[44] More recently, Stephen Gregory has critiqued the gaze of social scientists on the black urban poor for its tendency to "only reinforce stereotypes about urban poverty, pathology, and chaos" while overlooking the vibrant ways the poor often survive and resist injustice and their sophisticated understanding of relations, as evident in the activist coalitions they build across gender, class, and ethnic boundaries in their home spaces. This "agency-oriented" perspective has done much to advance an understanding of majority-minority and intraminority relationships.[45] We should presume that this perspective could do the same for a clearer understanding of interminority dynamics. However, only sparse literature advances the perspective. With this book I attempt to help fill that void. In it I privilege moments and spaces that emphasize the complex personhoods of blacks and Latinos/as, and I convey a more agency-oriented perspective on how those two groups negotiate their similarities and differences in shaping a collective oppositional consciousness and culture.

The discourse on black-Latino/a conflict that I work against here reflects other discursive pressures, if not even political strategies, for maintaining white hegemony in what has been called this "post–civil rights" era. In the current moment, tales of minorities fighting over scraps fit neatly within the hegemonic discourse of postracialism and the more specific problem of "racial fatigue," a term I am introducing to describe a mental state originating from a popular belief among the U.S. polity that the United States has done all it can to address and remedy its history of racial inequality. Racial fatigue causes people to cringe at contemporary reminders that much work remains. Combined with the dominant tropes and stereotypes regarding the racially aggrieved that Gregory and others have critiqued, especially blacks and Latinos/as, the racial fatigue of many Americans thus may make black-Latino/a conflicts more revealing or important. Some people have grown so tired of blaming whites for racism that revealing how people of color oppress one another has become something of a cottage industry in academe and the popular media.

The literature on black-Latino/a conflict often manufactures, exaggerates, or overlooks data regarding the impact of the Latino/a boom on black unemployment, Latino/a voting habits, and black and Latino/a gang violence. In 2008 it was widely suggested that Latinos/as would not support the presidential campaign of Barack Obama because he was black. Ultimately, strong Latino/a support has been cited as one reason Obama won that campaign over Republican candidate John McCain.[46] There are also widespread misconceptions regarding black versus Latino/a competition over jobs.

Although Latinos/as and especially those who are immigrants are commonly depicted as stealing jobs from blacks, the steady loss of black jobs in recent decades has been the result of industrial downsizing and the outsourcing of manufacturing jobs to the global South.[47] Moreover, the most influential factor in high rates of black unemployment has been shown to be deeply rooted anti-black stereotypes harbored by some employers. By comparison, increased competition for jobs created by Latino/a population growth has had only a minimal effect on black joblessness.[48]

Some analysts have gone so far as to blame Latinos/as for a skyrocketing black prison population. George Borjas, Jeffrey Grogger, and Gordon Hanson argue that Latino/a immigrants taking black jobs is a primary reason many blacks had no choice but to turn to illegal activities such as making and selling crack cocaine for economic survival.[49] To argue that Latino/a population growth is the reason for high rates of black imprisonment overlooks the fact that the Latino/a prison population is skyrocketing as well.

A popular argument has circulated that Latino/a gangs immigrated from Latin America into the United States to practice "ethnic cleansing" as a method to eradicate black gangs from territories they seek to make their own.[50] To critique the ethnic-cleansing rhetoric surrounding gang violence, criminologist George Tita told a reporter, "You don't see these major black-brown wars, either within the context of gangs or outside the context of gangs."[51] In an earlier news story Tita said the vast majority of gang homicides are black on black or Latino/a on Latino/a. Latino/a on black and black on Latino/a violence is extremely rare but receives far more attention because, as Tita explained, "the rare events are more newsworthy."[52] Residents of Los Angeles–area communities have said the extra attention given to the rare events is a plot by the media and elected officials at race baiting an interminority conflict.

At a 2007 event to discuss this phenomena, Noreen McClendon, an African American, executive director of Concerned Citizens of South Central Los Angeles, and vice president of the Watts Gang Task Force, declared: "We need to go on the offensive to put an end to this idea of ethnic cleansing in L.A. . . . It is not happening."[53] McClendon said reports of Latino/a on black violence or vice versa are "blown so far out of proportion" as a component of a broader conservative agenda to depoliticize critiques of white supremacy and to distract and disable black civil rights organizations.

Considering these examples raises crucial questions: Why is black-Latino/a conflict considered more newsworthy, and how is such conflict being reported as a new kind of racial conflict with relatively thin evidence of its taking place in U.S. communities? Does it represent an affront to conventional wisdom regarding both groups? Or does it fulfill some other discursive desire to help ease anxieties produced by racial fatigue and encourage blaming victims for their own suffering? This is a claim that Claire Jean Kim has made with regard to black-Korean conflict in New York City.[54] In her "racial triangulation" theory Kim suggests that black-Korean conflicts are in large part produced by means of popular discourse and a gaze of white Americans upon deficient communities of color as two groups pitted against one another in a struggle for scarce resources. Concurrently, whites remain unchallenged in a supreme or apex position above that fray, and the colonial order is fortified.

BOOK DESIGN AND OUTLINE

This book conveys a logic and intervention similar to Kim's. With acute attention paid to Hall's suggestions regarding the significance of conjuncture and chronological and geographical specificity in analyses of race, this book's chapters present specific attention to changes and continuities over time in Baytown, Texas, my hometown, one among many blue-collar towns built in the early twentieth century around the oil-refining industry that dominates the Houston metropolitan area's southeastern region. Baytown is home to roughly 70,000 citizens and a large number of undocumented denizens, mostly from Mexico and Central America. Baytown's demography reflects the broader Houston area, at roughly 55 percent white, 30 percent Latino/a, and 17 percent black. As a town built around one of the world's largest oil refineries, the majority of its residents are either middle or working class.

A killing in Baytown in 2002 created the primary impetus for my arguments regarding how black and Latino/a people often think and act collectively based upon their common experiences in shared spaces. In January 2002 a middle-age Mexican immigrant named Luis Alfonso Torres was

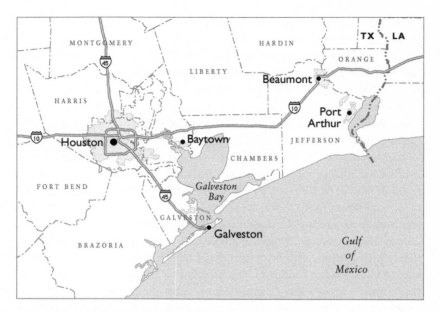

Houston Metropolitan Area to the Louisiana state line. Map by Molly O'Hallaran.

beaten and choked to death by four white police officers in Baytown, and his family was then denied justice in courts of law despite compelling evidence of police brutality. In response, black and Latino/a residents of Baytown and from across Houston joined forces in launching what I define as an "activist awakening" in Baytown.

The Torres case of 2002 offers a lens for viewing how ordinary, working-class residents of a local community become grassroots agents for social justice when government institutions prove insufficient to protect their civil and human rights. I use the Torres case and Baytown's history as a leitmotif or conceptual frame for addressing larger debates about demographic changes, interminority relationships, and the shifting nature of racial politics in the United States at large. Baytown's activist awakening was an exertion of hybrid subjectivities, a transracial consciousness of power representative of a "decolonial turn," a condition that Maldonado-Torres has described as comprised of "subaltern memories of suffering and displacement but also happiness and hope in the midst of challenges to human existence."[55] That activist awakening altered Baytown's social climate in an unexpected way and from an unexpected source. It originated in a moment that is often declared "post-racial" or "post–civil rights" and within which antiracist movements are often criticized as creating racial divisions rather than respected for critiquing them.

The activist awakening resulted from an interweaving and amalgamation of shared black and Latino/a memories of oppression and resultant subjectivities that manifested in a moment that is far more commonly described as being rife with black-Latino/a tensions and hostilities.

This activist awakening was the impetus for me to begin to more heavily ponder the influence of black history and black oppositional cultures on that particular expression of hybridity. What stood out as glaringly evident to me was that black leaders helped galvanize the protest movement and were often at the forefront of its most scathing critiques of white supremacy. It was not just from black political actors or black bodies, however, that Latinos/as drew added strength and purpose to their protests. Symbols of anti-black racism and black antiracism were also prominent in the signs and slogans used by Latinos/as to combat racism in that moment. Black political actors clearly manipulated memories of black history to better characterize Latinos/as as victims of racial oppression within the political imaginary of that community.

These types of discursive mutations stirred a series of questions regarding the significance of African American history in this neoliberal age. While it is common to hear suggestions that we should look beyond or expunge the black-white binary when assessing the social meaning of race, we would do so at the risk of discounting the very reasons this binary has been so influential. It is not that the extra attention supposedly afforded to blacks in general and African Americans more specifically has resulted in their being more empowered than other minority groups. Most socioeconomic statistics suggest otherwise, and blacks remain highly susceptible to state-sanctioned violence. I propose that it is more constructive to consider how the condition we understand as the black-white binary contributes to or is being blended into new racial knowledges, subjectivities, and maybe even transracial and transethnic subject positions—produced, as Mignolo explains, in the wake of local histories colliding with global ones under the rubric of globalization. In breaking down the black-white binary as a way of destroying it, perhaps it could be broken down as a deconstructive enterprise designed to reinterpret its origins, meanings, and significance within specific, contemporary, neoliberal frameworks. The goal is then not to diminish the significance of African American history within debates about the social meanings of race in the United States but to remix and reinterpret it.

Baytown's activist awakening affords an opportunity to do so. Beneath the expression of black-Latino/a solidarity that characterized the event lies a haunting essence of blackness that is in part unique to that community's historical development and location but that also may reflect the role African American history plays in structuring an understanding of racial politics in the United States generally. The role that blackness or collective memories of black history played in the activist awakening is what influenced me to expand the scope of this book. I highlight Baytown's activist awakening to map out a more diverse and extensive discursive terrain across which I have witnessed black and Latino/a subjectivities emulsify into a compound subject position that has produced unanticipated acts of resistance by unexpected alliances.

Chapter One lays out the broader geographic and discursive contexts within which I place the later evidence. More specifically, it introduces two terms, "foundational blackness" and the "racial state of expendability," that are used as the conceptual framework for the empirical evidence I analyze in each subsequent chapter. Chapter Two focuses on the role that state-sanctioned racial violence has played in shaping black and Latino/a subjectivities in Baytown and the general Houston area over time. It traces the relationship between this violence and the Houston area's development from a slave economy in the mid-nineteenth century into a center for the world's energy industry by the late twentieth century. The shared experiences of blacks and Latinos/as as targets and victims for this violence is an important reason, I argue, that they have been able to engage in collective acts of resistance more recently. For much of the area's history, anti-black violence was more rampant and the foundations for black resistance were stronger, leading to my contention that blackness bears an added moral weight in the Houston area's social climate.

Chapter Three focuses on the late twentieth and early twenty-first centuries. In it I demonstrate how police terror replaced vigilante terror as the primary mechanism for anti-black and anti-Latino/a injustice in the Houston area. This violence, combined with demographic shifts wrought by neoliberalism, the advent of hip-hop culture, and the proliferation of youth gangs in Baytown, allowed for black and Latino/a subjectivities to overlap and amalgamate with more intensity than ever before. One result is the new hybrid forms of subjectivity that manifested in Baytown's activist awakening.

In Chapter Four I demonstrate how Baytown's activist awakening was a clear manifestation of the historical processes previously outlined. I do so by detailing how the Torres case transpired and was politicized. I demonstrate the effects of hybridity and hybrid subjectivities in one space and moment.

In the conclusion I examine the "moral witness" concept as a way of theorizing the significance of Baytown's activist awakening beyond Baytown, Houston, and the South and within broader debates regarding postcolonialism. I borrow the term "moral witness" from Bhabha to suggest how artists and activists utilize memories of past barbarism to critique contemporary crises in both the private and public domains and refute the logic of postcolonialism in doing so. Moral witnesses, in sum, are the authors, scribes, or performers of decolonial knowledge; this chapter is designed to validate their significance within the realm of racial politics. In the conclusion I also draw critical attention to the role women of color have played in building activist coalitions against police terror in Baytown and communities across the United States. Women's contributions contrast with the male-centered discourse on black-Latino/a conflict and the nature of black-Latino/a solidarity.

CHAPTER ONE

FOUNDATIONAL BLACKNESS AND THE RACIAL STATE OF EXPENDABILITY

THIS CHAPTER HAS TWO CENTRAL PURPOSES. The first is to introduce the Houston area as a "contact zone," a term I borrow from Mary Louise Pratt to describe a space that is demographically, geographically, and historically unique for the kinds of interactions between black and Latino/a lives that I am mapping.[1] The chapter's second purpose is to introduce two conceptual models I have developed to make sense of these interactions and to describe their broader political significance. Those models are the racial state of expendability and foundational blackness.

The former is a model I introduce to suggest how expressions of black-Latino/a solidarity quite often emerge from outside the realm of resource competition, that is, as the result of a shared susceptibility to obliteration with legal impunity that has manifested in the late twentieth and early twenty-first centuries particularly in the form of state-sanctioned police brutality, a condition I explain as irreducible to and yet associated with a method of economic exclusion or exploitation. Such expendability is the result of how blackness and *latinidad* have been produced as either racial (blackness) or ethnoracial (*latinidad*) signifiers of deficiency and criminality within the assemblage, organization, and governing of bodies that constitute the South as a racial/colonial formation. These conditions have created a nexus for black and Latino/a subjectivities to amalgamate, resulting in a shared consciousness of racial power and an impetus for greater political cooperation.

I introduce the term "foundational blackness" to underscore the significance of anti-black racism and anti-black violence to this racial formation. The term suggests how African American history, or the normalization of anti-black violence in the region as an essential component of its law enforcement apparatuses and racial/colonial dynamics, has been significant both in concrete acts of violence and in the symbolic justification and glorification of such violence to the ways the South's growing Latino/a population has experienced the racial state of expendability. The term "foundational black-ness" also suggests the ways collective memories of black antiracism in the Gulf South, that is, an oppositional culture derived from African American history and responsiveness to expendability, have been a basis for how Lati-nos/as have developed their own methods of survival and resistance over time. In sum, a rich history of black activism and expressive cultures in the Houston area has had a significant influence on the ways Latino/a resistance to racism has been formulated and waged.

This influence has often been explicit and also implicit as a subliminal effect on how modes of Latino/a resistance have been imagined and performed in public and political domains. Foundational blackness, I argue, has been most evident as of late, in moments such as the Luis Torres case of 2002 in Baytown through which a strong expression of black-Latino/a solidarity emerged as the foundation for an activist awakening. Such moments demonstrate the cen-trality of African American history to the formation of Latino/a subjectivities in this time and place, an influence whose significance is being deepened as a result of the multilayered effects of neoliberalism and globalization.

THE WHITE ELEPHANTS

They are there. There is no denying them. Past and present tensions between blacks and Latinos/as do exist in the Houston area, in Texas, and beyond. As much as I aim to show recent exceptions to this phenomenon, it is significant and not to be ignored by those interested in understanding the dynamic and complex nature of racial politics in this post–civil rights nation.

Thomas Gugliemo, Ian Haney-López, Neil Foley, and Brian Behnken have demonstrated black-Latino/a tensions to be quite common in Texas during the early to mid-twentieth century.[2] Foley, Nicolás Vaca, Behnken, Tatcho Mindiola, Yolanda Flores Niemann, and Nestor Rodriguez demonstrate that these tensions have been prominent in the Houston area more contempo-rarily.[3] Foley contends that black-Latino/a tensions were so common nation-wide during the mid- to late twentieth century that they represent a "failed promise of black-Latino/a solidarity."[4] On a smaller scale, Behnken conveys that conflicts between the two groups were a reason they conducted separate and parallel civil rights struggles in Texas, generally failing to work together to effectively overcome similar obstacles since the mid-twentieth century.[5]

None of these conclusions is inaccurate. Foley's and Behnken's historical analyses are particularly useful and admirable. Their excellent archival research pinpoints how, where, when, and why black-brown tensions have developed historically within social movements and how those tensions have been detrimental to the broader goal of eradicating racial discrimination. These historians offer important reminders of why social movements cannot be romanticized, retrospectively, to the extent that important and often troubling realities about them are overlooked.

My goal is not to refute these conclusions. I aim to complicate them in four ways. The first is quite simple. While Foley and Behnken focus most of their attention on the leaders of civil rights organizations, labor unions, and intellectuals from the 1940s to around 1970, my work focuses much more on emergent expressions of black-Latino/a solidarities in the late twentieth and early twenty-first centuries and across a broader spectrum of social actors. The second way I complicate Foley's and Behnken's emphasis on black-Latino/a conflict is by challenging traditional academic methodologies and/or disciplines and especially the archival research of social-movement historians. Foley and Behnken are skilled and disciplined historians who generally analyze archives that others have normalized as sound representations of the desires and subjectivities of black and Latino/a populations overall. The two researchers' archival methods condense the ideological and imaginative domain of politics, reinforcing the very power/knowledge interfaces responsible for structural oppression from the outset.[6] They presuppose that one must be a representative of organizational or institutional units in order to have a significant voice in debates about the efficacy of black-Latino/a solidarity or even within racial politics at large.

Subaltern studies scholars have been critiquing this condition for some time now, conveying that a gaze upon organizations and political figures who aimed to reform liberalism and capitalism belatedly on behalf of select subaltern groups has actually contributed to the further marginalization of the subaltern within postcolonial contexts. In sum, the symbolic and structural architectures of colonial formations have been preserved by the very idea of belated inclusion into institutions or processes that oppressors recognize and define as representations of the political.[7] Belated inclusion thus created a new method through which the subaltern would be produced as perpetually deficient, not quite ready to initiate a meaningful challenge for equality, not yet capable of political efficacy, as achieving a progressive political consciousness only when it mimics the ethics and discourse of the very society responsible for its initial marginalization or displacement. The U.S. civil rights era fits within this critique. Gayatri Spivak's question "Can the subaltern speak?" has become eminent for ethnic studies scholars.[8]

The subaltern studies project becomes even more useful when coupled with a decolonial critique, a project to unsettle the truth-sanctioning protocols of Europe and to map out a more diverse representation of what constitutes the domain of politics, a representation of political possibilities grounded and harbored in the subjectivities of the masses and the dynamic ways they survive, adjust to, and resist marginalization in their day-to-day lives. Robin D. G. Kelley captures this decolonial essence when he explains, "Unfortunately, too often our standards for evaluating social movements pivot around whether or not they 'succeeded' in realizing their visions rather than on the merits or power of the visions themselves."[9] Kelley's intervention suggests that acts of resistance in and of themselves and regardless of their efficacy or longevity can be perceived as successful not by how they "win" equal access but by how they help transform an understanding of the origins of inequality and the language through which debates about such inequality are communicated. Social transformation in this regard is something that cannot transpire in an immediate shift of power through which the subaltern forms organizations that reform liberalism and capitalism and then rushes to integrate institutions from which they had been excluded. Rather, transformation occurs in a steady, sustained remaking of ethics from the ground up, a building process that unsettles the normative discourses that, if left without critique and seen as immutable, will only produce the subaltern as never quite ready, as always deficient.

Kelley's commentary reflects a prominent tension between ethnic studies and activists, a tension similar to what Laurence Cox and Colin Barker have described as a "parasitic" relationship of scholars of social movements and the activists who create, participate in, and maintain them.[10] Academics scrutinize and assess the successes and failures of social movements and yet are never quite attuned to the severe difficulties of those struggles, the courage and perseverance of those everyday and ordinary people who become voices of resistance in the spaces they call home and within which they have often been terrorized, their astute visions, the ebbs and flows of intragroup and intergroup solidarity they must manage, and the dynamism they have to maintain merely to organize collectives. Such dynamics are difficult to judge or read within archives. These conditions are exacerbated by the overwhelming lack of diversity within academe and especially a lack of black and Latino/a scholars who come from the violence-ridden, working-class communities. In this sense, the subaltern is far more often researched than a researcher, and this leads to grand neglect and misrepresentations of his or her complex personhood.

Ralph Ellison called attention to the growing schism in 1964 with his critique of social scientists studying black communities: "Prefabricated Negros are sketched on sheets of paper and superimposed on the Negro community; then when someone thrusts his head through the page and yells: 'Watch out jack, there are people living under here!' they are shocked and indignant."[11] Ellison's critique reinforces Cox and Barker's parasite thesis and their claims that "the primary 'community' that validates her or his work qua academic is that composed of other academics, who form their own hierarchies of reward and respect, and their own criteria of success."[12] So, the status quo is very much reinforced or reproduced within the privileges and lack of diversity in academe.

This tension is a reason fields like critical ethnic studies have developed as not only interdisciplinary but also rather antidisciplinary and a method to break down the borders that so often separate scholars from activists. Social movements are, after all, social in essence, meaning that they reflect the impulses and desires of populations and not just the thoughts and ideas of those who have been archived because they garnered the attention of white liberals who sympathized with their cause or white conservatives who sought to police and subdue them. By looking across and unsettling disciplinary protocols, the critical ethnic studies camp aims to disrupt academic imperialism and map out a more diverse discursive terrain regarding the political, one that unsettles the gaze upon mainstream civil rights organizations in particular, that troubles the truth-sanctioning protocols that emerged concurrent with European modernity and its colonial formations, and that incorporates a much more dynamic and critical interpretation of subaltern subjectivity as a harbor of and for political possibility. To be sure, this is a praxis that Stuart Hall and others at the Birmingham School of Cultural Studies advanced in the late twentieth century and that scholars like Americo Paredes were practicing decades earlier. More recently, Cynthia Young, Luis Alvarez, Laura Pulido, and George Mariscal have demonstrated how solidarity between blacks and Latinos/as has not failed but rather is a complex goal, a work in progress, a guiding vision, an imminence, an attribute of subjectivity, an element of complex personhood, and a dynamic component of how those groups have related to one another politically, over time, and always amid interminority tensions.[13] Each looks beyond the archives of civil rights or labor union leaders and more critically at fashion, music, literature, film, ethnography, oral histories, and public art, all media shaped by and generating significant visions of power, examples of possibility, and an emergent ethics that often has bonded African Americans, Latinos/as, Asian Americans, and Native Americans as a political collective.

The state was clearly wary of such possibilities. Mariscal and Alvarez suggest that one reason black-Latino/a solidarity was perceived as a failure during the mid- to late twentieth century is that the state heavily mandated that it would be. Black-Latino/a solidarities expressed in youth cultures, within grassroots and antiracist initiatives, and among students and administrators of public universities were seen as such a threat to the status quo that they were heavily policed and often violently undermined by state agents and agencies. Similarly, Pulido and Young demonstrate how the subjectivities and desires of Black Power, Yellow Power, Chicano Power, and Red Power activists in Los Angeles often blended together within a "U.S. Third World Left" during the 1960s and 1970s, a mixture of black, Latino/a, Asian American, and Native American solidarities attuned to and inspired by anticolonial movements across the global South. Demographic shifts and advancements in information technology (time-space compressions associated with neoliberalism), dynamics central to this book's design and purpose, have only enhanced this dynamism in the late twentieth and early twenty-first centuries, resulting in expressions of solidarity but also a proliferation of hybrid subjectivities and acts of progressive and diverse opposition.

The third way I complicate Foley's and Behnken's focus on black-Latino/a conflict is by critically scrutinizing how they conceptualize political solidarity or failure. I have made some reference to this problem already with my comments regarding the broader subaltern studies project. It deserves a more critical scrutiny, though. Borrowing from Jacques Derrida's deconstruction analytics and his theories regarding the relational nature of social knowledge and language, one cannot declare a social phenomenon to be a political failure without eliciting some scrutiny or questioning of what might constitute its success.[14]

According to the logic within Behnken's and Foley's analyses and considering the pervasive nature of racism, all antiracist movements in the United States, regardless of what activists or forms of activism characterized them, can be declared to be failures, as ineffective, or as failing to generate a kind of wisdom, comprehensive solidarity, and courage among all oppressed peoples that would result in monumental social transformation. Even if blacks and Latinos/as could work together comprehensively and within organizations, could this have reversed centuries of oppression within a few decades? There has never been an inclusive political solidarity within either population, much less between them. Support for or resistance to any political cause can vary even within the individual. What kind of political efficacy are the authors of the black-Latino/a conflict discourse in search of? Are they not imposing unrealistic expectations on groups they subsequently recognize as historically and often violently oppressed, traumatized, and marginalized?

Scholars of social movements routinely gaze upon the subaltern presumptively, with an expectation regarding how the scholars believe the subaltern should respond to oppression. When oppressed peoples, the objects of the research, do not respond to oppression in this way, those responses become the empirical evidence within what is often perceived as the latest innovation or unexplored terrain within social movement research. Such revelations, more-over, are implied as a set of instructions from which the oppressed can learn and grow, an implication that also presumes that the oppressed cannot learn and grow in such ways on their own.

My first involvement with scholarly research was as an object/subject in the 1980s, as a character in social scientific reports regarding the pathology of urban and working-class families on governmental assistance, which was a misrepresentation of my family, what we value, how we live. Even since I be-came an academic in the 2000s my family has been targeted for ethnographic research that misrepresents our dynamism and complexity, reducing us to mere victims of an oppressive criminal justice system, psychologically dam-aged and politically paralyzed, persons who have internalized inferiority and have thus engaged in acts of violent self-destruction. This ethnography was, ironically, conducted by a colleague of mine and was done discreetly. Being a character in my own colleague's narrative regarding the oppressed while also being his academic peer offers an intriguing lens for thinking about the postcolonial condition writ large, that is, of the effects and affect of subaltern voices being belatedly included into academe and ultimately of the need for paradigms like critical ethnic studies to provide a space for the subaltern to engage in a meaningful praxis of self-determination.

To delve a bit deeper into political theory regarding the politics of repre-sentation, the kinds of success or efficacy that authors of black-brown con-flict discourse refer to as "unreached" can also be interpreted as unreachable. The subaltern can never access universality—freedom, emancipation, and so forth—within a schema or system that is designed in opposition to them, that produces them as deficient by necessity. There has been extensive de-bate among political theorists regarding universality, or justice, as a myth underlying sovereignty and modern social formations, namely, liberal, capi-talist nation-states. Derrida, for example, has described the concept or condi-tion of justice as it is presupposed in and underlies political discourse within modern liberal social formations as à venir, that is, as "the very dimension of events irreducibly to come," a concept or condition that carries the ethical weight of imaginative imminence. Absolute justice, he argues, is something that would happen with immediacy and therefore is "incalculable," a concep-tual intervention suggesting that it is impossible to gauge or value the efficacy of social justice movements.[15] The function of justice, however, as a signi-fier of universality configured within the structural and symbolic architec-tures of modern states—some of which are also settler colonies—as Derrida explains, "requires us to calculate." Within those calculations, universality is then prohibited; it is filtered out by who is doing the calculations, privileged academics in this instance, and by the language and normative discourses regarding difference that those assessers appropriate as sound methodologies. Others have claimed that such calculations not only transpire within the spatial or temporal borders of modern nation-states but are a foundational element in the constitution of those nation-states or sovereignty in general. In this perspective, justice is a myth that depends upon the persistent discovery, creation, criminalization, and subjugation of an other who is, in essence, deficient; these calculations have occurred within the context of conquests and colonial formations the world over.[16]

By questioning whether racial justice is achievable within the philosophical and structural designs of modern, liberal nation-states, I do not mean to suggest that oppressed peoples are incapable of effecting social change or that they should abandon their efforts for inclusion and more equal access. I am, similarly to Kelley, merely calling attention to how resistance, psychosocial decolonization, the willingness and ability to confront potent forces of oppression in one's community are often victories in and of themselves for the subaltern. Resistance is a success in its existence, when it opens space for a different conversation to take place, when it gives a new language regarding power, when it integrates an alternative representation of ethics within political debates, and when it allows for a more diverse set of subjectivities to be heard and taken into account within those conversations. Acts of resistance are part of a process; they are part of what Glenn Coulthard describes as "transformative praxis," that is, a form of self-determination that untethers subaltern subjectivity from the power/knowledge interfaces of colonialism and the kinds of subjection that they produce.[17] Resistance, as transformative praxis, does not transform society instantaneously but is an element of the kinds of societal remaking, an incremental transformation from the ground up, one relationship at a time, an evolution captured by Derrida's dynamic description of justice as "'perhaps' . . . one must always say perhaps for justice."[18]

FIGHTING FIRE WITH WATER

In some cases, the hybridity established in black and Latino/a subjectivities during the mid-twentieth century was so influential that it blurred the borders between the groups, producing hybrid, grassroots, antiracist organizations that posed a threat to the status quo, were heavily policed and criminalized, and differed from the more prominent and/or mainstream civil rights organizations, intellectuals, judges, and labor unions that Foley privileges in his analysis. In Chicago during the 1960s, leaders from the Black Panther

Party, Young Lords (a coalition of Puerto Rican and Mexican American activists founded in Chicago), and the Young Patriots (a group of working-class whites) forged an alliance and started an organization they called the Rainbow Coalition. The organization was formed out of a realization of linked fates that members were already struggling for common goals and yet were doing so separately and within their racially or ethnically designated groups.[19]

The Rainbow Coalition raised the eyebrows of local and federal law enforcement agents who feared a united black-Latino/a political uprising and the politicization of black and Latino/a youth gangs in particular, largely due to the influence of charismatic leaders such as José "Cha-Cha" Jiménez and Fred Hampton. The life of the Rainbow Coalition was short due to the assassination of one of its leaders, Fred Hampton (also leader of the Chicago chapter of the Black Panther Party), by Chicago police officers in 1969. Jeffrey Haas has described his assassination as a concerted effort between the FBI and local police authorities to undermine a growing decolonial movement across the city of Chicago.[20] While Hampton is often remembered as having been assassinated for being a Black Power leader, those more familiar with his life and significance in Chicago realize that it was his ability and dedication to forge coalitions across racial lines and to advocate for comprehensive antiracial solidarity as connected to a sophisticated critique of capitalism that was most inspiring to youths of color and most threatening to the powers that be. Hampton's goals and influence are best represented by his own words. In a speech about coalition building and interminority solidarity appropriately titled "Power Anywhere There's People," he explains, "When I talk about the masses . . . I'm talking about the black masses, and the brown masses, and the yellow masses, too. We've got to face the fact that some people say you fight fire best with fire, but we say you put fire out best with water. We say you don't fight racism with racism. We're gonna fight racism with solidarity."[21] This statement reflects a decolonial ethics.

Hampton suggested that rather than merely seeking to replace white power with black power or with brown power, the Rainbow Coalition acknowledged that resistance comes from a concerted, antiracist, decolonial ethics. His is a critique of white supremacy that transcends racial, ethnic, and national borders and unsettles racial/colonial taxonomies; is a component of incremental social transformation originating in the most intimate of human relationships; and takes steps toward an imminent justice, *à venir*. Hampton's words verify the kinds of subjectivity and political vision I examine in this book as reflective of a decolonial or transformative praxis, the very will to resist. Considering Hampton's efforts to build black-Latino/a solidarity in particular and to blur the borders dividing the two groups, the price he paid for his efforts and vision of freedom, the inspiration he provided in life and in death, it is hard to consider his work as having failed. And yet, failure has been the dominant characterization of black-brown solidarities in the mid- to late twentieth century.

Social movements are not only about community activism or the development and naming of new organizations. Social movements are essentially complex social phenomena layered with variant instantiations and visions of justice, injustice, and freedom. Groups like the Rainbow Coalition emerged concurrent with vivid examples of black-Latino/a solidarity, if not hybridity, evident within expressive cultures. As activists like Fred Hampton were working hard and even dying to build black-brown organizational coalitions, artists like Gil Scott-Heron, Carlos Santana, Willie Bobo, Dizzy Gillespie, Chano Pozo, and Joe Bataan and groups like War, Tower of Power, Little Joe y La Familia, and Sunny and the Sunliners were blurring the boundaries between what was considered black and Latino/a and Asian American music, culture, history, and politics across the country.[22]

Even before the 1950s and 1960s there exists strong evidence of black-Latino/a solidarity in Texas and other parts of the South and Southwest. That solidarity always coincided with black-Latino/a conflict. It always will. Texas is a massive state geographically, second in size only to Alaska. Roughly 1,000 miles separate Houston, the state's largest city, on its eastern Gulf Coast, and El Paso, the westernmost city. The expanse opens much room for diverging histories, patterns, and conclusions regarding black-Latino/a solidarity even within the state. Throughout the mid-nineteenth century, black slaves fled the South and often sought refuge within Mexican and Native American communities in northern Mexico and across the central and southern regions of the Texas Republic. The most compelling piece of evidence of early solidarity between blacks and Mexican Americans and Mexicans and during the Reconstruction era is in *El Plan de San Diego*, a document written and disseminated in 1917 in the South Texas town of San Diego that called for a multiracial coalition of Mexican Americans, Native Americans, African Americans, and Asian Americans to take up arms against white oppressors in Texas and create a separate republic.[23] Decades prior, Mexican Americans and African Americans clearly realized their collective interests as they often joined forces to oppose the white Texan army during the Texas war for independence from Mexico in 1836.

Much of the impetus for that war and for the U.S.-Mexican war of 1846–1848 was that Mexico prohibited slavery in its territories and refused to return the more than 10,000 slaves who took the southern underground railroad to freedom in Mexico. This decision reveals a rather extensive element of black-Latino/a solidarity that, considering the context, is difficult to describe as a failure. Luis J. Rodriguez recently has explained that "Mexicans were willing to die so that blacks could be free."[24] And many of them did die. Thousands of blacks were willing to die alongside them and did so as they joined the Mexican army due to their resentment toward white slave masters in Texas and across the U.S. South. Anthropologist Martha Menchaca further demonstrates how the "racialization" of African Americans and Native Americans across the South and Southwest played a vital role in determining how Mexican Americans experienced racial oppression in Texas and elsewhere.[25]

In far West Texas, black soldiers stationed at Fort Bliss would seek refuge from Jim Crow segregation enforced by whites in El Paso by crossing the border into Ciudad Juárez, Mexico, to shop, recreate, and often live more freely among Mexicans. Accordingly, they found greater comfort and opportunity in Mexican communities than they ever experienced in their segregated home communities in the South. In that same El Paso–Juárez border region, black-Latino/a tensions developed after black soldiers were deployed by the U.S. Army to subdue the populist revolutionary hero Pancho Villa's forces during the Mexican Revolution. Tensions deepened after the Battle of Carrizal when the all-black Tenth Cavalry pushed back Villa's forces, whom many peasant and working-class Mexicanos/as on both sides of the border envisioned as a champion for the oppressed. Blacks were then stigmatized as having wrongly joined forces with their own oppressors. As David Romo describes this conflict, "The American military policy of pitting blacks against Mexicans on the border drove a wedge between two ethnic groups who might have otherwise collaborated against Anglo hegemony."[26]

The famous Harlem Renaissance poet Langston Hughes also recognized that being an African American in Mexico was often less restrictive on one's civil liberties than living in the United States. During his visits with his father in Mexico City as a teenager, Hughes took notice of the similarities among Mexicanos/as living in the U.S.-Mexican borderlands, the indigenous and Afro-descended peoples of Mexico, and African Americans living in the U.S. South. These transnational encounters influenced his subjectivity and how he envisioned himself as a man of color. The similarities Hughes encountered were so vivid that he later co-authored a children's book with Arne Botemps titled *Boy on the Border* to underscore those connections for the American literary audience and to raise awareness about Mexicanos/as and the borderlands. The book is about a young Mexican boy who joined his uncle's cattle drive from northern Mexico to California.[27] The book was left unpublished until 2009, when Maceo C. Dailey Jr. and his wife, Sandra Banfield Dailey, discovered it in an archive at Yale University.

These examples demonstrate how solidarity is a dynamic component of subjectivity, even when it is not acted upon organizationally or in ways that are understood to be politically relevant or successful according to hegemonic conceptualizations of what constitutes politics. Solidarity is far more a practice than a phenomenon to be measured as a failure or a success. Whether it is expressed in an intraminority or interminority framework, solidarity acts more as a verb than a noun. It can vary in individuals as much as it can between groups of individuals. Solidarity is an attribute of the daily lives and thoughts of the subaltern, even when he or she voices opposition to it. As it pertains to social movements, reminiscent of Gramsci's concept of "organic intellectuals,"[28] Laurence Cox and Caitriona Mullan describe solidarity as "hidden knowledges of situated social relations, needs, and struggles."[29] This position is generated "from the assumption that other people are in some ways quite well-informed about their own experience, needs and possibilities of action."[30] So, whether or not oppressed groups are engaged with a direct, concerted, or successful campaign to eradicate oppression, solidarity may still be a component of their subjectivity. The subaltern may be disadvantaged, but he or she is never ignorant or unwary.

THE RACIAL STATE OF EXPENDABILITY

The fourth way I complicate the discourse on black-Latino/a conflict is by advancing an alternative conceptualization of racial oppression or racism. Underlying most of the literature on black-brown conflict is the conceptual trope of resource competition. This trope or theoretical premise conveys that black and Latino/a subjectivities are forged primarily as they pertain to how each group is excluded from equal access to education, to economic competition, or to competition for political representation within a modern, liberal, capitalist nation-state. Success is then implied to be the equivalent of blacks and Latinos/as having better access to education, job competition, or political representation. Race, within this scheme, is conceptualized as a utilitarian discourse that is socially constructed to justify exclusion. This conceptualization has been the prevailing one among race and ethnic studies scholars since the mid-twentieth century and has been deployed largely as a method to debunk primordial definitions of racial difference.

New models by critical race theorists, however, are showing how race is more complex and insidious. It is, Hesse argues, a sociological underpinning or "attribute" of European modernity;[31] or, Ferreira da Silva argues in her concept of "raciality," race is a productive strategy of power, a modern knowledge form that enables and sets the groundwork for conditions like capitalist or liberal exclusion to transpire.[32] She defines raciality as an "onto-epistemological arsenal constituted by the concepts of the racial and the cultural, and their signifiers, those which produce persons (ethical-juridical) entities not comprehended by universality, the chosen moral descriptor of post-Enlightenment political configurations."[33] Ferreira da Silva's concept of raciality enables an understanding of race as a dynamic that is irreducible to what she describes in an earlier work as a "socio-logic of exclusion," or the idea that race is a mere category of difference socially constructed to justify conditions of economic exploitation and displacement.[34] Race, in sum, does not justify oppression. It produces it. Ferreira da Silva's concept of raciality accounts for the process through which groups like blacks and Latinos/as are produced only to be devalued and relegated to the "scene of nature," an essential component of Enlightenment thought and the domain of the subhuman or bloody savage deserving of either quarantine or obliteration. This devaluation and relegation is an inherent component of the political (juridical-economic) infrastructure of modern social formations and the "civil society" they are designed to protect.

Building on Ferreira da Silva, I argue that the foundational effect of raciality is a racial state of expendability, that is, a fundamental and existential life devaluation, a perpetual susceptibility to obliteration with legal impunity that allows for all other modalities of injustice, including exclusion and exploitation, to occur and endure. Death is the fundamental outcome of what race, as a form of knowledge, logically conveys and that it is designed to account for, produce, justify, or allow. The effects of race, as such, function without regard to one's class position, gender, sexuality, or citizenship status. Expendability is enhanced and has been pervasive in the United States as a settler-colonial nation.

In her analysis of the ideological foundations of U.S. white supremacy, Andrea Smith identifies "three pillars" undergirding how the United States operates as a prototypical settler-colonial state with a built-in propensity for continued and pervasive violence as a method of sustaining itself as a nation, a violence that is legitimized within its law enforcement and military apparatuses and that has been inflicted to a large extent on nonwhite persons and Native people in particular.[35] This violence is an element of the structure and/or design of the United States and is thus irreducible to a mere event or aberration. The violence then manifests through repetitive exhibition, the pervasiveness of war, a condition Walter Benjamin describes as "spectral violence," a ritualistic performance of obliteration that Fanon also has described as originating within the settler's pervasive "preoccupation with security" intended to communicate to the colonized that "he [the settler] alone is master."[36] Violence that Patrick Wolfe describes of settler-colonial formations is not an event but is central to the very structure of such societies.[37] According to Richard Slotkin, violence, in being repeatedly inflicted and romanticized within nationalist mythologies, is how U.S. sovereignty has been and is legitimated. He asserts that the history of U.S. nationalism can be mapped through a recurring "regeneration through violence."[38]

The expendability of blacks and Latinos/as is clearly evident in their histories. Across the South and Southwest, from the mid-nineteenth through early twentieth centuries, each group was a primary target for vicious lynching campaigns inflicted by white slavers and settlers in the name of Manifest Destiny.[39] From the mid-twentieth into the early twenty-first centuries, both groups have been the primary targets and most common victims of police brutality, a condition that has been addressed by human rights organizations the world over.[40] This history is significant to my analysis because the prevailing literature on black-Latino/a conflict implies that members of each group are ignorant of their expendability and/or that expendability has only a limited influence on their subjectivities, thus limiting the rationale for black-Latino/a solidarity.

All scholars make choices in how they represent the subaltern. We choose to exaggerate certain realities so as to gain the attention of our peers, to seek the approval of the editors of academic presses, or even to garner the attention of the mass media while ignoring or discounting the significance of other realities so as to support our central theses. I am no different and am equally guilty of spinning a narrative. I choose to privilege expressions of solidarity, to exaggerate their significance as a method of interrupting the deficiency discourse, to decolonize by giving subaltern communities the benefit of my doubt, even to the extent that I might gloss over significant elements of conflict in which they/we engage. I am not claiming that blacks and Latinos/as get along better in the Houston area than in other regions, nor am I refuting the existence of significant black-brown tensions in the Houston area or beyond. The narrative I present here is intended as an intervention to call attention to the diversity through which blacks and Latinos/as relate to one another politically and the courage it takes to address and resist expendability rather than to numb ourselves to it, which is so often the case.

BROWNING THE BLACK BELT

What is it about Baytown and the Houston area that makes a space for this kind of intervention? Houston is the fourth-largest U.S. city and sits in the

third most populous U.S. county. It is the largest city in the South, a quali-
fication that is sure to raise eyebrows considering that Houston sits, geographically, in the Southwest. Foley has accurately described the Central
Texas region where San Antonio and Austin are located as a border province
or "shatter belt" where the histories of the tense Latino/a-white relations of
the Southwest and black-white relations of the South overlap. Houston is a
few hundred miles east of that shatter belt literally and significantly east of it
figuratively.[41] Although more geographically Southwest, Houston's history
and social climate make it rather quintessentially southern. Part of that quali-
fication means that it has been home to a historically large and influential
black population and that it is in a region shaped by an enduring legacy of
rampant anti-black racism originating in the chattel slave economy. Houston
also has a rich history of black antiracism, that is, a history of black survival of
and resistance to white supremacy. Of the ten largest U.S. cities, Houston is
the only southern city and the only one born primarily from a slave economy.
Moreover, Houston was an important center for the Confederacy during the
Civil War, and some of the nation's largest freedmen's settlements, also called
"freedom colonies," formed near Houston in the postbellum period. These
details will be explored further in the ensuing chapter; I introduce them here
to reinforce why I am identifying the Houston area as a unique contact zone
for generating hybrid subjectivities.

Much of Houston's southernness has to do with the significance of slavery
to its early development. Houston historian Cary D. Wintz describes the city
and nearby Galveston Island as "the most important centers for slave trade
in Texas":

> From the beginning, slaves made up a significant portion of the population.
> In the censuses of 1850 and 1860, slaves comprised 22 percent of the city's
> population. Slavery was even more widespread in the plantation areas that
> surrounded Houston. In Harris County and the other counties that con-
> stitute the metropolitan area today, slaves accounted for 49 percent of the
> population in 1860.[42]

Baytown was one of those plantation areas that surrounded central Houston and the home of one of the region's most prominent slavers, Ashbel
Smith. The emancipation of Texas slaves in June 1865 (Juneteenth) led to a
booming African American population in the Houston area. Freed black men
and women from across the South envisioned the city as a refuge from the
kinds of isolation and terror they would face in the rural or plantation areas
of the region.

The story of novelist Sutton Griggs exemplifies Houston's significance to Reconstruction. Born in Chatfield, Texas, to former slaves, Griggs made Houston his home for long spells of his career as a pastor and writer. Griggs's novel *Imperium in Imperio* was a utopian narrative written in 1899 that called for a separate black state for all African Americans to be located in East Texas along the Louisiana border and the Gulf coastline. Houston would be the largest urban center and hub for trade and commerce for this separate black nation.[43] Griggs's novel is commonly cited as one of the first narratives regarding black nationalism in the United States and a work that inspired black-nationalist struggles decades later. As rural blacks continued to pour into Houston during the late nineteenth and early twentieth centuries, they established some of the nation's first black churches, newspapers, civic organizations, public parks, and chambers of commerce.[44] For much of that period, the Houston area was home to the largest black population in the entire South and one of the nation's largest. Today it has the nation's fourth-largest black population. The Houston area has been described as the birthplace of important black musical genres such as the blues, zydeco, and "dirty South" gangsta rap.[45]

The state's two largest historically black colleges or universities (HBCUs) are in the Houston area, clearly situating it as a center for black education and intellectual life in Texas and the South. Texas Southern University sits in Houston's historic Third Ward. TSU was founded in 1927 as the Houston Colored Junior College and is currently the third largest of eighty-four HBCUs in the country. TSU's Thurgood Marshall Law School has produced some of U.S. schools' highest numbers of black attorneys. The other Houston-area HBCU is Prairie View A&M University, founded in 1876 as the Agricultural and Mechanical College for the Benefit of Colored Youth. Prairie View A&M is now the eighth-largest HBCU in the country.

Geographically speaking, African American historians have long considered Houston the easternmost part and only major Texas city within the Black Belt, a region stretching from Virginia to East Texas that marks where the nation's slave economy was centered and where most of the U.S. black population has lived.[46] The Houston area is commonly described as part of the Gulf South, a region extending from Houston eastward along the coastline of the Gulf of Mexico across southern Louisiana and Mississippi and ending in coastal Alabama.

Samuel C. Hyde Jr. describes the Gulf South as "a backwater in the field of southern history" that has been long neglected.[47] The lack of attention given to this region by scholars is especially crucial considering that Houston is the largest city in Texas, in the Gulf South, and in the South and historically piv-

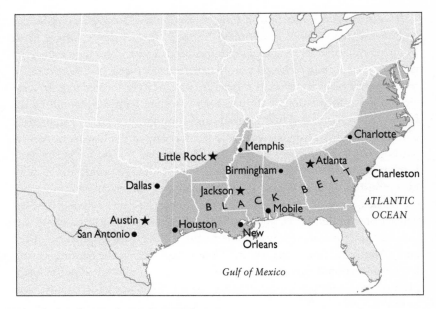

The Black Belt. Map by Molly O'Hallaran.

otal. Cary D. Wintz and Howard C. Beeth argue that Houston's rapid development as an urban region, its blue-collar social climate, its long-segregated educational systems, and rampant anti-black attitudes of Houston-area historians are reasons more attention has not been paid to black history in the region.[48] Only a few scholarly books have been published on black Houston in particular.[49] Likewise, few have been produced on Latinos/as in Houston.[50]

A series of incidents beginning in the late 1990s called more critical attention to the Gulf South and especially to its history of anti-black racism. These incidents include the dragging death of James Byrd Jr. by white supremacists in Jasper, Texas, in 1998; the controversy over public-housing desegregation and the Ku Klux Klan's intimidation of black residents in Vidor, Texas, in 1999; the "Jena 6" case in Jena, Louisiana, in 2006, in which six African American teens were jailed on charges of attempted murder for defending themselves in a fist fight against white peers threatening to lynch them; and the Hurricane Katrina disaster in New Orleans in 2005.[51] As an example of how popular culture often serves as an important medium through which black politics are produced and performed, the rapper Kanye West declared, "President Bush doesn't care about black people" during a live, nationally televised public service announcement to raise awareness and funds for residents of New Orleans.

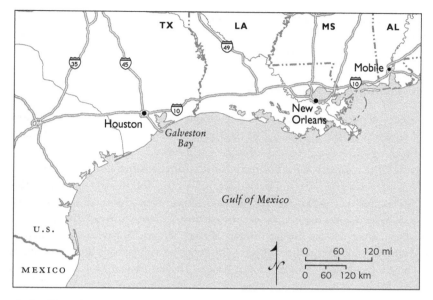

The Gulf South. Map by Molly O'Hallaran.

Two years after West's statement, one of Houston's most famous Latino/a hip-hop artists, Chingo Bling, rapped "A-yo Kanye . . . Bush don't like Mexicans either!" in a slow, bluesy, distinctively southern and Houston-styled rap song titled "Like This and Like That." The lyrics discuss Latino/a growth in the region and in Houston and New Orleans in particular.[52] Chingo Bling's lyrics depict Houston as home to the Black Belt's largest Latino/a population but also one of the largest overall among U.S. cities. While Latinos/as historically have been the largest minority group in Los Angeles and other metropolises in the Southwest, Houston's Latino/a population did not begin to numerically rival the city's black population until the late 1970s. For most of the twentieth century the Houston area's black population was nearly triple that of the region's Latino/a population. From 1980 to 2000 the Houston area's Latino/a population tripled in size, the most significant effect being that Latinos/as surpassed blacks as the largest nonwhite population at the dawn of the twenty-first century. The South's largest city has been Latinized.

TSU now enrolls the highest number of Latinos/as of all HBCUs in the United States. The history of that institution and the changing demographic make-up of its student body shed a light on the kinds of dynamics I analyze in this book, the relationships it produces, and the political possibilities that may emerge. Latino/a hip-hop artists like Chingo Bling, the son of Mexican immigrants, reflect how the rich expressive traditions of African American artists have had a strong influence on Latino/a art in the late twentieth and early twenty-first centuries.[53]

FOUNDATIONAL BLACKNESS

A central purpose of this book is to highlight black history's influence on how Latinos/as in the Houston area have experienced and considered the social meaning of race, an element of what I will describe as "foundational blackness." The inspiration for this term comes from the venerable African American poet and jazz artist Gil Scott-Heron. In 1978, following a violent protest against anti-Latino/a police terror in a community on the north side of Houston, Scott-Heron recorded a song titled "Jose Campos Torres." The namesake of that song was a Chicano veteran of the Vietnam War who was beaten to death by Houston police officers. The song has the famous lines "Common ancient bloodline brother Torres is dead . . . In Houston maybe someone said that Mexicans were the new niggers?"[54] Scott-Heron's pondering of whether Houston's booming Latino/a population represented "new niggers" suggests that Latinos/as were being relegated to the spaces and conditions originally designed to render the region's black population expendable. While Scott-Heron was not a historian and was not even from the region, his assertion is historically astute. He associated expendability with the distinctively southern and anti-black racial epithet "nigger" yet used the term to describe how Latinos/as were being similarly targeted for obliteration as their numbers grew.

In Scott-Heron's example we see a well-recognized black artist utilizing a black art form to symbolically connect the blood of a Latino/a with the much more recognizable river of blood that has been flowing from black bodies for centuries in the Houston area. Ultimately, Scott-Heron's "Jose Campos Torres" suggests that the kinds of hybrid subjectivity that I aim to fore-ground, developing from the Houston area's racial formation and location, might actually transcend that space and characterize a progressive perspective on racial politics that was more prominent in the United States during the late twentieth century but that tends to be far too easily overlooked in discourse on black-Latino/a conflict. Scott-Heron's use of the term "nigger" to describe the reality of anti-Latino/a violence in Houston and his suggestion that blacks and Latinos/as share a common "ancient bloodline," a primordial relationship derived from the history of slavery across the Americas, is reflected in D. Soyini Madison's definition of blackness as a racial signifier that is as much performed as it is embodied. She argues that blackness represents "a universal signifier of fear, danger, and threat across color lines."[55] While I feel that a similar argument can be made about indigeneity and other representations of difference, Madison's description of the particular moral weight associated with blackness and its political effect remains useful, especially in the South. The sense of fear, danger, and threat that I appropriate from Madison's model is one that not only demonizes black bodies in a white-supremacist world but also enables blackness to signify a strong opposition to whiteness and to racial injustice at large for and beyond black peoples. Blackness, in its performed more than embodied articulation, has become a dominant catalyst through which black and Latino/a subjectivities have been amalgamated and through which hybrid cultures are being formed. Building on Madison's and Scott-Heron's visions, the term "foundational blackness" conveys that over the course of U.S. history blackness has been transformed from an oppressive stigma into an inclusive formation that decisively transcends the "racial" boundaries of its original denotation.

On the one hand, "foundational blackness" suggests that anti-black racism has had an effect on how nonblack minority groups experience oppression similar to some of the aforementioned examples. On the other hand, this term suggests that blackness functions as an element within transformation praxis that is often constituted in the subjectivities of groups like Latinos/as who are nonwhite and generally considered nonblack in the U.S. racial order and nomenclature. The black-white binary is commonly critiqued by Latinos/as, Asian Americans, Native Americans, and Arab Americans as a hegemonic discourse that occludes the plight of other nonwhites; however, usually only the white side of that binary tends to be theorized for its hegemonic influence, while the black side remains fixated on the bodies of black victims. Whiteness, then, is signified as dynamic and politically salient or discursively influential beyond white bodies, while blackness is static, a signifier of victimhood, of death, of expendability as in Scott-Heron's use of the term "nigger" to describe the dead. Blackness is far too often locked into this rigid and corporeal signification to the extent that the presence of black bodies (of any hue) is often confused in white spaces as a sign of racial progress.

As a linguistic means to free blackness from this corporeal reduction and to accentuate its significance to oppositional cultures beyond the black-white binary, the term "foundational blackness" conveys that the collective memories of black suffering, survival, and resistance carry a heavy moral weight in U.S. political culture among minority groups. Scott-Heron's use of the term "new niggers" not only implies the newly expendable but also suggests a foundation from which black-Latino/a solidarities can be expressed. Foundational blackness is more complicated than the condition commonly referred to as "the black-white binary." It is a discursive condition through which that binary prohibits a more critical attention to nonblack minority groups including Latinos/as, Asian Americans, and Arab Americans. Foundational blackness represents a method and language through which the antiracist critiques from those same groups are developed and politicized. This process, combined with the similar expendability faced by blacks and Latinos/as in Houston and most U.S. cities, helps fuse black and Latino/a politics into a hybrid subjectivity, allowing the groups often to act in unison while also providing them with a (subject) position from which to act.

To a considerable extent, foundational blackness is rooted in popular perceptions about the originating moments of each minority group's history. Native Americans are frequently perceived as victims of violent conquest and removal yet also as a population too small to play a dominant role in debates about civil rights. In turn, the large Latino/a and Asian American populations are often, and cynically, seen as immigrant newcomers to the United States and therefore as groups that have willfully exposed themselves to racism while in search of the American dream. By comparison, African Americans are generally understood as a people whose history begins with the unquestionable act of force that is chattel slavery, an originating moment that denied any choice. This contrast in the perceptions of different ethnic groups could be described as a force-choice binary and often allows for blacks to monopolize the role of victim within civil rights debates while Latinos/as and Asian Americans are displaced, made to wait in line before entering many conversations regarding civil rights, and reduced to a state I describe as one of being racial outsiders.

The force-choice binary is a discursive condition, then, or a kind of controlling social logic that produces or allows for the black-white binary to be hegemonic. To be sure, Chicanos/as, Boricuas, Dominicanos/as, and other Latino/a subgroups have actively contested this condition for decades now. During the Chicano/a movement, activists popularized the slogan "We didn't cross the border, the border crossed us" to accentuate the violent forces of conquest and imperialism as the originating moments in their history. Because Latinos/as and Asian Americans did not become large components of the Houston area's demography until the 1980s, although they had some presence earlier, and because slavery, Juneteenth, and Jim Crow were so important to the area's racial formation from the mid-nineteenth century onward, the force-choice binary is more influential in that region—and consequently why blackness carries added weight in structuring the politicization of race there.

Popular culture plays an equally important role in configuring the kind of moral weight I associate with foundational blackness, whether in or beyond

Houston. Richard Iton demonstrates that black popular culture, for better or for worse, has often served as the primary medium through which narratives of black suffering and resistance have been expressed in U.S. culture at large and elsewhere and implanted in the popular political imaginary.[56] More narrowly, many Americans have learned about the horrific nature of slavery and Jim Crow from popular culture such as the blues, literature, hip-hop, television programs, and Hollywood movies. The importance of Houston to the development of the blues, gospel, soul, zydeco, and "dirty South" music genres strengthens this association. The English-speaking characteristic of African American political culture arguably makes it more compelling, or simply comprehensible, to most other Americans. By comparison, the largely non-English-speaking bases of Latino/a, Asian American, and Native American political cultures could be one reason much of the U.S. public so easily ignores their histories of oppression and resistance and these groups have not been more central to civil rights debates. On a national and international scale, U.S. black popular culture has provided sounds and language that have been used for counterhegemony struggles the world over and in ways incomparable to U.S. Latino/a cultures of opposition.

As a result of this complex cultural-historical constellation, Latinos/as in the Gulf South are influenced by black political cultures that are organic to the area and in turn strengthen black antiracist politics and blacks' struggles against white supremacy. These Latinos/as often transcend their position as racial outsiders by associating with the more pronounced history of African American oppression in the region in addition to the black oppositional cultures that it has birthed. This association does not always result in explicit expressions of black-Latino/a solidarity, but it is a dynamic that deserves scrutiny within debates about the phenomenon.

By emphasizing the influence of black history on Latino/a subjectivities in Houston, I will still be critiqued by scholars working in fields like Chicano/a studies and Latino/a studies for discounting the significance of Latino/a history in the region. For justifiable reasons, Latinos/as have often vigorously contested suggestions that they are either copying or are unduly appropriating African American political culture because they lack the knowledge or wherewithal to challenge oppression in their own ways.[57] There is a vibrant history of Latino/a resistance in the Houston area that should not be discounted. Beginning in the early twentieth century, pioneering Latinos/as in the region built *sociedades mutualistas* (mutual aid societies) that bonded families together in solidarity and created a base for Latino/a communities to both survive and resist. In the mid-twentieth century, Houston-area Latinos/as engaged in important civil rights activism. Some of this activism did indeed involve Latinos/as distancing themselves from blacks as a method to whiten themselves as part of a grander assimilationist strategy.[58] Soon thereafter, many Latinos/as in Houston participated in the Chicano/a movement and embraced discourses of cultural nationalism that were popular across the U.S. Southwest at the time as methods to critique white supremacy, to oppose assimilation, and to distance themselves from associations with white privilege.[59] Their interventions have been heroic and should not be glossed over.

As heroic as that activism was, however, Houston's Chicano/a movement did not match the magnitude or influence of San Antonio's Chicano/a activism during the same period, which deepens the symbolic divide between the South and the Southwest. David Montejano has asserted that the successes of the Chicano/a movement in San Antonio set an example for and even enabled other successful struggles across the Southwest. San Antonio's Chicano/a movement, he argues, was pivotal to Latino/a empowerment across the country. It influenced the change from an at-large electoral system to single-member districts that allowed for Latinos/as to be elected to important political offices, the organization of La Raza Unida political party, and the establishment of the Southwest Voter Education Project, an initiative that led to epic moments in the history of elected Latino/a leaders in Texas and across the Southwest.[60] Montejano helps to better center Texas within debates about the Chicano/a movement. And yet there is no mention of Houston in his analysis. This absence is not the result of his neglect; rather, there is just not as much to discuss regarding Chicano/a activism in Houston when compared to the activism across cities like San Antonio, Los Angeles, and Denver—all cities that Montejano describes as "urban hubs" for the Chicano/a movement.

By comparison, Houston was more significant for its African American civil rights and Black Power activism. San Antonio's Chicano movement created a political power base that enabled the landmark election of Latino/a leaders like Henry Cisneros, the second Latino/a ever elected as mayor of a major U.S. city. Civil rights activism led to the election of black political leaders from Houston like lawyer Barbara Jordan. In 1966, fifteen years before Cisneros's election, Jordan became the first African American elected to the Texas Senate since Reconstruction; she went on to become the first southern black woman elected to the U.S. House of Representatives. Montejano argues that part of the reason Chicanos in San Antonio were so dedicated to social change is that they were inspired by and borrowed from the black civil rights struggle in the South, especially pertaining to the issue of single-member voting districts.[61]

Foundational blackness is not a permanent or static condition. It is an epistemological signifier that calls attention to a certain configuration of time, space, demographics, and politics—that is, what Stuart Hall would describe as a conjuncture from which hybrid subjectivities have been generated.[62] The oppression or resistance of Houston-area Latinos/as was never dependent upon the prior oppression or resistance of Houston-area blacks. But the latter has influenced the former to a degree worth considering.

AGAINST THE "LATINOS-AS-WHITE" THESIS

If anything, the concept of foundational blackness certainly puts an interesting twist on ongoing debates about the place of Latinos/as within the U.S. racial order. Conversations about Latino/a identity have most commonly described it as produced by discourses of cultural nationalism, vibrant transnationalism, or proximity to whiteness that has been systematically denied to African Americans. Latinos/as are often depicted as being like many European immigrants who initially experienced ethnic prejudice in the United States: they will one day be absorbed into the white population.[63] For clarity I will refer to this as the "Latinos-as-white" thesis, a term I appropriate from René Francisco Poitevin.[64] Latinos/as are often described as a population that exists in a "racial middle ground" between blacks and whites, a space within which Latinos/as can claim or "pass" (phenotypically) as white more easily than blacks due to the hegemonic influence of the "one-drop rule" in U.S. history. Also known as the rule of hypodescent, this racial categorization during Reconstruction specified that a person with "one drop of Negro blood" was not white and thus not entitled to full civil rights. As a result, this "passing" phenomenon is often cited as a reason Latinos/as will increasingly enjoy the fruits of white privilege as they grow in number.[65]

Arlene Dávila, however, has recently argued against the Latinos-as-white discourse by suggesting that a "Latino spin" manufactured by mass media and marketing pressures ignores the diversity of Latinos/as as well as the extent of anti-Latino/a injustices over time. She explains that "Latinos are a primarily non-European mixed, brown and black racialized people," making them "not so easily 'whitened.'"[66] While I agree with Dávila's critique and especially how it aims for a more critical perspective on ways Latinos/as are racialized in the United States, its logic tends to reinforce the very power/knowledge schema that she, like most ethnic studies scholars, attempts to unsettle. It adds legitimacy to the condition we are attempting to delegitimize. In sum, the more we identify race corporeally, by skin hue or hair texture, as empirical evidence of racial difference that attains a social if not political significance within a hierarchy of socially constructed categories (what Omi and Winant refer to as "racial formation"), the more we enable the social logics that have resulted in racial oppression from the outset of modernity, that is, the more we reinforce a colonial assemblage of racial bodies. Hesse says contemporary racial or ethnic studies scholarship

> tend[s] to incorporate a residual empiricist reliance on the reduction of race in analysis to visible, corporeal difference. What I am suggesting is that the critical concept of race though assuming the discrediting of the biological idea of race nevertheless retains this formulation, surreptitiously as part of the critical purchase on race as the object of its critique. If the explanatory test of these studies is to rethink the concept of race as modernity without relying on the biological referent, then as with ethnographic/policy oriented race/ethnic studies in general, they have not met this test . . . [C]olour coded physiognomies or embodied ethnicities generally become privileged for the critique of race as a contested signifier.[67]

Whiteness is thus bolstered as a signifier of full belonging or citizenship in the United States by way of an empirical gaze upon the "nonwhite" characteristics of the Latino/a body and as a method to illuminate the racial oppression of Latinos/as that is implied to be similar to that of African Americans or Native Americans.

One result of this is that Latinos/as, in their attempt to challenge the Latinos-as-white thesis, often excavate examples of black or indigenous ancestry to legitimate themselves as racial others in the United States.[68] Their impulse is evident in a wave of recent literature on Afro-Latinos/as and in the attention given to an exhibit titled "The African Presence in Mexico" that toured the United States with stops at the DuSable Museum of African American History in Chicago, the Smithsonian Institution's Anacostia Museum in Washington, D.C., the National Mexican Museum of Art in Chicago, the African American Museum in Philadelphia, and the Museo Alameda in San Antonio. The exhibit has been promoted as a groundbreaking demonstration of the black diasporic presence in Mexico and Mexicanos/as. The significance of this exhibit is that Mexicanos/as make up the majority of Latinos/as in the United States but are rarely considered part of the black diaspora, genetically speaking.

On three occasions I have been invited to give a keynote lecture on contemporary black-Latino/a relations at openings of the exhibit. It focuses on Latin American history specifically during the colonial period, but I am not a historian and certainly not of colonial Latin America. The reason for my repeated invitations, however, lies in the implicit political impetus tied to the display of African ancestry among Latinos/as. Curators are quite aware that the exhibit will stir as many questions about contemporary U.S. black-Latino/a relations as it will about the history of slavery in Latin America. The genetic blackness of Latinos/as is being presupposed as a social fact that will contribute toward more harmonious relationships of African Americans and Latinos/as in the United States. I certainly hope that it does. But I think the presupposition is misguided and can be politically counterintuitive.

Black-Latino/a "relations" often occur within singular Latino/a subjects. The black roots among Latinos/as are indeed a significant and yet a historically neglected phenomenon. They deserve a more critical scrutiny, and I have dedicated much of my time, thought, and resources to helping illuminate the neglected histories and realities. I worry, however, that black-Latino/a solidarity is being presupposed as deriving from biological facts, as a condition that happens within the individual Latino/a subject and that reinforces the logic of racial differences as primordial or corporeal rather than reflective of a form of knowledge that identifies differences in bodies, behaviors (ethnicity), and space, racial taxonomies that Hesse describes as "constituted through the colonial designations of Europeanness and non-Europeanness, in verbal assemblages of social, economic, ecological, historical, and corporeal life."[69] The "black blood" or black bodies social logic is not the kind of foundational blackness that my work accentuates. I focus on subjectivity forged collectively and/or across racial or ethnic boundaries or populations and through a wariness of expendability, while this other paradigm focuses heavily on DNA within the human body and in its phenotypical manifestations concurrent with a desire for mere political recognition within the state's racial order.

In my analysis of solidarity, blackness is a condition that is as much discursive and performed as it is embodied or corporeal. What gets left out of corporeal debates is a focus on how racial difference is imagined and instantiated in acts of racial exclusion and terror and thus how such shared experiences among blacks and Latinos/as implant solidarity as a hidden knowledge within their subjectivities. That kind of hybridity, derived from shared experiences and memories, is far more powerful for building political coalitions for fomenting resistance than is the black biological ancestry of Latinos/as. In other words, we cannot merely assume that acts of interminority solidarity will emerge from drops of black blood in Latino/a bodies or vice versa.

The other detrimental effect of overaccentuating Afro-*latinidad* is that Afro-Latinos/as are distinguished as "having race," similarly to African Americans. This division is also due in large part to the hegemonic influence of the one-drop rule or hypodescent in U.S. history. The suggestion has the adverse effect of whitening the general and non–Afro-Latino/a population. Lawrence Wright has argued, regarding how Latinos/as get lost within debates about the significance of race in the United States, that "the great preponderance of Hispanics are mestizos—a continuum of many different genetic backgrounds. Moreover, the fluid Latin-American concept of race differs from the rigid United States idea of biologically determined and highly distinct human divisions."[70]

Most Latinos/as are, then, locked into a condition of not only racial outsidedness but also a kind of racial purgatory in that a large segment of the U.S. polity cannot decide whether Latinos/as qualify as a racially oppressed group like blacks or whether they should more commonly be associated with white oppressors. Much of this double bind is the result of uncritical perspectives regarding the origins of Latino/a history. As a result, Latinos/as are often uncritically linked to whiteness whenever their biological blackness or their indigenous ancestry is not being accentuated. George J. Sanchez offers a similar explanation for how Latinos/as are often written out of racial debates and uncritically linked with whiteness. He contends that because of the black-white binary generally and the one-drop rule in particular, "the racially mixed background of most Latinos/as in the United States, coupled with the more fluid ascriptions of racial categories in Latin America, has left Latino understanding of race at odds with U.S. racial descriptions."[71] Although Sanchez is describing how Latinos/as should be more critically considered within debates about race in the United States, he also conveys some rationale for how and why blackness functions as a discursive tool manipulated by Latinos/as to better integrate these debates.

As blackness has been constructed to be so clearly antithetical to whiteness in the U.S. racial formation and as the one-drop rule has been so deeply influential on how race is perceived and politicized in the country, blackness (in the more discursive or performative definition on which I am focusing) then often functions as an anchor to which a consciousness of anti-Latino/a racism is discursively tethered. It does, at least in many of the examples in this book that suggest that blackness has a discursive influence on Latino/a subjectivities. Memories of black history, black political leaders, and black expressive cultures have become heavily influential in how Latinos/as engage in a politics of antiracist resistance. This is especially true in metropolitan regions like Houston where anti-black racism and black antiracism are so clearly mapped out across a discursive terrain regarding the social meaning of race. Foundational blackness can then be interpreted as either a regressive or a progressive condition, although here I privilege its progressive characteristics. Foundational blackness verifies how *latinidad* is often uncritically politicized, and yet it also marks a representation of hybridity that can potentially transform how race is politicized at local, regional, national, and even international levels.

Despite the potential I see in the hybridity produced in part by foundational blackness, a more critical perspective on how *latinidad* has been racialized is still necessary. This perspective should be comprised of two components. The first is an acknowledgement that the sustained history of state-sanctioned exclusion, displacement, exploitation, incarceration, and obliteration of Latinos/as in the United States does not correlate with white privilege. In fact, it makes Latinos/as seem far more similar to blacks than to whites, and this is especially true in the Gulf South. This first component is a primary logic for black-Latino/a solidarity emerging in a community like Baytown. As I will discuss in more detail, it is not DNA or blood type that has produced black-Latino/a solidarity but the types of bloodletting (violence and obliteration) in which blacks and Latinos/as have been targeted and victimized within settler-colonial formations that have instilled in them similar sets of memories. The memories have produced similar subjectivities. The subjectivities have often resulted in expressions of black-Latino/a solidarity and resistance, as evident in Baytown's activist awakening of 2002 and the broader and more diverse discursive terrain regarding black-Latino/a hybridity within which I situate it.

The second component of my argument regarding a more critical perspective of *latinidad* has to do with its racialization and the relationship of race and ethnicity as it applies to the Latino/a population and history. In his critique of the Latinos-as-white thesis Poitevin appropriates the work of historian David Roediger, who analyzes how whiteness has functioned in the assimilation tactics of various immigrant groups in U.S. history. Roediger concludes that the relationship between race and ethnicity has always been "messy," meaning that there is no general way to assess this relationship, as it has produced different outcomes by group, period, and region.[72]

The relationship of race and ethnicity as it applies to Latinos/as, however, seems to have remained quite clear and comprehensive. Discourses of white Anglo-American supremacy were cemented as characteristics of U.S. nationalism in direct opposition to Latinos/as (specifically Mexicanos/as) during the mid-nineteenth century and as the current U.S.-Mexican border was being established.[73] Arnoldo De León and Reginald Horsman both have argued that as whites began to migrate to places like South and Central Texas to fulfill their Manifest Destiny, Mexicans stood in their way, thus creating the impetus for the production of demonic and anti-Mexican discourses to justify the subsequent removal and/or obliteration of Mexicans.[74]

The racialization of Mexicans as a natural threat to nation building during the mid-nineteenth century is important for thinking about the racialization of *latinidad* at large because of the symbolic significance of the border demarcating Latin America from the United States. But it is also significant in that two-thirds of Latinos/as in the United States today are of Mexican origin. From that period onward, a proximity to whiteness has at no point granted Latinos/as immunity from the racial state of expendability, as evidenced in how they have joined blacks as the primary targets for lynching, police brutality, and other violence throughout the nineteenth, twentieth, and now early twenty-first centuries. Latinos/as are hence like blacks in being perceived as internal threats to law and order. However, they also are like Arab Americans and Asian Americans, who are perceived as foreign threats. Latino/a expendability thus stems from two normativities.

In more recent decades a rise in xenophobia and U.S. nationalism, coupled with the stigma of Latinos/as being categorized as "illegal aliens," has only exacerbated the vulnerability to police terror of all Latinos/as and specifically of Mexicanos/as and Central Americans who are stigmatized as illegal aliens. The recent U.S. war against illegal immigrants can be interpreted as a condition that has made Latinos/as the most common victims of racial profiling and police brutality in the country. Border militarization has produced a Latino/a death toll of roughly a thousand victims a year since being implemented as a law enforcement strategy in the mid-1990s.[75] Anti-Latino/a hate crimes have increased more than 40 percent in recent years largely as a result of rampant xenophobia across the United States.[76] Twenty state legislative bills were introduced or passed across the United States since 2008 to enable or encourage law enforcement agents to suspend protocols of the U.S. Constitution and to police "illegal" immigrants by racially profiling all Latinos/as. Arizona was the first state to pass such legislation and was followed by Georgia and Alabama.

Recent anti-Latino/a directives across the South suggest that there has been a shift away from demonizing blacks alone and toward identifying Latinos/as as well as threats to sovereignty. The measures have resulted in conditions of policing and hypersurveillance that Maureen Costello, director of the Southern Poverty Law Center's Teaching Tolerance project, has described as the "new Jim Crow" and African American hip-hop artist Talib Kweli has called "Jim Crow en español."[77] Lekan Oguntoyinbo argues that Alabama's new anti-immigrant bill evokes and gives new life to its old Fugitive Slave Act, as it criminalizes anyone who grants refuge to undocumented immigrants.[78] Others have claimed that these initiatives are designed to control and exploit Latino/a workers or to "bring back slavery for Latinos."[79] Reminiscent of Scott-Heron's commentary in 1978 linking the plights of blacks and Latinos/as, these qualifications have been articulated as a method to connect Latino/a lives to conditions all too familiar to blacks in the South and as a way to stretch the meaning and significance of black history beyond the bodies of African Americans and focus attention on a more collective and expansive antiracist agenda fit for twenty-first-century realities.

The racialization of *latinidad* and the blurring of the line between race and ethnicity as it applies to where Latinos/as fit into the U.S. racial order were put on display with clash-of-civilizations theorist Samuel Huntington's assertion in a 2004 article that Latino/a population growth poses the primary threat to U.S. national identity: "Unlike past immigrant groups, Mexicans and other Latinos have not assimilated into mainstream U.S. culture, forming instead their own political and linguistic enclaves—from Los Angeles to Miami—and rejecting the Anglo-Protestant values that built the American dream. The United States ignores this challenge at its peril."[80] To accentuate the kind of threat Latino/a growth presents in the United States in a racial sense, Huntington contends that "the cultural division between Hispanics and Anglos could replace the racial division between blacks and whites as the most serious cleavage in U.S. society." The lines between race and ethnicity with regard to Latinos/as are clearly blurred in his xenophobic rant.

Huntington's warning about America's future stirred intense political debates not only because to progressives he sounded ridiculous; it also did so because Huntington's essay functioned as a literal call to arms to many conservative Americans who already embraced an image of Latinos/as as a threat to the moral and ethical foundations of U.S. nationalism and sovereignty. The result of this hegemonic discourse has been support for an assortment of draconian measures that have criminalized Latinos/as across the country, often leading to mass incarceration, wholesale deportations, a rise in police brutality, and increased vigilante violence against Latinos/as. Besides the pigment of the skin on many Latinos/as' bodies, it is also the memories, traditions, and languages expressed from those bodies that are perceived as a threat to the mythological America's (Anglo) national identity and ethos. The increasingly transnational nature of the U.S. Latino/a population, the more vibrant links being established between Latinos/as and Latin America as a result of migration and information technology, only exacerbate this tension. Again, the white privilege of Latinos/as seems rather impossible in this context. The border, in its symbolic significance, disallows it.

Beyond the racial state of expendability, the closer proximity to whiteness that Latinos/as supposedly have enjoyed since they were defined as legally "white" in 1898 does not seem to offer Latinos/as any advantage with regard to resource competition. Employed Latinos/as rank below employed blacks in income levels,[81] a statistic that can be cited to suggest that Latinos/as represent the most impoverished population in the United States. This statistic does not account for the millions of undocumented Latino/a workers living in the United States who are vital to the national economy, a group that would probably push the income levels even lower. Latinos/as have the least health insurance coverage of any group in the United States, have the lowest levels of education, and are the least politically represented by percentage of the U.S. population they comprise. While educational achievement has been improving for blacks and whites in the United States, it has continued to decline among Latinos/as, who drop out of high school at 2.5 times the rate of blacks and 3.5 times the rate of whites.[82] My own professional field, academia, is seriously deficient in Latino/a representation; in college and university faculties, Latino males are among the rarest members of all.

The historical and contemporary circumstances are reasons Latinos/as do not compare well with those southern and eastern European immigrants who entered the United States as nonwhite and yet became white over time. In his analysis of Roediger, Poitevin explains that the 13 million southern and eastern European immigrants who arrived in the United States between 1886 and 1925 became white as a result of two conditions. The first was that they comprehensively embraced anti-black racism as a method to distance themselves from the one group that was constructed as the clear antithesis to whites and whiteness at the time. The second condition was that state laws and federal programs rewarded immigrants for their anti-blackness by providing them with structural privileges.[83] This indeed took place as part of FDR's New Deal as the state worked to strengthen "white unionism" by excluding black, Asian, and Latino/a workers. The state funded and enforced the development of segregated neighborhoods for European immigrants through restrictive covenants, redlining, and other maneuvers. Considering these conditions, while there are examples of Latinos/as harboring anti-black sentiments and distancing themselves from blacks in Houston and elsewhere to become "more white," the rewards for these actions are, generally, still void. Poitevin argues, "There is no Latino 'New Deal' channeling hundreds of millions of dollars for new Latino housing (as happened with European immigrants), or New Deal–type legislation geared toward giving Latinos the upper hand against other groups on labor issues or government assistance programs. If anything the exact opposite is true: New government policies have been aggressively criminalizing Latinos."[84]

The state is, therefore, not rewarding Latinos/as for claiming whiteness but is instead continuing its legacy of exploiting, scapegoating, and marginalizing them for the ways they are perceived as nonwhites, non-Americans, and a perpetual border nemesis. Neoliberalism (globalization) has only exacerbated this condition.[85] Certainly, Eduardo Bonilla-Silva has shown, lighter-skinned Latinos/as have benefited from appearing whiter in the United States.[86] But lighter-hued blacks have benefited as well. Lighter skin tones within the African American community correlate with better socioeconomic outcomes, higher educational levels, and even shorter sentences for crimes when compared to darker-hued blacks.[87] As antithetical to whiteness as blackness has been constructed as the result of the one-drop rule, this does not discount the hegemonic influence of whiteness over black people in the United States. In fact, because much attention is given to the racial whiteness of Latinos/as, perhaps more critical attention should go to the ethnic whiteness or statism of blacks and especially African Americans, a group that often vocalizes the same kind of xenophobic sentiments associated with conservative whites. An African American has been elected president. If the White House is not a symbol of white privilege, then I am not certain what is. Perhaps, then, the black-white binary affords African Americans a closer proximity to whiteness when compared to Latinos/as or Asian Americans, who are commonly stigmatized as immigrant newcomers and hence not part of any binary discourse regarding civil rights in the United States.

As Latinos/as are so often described as racially whiter than African Americans, perhaps one also can make the case that African Americans are more ethnically white than Latinos/as and largely because of the intense time-space compression wrought by neoliberalism. After all, whiteness has been coterminous with being Anglo-American in how it has been constituted in the U.S. racial formation. As neoliberalism has increased anxieties regarding the waning of U.S. national identity and sovereignty, the black-white binary often appears to have mutated into a post–civil rights black-white alliance against foreign invasion. There are, to be sure, important exceptions to this outcome. Nonetheless, an argument can be made within this context of scrutinizing statism and the influence of whiteness within "minority" populations.

European immigrants utilized blackface minstrelsy as a method to become more American and hence more white; the same kind of procedural outcome has never been associated with Latinos/as in the more than 150 years of their being associated with whiteness in the United States. Latinos/as are decisively different from white youths who have appropriated blackness by way of hip-hop culture in the late twentieth and early twenty-first centuries. Latino/a youths helped invent hip-hop culture alongside blacks and popularized much of the dance and visual art elements of the genre.[88] The black and Latino/a foundations of hip-hop shed a light on the common struggles of the two groups and highlight the ways expressive cultures often serve as a primary medium to engage in racial politics. Greg Tate suggests that nonblacks who appropriate black culture do so with "everything but the burden."[89] By comparison, a more critical analysis of Latino/a history suggests that Latinos/as appropriate blackness, through hip-hop or any other medium, with the burden included as well as the additional burden of being considered foreign others.

The historical nonwhiteness of *latinidad*, and especially how this condition has been in part derivative of anti-black racism in U.S. history, provides the sociological grounds for the arguments I am attempting in this book. It is the overlapping and shared history of oppression of blacks and Latinos/as that has provided for a set of memories that fuse together black and Latino subjectivities. Foundational blackness, as it applies to my reading of Latino/a subjectivity and politics, does not entail Latinos/as advancing "on the backs of blacks," as Toni Morrison once said with regard to white immigrants to the United States and their relationship to African Americans.[90] It also is more complicated than Latinos/as simply borrowing from blacks in the ways they engage in racial politics. Foundational blackness entails Latinos/as realizing their linked fates and shared expendability with blacks and understanding the hegemonic influence of conditions such as the black-white and force-choice binaries. The subjectivities birthed from these power/knowledge interfaces often result in Latinos/as building with blacks and often from or through blackness a new kind of hybrid political subject, subjectivity, and oppositional culture that I find politically relevant enough to privilege for the sake of stirring debate.

CHAPTER TWO

BLACK GOLD AND BROWN BODIES: EARLY BAYTOWN

I SET OUT FOUR OBJECTIVES IN THIS CHAPTER. The first is to demonstrate that anti-black violence was foundational to how communities like Baytown were established during the late nineteenth to early twentieth centuries. That barbarism was primarily exercised in the form of vigilante and police terror during the mid-nineteenth to mid-twentieth centuries. Important gender and sexual dynamics characterized this violence, as it targeted black men in particular and was often legitimated as a necessary method to police and repress black masculinity as a potential emblem of black empowerment that unsettled white-supremacist discourse. At the time, Latinos/as were either nonexistent in certain communities or represented only a very small percentage of the population.

The scant Latino/a presence in early Baytown and in other Houston-area communities was a reason blacks and especially black men bore the brunt of the violence inflicted to segregate communities during the Reconstruction era. To be sure, this was also the result of the lingering tensions of the U.S. Civil War and for which communities like Baytown were quite important. The expendability of the region's black population reflected the social climate of the entire Gulf South during that period.

This expendability was and is as much a structural as it is a symbolic condition. I borrow the term "symbolic violence" from Pierre Bourdieu to convey how expendability structures subjectivities and relations of power in any given social formation.[1] Symbolic or "soft" violence is always connected to concrete acts of violence, or what Bourdieu refers to as "hard" violence, in a society. They are dual components of a system of "social control." Acts of systemic hard violence become justified or normalized, symbolically, within a community as part of its modus operandi. This normalization then generates the potential for more hard violence as a political apparatus, a method of social control. The effects of symbolic violence are evident structurally and psychosocially. Colaguori explains the significance of Bourdieu's concept of symbolic violence to analyses of subjectivity:

> Its power lies in the fact that it is embedded in the forms of subjectivity that serve to maintain the social order . . . As Foucault made clear, subjectivity implies the subjection to an order of power of some sort. And, symbolic violence is one way of speaking about a subjectivity that is socially regulated via an order that reproduces social domination.[2]

Applying this concept to my analysis of how and why anti-black racism was so central to the Houston area's early racial formation, this chapter demonstrates how this articulation of soft violence has been embedded in the iconography and social climate of the region. The iconography clearly glorifies the Confederacy in addition to local slave owners and other white-supremacist figures who gained notoriety in defense of slavery and segregation. This was especially true in Baytown, where nostalgia for the Old South is quite pronounced and is evident in the names of public schools, other institutions, and historical markers. Both Richard Slotkin and Marita Sturtken have shown that the public iconography of any social formation offers a clear view of the types of values it privileges and behaviors it has normalized.[3] The iconography helps map out the contours of symbolic violence and gives an indication of whose lives have been rendered most expendable in hegemonic narratives regarding the origins of sovereignty.

My second objective in this chapter is to demonstrate that the practice and normalization of anti-black violence helped structure how Latinos/as experienced, considered, and responded to racial oppression in early Baytown and in Houston. While I could find no evidence of Latinos/as being lynched or brutalized like blacks were, this does not mean they were immune from violence. What it does seem to suggest is that anti-black racism was so profound in the early history of communities like Baytown that it had a supplementary disciplinary effect over their much smaller Latino/a populations. Coupled with explicit examples of rampant anti-Latino/a sentiment, the violence targeting blacks that was glorified in the region's civic iconography also terrorized Latinos/as. It was a foundational element to how they experienced segregation, exclusion, and exploitation.

The third objective in this chapter is to demonstrate the effects of anti-black violence on Latino/a subjectivities. There is some evidence, for example, that grotesque public acts of anti-black violence were explicitly intended by whites to terrorize blacks and Latinos/as. There is also evidence that this maneuver was successful, as acts of anti-black violence would spur Latinos/as to deploy tactics like those blacks used for surviving and coping with the racial state of expendability for roughly fifty years prior to the establishment of Latino/a communities or barrios. After Juneteenth, some of the largest freedmen's settlements in the entire South arose in the Houston area, including those around early Baytown. The settlements were spaces where blacks attempted to insulate themselves from the terror of lynchings and other dangers and build strong bonds among families as an element of survival and uplift. Roughly a half-century later, Latinos/as followed suit, building barrios where their families bonded for self-help, mutual aid, and perseverance.

Certainly, the wariness of expendability of early Baytown's Latino/a residents could have originated from other parts of Texas where Latinos were being lynched as often as and even more so than blacks in the South. But we cannot discount the effects on Latinos/as of the Houston area's early anti-black social climate, a deep-seated dedication by whites to maintaining a social order related to the plantation economy of the Confederacy. The destruction of black lives and decimation of black bodies were the primary signifiers of symbolic violence in early Baytown and Houston. There is no way Baytown's and Houston's Latino/a pioneers were unaware of what was transpiring around them. This history is a moment when a hidden knowledge of black-Latino/a solidarity influenced the subjectivities of both groups.

My fourth objective in this chapter is to demonstrate how the deeper roots and nature of anti-black racism in the Houston area played a role in spurring more defiant acts of black antiracism roughly a century prior to acts of Latino/a antiracism. This chronological differential is not a sign of the passivity or whiteness of Latinos/as. It should instead be read as a reflection of demographic and historical realities. Blacks experienced violent oppression for much longer than did Latinos/as and had a stronger numeric presence to engage in acts of resistance far sooner than Latinos/as would.

SLAVERY AND EARLY HOUSTON

Unlike in other parts of the South, chattel slavery was not central to the region where Houston arose until the mid-nineteenth century. Texas was claimed by Spain in the early 1500s, but Spanish settler colonialism did not begin until the 1690s.[4] Texas was part of the kingdom of New Spain until 1821 and became part of the newly formed Republic of Mexico after Mexican independence and the first Mexican constitution in 1824. It remained part of Mexico until 1836, when it became the newly formed Republic of Texas, then annexed by the United States in 1845.

Slavery did not proliferate in early Texas until the arrival of Anglo-

Americans and other non-Spanish European settlers in the early 1800s. The region that would become the Houston area began to develop as a center for the Gulf Coast slave trade after the Louisiana Purchase of 1803. As Louisiana was added as a Southern slave state, New Spain sought to distinguish itself from its new eastern neighbor by issuing Article 28, a colonization law, on June 28, 1821. The law declared that any slave who migrated across the U.S.-Spanish border (today's Texas-Louisiana border) would be immediately emancipated. It also freed slaves' children over the age of fourteen.[5]

The declaration sparked a mass migration of runaway slaves across the border and into upper and coastal East Texas; many joined Native American communities to resist white slave hunters, an early example of solidarity induced by expendability. The demography and social climate of East Texas began to change rather dramatically in 1809, years prior to the 1821 decree, when the Spanish governor of Texas began to allow white U.S. slave owners to enter their territory in pursuit of runaway slaves. While this decree violated the Spanish viceroy's general policy on immigration, the governor's ruling allowed for the migration of whites into Texas over the next few decades. The biggest wave of white immigrants began to arrive after Mexican independence in 1821 when Stephen F. Austin established a settler colony in Central Texas. Austin's colony set the stage for a substantial increase of white slave traders in Texas, an increase that also encouraged desires among white settlers to claim Texas from Mexico.[6]

Austin allowed settlers to purchase fifty acres of land for each slave they owned.[7] The Mexican state of Coahuila y Tejas threw a wrench into Austin's plans in 1827 when it outlawed slavery in all forms; Mexico's emancipation proclamation followed in 1829. Austin's settlers were given a one-year grace period to comply with the law. Approximately 5,000 slaves did not wait that long and simply left plantations knowing there was little their owners could do to stop them. Many fled to the interior of Mexico and were granted citizenship and land by the Mexican government.[8]

This galvanized Austin's white Texans to declare their independence and launch a war against Mexico in 1835. The war elicited some of the first and most significant coalitions between blacks and Latinos/as in the region. Hundreds of runaway and freed slaves not only fled to the interior of Mexico but also took up arms against whites, joining the Mexican army in its campaign to subdue the rebellion.[9]

Blacks and Mexicans launched an uprising in 1835 in a community along the Brazos River. A group of roughly a hundred former slaves planned a preemptive strike against their previous slave masters after hearing that Mexican troops were approaching the area to seize it from white landowners and to allow them to leave without fear of violent persecution. Rather than wait for Mexican troops to arrive, the blacks decided to set the stage for the concerted victory with Mexicans by launching the attack. Their strike was mistimed. Major Sunderland formed a white militia that squashed the rebellion, resulting in more than a hundred of the rebels being whipped to death and others lynched.[10]

The Texas-Mexico war ended with the Battle of San Jacinto, near what is now Baytown, when the Texas army surprised a Mexican regiment while its men rested under some trees. The Independent Republic of Texas was established, and the San Jacinto monument looms high over Baytown and the Houston area as a monument to settler colonialism, the tallest monument in North America.

The "city to be" of Houston was established in 1836 by the Allen brothers, real estate speculators from New York, just months after the Battle of San Jacinto. They named their more than 6,000-acre purchase after General Sam Houston, the victorious commander of the Texas forces and the Texas Republic's first president. The site was but a small trading post for barge traffic on the tranquil waters of Buffalo Bayou at the confluence of the White Bayou. Houston became the first capital of Texas, and Texan leaders were eager to construct it into an admirable capital city. The hot, subtropical climate and swampy terrain made this goal particularly difficult from the outset. Black slaves and Mexican prisoners of war were forced to clear land and begin construction on the town's infrastructure. Kenneth W. Wheeler, one of the earliest historians of the region, contends that "no white man could have worked and endured the insect bites and malaria, snake bites, impure water, and other hardships."[11]

Their forced labor is an example of the common plight and position of blacks and Latinos/as in early Houston. It represents, moreover, a moment when Latinos/as were enslaved alongside blacks, just a few years before Latinos/as would be defined as legally white by the state of Texas. Despite the presence of Mexican prisoners of war in early Houston, Latinos/as did not begin to constitute a sizable population in the Houston area until the early 1900s. The region's black population, however, grew rapidly as the number of slaves in Texas grew roughly from 500 in 1825 to 12,000, the majority of them in the Houston area, on the eve of its annexation by the United States in 1845. The annexation of Texas as a state provided even more room for slavery to expand as it opened up a vast new western territory for southern slavers. As a result, the number of slaves in Texas grew dramatically, from 12,000 to roughly 250,000 by the middle of the U.S. Civil War, giving Texas the tenth-highest slave population in the nation and making it ninth among all U.S. states in the percentage of white families that owned slaves.[12]

More than half the slaves in Texas lived on cotton, corn, rice, and sugar plantations along the Gulf Coast and in upper East Texas. At this time, the area that would eventually become the city of Baytown was still sparsely populated, swampy territory outside of central Houston. Its population was concentrated around small rice plantations and a few brick-making enterprises along Cedar Bayou and Trinity Bay on what is now its eastern border and Black Duck Bay in today's western Baytown near the San Jacinto monument.[13]

The current city of Baytown, consolidated in 1948, encompasses three early settlements—Pelly, Goose Creek, and Baytown. In 1850 the area's population consisted of no more than fifty white families, a total of roughly 280 whites, and 90 black slaves. No Latinos/as or American Indians were reported to be living in the area at the time. The most prominent slave owner in early Baytown was Ashbel Smith, who owned 32 total slaves. He used slaves to cultivate his 300-acre plot of land and tend 180 head of cattle in what is now south Baytown along Goose Creek. John Rundell owned the second-largest number of slaves, at 12 total, most of whom he used to cultivate his 60-acre cotton plantation in what is now northwest Baytown in an area commonly referred to as Brownwood. David Burnet owned 2 slaves and a 2-acre farm.[14] Smith, Rundell, and Burnet are key figures in Baytown's civic iconography and are memorialized as Baytown's founding fathers. One of Baytown's oldest and largest elementary schools was named in honor of Smith. A large building at Baytown's local community college, which itself was named after General Robert E. Lee of Civil War fame, bears Rundell's name. One of the numerous bays from which the name Baytown originates is named for Burnet, who would serve as interim president of the Republic of Texas.

The Houston area began to evolve into a center for black life in Texas during the early years of U.S. statehood. Texas was unique among all slaveholding states for the size of its urban slave population, most of which resided in the Houston area.[15] Texas had the only slave population in the country that grew throughout the 1850s, with most of the growth taking place in the Houston area. Texas's annexation by the United States and the subsequent growth of its slave trade did not put an end to black resistance or coalitions between blacks and other groups of color. Many slaves continued to flee the Houston area and other parts of East Texas and travel to Mexico, where they often established their own communities near Mexico's northern border. By 1850 an estimated 3,000 slaves had successfully escaped to Mexico, and an additional 1,000 crossed into Mexico between 1851 and 1855. Black Maroons from Texas joined the migration of black Seminoles from Florida led by John Horse, who migrated westward to Texas and then southward to Mexico to establish towns such as El Nacimiento de los Negros Mascogos, just south of the Texas border in the Mexican state of Coahuila, where their Afro-Mexican descendants continue to live.

Again, this migration demonstrates that despite language and other differences, historically blacks recognized their commonality with Mexicanos/as—their expendability. The potential for solidarity between blacks and Latinos/as in early Texas was so strong that whites established explicit measures to prevent it. In 1854 a group of white vigilantes from the town of Austin acted to drive poor Latinos/as from the area and lynch those who resisted. While such an action was indeed fueled by their general disdain for Latinos/as, it was primarily driven by their fears that Latinos/as would encourage or assist in slave revolts.[16]

In 1866 white residents of Colorado County near Houston lynched several slaves and forced Latinos/as to flee after they learned of an alleged plot to arm hundreds of slaves and help them escape to Mexico. Because blacks were lynched in this case while Latinos/as were only driven from town does not mean Latinos/as were immune from violence; it calls attention to the fact that anti-black violence was more rampant than anti-brown violence during the late nineteenth century and more foundational to the racial ordering of that regional space. This was, at least, the case in parts of Texas including Houston and other areas of East Texas where blacks predominated. In some of South and Central Texas where Latinos/as far outnumbered blacks, Latinos/as were the primary targets.

Their shared experiences underscore the positions that blacks and Latinos/as occupied in the racial imaginary of early Texas. They also verify how Latino/a experiences with whites were often built upon practices and normative discourse originally designed to subjugate blacks and Native Americans. Horsman, a historian of racial discourse of the region and the period, comments that "Americans had two immediate racial models—the Indians and the blacks"—from which to borrow in their construction and perception of Latinos/as, specifically those of Mexican descent, in Texas.[17] De León notes that links between blacks and Latinos/as were so apparent to many whites that they commonly perceived the two groups to be biologically related. In fact, white political figures, scholars, and journalists often described Latinos/as as "half negro, half Indian greaser" or a "mongrel race" born from sexual encounters between blacks and Native Americans who inherited the worst traits of both sides of their genealogy.[18]

This imagined biological link between blacks and Latinos/as further fueled suspicions of Latino-led slave revolts. As much of the recent literature on Latino/a racial identity accentuates the access to whiteness and occupancy of a middle ground between whites and blacks, it is interesting to note that Latinos/as originally entered U.S. racial discourse as a group that was biologically inferior to blacks and Native Americans. This imagined biology represents yet another example of foundational blackness; as whites began to act upon their mythologized Manifest Destiny they drew on demonic images of blacks and language derived from black-white tensions in the South to demonize Mexicanos/as in the U.S. Southwest. The resulting experiences of Mexicanos/as were not dependent upon black history but were informed and structured by it. Menchaca has explained this early relationship, demonstrating how African American history helped determine the racialization of Latinos/as in Texas.[19]

The U.S. Civil War had a profound effect on early Houston and what would become Baytown. Texas seceded from the United States in 1860 and joined the Confederacy in the war against the Union. Many residents of early Baytown volunteered to serve in the Confederate army. The owner of the most slaves in Baytown, Ashbel Smith, was apparently so dedicated to the Confederate cause that he organized a local Confederate guard and named it the Bayland Guards. Smith recruited and gathered men from across Harris and Chambers Counties and on April 27, 1861, inaugurated a military training program for them at his Evergreen Plantation (now a golf course). As a reflection of Smith's connection to the elite of the region, his Bayland Guards included three men who were sons of two Republic of Texas presidents, Sam Houston and Anson Jones. Upon completing their training, the Bayland Guards were incorporated into the Confederate forces as Company C. They played a significant role in the battles of Shiloh, Corinth, and Hatchie Bridge in 1862.[20]

On September 18, 2010, the Bayland Guards were honored in a ceremony to dedicate a historical marker issued by the Texas Historical Commission. The marker was issued as the result of a petition filed by the City of Baytown and was funded in part by local businesses. A year and a half earlier, on March 19, 2008, the City of Baytown hosted a ceremony to honor a Confederate shipyard on the southern outskirts of town and dedicate a marker also issued by the Texas Historical Commission as requested by the city. The Chubb brothers, who donated the shipyard to the Confederate cause, were shipbuilders from nearby Galveston Island. They moved to the area in the 1850s to form a shipbuilding business in what is now a recreational site known as Bayland Park near Baytown's frontage on Galveston Bay. As kids we called the area Red Hill and assumed that the name meant it was a good spot to catch redfish from the banks of the bay. During the Civil War the Chubb brothers offered up their property as a site to construct, repair, and station

Confederate gunboats that patrolled the coastal waterways of East Texas and southern Louisiana.[21]

The two recent ceremonies honoring Baytown's Confederate roots reflect the city's social climate, symbolic violence, and nature of expendability. The commemorations indicate a much broader tradition through which local public schools have been named in honor of slaveholders and Confederate War icons like Ashbel Smith in a way that communicates an explicit disregard for, if not hostility toward, the black population of that region in particular. Today, for example, Baytown's largest and oldest high school and community college continue to bear the name of Robert E. Lee, the heroic leader of the Confederate army. Images of and reverence to Lee and the Confederacy are so prominent in and around Baytown that they, arguably more than any other factor, have functioned as Baytown's branding image. Out of so many possibilities, the naming of important public education institutions in honor of persons who not only supported but also led efforts to permanently subjugate people of color communicates an outright devaluation of these people's lives and well-being.

I attended Robert E. Lee High School and Lee College. When I was a member of Lee High School's football team in the early 1990s, our entrance to Baytown's Stallworth Stadium to begin matches against other Houston-area high school teams was accompanied by our school band's exuberant performance of the song "Dixie" to accentuate the school's namesake and link to the Confederacy. Lee High School's football team is an emblem of civic pride and history in Baytown that is exacerbated by the significance of the sport to the region and to Texas. Thus, thousands of fans would cheer and wave Confederate flags to represent our school and its tradition. Witnessing a predominantly black and working-class athletic team enter a stadium to represent Baytown and encouraging fans with a song like "Dixie" clearly reflected the kinds of symbolic violence that had been normalized in my hometown. Our team was the pride of the community, and yet that same community also took pride in a history that denigrated people of color.

Texas bears the dubious distinction of being the last state in the country where slaves were emancipated. On June 19, 1865, about 2,000 Union troops arrived at Galveston Island to issue the Emancipation Proclamation some two years after it was delivered to other slaveholding states. The day of the announcement is still celebrated annually in Texas and other states as Juneteenth, an important turning point for blacks in the Houston area, especially in Baytown, and in Texas at large.

No region of Texas was more affected by Juneteenth than the Houston-

Galveston area. Houston became the receiving point for masses of blacks who fled the rural rice and cotton plantations of East Texas and the Texas-Louisiana coast to start new lives as freed men and women in Houston's growing urban core. Their exodus would forever change the demography and social climate of the Houston area. A letter published in the local *Tri-Weekly Telegraph* of July 7, 1868, described challenges many of Houston's new black residents faced:

> We cannot help but pity the poor freedmen and women that have left comfortable and happy homes in the country to come to this city in search of what they call freedom. Nearly all of the old buildings that were not occupied . . . serve as homes for these . . . people. Many of these buildings are not fit for stables.

Opinions publicly shared by many white Houstonians call further attention to the black-white tensions that Reconstruction brought. A white Houston woman commented on the tragedy of the Confederacy's demise in another letter published in the *Tri-Weekly Telegraph*: "I am a secessionist as firm and as unflinching today as ever. I will take my son and fly to the islands of the sea first, and live there in everlasting solitude before I will live the subject of a conqueror."[22]

There is scant evidence of whites' sentiments toward Latinos/as in the popular media of early Houston. The nature of the newspaper commentaries sheds a light on two things. First, it demonstrates how black freedom was automatically equated with black criminality or an innate threat to the civil order. Second, the commentaries reveal just how foundational black-white tensions were to the Houston area's social climate due in particular to its importance in the Civil War and the Confederacy. The very idea of blacks not being slaves was perceived as a crisis of sovereignty and an immediate threat to the livelihoods of white residents. It is in this social climate and space that Latinos/as would increase in number during ensuing decades.

FREEDMEN'S SETTLEMENTS IN EARLY BAYTOWN AND HOUSTON

Houston's black migrants after the Civil War established a foundation from which some of the most effective antiracist critiques and challenges have emanated. This foundation began with the establishment of some of the oldest, largest, and most influential urban black communities in the entire nation. Don Carlton and Thomas Kreneck describe how "an influx of black migrants

to Houston filled the growing demand for labor . . . As their numbers increased, blacks developed their own separate society."[23] The formation of
black communities began a pattern followed later by Latinos/as as each group
attempted to insulate itself from the overall conditions and form communities within which they would develop a legacy of self-help and mutual aid
that would eventually lead to more defiant acts of protest. This pattern was
perhaps never more visible than in the community of Freedmen's Town, built
and appropriately named by free blacks in 1866 on the southeastern outskirts
of what is now downtown Houston in an area designated as the Fourth Ward.
After Juneteenth, Freedmen's Town quickly became one of the South's largest
black communities and a center for black-owned businesses, religious institutions, and entertainment. By 1880 it was larger than any other black community in the South and was one of the largest black enclaves in the entire
country. Freedmen's Town was the first black community to have its own
newspaper, *The Informer*; its own park, Emancipation Park; its own chamber
of commerce; and its own school.[24]

Coupled with a growing demand for cheap labor, the lure of Freedmen's
Town and smaller black communities fueled a black population boom in
Houston during the closing decades of the nineteenth century.[25] As a result,
by 1890 blacks comprised half the total population of Houston, or roughly
20,000 persons, making Houston's black community one of the largest in
the South. In comparison, there were no more than twenty Latinos/as reported to be living in Houston at this time and likely none at all in what is
now Baytown.

Another significant freedmen's settlement was established on the outskirts of modern-day Baytown.[26] In 1889 former slave Simon Barrett and
his family—his wife, Eliza, their children Harrison, Frank, Tobias, and Anne,
and Anne's husband, Mack Eagleton—built a home on the banks of the San
Jacinto River on lands they purchased for fifty cents an acre from a white
farmer named Ruben White. Barrett's Settlement, as it was called, soon developed into one of the largest landholdings by a former slave in the region. Fleeing the repressive and dangerous conditions they faced in white-dominated
rural communities, black families migrated en masse to places like Barrett's
Settlement in search of new lives and opportunities. Many of them were able
to build homes for themselves out of lumber provided by a sawmill run by
Harrison Barrett. The Barrett family also owned and operated a gristmill and
coffee mill that employed many newly arrived blacks. Residents of Barrett's
Settlement constructed Shiloh Missionary Baptist Church. This institution
served as the center of social life in Barrett and surrounding communities for
decades to come and continues to be an emblem of black pride and uplift in

Baytown and east Houston. Compared to the more urban setting of Freedmen's Town, Barrett's Settlement's more rural and isolated setting likely prevented it from developing into a larger black enclave.[27] Barrett's Settlement would eventually become known as Barrett Station due to the building of a railroad station and post office there.

On August 8, 2009, descendants of Simon and Eliza Barrett commemorated 121 years since the establishment of that freedmen's settlement. They held a ceremony on the lawn of the original structure built by Simon Barrett and a reunion for the founding families of the community. There were no elected officials, no uniformed men, and no state flags at the ceremony. Compared to the city and state government-sponsored celebrations of the Dubb brothers' Confederate shipyard and the Bayland Guards just years earlier, the Barrett celebration was a grassroots effort. No plaques were dedicated, no state historical markers were placed, and no state officials attended. Instead, it was put on by the Barrett family and relatives of the numerous families that had come to call Barrett home.[28]

Prior to the establishment of sizable black and later Latino/a communities, flight seemed like the main strategy for surviving racial violence during the closing decades of the 1800s. Prior to emancipation in 1865, an estimated 134 black slaves were dispersed throughout early Baytown and no Latinos/as. Three years later only 74 blacks were counted as living in this area.[29] The depletion of Ashbel Smith's estate reflects the broader transformation of Baytown during the immediate postbellum years. By 1870, five years after emancipation, only three black families, a total of 19 free blacks, were living on Smith's property. Many of these were described as black servants of Smith or sharecroppers, and 3 of them retained his surname after being freed. By 1880 only one black family of 4 persons lived on Smith's estate. In the same year, the area of modern-day Baytown listed only nine black families and 52 total persons, again a sharp reduction in the black population.

The majority of the remaining black population worked as sharecroppers, domestic servants, or laborers in brick-making facilities that dotted Cedar Bayou. The demographic statistics are reflective of the Gulf South at large during the period. Most former slaves in rural locations like early Baytown fled to newly established black communities like Freedmen's Town in Houston or Barrett's Settlement. Urban spaces and freedmen's settlements offered them a respite from the terror they faced in rural communities around former plantations.

The economic Panic of 1873 contributed largely to the demographic shift, as many paid black laborers were dismissed and contracts with black sharecroppers were destroyed. Other factors were at play in the black population

decline as well. Although the details about it are sketchy, apparently a horrific public lynching took place in Baytown in 1868. According to a document containing oral history testimonies of some Baytown white residents,
an unnamed black man was beaten, lynched, and mutilated by a white mob
for alleged sexual advances toward a white woman. This incident and white
residents' celebration of it caused blacks in the area to flee in terror.[30] In an
instant, the demography of early Baytown shifted dramatically and in a way
that highlights the gendered and sexual dimensions of anti-black racial violence across the South.[31]

It seems likely that many of the black residents who left settled in central
Houston, likely in Freedmen's Town, a more urban setting that could protect
them from the relative lawlessness of rural areas outside the city. As communities like Barrett's Settlement and Freedmen's Town expanded, they apparently helped insulate blacks from violence and other injustices and served as
bases for political mobilization, development of mutual aid networks, and
construction of separate black economic, political, and social institutions.

A shift from an agricultural economy to one based on oil drilling, refining,
and exporting in the early twentieth century spurred a general population explosion throughout the Houston area. Baytown would play an essential role
in the area's ascendancy to the center of the U.S. oil industry. The oil boom
fueled the growth of the black and Latino/a populations in early Baytown.
Black and Latino/a laborers were essential in transforming the Houston area
from an agricultural economy into a national center for the oil and energy
industries.

As their numbers grew, so did the threat of white vigilante violence against
them. This common danger, I argue, came out of conditions designed originally to subjugate blacks. It thus provides an important example of how black
and Latino/a experiences overlapped. The violence continued to dispropor-
tionately victimize blacks, but Latinos/as would increasingly be subjected to
the same treatment as their numbers increased and they began to reside alongside blacks in segregated enclaves surrounding Baytown's industrial base. As
they had previously with the formation of black enclaves like Freedmen's
Town and Barrett Settlement during the mid- to late 1800s, blacks and Lati-
nos/as responded to rising racial tensions in the early 1900s, specifically the
threat of vigilante violence, by struggling to establish their own ethnic communities away from whites.[32]

The discovery of a large oil field in 1901 at Spindletop, ninety miles east
of Houston near modern-day Beaumont, Texas, was the catalyst for Houston's shift toward an oil-based economy. By 1900 Houston had a railway system and a banking infrastructure, as it was the major trading center for the

region's agricultural goods and services. The infrastructure made Houston a prime location to develop as the urban center for the growing oil-processing and -exporting industry. Two other factors helped fuel Houston's growth into the regional center for the oil industry. First, the white business and political elite of Houston lobbied state and federal officials for funds to improve nearby port facilities. They were given $1.25 million in 1910, the largest federal grant yet awarded at the time, to shape waterways into the fifty-mile-long Houston Ship Channel to Galveston Bay.³³ Its ship channel contributed to making Houston an economic and industrial center of the South and eventually an important base for the entire U.S. energy industry.

The second major development of this period was the discovery of new oil fields in the area. The largest of the discoveries occurred in 1905 at Goose Creek in what is now Baytown. The Goose Creek oil strike and others would create an even larger demand for labor in the Houston area, much of which would be filled by new waves of black and Latino/a migrants.

The development of the oil industry in Houston in the early 1900s coincided with the turmoil of the Mexican Revolution, leading to an influx of Mexican migrants to the Houston area. Like blacks in the late nineteenth century, many new Latino/a migrants to the Houston area established their own communities to provide them refuge and a base of empowerment primarily against vigilante violence. The largest and most prominent of these settlements was El Segundo Barrio in Houston's Second Ward, adjacent to Freedmen's Town and the Fourth Ward. By 1912 Latinos/as had built their own Catholic church and school in Segundo Barrio; both were named Our Lady of Guadalupe, and they became a base for Latino/a political empowerment in the region.³⁴ Some of the earliest Segundo Barrio residents formed a group called the Agrupación Protectora Mexicana for the distinct purpose of self-defense against lynchings that took place throughout central, eastern, and southern Texas regions. Guadalupe San Miguel notes that this was but one among many community-based organizations established by Latinos/as in early Houston.³⁵

Texas was known to be a state where much anti-Latino/a violence was concentrated, exacerbated by the violent force of the Texas Rangers. The statistics regarding Latino lynchings in the Southwest and black lynchings in the South are quite comparable. William Carrigan and Clive Webb demonstrate that while there were by far more lynchings of blacks in the United States from the mid-nineteenth century to the mid-twentieth century, Mexicanos were lynched at a higher rate per 100,000 of the populations of many Southwestern states than were blacks in many of the most brutal lynching states of the South.³⁶ In Texas, Latino lynchings were concentrated in the southern and central regions, with no clear record of Latinos being lynched in the Houston area. In response to these conditions in the borderlands, Segundo Barrio residents sent a delegation to El Primer Congreso Mexicanista in 1911, a forum in Laredo, Texas, to discuss the problems and challenges facing all Latinos/as in Texas. Houston's Segundo Barrio residents played a role in getting accused murderer and folk hero Gregorio Cortéz paroled from a Texas prison. Cortéz showed his gratitude by visiting Segundo Barrio upon his release in 1913; he was welcomed there as a hero as residents reportedly paraded him through the streets of their neighborhood.[37] Houston-based Latinos/as had a hand in forging *El Plan de San Diego*, the manifesto that called for a general uprising on February 20, 1915, by a "liberation army of Latinos, blacks, Japanese, and Indians" seeking independence from "Yankee tyranny."[38]

THE HOUSTON RACE RIOT

Houston's black communities experienced growth stimulated by the development of Houston's oil industry, and their growth appears to have encouraged resistance. In 1917 Freedmen's Town erupted in one of the most volatile race riots of the twentieth century as its black residents protested a legacy of racial violence and other injustices. Just months after the United States declared war on Germany to enter World War I, the U.S. War Department ordered that two military installations be built in the Houston area—Camp Logan and Ellington Field. Once Camp Logan was built on the northwest outskirts of the city, the U.S. Army sent its Third Battalion of the Twenty-Fourth Infantry, an all-black battalion initially formed during the U.S. Civil War, to guard the establishment. Many whites said they felt threatened by the presence of armed black soldiers, many of whom were ranking officers, and believed they would incite aggrieved black citizens to rebel. Robert Haynes, a historian who studied the Houston race riot, describes their concerns: "Many Houstonians thought that if the black soldiers were shown the same respect as whites, black residents of the city might come to expect similar treatment."[39] As a result, Haynes argues, Houston police officers and sheriff's deputies began to regularly harass and brutalize blacks and especially the black soldiers when they entered the city.

Feeling disrespected, a number of the soldiers began to openly express their resentment toward white policemen. In response, the sheriff of Harris County passed an ordinance prohibiting black soldiers from leaving Camp Logan and entering the city. This enraged black soldiers and civilians alike. On August 23, 1917, the tensions boiled over. The violence began when Houston police officers arrested a black soldier who came to the defense of a black woman whom the officers were assailing in Freedmen's Town. Corporal Charles Biltmore, one of the twelve black officers with the Third Battalion, went to police headquarters to inquire about the soldier's arrest. An argument ensued, and white policemen assaulted Biltmore. Biltmore was able to flee, but officers chased after him, firing at him three times. They eventually caught Biltmore when he was hiding in a house in Freedmen's Town and took him into custody.[40]

A rumor quickly reached Camp Logan that Biltmore had been shot and killed. In response, a group of Biltmore's soldiers marched on the police station to investigate. Soon thereafter, police officers along with an armed mob of white vigilantes marched to Camp Logan to confront black soldiers, who opened fire on the mob. More than a hundred armed black soldiers then marched toward downtown Houston and into Freedmen's Town, where they were joined by a mob of angry black residents. During their march, the soldiers killed fifteen whites, including four policemen, and seriously wounded twelve others. The U.S. Army sent in white troops to quell the rebellion and restore order. Once the violence subsided, the Third Battalion was sent to Columbus, New Mexico, where its members were tried before a military tribunal. The court indicted 118 of the men on charges of inciting and participating in a mass insurrection and convicted 110. Of these, 19 were hanged and 63 given life sentences in federal prison. Not one white officer or civilian in Houston was indicted on charges stemming from the violence.[41]

The Houston race riot calls attention to the link between demographic change and changing majority-minority relations in the Houston area. It shows that the growing black population often fueled a heightened urgency among whites to maintain control over public spaces and a greater willingness among blacks to combat such conditions. White efforts to maintain control often may have been motivated by a desire to abolish any perceived public display of masculinity among black men. In this sense, the Houston race riot seems to have been prompted in part by white reactions to black masculinity in the form of armed and decorated black military personnel.

A black woman named Hazel Haynesworth Young, who was twelve years old at the time of the Houston race riot and resided in Freedmen's Town, recalled in a 2007 interview how the presence of black soldiers in Houston was perceived in gendered and sexual terms by the black community: "I remember the race riot. It seems that they sent soldiers . . . some of those soldiers came to our church with the shiny boots and everything . . . the young ladies in our church were all trying to meet and get, I guess, a husband out of that group."[42] The riot indicates that blacks were emboldened by their increasing numbers, and this inspiration translated into a much more defiant stance against conditions such as police brutality. The riot resulted from a commitment to uplifting and defending themselves. It also emanated from an act of chivalry by the black soldiers, as Young explains it:

> They say that the soldiers had said something, or an officer had said something to say to a black woman. The soldiers resented what they were saying to the black woman. And that is how they say the riots started. And a lot of people, they said hid, were so afraid for their lives. They were trying to escape from the rising up, the shooting and all . . . I do not see why they would have sent soldiers down here in the environment that they knew was in the South, where they were not accepted at all because of the fact that they looked better and had better, I guess, accoutrements than the whites, and that is how those race riots started. I never will forget it and I just feel sorry for those soldiers who were court marshaled who had not done anything but they had all of them shot, which was such a terrible thing I felt as a child.[43]

As white supremacy is espoused in the glorification of white men, the confinement and often elimination of men of color has been a central component toward maintaining that form of hegemony and discourse regarding patriarchy and heteronormativity that are central to settler-colonial formations in the South. Although observers describe the presence of black soldiers in Houston as angering whites, the building anger is already evident in concerns expressed by whites to local media prior to the arrival of the soldiers. Many expressed fear of black hostilities toward whites and their desires for revenge. There is no evidence of Latinos/as stirring this same level of concern or animosity in Houston, likely due to their smaller numbers. The following editorial letter appeared in the *Houston Daily Post* just weeks before the riot. It was written by a white man in Blue Ridge, North Carolina, after he attended a conference of wealthy whites in Asheville, North Carolina. His letter warned white Houstonians of a looming danger of a black uprising:

> For three days, day and night, the sessions went on in the discussion of topics relative to mob violence . . . It was recognized that we are facing a crisis in the South, which is eating away like a hidden gangrene, to the un-doing of law and order, and which, if not arrested, must work ruin.[44]

Two days later, a letter appeared in the same newspaper written by a white landowner from Brenham, Texas, just north of Houston. It read, in part: "Willie Shears, an Independence negro, was shot to death at Caldwell Sunday night while resisting a deputy sheriff who attempted to arrest him. The coroner's verdict says it was a clear case of suicide."[45] While details of the case are obscure, the coroner's pronouncement that resistance to arrest was suicide illuminates the social climate that manifested in the Houston race riot of 1917. The story of Willie Shears's death suggests that any resistance by blacks against police aggression in early Houston was popularly perceived to be legitimate grounds for officer-assisted suicide. The Shears story does not suggest that Latinos/as who resided in the Houston area were immune to such tensions. Blacks were primary targets of violence, given the historical development of the Houston area, its location, and its demography during this period. Free blacks represented the main threat to white hegemony during this Jim Crow era in the South, and it was the subsequent hard and soft violence against blacks that played the most influential role in the racial ordering of early Houston and the Gulf South.

An oral history interview of J. W. Carroll, a resident of early Baytown, reveals the degree of expendability that persons of color faced in the early twentieth century, especially by white law enforcement agents who did not distinguish between blacks and Latinos/as, lumping them together into a category that he described as "coloreds."[46] Carroll grew up on and worked at a sugar plantation in nearby Fort Bend County, seven miles southwest of the town of Sugar Land and around twenty-five miles southwest of central Houston. The plantation was owned by T. W. House, a financier from England who migrated to Houston in 1838 and became a prominent businessman in the region. House acquired the Arcola Sugar Plantation in 1872 and quickly expanded production through the use of a convict labor system that was prominent across the South during the Reconstruction era as a replacement for slave labor. Carroll said black and Latino prisoners were housed together in the "colored building," the largest wooden structure on the House plantation.

Carroll's interview contains precise details of the mechanisms invented at House's plantation to torture and terrorize laborers, specifically "the coloreds" when they would "refuse to work." The mechanisms included various instruments of torture fashioned from farming equipment in addition to the kinds of "whippings" that took place there. Carroll described the macabre circumstances that unfolded when a "colored worker" would die as the result of torture: "When those people died, very seldom would anybody claim them. They had a colored cemetery out yonder. When one of those prisoners died, they told some of those trustees to go out there . . . and dig a hole and put him in it. He was just a dead man and that's all there was."[47] Carroll's testimony of how blacks and Latinos/as were housed, exploited, tortured, and even buried as coloreds sheds more light on their shared experiences with expendability in the Houston area.

Goose Creek oil field, 1915. Courtesy of Baytown History Museum.

THE BERT SMITH LYNCHING IN BAYTOWN

Although the Goose Creek oil field was the largest and potentially richest in the Houston area, up until the later months of 1912 it had generally failed to provide the yield that oil speculators predicted. The frustration apparently lasted until October 1912, when Goose Creek wells began to produce a record amount of crude oil. Reports of this dramatic increase were enough to spark a migration of white "wildcatters" (oil speculators) and "roughnecks" (oil drillers) to the Goose Creek field beginning in November 1912.[48]

On August 16, 1915, a hurricane struck the area, causing extensive damage to oil-drilling operations in Goose Creek and the vicinity. The hurricane motivated many white workers and their families to move inland and to the east of the coastal oil field, where they were better protected from flooding and wind damage. A few months after the hurricane, a note in a local newsletter, the *Cedar Bayou Weekly*, reflected optimism about the oil field's resurgence: "Goose Creek is not dead yet, we can see 25 rigs most of them producing oil. Mr. Rucker has a drill running and we expect a gusher at anytime."[49] Inland white settlers established Pelly and Goose Creek, and the two towns grew rapidly in 1916 when the Gaillard #1 oil well began producing 8,000 barrels a day. Subsequent oil strikes that year helped increase the Goose Creek field's production from an average of 700 barrels a day in 1915 to 5,000 barrels a day by the end of 1916. On August 3, 1917, the Sweet #11 well blew and spewed roughly 25,000 to 30,000 barrels of oil over the area for the next three days.[50]

Goose Creek grew into one of several oil boomtowns on the outskirts of central Houston from 1912 to 1919,[51] and whites continued to dominate the population. By 1917 Goose Creek had its own Main Street, with a grocery store, barbershop, furniture store, boarding house, and post office. As oil-drilling operations increased in early Baytown, blacks from East Texas and western Louisiana began to migrate there in search of jobs, as did Latinos/as from Central Texas, South Texas, and northern Mexico. Denied the opportunity to drill for oil, most of these black and Latino/a newcomers assumed roles as cooks, janitors, servants, construction workers, delivery persons, and even entertainers in the oil-field labor camps and in other local businesses.[52]

The desires of whites to maintain power and control over public spaces appeared to increase with the influx of blacks and Latinos/as. Unlike Houston, early Baytown lacked a local police force to help them do so. White residents of Pelly and Goose Creek turned to vigilante violence to help maintain the status quo privileging whites. A few months prior to the Houston race riot in 1917, the Goose Creek oil fields were the site of one of the most horrific, albeit lesser known, lynching incidents in the region's history. It began when the wife of a white oil worker named Red Cowart alleged that a black man entered her tent in a labor camp while she slept. A black man worked as a cook for a white oil contractor named Robert Lyons. The cook became the prime suspect. In the *Houston Chronicle*'s coverage of the incident he was referred to simply as the "Negro assailant" whose "name was unlearned." The "negro assailant" was later identified as Bert Smith. Bert's surname suggests that he once lived on Ashbel Smith's plantation or was the progeny of someone who did.

The suspect and victim was a person whose name was at first unknown or obscure to local law enforcement officials, to those among whom he lived, to journalists, and even to his employer, signifying the extent of the racial state of expendability or devaluation that blacks faced during the Reconstruction Era in early Baytown. A person of no official or recognizable name can be theorized as the equivalent of a pet or even of livestock within the minds of whites and the plantation bloc of the early twentieth-century Gulf South.[53] Smith was reduced to a form of being that was primordially unqualified for human much less civil rights. He was an existential nobody, and in the end not even his body remained.

Smith was arrested by Harris County Deputy Sheriff Veale and two assistant deputy sheriffs the morning after the alleged incident and jailed in Goose Creek. The sheriff and his deputies heard that most drilling rigs in the Goose Creek oil field were shut down and men were gathering to march into town, and the lawmen feared they would not be able to deter a mob from lynching Smith. A mob of roughly 1,000 white oil-field workers subdued the sheriff's deputies, "battered down the doors of the jail," and took Smith into custody. According to the news coverage, they dragged him "about half a mile into the timber where they hanged him from a tree."[54]

Oral history testimonies say Smith was not only lynched but that his body was mutilated and then burned in a horrific, celebratory display of racist fury. It is also alleged that a local journalist was able to take pictures of the incident. The lynch mob, however, seized his camera and destroyed it. Members of the lynch mob severed all telephone lines in Goose Creek in an effort to prevent any intervention from Houston-based law enforcement officials or exposure of their deeds by Houston journalists. Justice of the Peace J. L. Thomason from the neighboring community of Crosby happened to be in Goose Creek that day. He had to walk "several miles into the country," to find a telephone connection to inform the county sheriff of the impending lynching. His phone call, however, was too late, as Sheriff Hammond and his deputies arrived to find Smith's charred and mutilated body and the remains of the celebration. A grand jury convened by the Harris County District Attorney's office to investigate the lynching ruled to "no-bill" the fifteen men arrested for the murder, exonerating all of them.[55]

As happened after the lynching incident of 1868 in Goose Creek, many blacks fled the area after the Smith lynching, according to at least one white resident at the time, and some presumably sought refuge in black enclaves of the region like Barrett's Settlement and Freedmen's Town. Garrett R. Herring witnessed the Smith lynching from a window at the "old Wiesenthal Drug Store." He recalled its effects on the demographics of early Baytown: "We had a negro porter working for us. And all the negros [*sic*] left town. They were really frightened."[56] In an interview twenty-four years earlier he said, "There were never many negroes living here, but a number of earlier ones moved away after the lynching. More Mexicans used to live in Baytown; however, around 1920 jobs were scarce and some roughnecks ran some Mexicans from their jobs."[57] Herring's mention of Mexicans in early Baytown in connection to the lynching of a black man offers additional evidence of how much the two groups were linked by their expendability. Margaret Swett Henson, author of the first historical study of Baytown, supports Herring's observations. She found that an armed mob of white workers marched through town in 1920 in a direct act to intimidate Latinos/as.[58] The lynching of blacks, therefore, was considered a form of disciplinary control over the growing Latino/a population as well.[59] It seems more than safe to assume that Latinos/as paid critical attention to events like the Smith lynching and that the horror signified by the case indeed influenced how they would respond to later acts of intimidation.

When viewed comparatively, the Smith lynching and the Houston race riot indicate that demographics help determine the level and nature of single ethnic group responses to racial violence. The Smith lynching took place in a location with a small black and even smaller Latino/a presence. The Houston race riot, just months afterward, provides quite the contrast. It transpired in a location that not only had a more sizable black population but that also was home to a large and influential black community. This stronger presence may be one of the many reasons the response of blacks in Houston was one of defiance and armed resistance rather than flight.

Lynchings of black men in the Gulf South and lynchings of Latinos in South and Central Texas were motivated by intersections of race, gender, and sexual meanings. The similarity was made quite evident within popular culture and, namely, in two films directed by D. W. Griffith, who is best known for his 1915 film *Birth of a Nation* and the hysteria that it fueled about black integration. His film *Martyrs of the Alamo* was released the same year and eclipsed by the former. *Martyrs of the Alamo* cast the famed battle of the Texas-Mexico war in a way that followed much of the plot popularized in *Birth of a Nation*. It depicted the Battle of the Alamo as a struggle of humble and morally sound white frontiersmen like Bowie, Crockett, and Austin to protect their wives from the sexual aggression of drunken and often drug-addicted Mexicans. In the film, Mexican sovereignty was reduced to the right of Mexican men to sexually violate and corrupt the bodies of white women, the same narrative Griffith construed to describe the postbellum South. A subtitle from an early scene in *Martyrs of the Alamo* reads: "Under the dictator's rule the honor and life of American womanhood was held in contempt."[60] Hence, the Battle of the Alamo was retold in a way that allowed the bloodshed of that military conflict to mean an effort to prevent blood mixing through sex rather than a battle over the right of Austin's settlers to own and exploit slaves.

The similarity in the plots and purposes of *Martyrs of the Alamo* and *Birth of a Nation* was so clear that Griffith used the same actors in both films. Walter Long in *Birth of a Nation* played the character of Gus (also known as Black Buck), the leader of a band of renegade blacks who hunted down white virgins; he also played General Santa Anna in *Martyrs of the Alamo*. Long played Gus in blackface created by black shoe polish and played Santa Anna in brownface using brown shoe polish. His portrayal of Santa Anna resembled the character Gus; in one scene Santa Anna was portrayed as "an inveterate drug fiend, the Dictator of Mexico also famous for his shameful orgies."[61] This scene was accompanied by images of Santa Anna intoxicated and literally drooling over the white women he captured at the Battle of the Alamo and held as sex slaves in his quarters near modern-day Baytown at the site of the later Battle of San Jacinto, after which he would surrender to General Houston's forces.

BLACK GOLD AND WHITE RAGE

Given the common demonization of blacks and Latinos/as in popular culture, it should cause little wonder that both groups faced the persistent threat of violence in daily life. In early Baytown the threat was quite apparent in the workplace. In late 1916 white oil-field workers throughout the Houston area organized their first union under the Texas State Federation of Labor and the Houston Trade Council. By this time, all workers at the Goose Creek oil fields were employed by either Humble Oil Company or Gulf Oil Company. Both allowed their employees to join unions. Faced with a higher cost of living and increased production due to World War I, union members demanded a raise and official recognition of their organization. Although some Humble and Gulf executives were willing to initiate a small wage increase, the union called for a general strike. On November 1, 1917, more than 2,000 white workers walked off the job.[62]

The strike brought unemployed men to Goose Creek, some of them black or Latino, looking to fill the jobs left by striking workers.[63] Humble and Gulf hired some of them as "scab" or replacement laborers. Fearing that they might lose their jobs permanently, many of the men on strike sought to return to their jobs within a week. Humble executives worried that the striking workers would commit mob violence, and they had large military-style barricades erected and hired a security force to protect company property. They also paid for two companies of a U.S. Army infantry division stationed at Camp Logan in Houston to come to Goose Creek in hopes of deterring a possible riot by angry white workers.[64] The racial implications underlying and fueling the tensions are clear. Considering the history of racial hostility in the area, company officials presumably expected that striking white workers would be incensed because some replacement workers were black or Latino.

When the strike was called off in January 1918, the union had made little to no gains and one-fourth of the striking workers had lost their jobs, largely, as it turns out, to white farmers from throughout the region who were hired as scabs.[65] The workers, however, were able to remove part of the black and Latino workforce and to solidify the threat of violence as a viable option for social and economic control.[66] In this moment the threat of racial violence had an economic logic tied to it. As in other instances, the threat was allowed by an underlying and prevailing perception of blacks and Latinos/as as subjects to whom justice did not apply due to their racial otherness.

As Baytown was transformed from a rural oil-drilling site into a base for Houston's oil-refining industry, its Latino/a population grew substantially. As it did, Latinos/as would come to experience the forms of subjugation with which blacks in the South and Latinos/as across the Southwest had become all too familiar. They would begin to develop similar strategies of survival and resistance. Latinos/as would begin to build segregated neighborhoods and insulate themselves from the expendability they faced in the community at large, as blacks had built enclaves such as Barrett's Settlement and Freedmen's Town decades prior.

By 1918 the oil field in Goose Creek proved to be much less abundant than expected. This realization led many white oilmen and workers to abandon it and migrate to oil fields in West Texas in search of better prospects. Black and Latino workers did not go, as they were generally prohibited from drilling for oil and instead were hired as service employees. At the same time, Humble Oil Company turned toward refining crude oil and initiated plans to build a large refinery in Baytown. The completion of dredging the Houston Ship Channel in 1914 helped make this project feasible, as it enabled large cargo ships to reach the Goose Creek area to export refined oil and gas.[67]

Humble Oil Company broke ground on its refinery construction project in the fall of 1919. Initially the company faced two obstacles: a swampy site polluted by oil, tar, and toxic chemicals and an insufficient labor force for the difficult initial phase of construction. Humble hired the black and Latino workers leftover from the oil boom and recruited others from the rural communities of East, Central, and South Texas. The company signed up workers from outside of Texas as well, particularly blacks from western Louisiana and Latinos from Mexico, to come to Baytown and begin construction of the refinery.[68]

The influx of blacks and Latinos/as altered the demography and social climate of the Goose Creek area. By the end of 1919 more than half the workers at the refinery construction site were black or Latino. This was a rather dramatic shift, considering that the workforce for the earlier oil drilling and excavation was largely white. The Houston area witnessed a small Latino/a population boom due to a steady stream of people escaping the turmoil and effects of the Mexican Revolution of 1910–1917 and seeking jobs in the burgeoning oil industry.[69] Established black communities like Barrett's Settlement, McNair, and Oakwood absorbed the steady stream of black workers moving into early Baytown from rural areas of eastern Texas, southern and western Louisiana, and southern Arkansas. Latinos/as, however, were just beginning to establish a solid footing in early Baytown and were often forced to live within the grounds of the Humble construction site or in makeshift tent communities that dotted the area.

Before 1918 most of the white construction workers employed by Humble were housed in Army-issued surplus tents in Goose Creek and were transported daily to the refinery construction site on a train contracted by Humble. By the early 1920s the Humble Oil Company refinery began to assume a more paternalistic relationship with its white worker population as it constructed many of the social, political, and economic institutions that helped shape Baytown's civic life and make it into a quintessential company town.[70]

While black and Latino workers were generally left to fend for themselves, white workers benefited from the benevolence and charity of Humble Oil Company. As the refinery expanded, Humble began to purchase land in the area to develop new neighborhoods for its growing white employee population. From 1918 to 1922 Humble constructed permanent dormitories for white workers as well as row houses made of wood or stucco for workers with families, all located near the refinery. It built a general store, drugstore, meat market, and gas station. The families of white Humble workers were given a monthly credit for supplies at these stores and were fed at any of four large mess halls for a discounted price. Humble maintained their homes, provided clean water and sewage services, paid their utilities, and even delivered fertilizer to aid the cultivation of home lawns and gardens.[71] The community that Humble built surrounding its refinery was called Baytown, the name that would eventually be appropriated for the entire city.

Black and Latino/a families were excluded from all of these resources. Their exclusion is a major reason blacks and Latinos/as depended heavily on one another to provide more sustainable living conditions for their families. There is also some evidence that blacks were given more opportunities than were Latinos/as in early Baytown. In 1920 a white man named H. K. Johnson Jr. allotted lands he had inherited to sell to black workers for a discounted price. Johnson's decision reportedly stemmed from the guilt he faced in being the heir to the fortunes of a former slave-owning family. Many black workers took advantage of Johnson's offer and established a small black community on the outskirts of modern-day Baytown that they named Harlem.

Compared to the housing options afforded to blacks, the labor camps where most Latinos/as lived within the refinery suggest that they were considered a temporary worker population to be exploited and then removed. They were particularly vulnerable to exploitation. J. W. Carroll, a Humble employee who came to Goose Creek in 1917, described the arrival of some of Baytown's first Latinos/as. He said a labor recruiter would travel to Eagle Pass, Texas, a town bordering Mexico, every Monday and return to the refinery on Saturday. Carroll said the recruiters

would bring two or three coaches of Latins up here. And they'd have everything they owned with them. The old lady would have two or three children draggin' 'em around. The old man would have a lantern and two or three frying pans and a dead roll of old clothes. They all had tags on 'em and they'd march 'em out to those tents. That's what they lived in.

The Latino workers were paid thirty-five cents a day, the same as the black workers. White workers like Carroll received fifty to eighty-five cents a day. Carroll said the "Latin" workers began indebted to the company, as they were given a coupon book with which they could buy food and supplies at the local commissary. The coupons, however, were deducted from their future pay. So they would spend most of their first few years just trying to work themselves out of debt, a condition equivalent to sharecropping and other forms of indentured labor. Latinos/as were also distinct from other groups in that entire families would live in tents, while black and white workers who lived in company tents were single men who had just arrived.

As the black and white population of the camps decreased, Latinos/as remained and renamed their community El Campo (The Camp) in 1918. Like residents of the black communities of Oakwood and Harlem and reminiscent of Freedmen's Town and Barrett's Settlement, residents of El Campo developed a profound sense of solidarity that they used to make the most of their living conditions and set the stage for future improvements. In its earliest years, El Campo lacked running water, electricity, sanitary sewage service, and access to medical facilities and public education.[72] Latinos/as' living predominantly in tents within the refinery grounds does not suggest that they benefited from white privilege in any form or when compared to blacks.

While they struggled for sustainable living within their segregated communities, blacks and Latinos/as functioned as a single unit at the workplace. At the Humble refinery worksite, black and Latino workers performed the most grueling jobs of building roads from the refinery tanks to the docks where ships could be unloaded of cargo and loaded with crude or refined oil. Their duties were among the least desirable and most dangerous due to the swampy and polluted terrain. Blacks and Latinos/as were denied the opportunity to take the aptitude tests used to place workers in higher positions according to skill, the most coveted position being first-class machinist.[73]

Segregation increased as the Humble refinery expanded and became one of the largest and most productive oil refineries in the Houston area. In 1924 Humble purchased 119 acres just southeast of the refinery and divided the property into 600 plots that the company then sold to its employees by loans it provided. The loans were restricted to whites only, excluding "blacks, Mexicans, Chinese, and Japanese." The lots ranged from $450 to $800, depending on their size and location. To encourage development in this community, Humble constructed streets, alleys, storm and sanitary sewers, a water system, and electricity in each residential area. It built a hospital in 1923 that soon became recognized as one of the area's most advanced medical facilities. Humble officials set out to promote social life among residents by constructing a community house in 1924 that would serve as the venue for dances, movies, holiday parties, and boxing matches. The Humble Community House served as headquarters for new civic organizations such as the Baytown Country Club, Women's Club, Veterans of Foreign Wars, and Baytown Volunteer Firemen.[74]

THE BROWNING OF EARLY BAYTOWN

Discriminatory conditions fueled the resilience and frustration that characterized Baytown's early black and Latino/a communities as well as intragroup solidarity in each community. During this period Latinos/as in Baytown began to develop their own community spaces within which they would establish a legacy of self-help and mutual aid like blacks had done in Freedmen's Town and Barrett's Settlement and Latinos/as did in some parts of Houston. Residents of El Campo in Baytown organized a community-based self-help or mutual aid organization they named the Sociedad Honorífica and renamed the Sociedad Mutualista Miguel Hidalgo in 1918. This organization was similar to those formed in Segundo Barrio in Houston. The development of these groups throughout the Houston area exemplifies the ways Latinos/as bonded and worked collectively in the face of acute discrimination. Members of Baytown's Sociedad Mutualista pooled their resources to build housing, conduct cultural events, and provide welfare, education, and even a health-care fund to transfer sick residents to the county medical facility in Houston in the case of emergency. Like blacks, Latinos/as were denied access to the hospital built by Humble. The Sociedad Mutualista Miguel Hidalgo established a bereavement fund to aid widows of men killed at the job site.[75]

Humble's Community House for its white employees and families was one of the more impressive brick buildings in the region. For its black and Latino workers, Humble built Community House #2, a wooden structure that was far less elaborate. Latinos/as gave the building an alternate name, El Salón, to highlight its significance to their community. El Salón became a space for the mixing of black and Latino/a subjectivities. Latinos/as had a stronger affiliation with the building because it stood in direct proximity to them in El Campo. Many black workers lived outside of the refinery grounds and in older black communities. Cinco de Mayo and Juneteenth celebrations would

Socieded Mutualista Miguel Hidalgo members in El Campo. Courtesy of Baytown History Museum.

El Campo, the Latino/a labor camp on Humble company grounds, 1918. Courtesy of Baytown History Museum.

Fiestas patrias celebration, 1919, sponsored by the Sociedad Mutualista Miguel Hidalgo at El Salón, Humble's Community House No. 2, in El Campo. Courtesy of Baytown History Museum.

take place at El Salón within several weeks of each other. Both groups viewed the structure as a home space where families could come together to celebrate ethnic customs and holidays.

Members of the Sociedad Mutualista Miguel Hidalgo hosted theatrical plays at El Salón that depicted Mexican history and the plight of Latinos/as in the United States. Excluded from membership in the male-dominated Sociedad Mutalista, Latinas from El Campo organized their own subchapter, the Ladies Auxiliary. They elected officers and concentrated their efforts on promoting Mexican culture, education, and recreational activities for children of El Campo.[76]

The founding president of the Sociedad Mutualista Miguel Hidalgo was Ernesto Nieto. His history illustrates the Latino/a experience and spirit of cooperation in early Baytown. Nieto was born in Veta Grande, Mexico, in 1890. In 1908 he migrated to the U.S. border town of Eagle Pass, Texas, in search of employment. There he married Gertrudis Campos in 1914; eventually they had twelve children. Upon hearing of abundant jobs at the Humble oil refinery, the Nietos moved to Baytown in 1919. Like most other Latinos/as, they settled in El Campo and Ernesto began working on the refinery construction crew. He soon became recognized as a community leader in El

African American employees, family members, and friends at a dance at El Salón, early 1950s. Courtesy of Sterling Municipal Library, Baytown.

Campo and spearheaded the initiative for Latinos/as to organize a mutual aid organization.[77]

Blacks continued their long legacy of self-help and mutual aid. By the time Mexicanos/as in Baytown started their mutual aid societies, large black communities like Barrett's Settlement and Oakwood had been in existence for some time. During the 1920s those communities began to make tremendous strides in their struggles for access to medical care and public education. In 1922 three black women residents of Oakwood—A. J. Johnson, Norah Davis, and Addie Rowls—began to circulate a petition calling for the establishment of a school for black children, considering that they, along with Latinos/as, were denied access to Baytown's public school system. As a result, the Goose Creek School for Coloreds was established and began to conduct classes for black students at the all-black Mount Rose Baptist Church in Oakwood. The church was like Mount Shiloh Church in Barrett's Settlement in that it served as a center for black civic life in early Baytown. Tilly Brown was the school's first teacher, Annie Bell Edwards was the school's first principal, and another teacher, Bertha Davis, was added soon thereafter. The Goose Creek School District purchased a building in Oakwood in 1923 to house the School for Coloreds.[78]

Latinos/as were slower to gain access to public education. In 1928 Baytown's Mexican School was established on land donated by Humble Oil Company. Unlike the School for Coloreds, the Mexican School suffered from neglect and lacked electricity, gas, water, sewage, supplies, and even teachers until 1930. The school did not have a full-time principal or administrator until 1937. The slower development of schools for Latinos/as and their deprived conditions have been explained as the result of various factors. Some early Latino/a residents said language was a factor, as there was a dearth of qualified Spanish-speaking teachers in the region. Others have said it was a general perception of Latinos/as as a perpetually foreign population whose residence there was only temporary. According to this logic, there was thus no perceived need to educate Latino/a children if their families would eventually return to Mexico. On the first day of classes at the Mexican School, seventy-two children arrived, many of them in their late teens who had never attended any form of schooling.[79]

The Mexican School expanded in the 1930s and was provided electricity and plumbing by the City of Baytown. It was renamed in honor of Lorenzo De Zavala, a Mexican politician who sided with the Texan army against Mexico during the Texas war for independence. Latinos/as organized their first Parent-Teacher Association, and Jessie Pumphrey was named the school's permanent principal. One of Pumphrey's platforms was pushing an English-only rule in the school because she considered assimilation and de-Mexicanization the only hope for Baytown's Latino/a youths.[80]

Besides its symbolic racial and ethnic boundaries, El Campo was demarcated and surrounded by a chain-link fence that Latinos/as were not to pass beyond unless they were entering the oil fields to work. Ruben De Hoyos was raised in El Campo; after serving in World War II he worked at the Humble oil refinery. During an oral history interview with me, he commented on the segregated boundaries of Baytown during his childhood: "[Whites] made it clear to us that if they caught you outside the fence you could take a bad beating . . . Even though I was just a kid, I remember being scared of dying or get-

Baytown Mexican School's original plaque, now housed at the Baytown History Museum. Photo by the author.

ting hurt if I ever left El Campo. . . . A lot of them were just waiting for the chance to catch us in the wrong place. El Campo was our home, but it also felt like a prison camp."[81]

Forced segregation may be one reason blacks and Latinos/as did not collaborate more often politically during this time:

> One reason that we did not work with blacks is that we never saw them even though the black section was just across the street. Every now and then, we'd run into each other, but the only place blacks and Latinos encountered each other was at the refinery and in there, white foremen did not allow too much communication between the groups. We had separate lockers, restrooms, and even separate drinking fountains which were labeled black or Mexican. I think they kept us apart because they feared an uprising.[82]

In the early 1920s Humble began to demolish El Campo as the refinery expanded, and its residents were asked to move to make way for Humble's new company neighborhood, reinforcing yet again the expendability of El Campo's residents. In return, Humble designated a small plot of land on the outskirts of the new neighborhood near the railroad leading into the refinery and helped build a series of streets named after various types of trees. The land was formerly the company waste reservoir, a dump for domestic and industrial waste. Hilda Martinez, a lifelong resident of Baytown, said as Latinos/as moved into the area and began to build their homes there, they referred to the new enclave by its previous name, El Bote, which in English means "The Dump."[83] Their choice of this name for their neighborhood suggests that they were quite aware of their expendability and understood their lack of white privilege. Although use of this nickname has waned over the years, El Bote remains home to a large proportion of Baytown's Latino/a immigrant workers and their families.

THE KKK IN EARLY BAYTOWN

As the refinery's operations expanded and blacks and Latinos/as increased in number, whites appeared more determined to maintain unjust conditions and more willing to use violence to do so. By May 11, 1920, the Humble refinery was completed and in full operation as the largest of its kind in the region; that year the area immediately surrounding the refinery was officially named Baytown. In 1921 layoffs in the region's other oil fields motivated many white workers to come to Baytown for jobs in the new refinery. Upon learning that some jobs they coveted were occupied by workers of color, hundreds of whites armed themselves and marched to the refinery gates, where they reportedly threatened to attack minority workers who did not abandon their jobs and leave town. Humble company officials and local law enforcement officials turned a blind eye to the vigilante threat, and the mob was relatively successful in getting Latinos/as and blacks to leave.[84]

In October 1921 white terrorists became even more focused and organized by forming the Goose Creek Klavern of the Ku Klux Klan. Consenting white residents justified the establishment of the Klan in Baytown as an effort to protect "morality, law, and order" and to preserve "crumbling Victorian standards" during a time of tremendous political, economic, and demographic change.[85] The establishment of the Goose Creek KKK Klavern was but a part of a much broader initiative to implant the KKK as a political entity in the Houston metropolitan region and Harris County.

Houston's KKK, Sam Houston Klavern No. 1, is reported to be the first in Texas, established in September 1920. The first KKK act in Houston was a march on November 27, 1920, of approximately 200 men through central Houston to announce the Klan's arrival. A few days earlier, KKK leader William Joseph Simmons had given a speech at Houston's First Christian Church titled "The Ku Klux Klan: Yesterday, Today, and Forever."[86] Soon after this, the KKK conducted mass initiations of thousands of Houston-area residents at a time. One event in December 1921 was attended by an estimated 5,000 or more Klansmen and witnessed the initiation of 2,051 new members. Houston police officers reportedly provided security for the event.[87] Kenneth Jackson, a Houston-based historian, estimated the total membership of Houston's KKK Klavern at around 8,000 between 1915 and 1944.[88] The *Houston Chronicle*, the area's explicitly anti-KKK newspaper, gave a much more conservative estimate, numbering Houston's KKK membership at around 4,000 total, with Goose Creek (early Baytown) accounting for more than 1,000 members.[89] Regardless of their accuracy, these statistics suggest there was heavy KKK support in Baytown compared to the general urban region, considering Goose Creek's much smaller overall population.

The notion of maintaining Victorian standards that was being promoted by Houston-area KKK chapters did not result in a lessened focus on maintaining racial segregation—it was a goal inherently linked to a desire for the disciplinary and biopolitical mechanisms normalized to maintain a racially pure white society. Since white women, specifically their bodies, were the fundamental resource or vessel for the reproduction of a racially pure society, much of the Klan's activities in the region stemmed from a desire to either protect white women from black men or to regulate them from performing immoral acts with other whites. Houston became the home base for *Colonel*

Mayfield's Weekly, a periodical distributed throughout the region that was published by editor Billie Mayfield as the voice of the KKK's mission. The periodical declared in a 1921 issue that "the community in which the Ku Klux Klan
exists . . . is no place for the white man who consorts with negroes." I could
detect no mention of the region's KKK Klaverns or the *Colonial Mayfield's
Weekly* voicing a concern about Latinos/as. This absence seems to be more a
reflection of demography than anything else, as the Latino/a population in the
Houston area at the time paled in comparison to the region's black population, which was one of the largest in the country. Latinos/as were seemingly
so few in number and thus so tangential to the social climate of the South to
raise much alarm among local white supremacists.

One of the more vicious acts of KKK violence in the Houston area is emblematic of its explicit anti-black nature. A black dentist, J. Lafayette Cockrell, was abducted by Klansmen in central Houston at gunpoint, driven to
a rural location near the town of Pearland, and castrated. One week earlier,
Cockrell had pleaded guilty in a local court to having a relationship with a
white woman and paid a fine. Klansmen apparently did not think the fine was
a heavy enough punishment. News of Cockrell's abduction and castration no
doubt angered many black residents of central Houston and stirred fears of
a riot. No riot ensued; instead, local historian Casey Greene reported, many
"leading blacks" left the region as a result of this case.[90]

The Goose Creek Klavern legitimated itself by claiming that Baytown
lacked its own local police force and needed a vigilante group to maintain social order. W. O. Tidmon settled in Baytown in 1917. In an oral history interview conducted in 1976 regarding the KKK in Baytown, he recollected, "We
had no law enforcement . . . the respectable lady could not walk down Texas
Avenue without being insulted or seeing a fight."[91] Tidmon's testimony suggests that the KKK did not have a racist agenda per se. However, J. W. Carroll
reported that "their primary targets were negros and Catholics."[92]

Support for the KKK was widespread in the white community of early
Baytown. Henry Cathriner, one of the city's first automobile dealers, opened
his business in 1918 and became the first president of the Baytown Shrine
Club and the Baytown Chamber of Commerce. During an oral history interview in 1956 he said, "The Ku Klux Klan started around 1918 and did a wonderful piece of work keeping the undesirable element of the population under
control. No police, county reps, or law enforcement agents existed. Therefore, prominent men organized a Ku Klux Klan."[93] Cathriner's suggestion
that the KKK was present in Baytown beginning in 1918 suggests that it
might have predated the establishment of the Sam Houston Klavern No. 1 in
central Houston. His statement that "prominent men" established Baytown's

Ku Klux Klan rally in early Baytown, ca. 1920. Courtesy of Baytown History Museum.

Klan chapter shows that it was an organization formed by elites there and had strong support in the community as a de facto law enforcement agency. This assertion counters the common impression of the KKK as an expression of working-class white sentiments. And yet not all whites were sympathetic to the KKK's activities in Baytown. Bess Shannon, who lived near the Goose Creek oil field as a child, said during a 1956 oral history interview that "to the oil field people, the Ku Klux Klan was a terrifying group; one never knew what it would do next. One would wake up in the morning to see posters planted which had not been there the night before."[94]

As was customary throughout the South, Baytown's KKK did much to reinforce the terror and garner consent for it through public relations campaigns. On May 28, 1921, Klansmen announced their presence in the community by holding a parade through the center of town and down what is now Texas Avenue. Klan parades became a tradition in early Baytown and were held nearly every Sunday. The Klan sponsored large, all-day barbecues and festivals for whites only. Resident Chris Myers described one such festival during an oral history interview in 1956, as originally transcribed:

> The Ku Klux Klan dominated the town politically, socially, and economically from 1920–1924 . . . The openness of the Klan operations in the com-

munity might be illustrated by the fact that the Klan held a large barbecue at the present site of Robert E. Lee [high school]. Teen beeves, twenty goats, and other large quantities of food were needed to feed the large and all day gathering.[95]

The festival was a distinctively anti-black celebration complete with Confederate flags and iconography throughout. *Colonial Mayfield's Weekly* was a significant recruitment tool and form of publicity for the KKK in early Baytown and was said to be widely available.[96]

The Klan received plenty of support from Baytown's white residents—so much so that many local political and economic elites reportedly assumed key roles in the Klan leadership. Ross S. Sterling, president of the first board of directors of the Humble Oil and Refining Company and clearly a most influential person in Baytown at the time, was rumored to be one of the first men initiated into the Klan and one of its early leaders.[97] This rumor was backed by a letter published in the *Houston Chronicle* in January 1923 that listed prominent Houston-area residents as KKK members. Sterling's name was on the list along with two county judges, a police chief, the county sheriff, a county clerk, and several clergymen, attorneys, and businessmen.[98]

At least one early resident, M. Ardella Grant, described how Humble Oil Company executives bolstered the KKK in Baytown's political economy.[99] The representation of Humble Oil Company in the Klan was so large that its officials used company facilities to recruit or pressure workers to join. Humble officers were known to put written messages in the watch boxes and lockers of Humble employees encouraging them to become active members.[100] Grant recollected the Klan's influential presence at the Humble oil refinery:

> Workmen would find warning notes in their watch case or billfolds advising them to join the Klan. When they would go to the company office to get their checks or attend other matters of business, statues of Klansmen arranged in a semi circle on a desk or table showed where the company's sympathy lay. The coercive membership drive extended even to the ministry.[101]

Grant's comment regarding the ministry supports the idea that Baytown's Klan had strong support in local Protestant churches whose clergymen assumed important roles in the Klan hierarchy. Grant recalled that Klansmen marched weekly into church ceremonies dressed in full regalia, carrying flowers and Bibles, and offered monetary contributions to the head pastors.[102]

The Klan was notorious for placing large barrels of tar near black and Latino/a communities as a reminder to residents that if they got out of line, they would not only suffer physical beatings but also be covered in hot tar or crude oil. Baytown resident and former Klan sympathizer Omar Dyer said such gestures were intended to make it clear that "we [whites] know what to expect of them [minorities] and they know what to expect of us."[103]

During these years Klan activities went unpunished largely because the Harris County sheriff, sheriff's deputies, district attorney, some county judges, and other civil authorities were active Klan members. This changed in January 1923 after Klansmen kidnapped and beat a local white woman for alleged sexual promiscuity. A group of concerned citizens hired a private investigator to gather information about the incident. He presented his research to a grand jury convened by District Judge C. W. Robinson, one of the few civil authorities in the region known to oppose the Klan and its activities.[104]

Judge Robinson's initiative led to the arrests of several Ku Klux Klan members in Goose Creek, galvanizing the protests of Klan supporters in the area. Susan Blankenship, a local historian, asserts that more than 600 supporters from Goose Creek, Pelly, and Baytown marched on the jail where the Klansmen were being held to demand their release.[105] A story in the *Houston Press* commented on this support, describing how the "prisoners were serenaded by a band, furnished with feathered beds, electric fans, fried chicken, and other comforts."[106]

Ultimately, Judge Robinson's campaign against the Ku Klux Klan in Goose Creek was relatively successful. Blankenship has found that the campaign publicly aired horrific details regarding clandestine Ku Klux Klan activities, resulting in a steady decline in support across the populations of Goose Creek, Baytown, and Pelly.[107] By 1924 the Goose Creek chapter of the Klan had officially disbanded. And yet popular opinion in Baytown suggested that this did not necessarily put an end to the Klan's influence. Grant said that as far as she knew, "none of the Goose Creek Klan leaders ever withdrew their membership in the Klan [despite] the public statement that they had withdrawn."[108]

The Great Depression that began in 1929 and lasted throughout the 1930s was not as destructive to the Houston-area economy as it was to other regions in the United States, largely because the federal government issued several laws and regulations to protect oil- and gas-producing industries from failure. The federal government distributed funds to state and local government offices in an effort to improve the area's infrastructure so the oil industry could expand. Since the Houston area's economy was based mostly on the oil and chemical industries, communities like Baytown directly benefited from the government concessions. Despite this, the Depression era did result in some layoffs at the Humble refinery in Baytown.

Latino and black workers bore the brunt of the cutbacks, while white

Matías Galván receiving his thirty-year pin from Humble Oil Company executives, 1949. Courtesy of Baytown History Museum.

workers were offered aid and concessions by Humble corporate heads. Beyond the workplace, Humble reduced rent prices for white workers living in housing owned by the company and deferred payments on mortgages the company financed. Humble replaced much of its historically black and Latino maintenance and construction crews with displaced white workers. It retained some black and Latino workers, however, to conduct the most brutal and undesirable jobs as contract laborers.[109]

This strategy is most evident in a statement released by Humble in a corporate newsletter explaining the need to retain workers of color: "Colored people were well fitted to do certain work in the refinery such as janitor, labor, mule handler, etc." J. W. Carroll described the scene at Baytown's Humble oil refinery in the early to mid-twentieth century: "It was very, very segregated . . . the toilets were white, black, and Mexican. There were no black and no Mexican that never progressed past a labor job until way up yonder and until they started all this equal rights opportunity whatever it was . . . and a lot of them were very skilled mechanics and so forth, the Latins and some of the darker ones. They were just as skilled as anyone else."[110]

Aron Mathews, who migrated to Baytown from Louisiana in 1919, was hired by Humble in the early 1920s. He was the first black man to attain twenty years of employment and was still performing much of the intensive menial labor that he had performed when he began working at Humble.[111] Mathews's story was not too different from what most workers of color faced in Humble's early history. Matias Galván was the first Latino recognized for thirty years of service as a laborer. He was hired by Humble in 1919.[112]

One method Humble used to lay off its workers of color during the Depression years was eradicating their jobs on days when they were sick or disabled. This was done at a time when some of Humble's first black and Latino workers could no longer perform the physical labor to which they were relegated. In 1937 Humble issued a decree that halted the hiring of Mexican workers outright, which company officials justified based on the inability of many of them to speak English. The decree made the seventy-two Mexican workers already at the refinery particularly vulnerable to discrimination, locking them into menial labor positions and preventing their promotion. Michael Botson, a former union organizer and a labor historian, wrote an important essay on labor organizing in Baytown in which he argues that Humble's Mexican workers "suffered racism that was by degree far worse than blacks when factoring in the ingredient of xenophobia."[113]

In the face of discrimination, blacks and Latinos/as continued to develop their own political, social, and economic institutions within their communities. Denied membership in the Humble Employees Labor Union, also known as the Humble Club, blacks formed the Baytown Refinery Club as a mutual aid and self-help organization. They pooled resources to provide recreational and social events for themselves and their families and to improve the living conditions in black neighborhoods. One prominent event sponsored by the Baytown Refinery Club was the annual Juneteenth celebration commemorating the emancipation of Texas slaves. Baytown's Juneteenth celebration became one of the biggest and most popular of its kind in the Houston area. Many whites in Baytown became wary of such large dem-

Black workers cleaning the inside of an oil tank at the Humble refinery, 1946. Courtesy of Baytown History Museum.

onstrations of black cultural pride. A note of relief and congratulations published in the company newsletter, the *Humble Bee*, after the Juneteenth celebration of 1928, evidences this well:

> The people of Baytown are glad to know that the colored population knows how to behave themselves. The company is greatly pleased with the manner in which the celebration went over. Such occasions as that, cause the company to feel more confidence in their colored employees. The colored employees have shown that they can conduct themselves properly during their biggest day of the year when the opposite is usually true.[114]

I could not find attention of this sort given to Latino/a cultural events in the Humble Oil Company archives. Again, this might suggest that blacks were given more attention, if not opportunity, within the corporation. Three years later the Humble workers union newsletter, the *Goose Creek Gasser*, was more frank about white fears of supposed black sexuality during the Juneteenth celebration in an article titled "Juneteen Has Inspired Many Colored Boys to Slip from Righteous Bondage." The article indicates an uneasiness of whites toward black social or economic mobility in Baytown during the 1930s that was couched in the language of gender and sexuality.[115]

Whites apparently had more to fear, as signs of black progress were evident throughout Baytown in the 1930s. In 1927 Ernest A. Archia moved to Baytown from Houston and was named principal of the Carver School in Oakwood; he would become an important leader for blacks throughout the area. During Archia's tenure as principal in the 1930s, he raised funds to add two new buildings to the campus and extended the school's academic levels to include ninth and tenth grades. Under his supervision, Carver was recognized as one of the best black schools in the state. Archia spearheaded an effort to build an elementary school in Baytown's other predominantly black community, Harlem, renamed McNair for a nearby train depot. The McNair School for Colored opened its doors to students in 1937. With this opening Baytown had two black schools, while Latinos/as had the Mexican School on Humble Oil Company property. Archia obtained electricity, water, and sewage disposal for the residents of Oakwood during the 1930s. McNair residents pooled their resources to build Antioch Missionary Baptist Church in 1928 and McGowen Temple Church of God in Christ in 1932. McNair obtained its first water lines in 1929 and electricity and sewage disposal services in the early 1930s. The community's spirit of self-help stimulated Baytown's first signs of political organizing. In 1932 McNair formed its own chapter of the NAACP, with Cephus Dubose serving as first president and Sherman Gray Jr. as vice president. The group disbanded during the 1950s.[116]

Latinos/as made strides as well in the 1930s and 1940s. The Mexican School, later Lorenzo De Zavala Elementary, graduated its first class in 1937. Later students of the elementary school went on to attend Baytown's Robert E. Lee High School, even though it was designated for white students only. This was a result of the *Mendez v. Westminster* decision of the Ninth District Circuit Court in California in 1947, a predecessor of the landmark 1954 *Brown v. Board of Education* decision in the U.S. Supreme Court. The Westminster decision allowed for Mexican Americans to integrate white schools years before blacks based in part on the argument that Latinos/as could be considered white. In Baytown this development apparently produced a rift between Latinos/as and blacks, as a black resident recalled: "Latinos were able to desegregate the schools much earlier than blacks, and this led to some mistrust of them because a lot of blacks felt left out and felt that Latinos were either growing closer to or forming alliances with whites."[117]

While the disparity suggests a form of Latino/a empowerment and black disempowerment, there also is evidence that the prolonged segregation of blacks in Baytown allowed for them to strengthen politically as it provided a logic for the reinforcement of mutual aid and self-help practices. Black schools were constructed decades before the Mexican School, which was built by Humble and the Latino/a community for the children of refinery workers in Baytown.[118] When the Mexican School was built it lacked electricity, sewage, supplies, and often even teachers. By comparison, black schools in the region were making vast progress, were far better resourced, and benefited from black teachers who were graduating from teacher-education programs in historically black colleges and universities across the South. Carver High School was lauded as one of the region's best schools, and black children from across the Houston area and Gulf South traveled long distances to attend it. Latinos/as had no high school to attend in Baytown until they were allowed to integrate Lee as a result of the *Westminster* decision.

So a case can be made that integration afforded Latinos/as an opportunity that blacks already achieved to a degree. Much of the situation is reflected in media comments aired in 2002 in commemoration of the thirty-fifth anniversary of the desegregation of Lee High School. On Saturday, June 22, 2002, roughly 300 graduates of Carver High School gathered to honor their struggle at the site where Carver once stood. After being offered the option to attend Robert E. Lee High School alongside white students and the few Latinos/as who had begun attending, many Carver students preferred to stay at Carver. That group included class valedictorian Mella Jenkins, who explained retrospectively, "This was in the midst of the civil rights movement. We were fighting for integration: Why stay? We knew about the political climate. Carver was a very good school and we wanted to stay."[119] While it would be easy to suggest that Latinos/as did not harbor similar attitudes because they desired to claim whiteness through integration, in Baytown there was no "good school" for Latinos/as, no high school for them to stay in or graduate from. Attending white schools like Robert E. Lee High in Baytown was their first opportunity at a decent education, while blacks had achieved a semblance of this opportunity and could boast about attending one of the best schools for blacks in that entire region.

Jenkins's statement about wanting to stay at Carver suggests that even when Baytown residents understood that the winds of change were blowing nationally with the civil rights movement, they also understood the cold winds of Baytown's social climate and its tradition of isolation and hostility toward blacks in particular. Even when sacrifices were being made by activists elsewhere to give them the option to desegregate, they chose not to with a clear knowledge of what life in Baytown was like. Eugene Washington, arguably the most famous Carver graduate due to his success as a star for the National Football League's Minnesota Vikings, commented like Jenkins that Carver students felt they were getting a better education than they would have received in integrated schools, especially one named after a Confederate war hero that prided itself in upholding Southern tradition, as was the case with Lee High School. At Carver, Washington said,

> [w]e learned that we were valued, that we were expected to learn and to perform to the highest of standards. We were encouraged to strive for excellence and especially excellence in education. We were told that you can have an education and not be free. But, you cannot be free if you do not have an education.[120]

Carver alumna Annie White more critically questioned the effects of integration for black students over time as she recollected about her Carver experience:

> In some ways, it was better then than it is now for the black kids. Integration was good but it wasn't all good. At Carver, we were more like a family than a school. You felt the teachers were a second set of parents. They really went out of their way to help you. They made an effort to help you along and it was difficult.[121]

Some black students who chose to integrate Lee High School did so with an activist's conviction. Vernon King, a member of the first group to attend Lee, said he felt a sense of duty to represent not only Baytown's black residents but also blacks in general: "I had the chance to dispel some of the myths about black students." One of his most poignant recollections was in taking a world history course at Robert E. Lee High School and making interventions during a class dialogue despite being the only nonwhite person in the classroom: "A situation like that brings out the inner strength that you have. When I heard negative comments, I just worked harder to continue to produce quality work."[122]

Despite Latinos/as' access to mainstream educational facilities, very few of them actually attended those schools in the 1940s and 1950s. Because the Mexican School did not offer education beyond the sixth grade, many young Latinos/as decided to instead join the military or the industrial workforce. During that period blacks continued to graduate from Carver High School in far larger numbers than Latinos/as ever did from Lee High School. Still, Latinos/as made strides within their own segregated institutions and enclaves. In 1937 an all-female orchestra, La Tipica Orquesta Femenina, was formed at De Zavala School. La Tipica would go on to garner much acclaim among Houston-area Latino/a communities and became a symbol of Latino/a pride for Baytown.[123] Denied the opportunity to participate on athletic teams sponsored by Humble Oil Company, Latinos, through the aid of the Sociedad Mutualista, established their own baseball team, named Humble 997 after a particular grade of oil produced at the refinery. The Humble 997 team not only provided a recreational outlet for Humble's Latino/a employees but also became a source of community pride as it gained a reputation as one of the best teams of its kind in the region. In the late 1930s Latinas of El Bote organized a parents' committee (name unknown) to push for improvements of the educational opportunities at De Zavala School.[124]

Jose and Virginia Moreno opened the area's first Latino/a restaurant, the Cuahtemoc, on July 20, 1938, in a predominantly black community.[125] Virginia was the daughter of an early Latino migrant. During an interview in 1980, she said her family fled the violence of the Mexican Revolution and worked as sharecroppers in South Texas during the early twentieth century. The family's work often was uncompensated by white farm owners: "They were slaves . . . they were slaves and that's all." Moreno said her family left South Texas after Texas Rangers "burned down all of our houses." Her father and uncle began to work in a lumber mill in Voth, Texas, near Beaumont and the Louisiana border, and the family soon followed. Tired of that work, her father moved to Baytown in 1926 and established a small dry goods store near El Campo in the newly established Latino/a community of El Bote. The store sold goods to the growing Latino/a community and sponsored entertainment events such as Sunday-night dances. Moreno remembers early Baytown as racially tense: "It was clear that the English speakers did not accept us here."[126]

Luciano and Manuela Gonzalez opened another Latino/a-owned restaurant, Gonzalez Restaurant, near the gates of the Humble oil refinery. It became a favorite eating establishment for the Latino/a community as well as a cultural center and symbol of community pride for Latinos/as.[127] Gonzalez Restaurant was a favorite among blacks as well. Luciano and Manuela were known for their acceptance of blacks in their restaurant at a time when blacks' choices were very limited by Baytown's rigid Jim Crow–style segregation. Gonzalez Restaurant was perhaps the only place in town where blacks and Latinos/as would dine together on a regular basis and where blacks could eat at a restaurant outside of black neighborhoods. During a celebration in 1998 commemorating the history of Baytown's Latino/a population, Luciano and Manuela Gonzalez were remembered as "being minorities themselves. They were sensitive to unjust discrimination, and in their own quiet way, they stood up for their rights and the rights of others."[128]

Gonzalez Restaurant in Baytown contrasted the realities of black and Latino/a tensions in other parts of the Houston area. Mindiola, Niemann, and Rodriguez have argued that Houston-area Latinos/as actually participated in

La Tipica Orquesta Femenina, Baytown, 1937. Photo courtesy of Baytown History Museum.

Humble 997 baseball team, 1938. Courtesy of Baytown History Museum.

Jim Crow segregation toward blacks, with one Houston-based Mexican res-taurant chain denying service to black customers until 1964 and the passage of the U.S. Civil Rights Act.[129] Baytown's Gonzalez Restaurant demonstrates a different reality. It openly served blacks beginning in 1938 and was one of the only eateries that did so in the region.[130]

WORLD WAR II AND BAYTOWN'S ECONOMIC BOOM

The transformations that characterized this period and culminated with Bay-town's demographic changes, gang explosion, and anti-gang crackdown originated during World War II. The start of the war brought some economic relief to workers and their families in Baytown largely because the Humble oil refinery played a crucial role in the Allied war effort overseas. In 1942 the U.S. Department of Defense contracted Humble Oil Company to construct a synthetic rubber plant as well as to produce 100-octane aviation fuel and the chemical compound toluene, a key ingredient for TNT (trinitrotoluene), the primary explosive agent used for making bombs.[131] Indeed, Humble Oil Com-pany's Baytown refinery produced more 100-octane fuel and toluene than any other refinery in the world throughout World War II. A Humble representative said, "The TNT in approximately two-thirds of the bombs dropped, shells fired and torpedoes launched by the U.S. military in World War II was manufactured from BOW [Baytown Ordnance Works] toluene."[132]

Humble needed a much larger workforce to meet the increased wartime demands. Its labor shortage was exacerbated when 29 percent of its full-time and unionized employees, most of them white men, were drafted for military service.[133] To recruit 1,000 new workers by July 1, 1944, Humble advertised in newspapers throughout the region that "almost any man under 45 years of age or any woman under 35 years of age who can meet our physical requirements will be accepted."[134] Blacks from East and Central Texas and western Louisiana flocked to Baytown for new jobs in the booming wartime energy industry. White women from the immediate area also entered the industrial labor pool in record numbers.[135]

The increase in Humble's black and Latino/a worker population during the war was not without tension. In November 1943 the Congress of Industrial Workers (CIO) was attempting to organize workers at the Humble refinery. Company executives warned white workers not to support the CIO because the union planned to empower black workers in particular.[136] To do so, they hired journalist Clifford Bond, the former publisher of a local newspaper. In a series of bulletins distributed within the refinery, Bond race-baited the conflict, stating that the CIO's vision of racial equality "will not work in this Southland of ours." He continued, "The CIO already has a large block of votes in the refinery in almost 100% of the Negro workers, whom they [CIO] have blinded with promises of complete social and industrial equality with white people, both men and women."[137] Bond combined his race-baiting with red-baiting, warning white workers of a secret alliance between the Communist Party and black workers: "Long ago the CIO entered into a three way agreement in which they were joined by the Communist Party and powerful representatives of the Negro race. This unholy three has its purpose as the complete control and subjection of the United States after the conclusion of the war."[138]

The CIO responded to this and other tactics of intimidation toward black and Latino/a workers at Humble by filing a complaint with the Federal Employment Practices Committee (FEPC). The FEPC report warned that Bond's bulletins contained "an incitement to violence against Negro workers . . . a gross irresponsibility creating disunity among works and retarding the war effort."[139]

Botson contends that a race riot in Beaumont in 1943 created fears of violent clashes between blacks and whites in the Houston area during the war.[140] Humble refinery superintendent Gordon Farned focused more on Mexican workers due to his fears of a violent uprising by blacks. Historian Emilio

Zamora quotes Farned's response to the FEPC report as saying, "It is an undeniable fact that the Anglo American workman and the public generally, exclusive of the Mexican[s] themselves, do consider themselves to be superior mentally, physically and socially to the Mexicans."[141] While Humble management highlighted the empowerment of black workers by the CIO as dangerous, the empowerment of Mexican workers was being described as a direct insult toward white workers. In yet another inflammatory company bulletin, Farned explained that the CIO's support of Mexican workers "would most certainly start serious hostilities and lead to a harmful conflagration."[142]

Humble's World War II expansion undoubtedly contributed toward doubling the population of Baytown from 1930 to 1950, the fastest growth in the area's history.[143] The company's wartime contributions were recognized by the Pentagon with the Army-Navy E Award for productivity.[144]

The return of black and Latino veterans to Baytown after the war created a base for political empowerment and community development. Still excluded from Baytown's public schools and unable to purchase land or homes in any of the preferred areas of town near the refinery, Latino war veterans pooled their resources together to purchase land and build homes in an undeveloped area known as Linus, or among Latinos/as as Linos, northeast of the Humble refinery. In an effort to instill a new sense of ethnic pride in Linos, they named streets after men recognized as heroes in Mexican history like Hidalgo, Juárez, Morelos, Moctezuma, and Zaragoza.[145]

As the refinery expanded, the environmental hazards it produced did also. By the 1940s whites had begun moving away from the neighborhood of West Baytown to newer developments on the northern and eastern sides of town that were farther removed from the refinery. In their absence, Latinos/as began to leave communities like El Bote to take up residence in homes and neighborhoods from which they had previously been excluded. Basically, only when whites no longer desired living there could Latinos/as move into that part of town. This smaller-scale migration began a process through which West Baytown became the center for Latino/a life in Baytown. Today, it is simply known as Old Baytown, or OBT.

Baytown's black communities likewise grew and progressed during the postwar years in response to various domestic and international social forces. In the early 1950s black war veterans led an effort to purchase prefabricated housing units previously used as temporary dormitories for Humble labor gangs and relocate them to McNair, formerly Harlem, which had been growing since the early 1940s as a result of Humble's wartime production and employment push. Taking advantage of lower down payments available for military veterans, black war veterans helped fuel the development in 1956 of a new black community named Central Heights, near Oakwood, Old Baytown, and the Humble refinery. At that time, a down payment on a new home in Central Heights was $450 for military veterans.[146]

As during the 1920s, 1930s, and 1940s, the establishment of new black and Latino/a enclaves like Central Heights and Linus and the expansion of old ones like Oakwood, McNair, and Old Baytown insulated black and Latino/a communities from the pressures they faced in the larger community. The developments empowered black and Latino/a workers as World War II veterans pushed for changes at the Humble refinery and in their communities. Black and Latino veterans were especially concerned about the limitations they encountered to advancing beyond positions of laborers at Humble, even when many of them were highly qualified for more advanced positions as craftsmen.[147]

FROM WHITE HOODS TO GOLD BADGES

Historically, police departments in the United States have played an important role in instantiating and enforcing the racial state of expendability. Police, moreover, have been an integral tool for the racial ordering of society, and their ranks have often been comprised of the most vehement segregationists. During the late eighteenth and early nineteenth centuries, police departments were initially established to discipline the growing working-class populations and to control public spaces in industrial cities. Since relations of power in the United States have been organized along class lines but also along the lines of race and other socially constructed categories of difference such as gender and sexuality, in practice the police have helped to maintain a racist, classist, and sexist status quo.[148] In this sense, Kelley has noted, police brutality in the second half of the twentieth century inherited the role and function of mob vigilante violence, or lynching, during its first half.[149]

From 1950 to 1960, like the white vigilantes before them, Baytown's all-white police force appeared to some people to target signs of perceived black and Latino masculinity in an efforts to maintain societal control. Returning black and Mexican American war veterans, with their ethnic/racial pride and slightly enhanced economic mobility, symbolized a masculinization of peoples who in a sense had been emasculated by Baytown's white male and mythical patriarchal tradition. The contestation between white and nonwhite expressions of manhood led to a heightened threat of racist police terror and hence provides good insight into how the racial state of expendability is comprised of strong gender and sexual characteristics.

Ruben De Hoyos described returning to Baytown after the war and readjusting to civilian life in his hometown. He recalled that one of his earliest encounters with a Baytown police officer occurred when he befriended a young white woman in the early 1950s:

> In the early days most police officers were really bad. They would rather hit or beat a guy rather than talk to him especially when there was a black or Hispanic with a white woman. They really did not like that. I saw this happen many many times. I also know because it happened to me personally. I met this white woman at a place and a policeman came in. He didn't talk to me but approached her. He didn't know what the situation was, whether we were old school friends or what. He came in and said, "What are you doing with this Meskin?" He took her off to the side and told her something then she came back to tell me "I've got to go." So evidently, he told her not to be seen with no Mexicans and made that clear to me with the way he stared. As a World War II veteran, these incidents angered me. I felt like I deserved more respect.[150]

The transition from vigilante violence to policing as a method of maintaining segregation is evident in the details of how Baytown's first police force was formed. On the one hand, supporters and members of early Baytown's KKK Klavern justified the organization as an ad hoc police force, necessary due to the geographic distance between Baytown and the county sheriff's office in central Houston. On the other hand, the recorded memories of some of Baytown's police veterans illuminate how the area's growing Latino/a population was seen as a menace. A history of the Baytown Police Department written by a former police captain suggests that the police were formed as a direct reflection of power dynamics already at work in the community at large. In that historical account, Gordon Lannou, who was hired in October 1947 as one of Baytown's first police officers, described joining the force: "Back then they asked you if you wanted to be a policeman and if you said yes they had you sign a paper, gave you a badge and a uniform, and told you to get to work. There was no formal training to speak of."[151] It is hard to imagine that this procedure applied to all men in Baytown.

CHAPTER THREE

SUBJECTIVITIES, CHOPPED AND SCREWED:
NEOLIBERALISM AND ITS AFTERMATH

IN THIS CHAPTER I ARGUE THAT NEOLIBERAL shifts affecting the U.S. oil industry in the late twentieth century contributed to the kinds of hybrid subjectivities and increased expressions of black-brown solidarity that began to emerge in Houston-area communities. The shifts included an influx of more working-class African Americans and Latinos/as and the arrival of more immigrants from Latin America and the Caribbean who helped diversify politics in communities like Baytown.

When Baytown's and Houston's black and Latino/a populations surged after World War II, police brutality began to replace vigilante violence as the method through which the region's history of rigid segregation was maintained. Only now, blacks and Latinos/as were being targeted and victimized more or less equally. The increasingly shared experience of expendability, in addition to demographic shifts that placed blacks and Latinos/as in closer proximity within more mixed neighborhoods across the Houston area, often resulted in greater potential for expressions of black-brown solidarity if not the emergence of a hybrid oppositional consciousness and subjectivity. These mutations, I argue, were evident across a diverse discursive terrain but primarily in the advent of hip-hop culture in the Houston area and in the formation of youth gangs in communities like Baytown.

The title of this chapter is borrowed from D. J. Screw, a legendary mix-tape producer and sound engineer from Houston who is recognized as having invented the region's distinct, slow-paced, mournful brand of gangsta-rap music during the 1990s, a style that musicologists have described as an extension of the region's significance to the blues, soul, and gospel music genres. D. J. Screw perfected a style that is commonly known as "chopped and screwed," a method in which records are slowed to half their normal speed (screwed) and cut and spliced (chopped) with other sounds and samples, altered, and remixed as a new, hybrid tune to highlight certain beats or phrases that accentuate a song's originality beyond its original format.[1]

I borrow Screw's chopped and screwed methodology to highlight the effects of time and space being compressed between black and Latino/a subjectivities in Houston-area neighborhoods. The ethnic and racial boundaries, both symbolic and concrete, that divided the two groups in previous decades were being chopped up by demographic changes, mostly a Latino/a population boom, resulting in the subjectivities of the two groups being screwed or fused together in the neighborhoods, schools, jails, and workplaces where they increasingly shared space and interactions.

BAYTOWN IN A NEOLIBERAL GLOBAL ECONOMY

Many of the demographic shifts that took place in the Houston area from 1960 to 2002 were accelerated by a global economic crisis originating in the early 1970s. In 1960 Iran, Iraq, Kuwait, Saudi Arabia, and Venezuela formed the Organization of Oil Exporting Countries (OPEC) in response to U.S. President Eisenhower's issuance of quotas on U.S. oil imports from the Persian Gulf and Venezuela. Their main goal was to increase the price of oil exported from their countries to curb the effect of U.S. quotas on their economies. OPEC issued a petroleum policy in 1968 that caused a sharp increase in global oil prices. Arab-Israeli tensions following the Six-Day War involving Israel, Jordan, Syria, and Egypt in 1967 prompted OPEC's Arab constituents to form a subsidiary group called the Organization of Arab Petroleum Exporting Countries (OAPEC) in 1973. The first action of OAPEC was to issue an embargo on all oil exports to Western Europe and the United States because of their support of Israel during the 1967 conflict. The non-Arab members of OPEC did not participate in the embargo. Nonetheless, the embargo sparked a rise in energy prices worldwide, making the cost of industrial production more expensive throughout the world but especially in more prosperous industrialized countries like the United States. Within ninety days of the OAPEC oil embargo, global crude oil prices quadrupled.[2]

The United States and other world economic powers sought ways to gain more access to labor, resources, and markets in spaces where labor was cheaper and environmental restrictions and commitments to social welfare were less rigid. U.S.-based oil companies searched the globe for better access to foreign oil reserves and were aided by U.S. military might. U.S. oil companies, many of them headquartered in the Houston area, gained nearly $7 billion in engineering and excavation contracts at newly discovered oil fields in the Middle

East, in the North Sea, and from Malaysia to Indonesia. These drilling contracts spawned the development of various oil-related industries in the Houston area that created more than 200,000 jobs from 1970 to 1985, a level of job growth unparalleled in any other U.S. city. In light of these developments, most major U.S. oil companies either shifted their operations to the Houston area or buttressed their established headquarters there.

Standard Oil Company was the nation's richest and most powerful oil corporation at the time. It purchased Baytown's Humble Oil Company refinery in 1968 with plans to better secure itself in the Houston area. Standard then changed the Humble Oil Company to Exxon and made its Baytown refinery the flagship for its much more extensive global corporate interests. Exxon would merge with one of its largest competitors, Mobil Oil Company, in 1999 to form ExxonMobil, the world's most powerful energy corporation and one that set world records for profit margins for a single company.[3] The Baytown refinery has remained one of the corporation's largest.

The Houston area was in an economic boom while most of the United States was beginning to experience the ill effects of deindustrialization. By 1974 more than 30 percent of the nation's oil-producing and -refining industry was located in the Houston area; much of it was concentrated in Baytown as a result of the development of Exxon. By 1980 Houston ranked as the nation's second-largest port in total cargo exported. Baytown's geographical location along the deep-water bays from which its name derives enabled the refinery to continuously expand as massive oil tankers from across the globe found it quite easy to access.[4]

Industrial expansion created a huge demand for labor throughout the Houston area and prompted the largest population boom in the region's history. From 1965 until 1980 the population of the Houston Metropolitan Area grew by more than 60 percent. Its white population grew more than 30 percent, its black population 18 percent, and its Latino/a population more than 70 percent, the largest ever for Latinos/as in the region.[5]

The region's Asian American population boomed beginning in 1975 and continuing until the late 1980s. Vietnamese refugees poured into the Houston area, many joining Latinos/as to reside in historically black communities where housing costs were more affordable. Today, Houston's Vietnamese population is the nation's third largest.[6] The same way Latinos/as have been subjected to conditions originally designed to subjugate blacks in the Old South, Houston's Vietnamese population stirred the ire of white supremacists in Houston in the more cosmopolitan New South. The KKK shifted some of its attention from blacks to Vietnamese in the late 1970s. Klansmen held large rallies near coastal port communities like Baytown to intimidate Vietnamese fishermen, who were beginning to excel in the local shrimping industry.[7] In 1981 the fishermen organized the Vietnamese Fisherman's Association and filed a class-action lawsuit against the KKK; the lawsuit marked a significant moment in the history of racial politics in the region.[8]

THE CARIBBEANIZATION OF BLACKNESS

The increasingly transnational reach of Houston-based oil companies during the 1970s initiated a massive migration of black immigrants from the Caribbean. Immigrants from Trinidad and Tobago, Saint Croix, and Saint Lucia gave a different meaning to and perspective on the politics of blackness in Baytown that diverged from Gulf southern African Americans, yet they were not altogether distinct. Black immigrants from the Caribbean played a pivotal role in forming black-Latino/a coalitions and bringing new conflicts to the black community. While Salvadoran, Guatemalan, and Honduran immigrants to the Houston area had blended more harmoniously into the existing Latino/a neighborhoods, Caribbean blacks did not so easily blend into the African American structure of Baytown's and Houston's black populations. As a result, many Caribbean blacks chose to live in older Latino/a communities instead.

The Trinidad and Tobago connection to Baytown was particularly interesting and emblematic of the U.S. political economy of the late twentieth century. The relationship was forged by the more transnational reach of oil corporations like Exxon. Trinidad and Tobago became the home to large oil refineries maintained by U.S. corporations, one of the largest being the Point-a-Pierre refinery in southern Trinidad that was owned by Houston-based Texaco. Exxon based its drilling and refining operations in Trinidad and Tobago in the town of Sinclair. The island of Saint Croix in the U.S. Virgin Islands evolved into a center for oil production in the Caribbean when the Hess Corporation started construction on a large oil refinery there in 1967. The Hess refinery on the south shore of Saint Croix expanded rapidly into one of the largest of its kind in the Western Hemisphere and continues to be one of the world's top ten refined-oil producers. In 1998 Hess and Venezuela's state-owned oil company, Petroleos de Venezuela, merged to form HOVENSA. The transnationalization of Exxon, Texaco, and other U.S. energy companies during the 1970s and the growth of large refineries in places like Saint Croix and Trinidad and Tobago produced a channel for Caribbean immigration to the United States. Skilled refinery workers from those two island nations in particular flocked to Houston-area refineries. They did so presumably to cash in on higher wages than they would be paid for the same work at home.

It is difficult to enumerate just how many black Caribbean immigrants arrived in Baytown, since most were subsumed within the "black" category on U.S. Census rolls. The influx of black workers and families varied significantly from Baytown's existing African American community, since racial segregation had generally excluded the latter from the training and apprenticeship necessary to become operators at the refinery, while the former arrived in Baytown with those credentials and experience.

An oral history interview with Ron Hamilton, who migrated to Baytown from Saint Croix in the early 1980s, underscores these transnational connections. Hamilton was born in Saint Croix and moved to Baytown with his family for economic opportunities tied to the oil-refining industry, in which his father was already skilled. Upon receiving his education at the University of New Mexico, Ron Hamilton began work in Houston in the home mortgage industry and married a Latina. Hamilton tells some of his family's story:

> My parents and older brothers are from Saint Lucia and me and my brother were born in Saint Croix. Many people worked for Hess Oil Company in Saint Croix. My father, for example, worked for Hess as a skilled operator and he brought those skills with him to Baytown. The Hess plant temporarily shut down at some time in the late 1970s, so a lot of people relocated to Baytown to work out at Exxon and to do the same kind of work. Once a few people came, the rest followed, because those people had all the trade skills, welding, pipe, and etc. When people moved to Baytown from the islands, they came on a referral basis from other friends and family members. That is another reason there is a lot of island folks in Baytown.[9]

The settlement of black Caribbean families in historically Latino/a neighborhoods provided some of the earliest examples of explicit black-Latino/a solidarity in Baytown's history. The choice of black Caribbean families to settle in Latino/a rather than African American communities could have been made for a variety of reasons. A significant reason seems to be that they were more familiar with the foods offered in local markets and restaurants, the cultures of Latin America, and the Catholic faith many shared, with most of Baytown's large Catholic churches in Latino/a communities. The church that my own family attended, Saint Joseph's in Old Baytown, had a parish community that was a mix of Latinos/as, whites, and black families from the Caribbean.

Culture linked black Caribbeans to Latinos/as as much as blackness linked them to African Americans. Upon inquiring about the black Caribbean presence in historically Latino/a parts of town, Hamilton said religion and strong familial bonds of Caribbean peoples linked them to Latinos/as:

Many of the Caribbean people were Catholics, attending the Saint Joseph Church. As a result, many people lived in south Baytown where all the Mexicans lived because it was economical and because they understood that culture more than they understood American blacks. The bonds between Mexican families were also more familiar to those of us from the islands. We are also a tight-knit community.[10]

Tensions between Caribbean blacks and African Americans played a role in bonding Baytown's Caribbean population to Latinos/as, a condition that is quite common across the United States. Louis Chude-Sokei has found that "black immigrants from Africa or the Caribbean feel cramped by the narrowness of American racial politics, in which 'blackness' has not just defined one's skin color but has served as a code word for African American. To be heard and to be counted, these black immigrants must often pass as African American, sometimes against their will."[11] The unwillingness of black Caribbean or African immigrants to assimilate by performance of African Americanness, Chude-Sokei argues, stems from their desire not to have their own cultural and historical distinctions erased or to be subjected to stereotypes that often prevail regarding African Americans. Black immigrants are often cast as a black "model minority" that "don't have the 'chip' of racial resentment on their shoulder and exhibit the classic immigrant optimism about assimilation into the mainstream culture."[12] The ability of whites to capitalize on this dynamic while further demonizing African Americans is a sensitive issue among African Americans, and for good reason.

Outside of the workplace, Caribbean immigrants deployed contesting articulations of blackness in the ways they navigated Baytown's civic terrain, and this social dynamic bore an influence over black-Latino/a relations at large. My oral history interview with Hamilton provided ample examples of how this applied to Baytown. When I asked him if there was ever any division or animosity between African Americans and black Caribbean immigrants, he replied, emphatically:

Yes! That has always been an issue growing up in Baytown, since we as Caribbean people were freed from slavery many years before the American blacks were. When they were facing racial discrimination, we were running our countries. So, we came up here with a different mentality. We were proud and defiant. Many of our people never relied on the welfare system because we were used to making it on what we had and by helping one another's families. We were accused by American blacks of coming here and taking their jobs, which wasn't the case because the Caribbean blacks were skilled with crafts and many even college-educated. In fact, U.S. oil companies first came to us, before us coming to places like Baytown, and we ran their refineries in the Caribbean while they also harmed our natural environment. Here in the U.S. they only want blacks as maintenance workers, similar to how Mexicans are treated.[13]

Another interviewee, "Rude-Boi," was also born in Saint Croix and migrated with his family to Baytown, in his case at the age of three. When I asked him if there was any tension between African Americans and Caribbean blacks, Rude-Boi responded, "Yeah, all the time . . . One of the reasons why is because African Americans [called] anybody from the islands Trinis, or they made fun of the way they talk."[14] I asked Rude-Boi if the migratory experience of Caribbean blacks, their tensions with African Americans, and their connections to the global South influenced their relationship to Latinos/as. He responded, "Most definitely! They can relate more. That's why you see so many island folks in Old Baytown or in the Mexican part of the east side."

Netra Charles, another interviewee, offered a similar commentary on the connections among Caribbean blacks and Latinos/as.[15] Charles was born in Baytown in the mid-1970s. Her father is from Trinidad, and her mother is an African American from southern Louisiana. Upon graduating from Prairie View A&M University, Charles worked as a nurse in Houston. Her mother's family migrated to Baytown from Louisiana for jobs in the oil-refining industry during the early 1970s. Charles's father, a decorated U.S. military veteran, arrived in Baytown around the same time for the same reasons. Charles said she generally identified herself as "just black" but often specified that she was "mixed islander and Creole." Charles said her Creole heritage and maternal ties to the Gulf allowed her to pass as African American, giving her an insider's perspective on how African Americans viewed Caribbean blacks and vice versa.

Her Caribbean roots enhanced her relationship to Latinos/as. Some of her closest childhood friends were Latinas, and the bond they shared came very much from ethnic and cultural origins: "Our cultures were the same, and we were all brown women dealing with the same things in the South, so it really didn't matter to us that some of us were black and some of us were Latina. My dearest friend is a Latina, and we are actually more like sisters." Charles discussed the division between Caribbean blacks and African Americans:

As a youth, I remember being around African Americans who didn't know I was Trinidadian as well, and they would make remarks like, "Oh those people, islanders, think they are so much better than us" . . . or "So and so can't go outside on the weekday unless it's a school function" . . . It was mostly things of that nature between island folks and African Americans. African Americans saw island folks as too conservative.[16]

Charles said African Americans stereotyped Caribbean blacks as exotic and wild despite also labeling them as conservative. The contradiction puzzled her. She described another stereotype: "I would often hear African Americans making statements on how nappy Trinis' hair is . . . and stereotyping as if all islanders are rastas, and we know that that's not true." For their part, Charles said, "islanders see a lot of African Americans as lazy."

Although Hamilton and Charles drew distinctions between and even among Caribbean blacks and African Americans, their remarks also demonstrate how foundational blackness has functioned to erase some of those differences over time. Charles suggested that she would explicitly perform a regional African American subjectivity to avoid stereotypes regarding black Caribbean folks. Hamilton, however, objected to this maneuver:

> I think nowaday it is a lot different because everyone is so Americanized and have taken the way of the American blacks because they felt they had to fit in and belong to someone. As a result, the kids today do not have the same morals and respect that us immigrants had growing up. Many islanders have mixed with Americans, so the roots are almost all removed. You see the same thing among Latino families, I think. The kids become Americanized and forget about their cultures.[17]

Rude-Boi expressed that view as well, to an extent. He specified that the ages of Caribbean immigrants upon their arrival in communities like Baytown determined the degrees to which they could or would assimilate by becoming more African American. He said he arrived in Baytown at an early enough age to be able to cloak his Caribbean roots more easily, and this tactic benefited him in the long run.

These testimonies of first-generation black Caribbean residents of Baytown reveal an interesting relationship between race and ethnicity. Black Caribbean families adjusted to life in Baytown in part by linking themselves to Latinos/as. Those families found more familiarity with Latinos/as due to religion, food, music, and other cultural customs. Their links were enhanced because they, along with Latinos/as and African Americans, were susceptible to racial injustice. Over time, however, the rigid racial order of the South produced a collective consciousness among African Americans and Caribbean blacks with regard to race.

THE VIOLENT RESEGREGATION OF
BAYTOWN AND HOUSTON

Unequivocally, the demographic shifts of the late twentieth century heightened the tensions between police officers and Baytown's black and Latino/a populations. The tension resembled the earlier surge in vigilante violence and establishment of the KKK in response to the rapidly rising black population. In the late twentieth century, however, it was both blacks and Latinos/as who were being targeted as threats to the status quo.

Former Baytown Police Captain Michael Mihalik's history of law enforcement in Baytown implies a natural link between the rise of Latinos/as during the 1970s and 1980s, a threat of crime, and a consequent need for increased vigilance by police. Mihalik recalls, "By the 1970s, the area economy was booming and there was plenty of work for everyone, especially the police. By this time, a large Hispanic community was flourishing in Baytown, and the bars on Harbor Drive and Market Street . . . were now patronized by Spanish-speaking laborers."[18] The alarm associated with Latino/a growth in Baytown was evident across the Houston area. Dwight Watson contends that the Houston Police Department developed a special unit called "the Mexican Squad" that gained a reputation for aggression and brutality in Latino/a communities.[19]

The implication of Latinos/as as a natural threat to law and order reflects the ways blacks were stigmatized during the late nineteenth and early twentieth centuries as they escaped slavery and rural poverty to start new lives in oil boomtowns like Baytown. Tensions between communities of color and local law enforcement agencies continued over ensuing decades. On April 4, 1970, Bobby Joe Connor, an African American teenager, was stomped to death in the Houston Police Department's Galena Park substation by officers A. R. Hill and J. A. McMahon. Galena Park is a community about fifteen miles west of Baytown. Houston-based historian Tuala Williams reports that Connor was accompanied by another black teen, Larry Taylor, who was also the target of the officers' brutality but survived. Taylor, as quoted by Williams, described the killing: "We were repeatedly kicked with the heels of the officers' shoes . . . Bobby Joe fell on the floor . . . he was kicked when he didn't get up and [they] kept kicking him."[20] Connor's death created a furor across Houston and, Williams writes, began to stir activism in local black and Latino/a communities.

This effect of the Connor case is verified in an autobiographical essay of Houston native and Latino activist Travis Morales, a prominent figure in anti–police brutality demonstrations in the Houston area from the mid-1970s until the early twenty-first century when he moved to New York City. La-

menting Connor's death and similar cases and linking them to the vulnerability or expendability of Latinos/as, Morales describes the social climate of
the 1970s:

> These were the days when the KKK openly recruited in the police locker
> room. Back in the late '60s, a newspaper photographer had snapped a picture
> of a Klansman in his white robes getting out of an HPD [Houston Police De-
> partment] car . . . When shown this picture, then police chief Herman Short
> said, "I see no contradiction between being in the Ku Klux Klan and being a
> Houston police officer."[21]

The photograph Morales mentions was published as part of a controversial
exposé by photojournalist Ron Laytner that chronicled the lives of Houston-
area law enforcement agents who were also reportedly involved with the Ku
Klux Klan. The exposé was published in 1973 in the Paris-based *International
Herald Tribune*. Houston Police Chief Herman Short described the story as
fraudulent and said he conducted a two-week internal and intelligence review that provided no evidence of Klan activity within the HPD. However,
an article in the *New York Times* soon thereafter conflicted with Short's denial.[22] *Times* reporter Martin Waldron describes the arrest of Joseph L. Sulli-
van, a thirty-two-year-old HPD officer, as a member of a KKK "gang of
night riders" that "burned two homes of Negros and an elementary school
near Lake Charles, Louisiana in November, 1970 and January, 1971." Lake
Charles is approximately 100 miles east of Baytown and just across the Louisiana border.

With or without a link to the KKK, there was an indisputable tension between law enforcement and the Houston area's communities of color during
the 1970s. A survey conducted by the Houston Civilians Complaints Forum
indicated that most residents of a black community in Houston reported abu-
sive and insulting language and use of excessive force directed at them by the
police.[23] Reverend William Lawson, a black religious and civil rights leader
in Houston's Third Ward, said in an oral history interview, "I do remember
Herman Short and I do remember that he reflected the racist attitudes of
much of the south."[24]

Journalist Tom Curtis wrote an article on police brutality in Houston in
Texas Monthly magazine in 1977.[25] He interviewed emergency-room physicians at Houston's Ben Taub Hospital regarding the extent or frequency of
police-inflicted injuries they treated. The physicians told Curtis, "These things
happen just about every night . . . It's hard to imagine how someone would
get a three-inch gash in his scalp, a quarter-inch deep and bleeding profusely,

unless he was hit with a nightstick or a six-cell flashlight. But the policemen usually say, 'Oh, he fell down,' if I ask what happened, or 'He hit his head on the patrol car as he was going in the door.'"[26] Considering such phenomena, Curtis concludes, "Police brutality isn't limited to Houston, of course. But the sheer volume of incidents, the apparent shoot-first-and-ask-questions-later mentality, and the almost total absence of civilian control does appear unique among American cities."[27]

Daniel Bustamante, a Latino who moved to Houston from South Texas in 1969 and became a union organizer and civil rights activist during the 1970s, said during an oral history interview that he was initially alarmed by the Houston Police Department's reputation for corruption and violence: "When I first came here, the Houston Police Department had a horrendous reputation. There were lots of police homicides of prisoners."[28] Bustamante's next thoughts on this matter were of how he and other Latinos/as began to join forces with blacks to organize against the injustices: "We quickly became involved . . . with our black colleagues and picketing and protesting some incidents. Because of my political activism, I also became a victim of police issues." His comments support Arnoldo De León's historical account of Latino/a activists being terrorized by local police during the 1970s.[29] Bustamante went on to tell how in 1976 he and other Latinos/as filed a federal lawsuit against the Houston Police Department and the City of Houston after they were arrested for intervening in an incident in which Houston police officers were brutalizing a friend of theirs.[30]

The tensions would reach an apex the following year. In May 1977 three white police officers beat to death Jose Campos Torres, a twenty-five-year-old Mexican American and Vietnam War veteran. Torres was allegedly hostile toward police officers attempting to remove him from a bar that had closed for the night. Days later, his body was found floating down Buffalo Bayou, which runs through central Houston. An autopsy report showed that he had been brutally beaten.[31]

Political organizations like the League of United Latin American Citizens (LULAC) pressured authorities for a full investigation but were relatively unsuccessful, as only two of the six officers involved were charged with crimes. The two officers, moreover, were not charged with murder or manslaughter but with negligent homicide, an offense for which they were given one-year probations, with no jail time, to be served prior to their returning to work. The officers also were fined one dollar each, a measure that many viewed as a direct insult from the county judge. Houston's Mayor Fred Hofheinz was alarmed by the decision: "Something is loose in the city. That is an illness that has infected the police."[32] Other whites noted the injustice of the Joe Torres case. In his 1979 book on "things to be afraid of," writer Vance Muse declared that "Houston cops by many standards are the worst cops in the nation. They are disorganized, corrupt, poorly trained and, most pertinent to your fears, are over armed and brutal."[33]

According to De León, many working-class Latinos/as by that time had lost faith in civil rights organizations such as LULAC.[34] Frustrations with the Joe Torres case in particular culminated with a militant awakening for Latinos/as across the region. On May 8, 1978, one year after Joe Torres's death, hundreds of Latinos/as began to pelt police officers with rocks and bottles, turn over police cars and other city vehicles, and engage in other acts of militant protest during a Cinco de Mayo celebration at Moody Park on Houston's north side, all while chanting slogans like "Viva Joe Torres!" "Justice for Joe Torres!" and "A Chicano's life is worth more than one dollar!" Travis Morales was a participant in the insurrection and recalls the moment:

> At one point I turned around and there was a Chicano from the steel mill where I worked standing in the middle of the street holding a Mexican flag. He and some friends at a barbecue had heard about the rebellion on the news and drove across town to join it. Hundreds of people would chant, "Joe Torres dead, cops go free, that's what the rich call democracy!" Another participant commented, "It was like a festival out there. It felt good to be free, just for a while . . . Old men were coming out of their houses to shake their fists at the police and holler, 'We should throw you in the bayou!'"[35]

Daniel Bustamante recalled the Joe Torres case as a Latino/a political awakening in Houston:

> That [Moody Park rebellion] became a lightning rod for this community and we were very involved in the whole effort to not only protest what was happening but also to bring some kind of dignity to our community to ensure that we were respected. So, I was very involved in leading protest marches and just confronting the situation. We did a lot of work trying to make sure the communities were not scared, were able to successfully organize and protest without the element of fear because there was a lot of fear in our community and there was a lot of violence. There were riots on May 8, 1978 and I was right there watching this whole thing, just watching our neighborhood burn up. As a consequence of that, a lot of suffering to this day still exists.[36]

After three days of violent protest, troops from the Texas National Guard and local law enforcement agencies quelled the rebellion, eventually arresting twelve people for inciting the riot. The Moody Park rebellion bore much in common with the Houston race riot of 1917. Both were protests against police terror, and both transpired when a nonwhite population was experiencing a population boom. The much earlier date of the Houston race riot sheds light on how I am describing black history and politics as more foundational to the Houston area's racial formation.

The Moody Park rebellion became known far beyond the Houston area through jazz artist and poet Gil Scott-Heron, who produced the song and performance piece "Jose Campos Torres" on his now-classic 1978 album, *The Mind of Gil Scott-Heron*. Scott-Heron penned and recorded the song to honor Torres and more generally to call attention to the problem of police brutality across the United States. The lyrics are as follows:

> Brother Torres, common ancient bloodline brother Torres, is dead . . .
> The dogs rabid foaming with the energy of their brutish ignorance.
> Stride the city streets like robot gunslingers
> And spread death as night lamps flash crude reflections from gun butts and
> police shields . . .
> The mother fucking dogs are in the street
> In Houston maybe someone said Mexicans were the new niggers.

While the black population did not experience the same dramatic growth rate as that of Latinos/as in the Houston area during the 1970s, blacks were empowered in a symbolic sense by the nationwide civil rights and Black Power movements of the 1960s and 1970s.[37] Latino/a youths were similarly influenced by the broader Chicano/a movement. Their activism has been chronicled by historian Guadalupe San Miguel, among others.[38] There was not much evidence of the Black Power or Chicano/a movements having much of an impact on social life in Baytown. In fact, Baytown was void of significant activism in the mid- to late twentieth century outside of a few small local chapters of the NAACP and LULAC, none of which were sustained for long. Baytown, however, was certainly not void of racial tensions.

By comparison, some of Houston's older black communities were hotbeds for black militancy in the South during the 1960s and 1970s. In 1967, inspired by the nationwide spirit of black protest, black students at Texas Southern University in the Third Ward pelted police officers with rocks and bottles after the officers used excessive force to break up student demonstrations in historic Emancipation Park. Lawson recalled this incident: "Somebody had told the mayor and [police chief] Herman Short that there was a riot going on at Texas Southern . . . There was no riot . . . but the police came down in force."[39] He and others said the spirit of protest in black and Latino/a communities of the 1970s continued as more expressions of black-Latino/a solidarity in the 1980s, along with new and old black-Latino/a tensions. Lawson described relations this way: "It's a hot/cold kind of relationship. There are times when blacks and browns work together very well. There are times when they will be almost hostile towards each other."[40]

Much like Fred Hampton in Chicago, Houston's Carl Hampton (no relation) was a pivotal figure not only in organizing resistance against conditions like police brutality but also in forging multiracial and antiracist alliances. Carl Hampton was a native of Pleasantville, a community just west of Baytown and near Galena Park. Inspired by the Black Power movement as a teen, he traveled to Oakland, California, in 1969 to learn organizing strategies from the Black Panther Party for Self Defense. Hampton returned to Houston that year to establish a chapter of the Black Panther Party. His goals were impeded by a moratorium passed by the Black Panther Party in Oakland for establishing new chapters. Hampton, as an alternative, established the People's Party II and set up headquarters for his organization in Houston's Third Ward community.

Months later, the death of Bobby Joe Connor in Galena Park became a catalyst for Hampton and his new organization. At a rally he organized at People's Party II headquarters, Hampton expounded on the importance for black peoples to arm themselves in self-defense: "It's your constitutional right to defend yourself. The people sat around and let Bobby Joe Connor get stomped to death!" In that speech Hampton referred to growing tensions between his organization and the Houston Police Department, predicting that his activism would eventually cost him his life: "I gave up the idea of being an old man a long time ago. I know that they (Houston lawmen) are gonna attack this building." Minutes after delivering this word, Hampton was informed that lawmen were indeed poised for such attack. Hampton, along with other members of his organization (all armed), walked toward where the lawmen were positioned on a roof across the street. Shots were fired and Hampton was wounded. He died later at Ben Taub General Hospital at the age of twenty-one. Hampton's sympathizers have long considered his death a political assassination similar to the killing of Fred Hampton in Chicago the year before.[41]

Beyond the scope of Black Power, Carl Hampton was mourned because of his stress on coalition building among Houston's emerging activist scene in the late 1960s and early 1970s. Hampton was accompanied by Roy Bartee Haile, a member of the John Brown Revolutionary League established by white activists in Houston. Haile was wounded in the shooting incident in which Hampton was killed. Hampton was the pivotal figure in establishing the Rainbow Coalition made of the John Brown Revolutionary League, People's Party II, and Mexican American Youth Organization (MAYO) in Houston.

The ironies connecting Chicago and Houston are intriguing. Both cities produced Latino/a, black, and white activist coalitions in the late 1960s called the Rainbow Coalition. Each was led by a black man with the last name Hampton in a city where collective memories of anti-black racism and black antiracism were quite profound and where the Latino/a population was growing at an intense rate in the late twentieth century. In both cities, moreover, the Rainbow Coalition initiative was thwarted by police killings of those leaders of the same surname and in consecutive years. In sum, killing the black leaders of such coalitions seemed to seriously undermine the groups' capacity to continue.

Other black leaders, less militant than Carl Hampton, worked hard to establish coalitions with Latinos/as in the Houston area, an initiative sparked by their realization of the demographic changes that were afoot. Minister Wallace B. "Bud" Poteat, a religious and civil rights leader in Houston, used his Ecumenical Fellowship organization to advance the cause of poor African Americans and Mexican Americans who resided in the east end of Houston near Baytown in a community commonly described as the Latin American Channel due to its large and growing Latino/a population and proximity to the ship channel.[42] Foundational blackness was also evident in the work of civil rights activists in Houston-area Latino/a communities.

In 1967 Antonio Gonzales, a Catholic priest in Houston, announced that he planned to be the "Martin Luther King of Mexicans" in the Houston area.[43] He built this proclamation upon King's inspiration to encourage black-brown activist coalitions in local communities. Gonzales's declaration demonstrates how the Latino/a population mobilized collective memories of the black civil rights struggle in the South to create a space and a language for progressive Latino/a causes. Historian Robert R. Treviño has highlighted the evolving relationship between the Catholic Church and Latino/a civil rights struggles in the Houston area.[44]

Black educator and community leader Howard Jefferson commented on how Houston's Latino/a population boom since the 1980s put pressure on blacks to diversify their thinking and support coalition building:

> The dynamics are changing. I had to testify before a senate committee once and we were talking about getting black and brown judges, and I said to that committee, "Look at the enrollment of HISD [Houston Independent School District]. Just put the blacks aside for a while and just look at the enrollment.

Hispanics are 51% or 52%. The white people had better start making their friends before they need them because the population is increasing."[45]

Jefferson implied that whites needed to form alliances with Latinos/as or blacks before they formed their own that would displace white hegemony. He also suggested that wealthy whites, blacks, and Latinos/as in Houston aimed to falsely depoliticize race by suggesting that demographic shifts had transformed Houston's southern social climate to the benefit of nonwhites: "You hear people say race doesn't have anything to do with it. That is the biggest lie that has ever been told. It does have something to do with it. And if you would realize this, then we would have a place to start. How do we fix it for a level playing field?" One remedy he recommended was for black leaders to realize the importance of progressive black-Latino/a coalitions:

> Now, some time ago, we formed a black/brown coalition and we work very well with the Hispanics, the black community. Very well. There have been people trying to drive wedges in between us and about 2 years ago . . . I called a meeting of the black communities and the Hispanic community and got together on TV and said, "You are not going to drive a wedge between us."[46]

Houston-based Latino attorney and community activist Marc Campos, who hails from Baytown, offers a different perspective. He describes Houston as unlike most large cities in the United States due to its general lack of black-Latino/a conflicts: "I think we have truly been blessed that the city has not gone through a lot of the racial strife that other major cities have gone through in the United States."[47] Houston's rapid growth into a metropolis in the mid- to late twentieth century partly explains why it has avoided interethnic competitions that characterize older cities, but Campos gives more credit to Houston's blue-collar ethic for its reputation for solidarity. He says the leadership of two Houston politicians was pivotal toward building a strong case for black-Latino/a coalitions: "I credit two people and they are no longer involved in politics: Mickey Leland who died in 1989 and Ben Reyes . . . They worked together and they brought communities together, those two communities. And I think a lot of us learned there was no point in working against [one another]."[48]

The economic boom in the Houston area during the 1970s did not last long. Oil refineries like the Exxon refinery in Baytown were simply producing too much oil by the early 1980s, and other oil-related industries were producing more supplies than needed for new global oil-exploration and -production projects. This overproduction coincided with an acute deflation in the price of oil worldwide. In response to these global pressures, Houston-area oil companies laid off record numbers of their workers and drastically cut back on their production. Refinery production was cut from near 91 percent of total capacity in the 1970s to roughly 70 percent in the 1980s, a historic low. The Houston Metropolitan Area experienced a sharp increase in unemployment during the 1980s, some of it resulting from a shift as refineries relied more on seasonal and contract labor to save money.[49]

Because so much of its economic infrastructure was based in the oil industry, the economic downfall of the mid-1980s was particularly destructive in Baytown, and its unemployment rate often approached 15 percent. Considering that a large proportion of the labor force that arrived in Baytown during the boom of the 1970s was black and Latino/a, these workers were the hardest hit by unemployment because history and race had deemed them most exploitable. As a consequence, black and Latino/a residents of Baytown began to endure the same effects of economic decline evident elsewhere in the United States.

One of the most pronounced effects of massive unemployment in historically aggrieved communities of color across the country is the prevalence of underground economies. An aspect of the underground economy in the 1980s was the crack cocaine trade, which in part stimulated the militarization of public space by local police departments as the war on drugs escalated. Kelley comments on the effects: "The invention and marketing of new, cheaper drugs (PCP, crack, and synthetic drugs) combined with a growing fear of crime and violence, the transformation of policing through the use of new technologies, and the erosion of youth programs and recreational facilities have had a profound impact on public life."[50] Many of these campaigns originated during the Reagan administration when, Christian Parenti argues, the lines dividing military repression and policing were blurred to inaugurate a regime of social control in U.S. cities that was complicit with deindustrialization and the outset of a post-Cold War, neoliberal political economy.[51] The Reagan, Bush, and Clinton administrations used memories of civil unrest during the 1960s and 1970s—from anti–Vietnam War protests to racial power movements—to gain support from middle-class Americans by creating the mirage that their cities were under siege by disenfranchised black and Latino/a criminals undermining America's post-Cold War progress. Parenti says of the new regime of militarized policing that it is not about suppressing social movements as it was during the 1960s and 1970s: "Rather, it is about managing and containing the new surplus populations created by neoliberal economic policies, even when those populations are not in rebellion."[52]

FROM WHITE LYNCH MOBS TO BLACK LYNCH MOBS

Beginning in the late 1980s, Baytown became embroiled in violent turf wars among rival neighborhood gangs. Neighborhood boundaries that initially were erected by white racists were now patrolled and defended by black and Latino/a youth gangs. Old Baytown, the largest and oldest Latino/a neighborhood, situated at the gates of the Exxon refinery, was renamed Barrio Trece, the home turf of OBT, one of the largest and reportedly most violent youth gangs in the entire Houston area. The OBT gang embodied the demographic shifts of the 1970s and 1980s. It was composed predominantly of Mexican Americans, Mexican and Central American immigrants, and a few black Caribbean immigrants, reflecting the influx of diversity into the previously Mexican American community driven by neoliberalism. Rival Latino/a gangs the East Side Locos and the Pelly Rats established and defended their turfs in smaller poor and working-class Latino/a communities around town. Most working-class black communities in Baytown underwent a similar transformation. Historically black neighborhoods like Oakwood, McNair, and Barrett were soon identified as strongholds of rival black gangs such as the McNair Lynchmob and UNLV (an acronym for Underground Niggas Living Violence). Each of these names was listed by the Baytown Police Department as an organized crime outfit. This official list was published in the local newspaper on a few occasions and remains registered with the Texas Department of Justice in its organized crime database.[53]

Baytown rapidly gained a reputation as the Houston area's most gang-ridden community. For an exposé about Baytown's gang problems by the *Houston Chronicle* in 1991, Jeorrick High, one of UNLV's founding members, was interviewed by journalist Cindy Horswell. She wrote:

> High was the one to name it "UNLV." On the surface, it appeared the gang was named after the University of Nevada at Las Vegas, basketball champions that season. But, High says, his acronym stood for something more ominous: Underground Niggers Living Violence. His gang lived up to the last word of its name—pouncing on outsiders caught wearing UNLV garb, burglarizing dozens of homes, peddling drugs and waging war against the McNair Lynchmob, a rival gang from Baytown's Ross S. Sterling High School across town.[54]

High was often the focus of media attention on Baytown's gang problem. His paraplegic condition was the result of a drive-by shooting by members of the McNair Lynchmob in 1990. His testimonies about gang life from his wheelchair were often seen as a compelling narrative about urban strife in the Houston area. A biography of High was designated as a teaching tool to steer youths away from gang violence.[55]

UNLV's rivals, the McNair Lynchmob, also chose a name that deserves scrutiny considering the historic context and locale from which it emerged. On the one hand, it symbolizes the history of lynching in communities like Baytown where lynch mobs once terrorized the area's black and Latino/a populations. On the other hand, it symbolizes the effects of expendability on subaltern subjectivity, an internalization if not defensive numbness to the threat of obliteration with impunity, a psychosocial adaptation that influences subaltern subjects themselves to become violent against one another.

I borrow this interpretation from Fanon and his concept of "epidermalization." Central to Fanon's *Wretched of the Earth* (1963) was his argument that settler-colonial formations are established and maintained through the practice and pervasive threat of violence toward natives. Granted, it is not easy to apply Fanon's theories regarding colonial formations in North Africa and the Caribbean to the Houston area. The application, however, is not far-fetched considering the racial violence and segregation of the Gulf South's historical development as a settler-colonial formation. Building on Fanon, and in a previous essay published on gang violence in Chicago,[56] I have argued that expendability is then a defining element of subaltern subjectivity, that communities structured by histories of explicitly violent segregation are wary of their susceptibility to violence with legal impunity. It is a violence inflicted primarily by state agents or vigilantes the state has either supported or purposely ignored. Such has been the history of Baytown.

Fanon asserts that a detrimental effect of expendability is that the subaltern normalizes it psychologically as an element of survival. This, he argues, is an intended outcome and a method of maintaining social domination. In *Black Skin, White Masks* (1952), Fanon refers to this condition as an element of epidermalization, also often referred to as "lactification," or the psychological internalization of inferiority and expendability. It is then not only a violently enforced spatial segregation that is fundamental to settler colonialism. Such social formations are also dependent upon a temporal segregation, an alienation from self that occurs within the psyche of the subaltern; he or she must adapt to being expendable, that is, to the reality of being a subject whose death is preauthorized with legal impunity, which in communities like Baytown is evident even within a community's civic iconography and related history. An intended consequence of this alienation and epidermalization, a component of the sociological architecture of settler colonialism, is that the subaltern embraces violence as an ethic of (false) empowerment, a violence that he or she inflicts toward his or her peers. Fanon describes the dynamic in *Wretched of the Earth*:

> While the settler or the policeman has the right the livelong day to strike the native, to insult him and to make him crawl to them, you will see the native reaching for his knife at the slightest hostile or aggressive glance cast on him by another native; for the last resort of the native is to defend his personality vis-à-vis his brother. Tribal feuds only serve to perpetuate old grudges buried deep in the memory.[57]

I find Fanon's model particularly useful for understanding the outbreak of black and Latino/a gang violence in Baytown during the late 1980s and early 1990s. Most of the social science literature on gang violence suggests that it results largely from declining employment opportunities associated with deindustrialization. This was in part the case in Baytown. The relationship between youth violence and employment opportunities there, however, was more complex. It is true that there was an increase in unemployment, but it was not like what was transpiring in cities like Chicago or Detroit where much of local industry was dependent upon manufacturing. In fact, Baytown's unemployment figures indicated a shift from full-time and unionized employees to a contract labor pool hired seasonally. Contractor jobs at refineries were always there and continue even amid broader economic crises. This is true in the current economically tense moment as well. CNN recently highlighted the Houston area and Baytown as an aberrational space within the United States due to its abundance of jobs and a still expanding oil-refining industry despite the economic crisis of 2008 that placed many U.S. jobs in peril. Thus, even in the hardest of economic times, Houston and Baytown have been something of a refuge for unskilled workers.[58]

Another set of circumstances was at play behind Baytown's violent youth gang culture of the late twentieth century. I was a teen immersed within the gang violence of the era, although I was not a gang member. As mentioned earlier, that experience is the primary reason I fled my hometown. Refinery jobs were plentiful even for the most unskilled of my peers. Obtaining a refinery job required only being willing to work in the refinery and knowing someone who could reserve a spot for you on a working crew. Peers routinely left jail or prison and went straight to work at a refinery. This is still the case.

As a result, education was popularly perceived as a mere formality, a temporary distraction that stood in the way of our inevitable evolution into refinery workers like our fathers. A conversation among some of my peers at the time was quite telling and memorable. One was bragging about how he would graduate from high school early, at the age of seventeen, after completing a vocational training program that enabled him to accumulate credit hours through a local community college. Another peer responded to his bragging by asking, "What good is it to graduate early if you can't work at the plant [refinery] until you are eighteen? In one year, all you can do is get into trouble."

That conversation was memorable because it highlighted two things that we seemed to have normalized as inevitable in our lives: our expendability and an adult career as a blue-collar refinery worker. Granted, some of us, like so many youths of color, especially males, across the United States had grandiose dreams of careers in entertainment or professional sports, myself included. Such dreams were envisioned as our pathways out of Baytown. But the sure and more logical future was the refinery, especially considering its significance to our families and communities. The only alternative seemed to be the military, which many peers did join.

We generally saw college as a white people's endeavor except for those of us youths of color who were being recruited by colleges and universities as athletes. College was something that middle- to upper-class white kids and their parents knew about and had financial plans to ensure. The context of these limitations is what made life as a gangster attractive as an alternative. We saw what our fathers, uncles, and other male family members endured, the alcoholism and depression they suffered as shift workers at the refinery, the humiliations and terror they had to adapt to in workplaces that just decades prior had been the recruitment spaces for the KKK and that continued to expose them to routine racial insult and intimidation. We wanted more than differential inclusion into the local industrial economy. Our adoption of violence was a false method of empowerment laden with hypermasculine gestures. It was more reflective of epidermalization than it was of any other social phenomenon.

An oral history interview I conducted with Frankie Hildenbrand shed a light on these psychosocial conditions. Hildenbrand is a Latino born in Baytown in the mid-1970s and raised in Old Baytown, in the neighborhood that was originally called El Bote. At the time of the interview he was in his thirties and worked as an operator at a local refinery. The product of a broken home, Hildenbrand became involved in gangs at an early age. He decided to leave much of gang life behind upon being wounded badly in a drive-by shooting as a young teen and becoming a father a few years thereafter. He said gang activity put us on the map. Everywhere you went people knew about Baytown because of us. Even cops were scared of us. Little kids looked up to us like role models. I know that sounds messed up but it's really how it was. I guess we were tired of being seen as poor and dirty little Mexicans or blacks. We wanted something different than just working at the plant.[59]

After offering his commentary and without my request, Hildenbrand pulled down his shirt to show me scars on his neck and chest from the shotgun blast he suffered as a kid in addition to scars from other moments of violence. While pointing to his corporeal reminders of the difficulty of our youth, he said, angrily:

This kinda shit is like a badge of honor for us. That's how messed up things have gotten around here . . . to where we have nothing else to brag about other than being shot. After I got shot, more girls liked me . . . that ain't right. We all made stupid decisions as kids. I take responsibility for it. But all of this is a product of inequality. This city didn't provide much for us, so we created our own world, our own values.[60]

Hildenbrand shed light on how demographic changes in Baytown were resulting in mixed black-brown gangs across the city:

In the older neighborhoods like Old Baytown, Oak Addition, or McNair, you didn't see as much mixing between black and brown because of who lived there. There was even tension between the groups. Like here in Old Baytown, there were only two blacks our age that lived around us. Both of them were down with us Mexicans. They even acted Mexican because of where they lived, and this often caused them problems with other blacks from other neighborhoods. But in newer communities like on the east side of town, you had a lot of mixed communities where blacks and Mexicans lived more as neighbors, especially in the big apartment communities that they built on that side of town. So, what you saw from those neighborhoods was a lot more mixture between black and brown in cliques. You can see that in gangs like East Side and UNLV, which are black-brown coalitions. So, it was mostly about demographics. Other than that, I would say that there was never much serious beef between blacks and Mexicans. We were all in the same boat, really. Still are.

Baytown's high rates of black-on-black and Latino-on-Latino gang violence gave Baytown a reputation as one of the Houston area's most violent communities. From 1990 to 1994 Baytown had among the highest murder and incarceration rates per capita not only in the Houston area but also in the entire nation. From 1990 to 1995 the homicide rate in Baytown jumped nearly tenfold from previous years.[61] Baytown's gang problem was so acute that it was a feature story in Houston newspapers and television programs on more than six occasions.

In January 1987 a large photograph of members of Baytown's OBT gang captured the front page of the *Houston Chronicle*, accompanying an investigative report that covered the Houston area's spreading gang menace.[62] Baytown's black and Latino/a youths were becoming poster children for urban strife in the region. The photo and story focused on a smaller clique in the OBT gang that went by the name of the Royal Cruisers and was made up of blacks and Latinos. And yet the Royal Cruisers were still heavily influenced by Chicano gang culture, as evident in the slogans they used and borrowed from the "low-riding" or "cholo" culture that had become popularized on the U.S. West Coast. Thus, in keeping with Hildenbrand's description of Old Baytown, the black-brown fusion in the Royal Cruisers was accomplished by blacks adapting to Old Baytown's predominantly Latino/a influences. The Royal Cruisers' territory was the former neighborhood of El Bote, the Latino/a enclave formed near El Campo from an industrial waste dump used by Humble Oil Company.

The black youth in the newspaper photo is originally from Saint Croix and likely one of the black neighbors Hildenbrand mentioned in his interview. He presumably found more commonality with Latino/a youths in Baytown due to his Caribbean origins and his resentment toward African Americans for ridiculing his family's Caribbean accents and other characteristics.

In a follow-up editorial in the *Houston Chronicle*, the writer basically warned other Houston-area communities about what Baytown had become: "The Houston area has been blessedly free of the street gangs associated with other large cities. However, the rash of gang violence in Baytown . . . offers a pointed warning of the destructive potential of gangs if they are allowed to grow."[63] The young Latino seated in the middle of the *Houston Chronicle* photo looking away from the photographer and wearing a white hat is Calvin Carmona. He was widely known in Baytown by his street name, "Pajaro." Journalists interviewed him on two occasions over four years to discuss Baytown's street-gang culture.

Nearly twenty years after he debuted in the local media, in 2006 Pajaro and another man were charged with killing a thirty-four-year-old Latino named Jose Luis Castillo Jr.[64] Known as "Joey" to family and friends, Castillo's mur-

Royal Cruisers of the OBT gang, photo published with a front-page story in the *Houston Chronicle* of January 5, 1987, about gangs in Houston. The caption reads: "Angel Garcia, Calvin Carmona, Greaser Sandoval and Kilroy Randolph— Royal Cruisers gang members in Baytown." Garcia, Carmona, and Sandoval are of Mexican descent. Randolph is from Saint Croix. Courtesy of the *Houston Chronicle*.

der incensed and saddened much of the Latino/a community. He was a well-regarded resident of the Pelly side of south Baytown and was not considered to be involved with gang life. His father, Joe, owned a small trucking business and was well known throughout Pelly and Old Baytown for his contributions to a local softball league, for being the community's Little League coach, and for his volunteer work at Our Lady of Guadalupe Church. Joe Castillo was one of my father's first friends upon moving to Baytown, and his eldest son, Joey, was one of my first childhood friends.

The other man accused of killing Castillo was Victor Hugo Tarin. Carmona, however, was the only one detained and prosecuted, and Tarin remained at large.[65] The Castillo murder case suggests that Carmona could never escape the Pajaro persona he had created for himself that made him a media figure for Houston's gang problems. It seemed as if Pajaro arose from Carmona's alienation from himself and an inability to answer the question that Fanon suggests is the result of all settler-colonial formations: "In reality, who am I?" During an interview with reporter Cindy Horswell of the *Houston Chronicle* in 1991, Carmona offered some indication of how he was attempting to answer this question, yet he never quite arrived at the kind of decolonial conclusion that Fanon encouraged decades prior. Carmona indicated that he wanted to leave the gang life behind but saw no way out of it, no way to delink himself from Pajaro.[66] At the time of this second interview, he was twenty-one years old and serving a five-year stint in a Texas prison for attempted murder. During the interview he reminisced about his initial foray into Baytown's gang culture in the 1980s: "To tell the truth, I think we all knew sooner or later we would be in prison or dead . . . OBT's symbol was a skull, flanked by bat wings and pierced by a dagger. We wore the color black because it symbolized death. I thought I would die young." While Carmona indicated his wariness of expendability and alienation wrought by the terror of the spaces into which he was born and reared, he also revisited Pajaro's disdain for OBT's traditional rivals, the East Side Locos: "We just don't like each other. I hope the next generation takes up the fight. But it's up to them."[67]

Fifteen years after making that statement and now in his thirties, Carmona was charged with and found guilty of murdering Joey Castillo. I still do not know many of the details regarding this incident. But what I do know is that Joey was no gangster. He was a hardworking father and husband and is now dead, and his death has brought a tremendous hardship for his family and a mournfulness among those of us who knew and loved him. Carmona's arrest for Castillo's murder was the Hollywood-movie fashion that Pajaro seemed to long for, a product of epidermalization and evident in the interviews he gave the Houston media since the 1980s in which he identified famous mob figures as role models. Fleeing arrest for the Castillo case and hiding in a trailer in a rural part of north Baytown near Barrett, the area's original freedmen's settlement, Carmona holed up with a gun and had a standoff with the local SWAT team. Baytown was in the news once again for its violent crime, and Pajaro was again the center of this attention.

During Carmona's sentencing, Joey Castillo's older sister, Debra, stared directly at Carmona and pointed at him while stating, "My brother was known for his jokes and his barbecues. . . . You took my niece and nephew's father . . . That [twenty-five-year sentence] is a mere slap on your hand and a slap in the face to our family. You deserve life without parole."[68] Since it took place, Joey's murder has been memorialized in the local paper, the *Baytown Sun*, as a reminder of the lingering problem of gang life in Baytown. In 2009 Debra continued in the role of family defender and spokesperson: "I'll never forget this as long as there is a breath in my body and whenever Calvin Carmona comes up for parole I'll be there to fight it."[69] The Castillo case is only one among many that I could cite to demonstrate how black and Latino/a families in Baytown, my own included, have been affected by gang violence. As emotionally trying as this violence has been for all of us, both the killed and the killers are victims of a much more pervasive history of violence in Baytown, that is, the effects of expendability.

In the early 1990s, many of us began to make an attempt at decolonization, to rid ourselves of the alienation, and to begin addressing the true origins of our violent behaviors. At that time a team of social workers and educators organized a campaign to keep children from joining gangs. They called the initiative Gang Activity Prevention, or GAP. While it began as a grassroots initiative, GAP organizers were rewarded a $200,000 grant by the Texas Department of Human Resources. The government agency scrutinized GAP as a test model for possible statewide violence-prevention strategy. A stipulation in the grant was that GAP must seek out and employ persons from the violence-stricken communities it served who had attained a certain level of "street cred," because such qualifications would better enable them to influence children and steer them away from gang life.[70] I was in my late teenage years at the time and was recruited to work in GAP. Within a year I joined Jeorrick High as the GAP program's public-speaking team. Jeorrick and I were the black and brown faces of Baytown's first anti-gang initiative and among its first public examples of a black-brown political coalition. We worked on behalf of black and brown youths in our community while still trying to steer clear of the dangers of gang life in our own lives.

As part of our duties I routinely wheeled High into a civic organization's meeting to tell our stories and to ask for support and donations to our program. I would do most of the talking, with High propped on stage in his wheelchair to enhance the drama. The audience was always middle- to upper-class white men, most of them business owners and civic leaders. They were often moved to tears by our sad stories and wounds. They were often moved enough to write us checks and have their pictures taken with us. I have always imagined that those pictures have been mounted on the walls of their businesses as emblems of how they give back to the community. There was always something insulting about those moments, about those photographs, and now I know why. Those scenes reproduced a perspective of us and the communities we represented as deficient, reinforcing tropes of pathology and chaos through which the white civic and political elites gazed upon black and Latino/a peoples, exacerbating the discursive conditions that produced us as racial others, ultimately contributing to our expendability by placing them in a position as those who must control and oversee us because we presumably cannot control ourselves. As hard as High and I worked to curb violence among our peers, this was a difficult task, considering the intensification of tensions with local police. The tensions were certainly not limited to Baytown but were rife across the Houston area.

On April 13, 1990, a twenty-two-year-old black man, Tyrone Henry, was killed by an off-duty Texas Department of Public Safety officer. The officer was allegedly trying to calm a loud party that at the apartment community where he lived. He reportedly got into an argument of some sort with Henry, who was attending the party, and the officer shot Henry. He died on the scene. A year later, a Harris County grand jury decided not to indict the officer, a decision that reinforced a pervasive legacy of Houston-area law enforcement officers going relatively unpunished for brutality when compared to their counterparts in most large U.S. cities.[71] In response to Henry's death, a group of black residents of Baytown formed the Justice for Tyrone Henry Coalition. A spokesperson for the coalition, Jesse Shead, told local media, "There were five eyewitnesses who said the trooper should not have shot the young man. If not murder, then the trooper should have been indicted for voluntary or involuntary manslaughter."[72] Shead continued his commentary on a personal note: "Our system is broken. Two of my sons were there. It could have happened to one of them." This case is said to have prompted some of the first meetings among blacks in Baytown to discuss police brutality and consider organizing against it.

Other cases have revealed the similar plight of Latinos/as. On July 12, 1998, six members of the Houston Police Department's Gang Task Force Unit burst into the apartment of Mexican immigrant Pedro Oregon without a warrant and accused him of being a drug dealer and organized crime leader in what the Houston Police Department described as one of Houston's "most dangerous neighborhoods." They used this ascription to justify the excessive force waged upon Pedro Oregon as "self-defense."[73] Houston police officers shot at Oregon thirty-four times, fatally wounding him with twelve shots. Oregon, however, was found to have been unarmed, and there was no evidence of illegal drugs in his apartment.[74]

Furthermore, autopsy reports show that Oregon was trying to flee from the officers' aggression: the first shot entered the back of Oregon's head, the second the back of his wrist, the third the back of his shoulder, and the remaining nine shots were to the back of his torso as he lay facedown on the floor with his hands in front of him. The ferocity of the officers' attack was so extreme that one of them, a Mexican American, fired until his gun was empty, paused to reload, then resumed firing at Oregon. Despite all the compelling evidence of police brutality, Oregon's murderers were "no-billed" by a Harris County grand jury.[75]

A rally in Houston in 1999 to call attention to the Pedro
Oregon case and others involving police brutality. The sign on
the right has a picture of Pedro Oregon and a call for justice
on his behalf. The sign in the middle has a list of people
brutalized by police officers in the Houston area in 1999
alone. Three victims were Latino, and four were black. Photo
by the author.

The Oregon case represented a significant moment in the history of black-
brown solidarities in the Houston area. The Justice for Pedro Oregon Coalition was formed to raise awareness about this case and to aid the Oregon
family in seeking justice. The coalition was composed predominantly of veteran black and Latino/a activists from across Houston. Sandra Torres, the
younger sister of Jose Campos Torres, the man whose death sparked the
Moody Park rebellion in 1979, attended one of the public rallies organized
by the JPOC. She spoke at one, saying, "The way they killed Pedro Oregon,
it brings back memories. It seems like yesterday, how they handcuffed my
brother and then drowned him. It's like there's been no change at all."[76]

Two of the officers who shot Oregon were Latinos, a reminder of how
police terror does not require a white officer for it to reinforce the racial state
of expendability. In fact, in the face of rapidly changing demographics, the
racial state of expendability requires the complicity of nonwhites to retain its
power and structural influence. The increased aggression of cops of color is a
common theme in critiques of police terror within hip-hop culture, evident
in late-1980s and early-1990s tunes like KRS-1's "Black Cop," N.W.A.'s "Fuck
tha Police," and the Houston-based Geto Boys' "Crooked Officer."[77]

The threat of vigilante violence did not die out altogether with the rise of police brutality. I conducted an oral history interview with Alan Green, an African American in his thirties who after graduation from Rice University has worked as a television actor and Broadway musical performer and lives in New York City.[78] Green's family moved to Baytown from Pittsburgh in the late 1970s, and he spent his childhood there. His father purchased a home in a neighborhood predominated by upper-middle- and upper-class families. Green's family was different from most black families migrating to Baytown at the time. His father was a college-educated engineer who landed a coveted position at the Exxon refinery. Class privileges, however, did not make Green's family immune from Baytown's traditions, as he describes: "We lived in the biggest house in the neighborhood. Someone burned down the tree in our front yard a few weeks after we moved in."[79] While it was never specifically identified as a hate crime or an act of vigilante terror, Green's family remembered it as racial intimidation, as they were among the first nonwhite families to integrate the neighborhood and lived in the largest house there. Green recalled that they were only somewhat prepared for the reception in their new neighborhood: "My family was from up north. We were certainly not naïve about race issues, but we were still not fully accustomed to what it was like in the South. But we learned quickly."

Green indicated that his upper-middle-class status appeared to make him less authentically black in the eyes and minds of many of his white peers. When asked to discuss his views on racial politics in Baytown, Green replied:

I was accepted by certain white people. But the truth is most of them didn't count me as black. I was an exception because I didn't fit their racist ideas of what it is to be black. I was accepted only as an exception. I remember [a white female classmate's] dad throwing someone out of their house because he was black, while calling him a "nigger." I said to her [the classmate], "How can he say that in front of me?" She responded by saying that I didn't count because I wasn't black, which seemed like such an odd response to me at the time . . . I am sure I was inside of the home and not kicked out like the other black kids because my folks had a little money. But I didn't count as black to them. I think I would have rather been kicked out with the other black kids instead of receiving this whacked form of acceptance. That being said, there are several white people who I grew up with who are still in my life today who accepted me for who I really was.

Green's testimonies about life in Baytown bring up yet another aspect of the dynamism of discourses of blackness. I did not probe him on the issue of sexuality, yet he found it necessary to comment on it: "I wish I had the where-withal to come out while I was in high school. That would have really stirred up the pot." In making this comment Green suggested that in some ways his closeted homosexuality also dislocated him from being viewed as authenti-cally black in Baytown in similar ways as did his class status. In contrast, his abilities as an athlete in the popular sport of American football often func-tioned as his pass to blackness or acceptance among blacks: "The only reason why lots of kids couldn't get away with calling me 'faggot' is 'cause of my abilities on the football field. It was also one of the reasons why black folks didn't alienate me as much as they might have been initially inclined to do." In Green's testimony, besides his family's socioeconomic standing, his own athletic prowess in a sport that was deemed one of the utmost expressions of virility in Baytown and the Gulf South at large insulated him from some forms of anti-black racism as well as the rampant homophobia in Baytown and all ethnic communities. Green described his reticence on the issue as stem-ming from living in a blue-collar town in the South. In his eyes, he would have come out of the closet much sooner had there been a more prominent and visible gay community around him to facilitate and encourage that process.

Baytown's reputation for racial hostility and segregation carried over into debates about policing and other quality-of-life issues during the 1990s as the city sought to repair its image in the media. In 1990 a group of economic planners in Baytown hired the American Institute of Architects to conduct a survey of Baytown mainly to learn why it had a poor public image in the Houston area. The Regional/Urban Design Assistance Team (R/UDAT) re-port concluded that Baytown's main problems were racial tensions and a his-tory of segregation. The first paragraph in the report read:

> Baytown has a rich history worth discovering . . . One part of history worth remembering, in light of many of today's issues and conflicts, was that it was a racially and ethnically diverse history . . . It was, however, a segregated his-tory. Mexicans and Blacks lived in a separate—and most probably unequal—company town from the one the white workers lived in. This history is im-portant to remember because ethnic and cultural diversity have become an important issue in 1990 Baytown. As the minority population has grown in the 1980s—it has become clear . . . that much of the city's public and private leadership are still far from accepting the idea of racial and ethnic diversity as part of the city's image. Rather than being seen as a part of the community, as people who can contribute to the excitement and vitality of the city, Bay-town's Black and Hispanic population are widely perceived as a problem—either to be solved or to be ignored.[80]

The R/UDAT reporting team spent three years in Baytown interviewing its civic and business leaders—the mayor, the city manager, City Council members, the chief of police, Chamber of Commerce officials, and local educators—all members of a civic elite that had generally ignored or normalized racial tensions in the community.

VALDEZ IS COMING

In 1992 Baytown Police Chief Charles "T-Bone" Schaffer launched an initiative designed to eradicate Baytown's gang problem. He named it Operation Valdez after the movie *Valdez Is Coming*, which he recounted as one of his favorite westerns; the film is about a vigilante who took justice into his own hands on the wild western frontier. In a speech to the local Kiwanis Club, Chief Schaffer explained the need for Operation Valdez:

> No social problem and elements can justify gang members having their tennis shoes on the throat of the people of Baytown. We will stay on them because they are as illegal as the Medellín Cartel and I have no sympathy for them. They are my enemy and your enemy and we can't condone their existence.[81]

Comparing Baytown's black and Latino/a youth gangs to an organized crime community as extensive and infamous as the Medellín drug cartel of Colombia reinforced the R/UDAT report's conclusion that the city's black and Latino/a residents were perceived as a problem.

Operation Valdez was authorized by city and police administrators through existing state and federal statutes regarding organized crime. The enforcement of those statutes was very much influenced by Baytown's history of segregation and corollary racial tensions. A provision in the Texas Penal Code allowed any local law enforcement agency to define certain neighborhoods as "organized crime zones" or "hot spots."[82] As a consequence of the Baytown Police Department's appropriation of this legal stipulation as a component of Operation Valdez, persons caught standing in groups of three or more in a designated hot spot could be identified as conducting organized criminal activity and if caught committing a crime could be prosecuted to the fullest extent of state and federal statutes. In other words, by definition a person could legally be identified as a criminal suspect simply by wearing certain styles of clothing or occupying certain spaces. The stipulations authorized the Baytown Police Department to legally define a criminal street gang as three or more people having a common identifying sign, symbol, location, or leadership who regularly associated in the commission of criminal activity.[83]

The regulations permitted the Baytown Police Department to declare that the UNLV, the Pelly Rats, the East Side Locos, the Lynchmob, and OBT were street gangs deserving of force and policing that would otherwise be extralegal. Declaring Baytown's youth gangs organized criminal outfits allowed police officials to utilize the Texas Organized Crime Statute, which states that a crime is one degree more severe than it appears in the penal code if committed by a person identified in gang audits. The federal statute known as RICO (Racketeer Influenced and Corrupt Organizations), enacted to combat organized crime syndicates in northern U.S. cities in the mid-twentieth century, was used to exacerbate sentences.[84]

Operation Valdez's appropriation of the RICO statute and state laws enabled the Baytown Police Department to identify suspected gang members according to physical attributes and geographic space and to prosecute them to the most extreme extents of the law. In this situation, Mills's concept of the "racial norming of space" and of bodies clearly comes into play: "The racial norming of space is the process whereby racial knowledge is imprinted in physical spaces, which subsequently creates a set of expectations about the occupants of that space."[85] The spaces identified as hot spots in the 1990s were the same spaces where persons of color were segregated during the early twentieth century. Operation Valdez thus inherits the legacy of racial ordering, exclusion, and expendability in the Baytown area that constituted its development as a settler-colonial formation.

It is interesting to note that Baytown's chief of police announced Operation Valdez only after he held a historic meeting with what he described as "the black ministers" of Baytown. According to one of the ministers who attended that meeting, the cooperation between the police department and Baytown's black community was seemingly unprecedented: "It's going to take everybody coming together to change anything. Our city was in denial, not wanting to admit there was a problem. This was the first time police have met with our ministers and asked for their input."[86]

The involvement of Baytown's black ministers seems to suggest two things. First, the Baytown Police Department somehow knew it was about to embark upon a project that would stir cries of racial profiling and police brutality from communities of color. Second, it verifies the effects of foundational blackness, that is, the role that black history and political figures play as both moral authorities and the source of oppositional power in the community. Latino/a religious leaders were not consulted, although Latinos/as outnumbered blacks in Baytown; three of Baytown's oldest and most notoriously violent gangs were almost exclusively Latino/a; and each gang claimed predominantly Latino/a neighborhoods as its turf.

Homero Rangel, a Latino who was born in Baytown in the 1970s and spent his entire childhood there, shared his memories of life as a teen in Baytown in the early 1990s when tensions escalated as a result of Operation Valdez. At the time of my oral history interview with him, Rangel, a graduate of the University of Houston, worked at NASA and lived in Houston. He said, "The racial overtones mostly deal with the police. You hear about very little race incidents that don't deal with cops. I would say minorities are definitely profiled in Baytown . . . Baytown fares worse than most surrounding areas."[87] Rangel's testimony was interesting because I did not ask or probe him about police, racial profiling, police brutality, or expendability. I only asked him to characterize Baytown's social climate based on his personal memory. I asked about his perception of relationships between Baytown's blacks and Latinos/as. He responded, "I've always gotten along well with anyone, even whites, and try not to see race. But as far as I can remember the black and Latino/a people of Baytown have always been united. I mean, we live in different neighborhoods and I am sure that we disagreed about some stuff. But we always knew that we were up against the same issues."

As a supplement to Baytown's Operation Valdez, public schools in or near hot spots and even the local community college, also named in honor of the Confederate war general Robert E. Lee, were militarized in Operation Bright Star, in which armed police officers were stationed within the schools and classrooms and metal detectors installed at entry points of all buildings. Baytown's school superintendent, Harry Griffith, justified these measures at Baytown's public junior high and high schools: "I think we can do it aesthetically so that it does not appear Gestapo-offensive." He also said, "We are living in the most violent society in the world."[88]

My 2009 oral history interview with "Capone," an African American born in Baytown in 1972, demonstrates how Baytown's war on gangs exacerbated the racial profiling and subsequently reinforced the racial state of expendability in Baytown for black and Latino/a youths in the early 1990s. Capone's family migrated to Baytown in 1969 in search of opportunities in the city's expanding industries. Capone's family was middle class, but his parents chose to live in Central Heights, one of Baytown's historically black and predominantly working-class communities. Their home was always a gathering place for black and Latino/a youths in that community and others, as Capone's parents were very welcoming and generous toward them.

When I asked him to describe his memories of the racial climate in Baytown, he mentioned the commonalities faced by blacks and Latinos/as: "The ordinary black or Hispanic got it fucked up down there."[89] When I asked him to elaborate on how he saw the plight of the ordinary black or Latino/a resident, Capone responded, "Well, they don't have any opportunity unless they know someone. And growing up with East Side against Pelly and Old Baytown [gang rivalries], they can't seem to advance and prosper. We [blacks and Latinos/as] were all labeled. . . . but by being good in sports, we sometimes got looked over." Capone's remarks suggest that most black and Latino/a youths who suffered from a lack of resources and were not athletically gifted were stuck with the gang tensions they inherited in rival neighborhoods. I asked Capone more specifically to share his memories of relations between police officers and youths of color. He responded, "It's no good. They [youths of color] are labeled off the top if you are in a certain neighborhood or certain part of town. You are already labeled as criminal and it didn't even matter if you committed a crime. Just being brown was seen as a crime to 5-0 [police]."

BROWN BLACKS AND BLACK BROWNS

Baytown's gang culture revealed an enhanced amalgamation of black and Latino/a subjectivities, exposing how black and Latino/a youths envisioned themselves as a panracial group whose histories and struggles were the same and who viewed the social world through the same lens. This shift, I argue, is partially the result of demographic changes. As many of Baytown's black and Latino/a neighborhoods began to become more mixed, their youth gangs were integrated as well. Gangs from those communities would not identify themselves as black or Latino/a but instead found strength in being multiracial and multi-ethnic. Many times the gangs were composed of smaller black or Latino/a cliques that came together in defense of a common territory. The identification of Baytown's new east- and north-side apartment communities with gang crime became so prominent that the Baytown Police Department continues to consider the number of apartment complexes and residents in them as important statistics in its yearly crime analysis.[90]

The development of mixed black and Latino/a youth gangs in Baytown's newer apartment-complex communities was frowned upon by an older generation of gang members who were accustomed to more rigid patterns of residential segregation. A Latino and former gang member who grew up in a low-income apartment complex on the east side of Baytown like the one of my own childhood commented on tensions with the older OBT gang: "Those old fools call me 'nigger lover' because some of my boys are black and because I listen to rap music. What else am I gonna do? We all grew up together in the projects playing ball and shit. I don't even speak Spanish."[91] A black resident of Baytown, "Big Mike," told me that much of the hybridity that characterized Baytown's mixed black and Latino/a neighborhoods was repressed within the Texas penal system. At the time of our interview, Big Mike was in his mid-thirties and had just been released from prison. He was working at an area refinery, had just married, and was a devout Christian. He described prison relations between blacks and Latinos/as:

> The prison system messes all that up. You know how we're all cool here in Baytown and we get down for one another? Well, you can't do that in the system. You can only get down with your race. It's segregated by black or Mexican. Like, if you and I went in together, I'd have to act like I hated you [as a Latino] just to survive in there. I would probably even have to fight you to prove that you were no longer my homeboy.[92]

The influx of black Caribbean families into Baytown's historically Latino/a communities presented a few interesting dynamics as well. OBT, Baytown's oldest gang, historically connected two smaller cliques, the Royal Cruisers and the Latin Lords. It witnessed a faction of young residents shunning allegiance to the organization because older OBT members were often overtly hostile toward blacks, although one of OBT's founding and more prominent leaders, Leroy Randolph, is black.

Randolph is commonly recognized by his street name, "Psycho," and was one of the men depicted in the original 1987 story and photograph in the *Houston Chronicle* on Baytown's gang menace. Randolph's blackness amid his Latino/a peers stood out to reporter Cindy Horswell in quoting him: "'We're not going to start nothing [with the East Side Locos], but we'll be waiting,' agrees Leroy Randolph, one of the few blacks from O.B.T."[93]

Like his good friend and gang mate Calvin "Pajaro" Carmona, Randolph lived his life as another persona, that of Psycho, the product of his alienation produced by settler colonialism and expendability. And like Pajaro, Psycho was one of Baytown's gangster icons due in large part to the media attention they both garnered beginning in the 1980s. Together Pajaro and Psycho were an iconic brown-black duo in the community, only in a far different way than Jeorrick High and I were as the GAP program's public-speaking team. Psycho's name came up during an ethnographic interview with another Baytown native, Felipe, in anthropologist Howard Campbell's 2009 book about the illegal drug trade in Texas, *Drug War Zone*.[94] Felipe agreed to be an ethnographic subject because of his felony arrest for illegal drug distribution. Felipe's parents, a Chicano and Chicana, migrated to Baytown from El Paso in the early 1970s in search of work in the refining industry. Although a graduate of a public university in Texas, Felipe shunned these resources to embrace a criminal underworld that social scientists most commonly associate with the urban underclass, those economically displaced by deindustrialization. His story reads as an example of the psychosocial effects of colonialism, discussed earlier, and the internalization of inferiority.

Felipe's testimony offers an interesting perspective on aspects of hybridity and hybrid subjectivities: "I grew up in a very southern, Texas atmosphere. I always identified as Mexican although I didn't know a lick of Spanish. I looked Mexican, but I never really knew what real Mexicans were . . . Both of my parents were bilingual, and they spoke Spanish during arguments so us kids wouldn't understand."[95] As an alternative, his subjectivity was strongly influenced by what he referred to as a "Blaxican culture" of the Gulf South: "Houston-area Mexicans are probably the blackest Mexicans."[96]

The area also produced Mexicanized blacks, as Felipe explained: "Growing up, some blacks would cross over into Mexican culture, and vice versa. You'd see a Chicano with gold teeth and talking southern black. I knew one black guy named Psycho who was an all cholo-ed out black dude."[97] Little did Felipe know that Psycho's camaraderie with Latinos/as and his embracing of Latino/a culture likely also reflected Psycho's Caribbean origins. Like the aforementioned Baytown residents Ron Hamilton and Rude-Boi, Psycho had roots in Saint Croix. Apparently he, like they, found some comfort in Baytown's Latino/a neighborhoods. But Psycho took his connection to Latinos/as to an extreme. He was reputed to have an explicit hostility toward African Americans that some claim was the result of his being ridiculed by some of them as an exotic foreigner with a strange accent. Psycho was notorious in Old Baytown for outlawing rap music from being played at any house party.

In fact, Psycho often sang lead vocals for a death-metal group from OBT called Los Mariachis from Hell. I attended a house party in OBT once and witnessed Psycho perform the lead vocals for a song he titled "East Side Sucks," in which he rails against the rival East Side Locos over a few simple guitar riffs modeled after the band Black Sabbath from Birmingham, England. Psycho put on his favorite dark sunglasses and sang over a slow, Black Sabbath–style distorted rhythm. The song had only one verse that Psycho sang repeatedly in a voice that sounded like rock singer George Thorogood's:

Let me tell you a lil' story
About some Putos.
The East Side Sucks
Burn in Hell.

Witnessing a tall, lanky, dark-complexioned black man from Saint Croix with a face scarred by gang violence inflicted in battles with a rival Latino/a gang perform this song about those rivalries and using Chicano slang words from the Southwest and West Coast to do so offers a quite compelling example of the types of ethnic fusions taking place in Baytown's gang culture of the late 1980s. These fusions arose from a variety of political-economic shifts, primarily demographic but also from symbolic hybridities, that is, what Stuart Hall refers to as "new ethnicities" emerging from the intense cultural exchanges and technological developments of the late twentieth century, border knowledges and discourse that unsettle the rigid racial hierarchies and subjections necessitated by settler colonialism the world over.[98]

Hip-hop culture has been described as an essential lens for understanding the challenges faced by working-class blacks and Latinos/as in postindustrial American cities during the 1980s and 1990s.[99] It has also been described as a symbolic or discursive portal through which disenfranchised youths of color voice their concerns and air their grievances to a nation that essentially shuns them. Houston's hip-hop scene offers a lens for viewing the facts of life during the 1980s and 1990s and gives insight into how the history of the art form pushed youths of color to boast about their resilience to racial inequality.

One of the Houston area's first rap groups originated in Baytown and was composed mainly of Caribbean immigrants. RMG was formed in the early 1980s by Baytown teen Romany Malco, whose parents migrated to the United States from Trinidad and Tobago. After finding some success on the local music scene, Malco moved the group to Los Angeles and changed its name from RMG to the College Boyz. While in L.A. they signed a lucrative record deal with Virgin Records and released the single "Victim of the Ghetto," a tune that chronicled much of what Malco had witnessed of life in Baytown for youths of color. "Victim of the Ghetto" became the number-one tune on the *Billboard* rap chart in 1992. The College Boyz disbanded in the mid-1990s, and Malco worked as a music producer in Los Angeles. Today he is an actor in television shows and Hollywood films.

Outside of Baytown's early hip-hop scene, the Houston area would become significant to the hip-hop world in other ways. One of the nation's preeminent gangsta-rap acts was the Geto Boys, from the southeast side of Houston near Baytown. The Geto Boys group was formed in 1986 in Houston's Fifth Ward neighborhood by African American entrepreneur James "Lil' J" Smith, also known as J. Prince and Prince James. Smith formed Rap-A-Lot Records, one of the nation's first exclusively black-owned independent rap music labels, to promote his new group of Houston natives Willie D. from the Fifth Ward and Scarface from South Acres with Bushwick Bill, a Jamaican immigrant from New York who moved to Houston as a teen. The Geto Boys' debut album, *5th Ward Chronicles: Making Trouble*, created a buzz in Houston and New Orleans. A distribution deal with Warner Brothers Records in 1990 gave the Geto Boys a broader following and exposed them to a national audience. The Geto Boys, along with Los Angeles groups N.W.A. and Ice-T, were pioneering gangsta-rap acts in the United States. Like that of their peers, much of the Geto Boys' early work glorified violence toward and exploitation of women.

The Geto Boys, like N.W.A., offered critical social commentary about race and particularly police brutality. This was evident in songs like "City under Siege," which highlights the advent of militarized policing in working-class black and Latino/a communities in Houston and explains it as a direct result of the neoliberal domestic and foreign policy of the Reagan and Bush presidencies.[100] Their song "Fuck a War" rails against military recruitment in Houston's working-class black and Latino/a neighborhoods, a highlight being when Bushwick Bill critiques U.S. imperialism in the Middle East by shouting, "I ain't fightin' for no god damn oil!" The 1993 single "Crooked Officer" was yet another vivid critique of police brutality, and "Eye 4 an Eye" in 1998 was the Geto Boys' response to the dragging death of James Byrd Jr. That song swore violent revenge on behalf of the Byrd family and against the Houston area's white-supremacist tradition, which Geto Boys member Willie D. describes as persistently tormenting "niggas and vatos"—blacks and Latinos/as. The tune closes with Willie D. challenging "rednecks" on behalf of blacks and Latinos/as: "You wanna race war? U got it. I ain't scared of you muthafuckas."

The Geto Boys' 1996 song "The World Is a Ghetto," which samples the 1972 original by War, links the expendability of blacks and Latinos/as in Houston to populations of color in the global South. The lyrics sung by Bushwick Bill suggest that the United States offers little refuge to immigrants and refugees from the racial state of expendability, a condition familiar to U.S. black and Latino/a populations: "Fools fleeing their countries to come here, black. They see the same bullshit and head right back. They finding out what niggas already know . . . the world is a ghetto." While the word "nigga" is most commonly associated with blacks and especially African Americans, Bushwick Bill uses it to signify blacks and Latinos/as. The racial and ethnic connotation appears in its lyrics about police brutality in Houston: "They got crooked cops, working for the system. Makin' po' muthafuckas out of victims. But don't nobody give a fuck about the po'. It's double jeopardy if you're black or Latino."

Geto Boys' most famous work, "Mind Playing Tricks," reached number one on the U.S. *Billboard* music charts in 1991. It delves into the psychosocial effects of expendability with a dark tone, eerie melodies, and slow cadence of macabre lyrics, reflecting the region's social climate and history. Music journalist Sasha Frere-Jones of the *New Yorker* magazine described "Mind Playing Tricks" in 2005 as "a slow, mournful plaint . . . [that] relied on long, harmonically complex guitar samples—a departure from the short horn bursts and rapid drums then dominating hip-hop. If the song had an antecedent, it was the blues, not music you might have heard in a disco."[101]

Frere-Jones's commentary correlates to Rick Mitchell's claim that Houston is the true blues music capital of the world.[102] The same neighborhood that produced the Geto Boys and Rap-A-Lot Records, the Fifth Ward, was also the birthplace and home to Peacock Records and later the Duke-Peacock record label in the mid-twentieth century. Peacock was a gospel music label founded during the 1940s. It merged with Memphis-based Duke Records in 1952, and Duke-Peacock began to specialize in Houston's brand of more soulful and patient blues music. The Duke-Peacock merger made it the largest black-owned record label in the country before the rise of Detroit's Motown label in the 1960s. Some of its most successful recordings were Johnny Ace's "Pledging My Love," Junior Parker's "Drivin' Wheel," and Bobby "Blue" Bland's "I Pity the Fool." Mitchell wrote that these recordings "defined a new sound in popular black music, marking the evolution from the rough-and-tumble, electrified Delta blues coming out of Chicago to a jazzier, more sophisticated, uptown R&B style."[103]

One of Duke-Peacock's stars during the 1950s and 1960s was Buddy Ace, "the Silver Fox." He was born in Jasper, Texas, and raised in Baytown since early childhood; he graduated from Baytown's Carver High School. Buddy Ace became part of the Duke-Peacock roster in 1955. Other noteworthy blues artists to have emerged from the Houston scene were local guitar legends such as Lightnin' Hopkins, Clarence "Gatemouth" Brown, "Texas" Johnny Brown, Johnny "Guitar" Watson, Albert Collins, Johnny Copeland, Joe "Guitar" Hughes, the TSU Toronadoes (a pioneering blues and funk band), and Pete Mayes. Houston also produced a long list of notable blues vocalists, including Beulah "Sippie" Wallace, Willie Mae "Big Mama" Thornton, Esther Phillips, Katie Webster, Amos Milburn, Charles Brown, Ivory Joe Hunter, Percy Mayfield, and Archie Bell and the Drells.[104]

In addition to the Silver Fox, Buddy Ace, Baytown produced another important soul-blues singer. "Joe Tex" was born Joseph Arrington in Baytown in 1933. He attended Baytown's Carver High School, where he was mentored by Mattybelle Durkee, an iconic black educator and Baytown native. Durkee taught Arrington along with Buddy Ace and another blues artist, Charlie Jones. Joe Tex recorded a string of hit singles. Much of his notoriety is tied to his rivalry with James Brown that stemmed from Tex's claim that Brown stole his dance moves—and his wife, apparently.[105] Beyond his significance to soul

Joseph Arrington, later known as Joe Tex, as a student at Baytown's Carver High School. Seated at the piano is Mattybelle Durkee, a Baytown native and a music teacher at Carver who mentored Tex and other artists in the blues and soul music genres. Courtesy of Baytown History Museum.

and R&B, Joe Tex is also widely credited by musicologists with inventing rap music. His 1965 hit record "Hold on to What You Got" included a rhyming monologue over the song's beat. The success of that song influenced Tex to offer more monologues in subsequent records. Tex described this technique as "rap" more than two decades before that genre became the phenomenon it now is.[106] An interesting twist to Tex's story is that he converted to Islam in 1966 and changed his name to Yusuf Hazziez. He abandoned his musical career and toured the United States as a spiritual lecturer on behalf of the Nation of Islam.[107]

The Houston area's blues tradition appears in the group UGK (Underground Kings) formed in 1987 by rappers Bun-B and Pimp-C in Port Arthur, Texas. Their notoriety among Houston-area hip-hop artists is second only to that of the Geto Boys. Port Arthur was another blue-collar city formed around the oil-refining industry and with a history like Baytown's. It is sixty miles east of Baytown and near the Louisiana border. UGK became well known in the southern rap game for albums like *Super Tight*, *The Southern Way*, and *Riding Dirty*. Compared to the Geto Boys, UGK's sound has an even heavier gospel and blues influence. Like the Geto Boys, UGK's political commentary often rails against police brutality, as in the tune "Protect and Serve."

After the Geto Boys and UGK, artists like the Trinity Garden Cartel, Street Military, 5th Ward Boys, Fat Pat, Big Pokey, HAWK, Yungstar, Tela, and South Circle reached some local success. Houston experienced a rap renaissance at the turn of the twenty-first century with artists like Mike Jones, Slim Thug, Trae the Truth, Lil' Keke, Chamillionaire, Z-Ro, and Lil' Flip. These artists dominated hip-hop record sales in the United States from 2001 to 2004, a moment Frere-Jones describes as "a musical hegemony that happens only occasionally in pop. Not since Nirvana made Seattle the capital of grunge, in 1991, have a city, a sound, and a significant chart presence been so closely linked."[108] He describes their sound:

> Unhurried and woozy, as if it had been left too long in the sun. . . . The easy finesse of Houston's m.c.'s can make East Coast hip-hop sound stressed out, uptight, or just plain square. The Houston sound is, above all, slow, a perpetually decelerating music that is equally good at conveying menace, calm, and grief. The city's heat seems to encourage both languor and soul-spilling; Houston m.c.'s rap charmingly about their possessions but are comfortable singing about death, racist cops, and life in prison.[109]

These qualities reflect the genre's blues origins. Mitchell writes that "the spirit of the blues can be felt in the slow-rolling, hard-banging beats of Houston hip-hop. It is not too much of a stretch to go from Juke Boy Bonner's 'Stay off Lyons Avenue' to Z-Ro's 'King of the Ghetto' and Trae's 'In the Hood.'"[110]

The renown of Houston-area rappers across the country and world and their dominance on the rap music market at the beginning of the twenty-first century were highlighted in *The Source* magazine's special issue of April 2006 dedicated to Houston's significance to the genre and industry. The magazine cover features most of Houston's rap legends, among them the Geto Boys and UGK along with newer stars, with the subtitle "Why Houston's Reign Won't Stop."

It did stop. The influence of those artists, though, still is seen in the rise of Latino/a hip-hop from Houston. More than a decade earlier, South Park Mexican (SPM) and Chingo Bling were the first Latino/a rappers from Houston to gain a national following. SPM was raised in the predominantly black working-class neighborhood of South Park in southeast Houston. His recording name, South Park Mexican, hints that he was among only a handful of Latinos/as in his community. After struggling in school, SPM began to work in area oil or chemical refineries; he said he could not tolerate the environmental hazards at the workplace.[111] He then turned to selling crack cocaine as a way to make a living and began to invest his earnings into recording rap music; with his brother he started his own record label, Dope House Records.[112]

By intention, there was nothing definitively Latino about SPM's first albums, *Hillwood* (1992) and *Hustle Town* (1995). During an interview by UGK's Bun-B, SPM explains some background: "First of all, I went to Woodson with Scarface [of the Geto Boys]. I went to Worthing [High School] with Cadillac Anderson [a pro basketball player from Houston]."[113] In linking himself to these local black celebrities, SPM sought to distance himself from being perceived as just a Latino artist. He offered more clarification of this: "I aint tryin to be the best Meskin rapper I aint tryin to be the best Latino rapper, knowhamsayin. I'm trying to kill 'em all."

John Nova Lomax, a Houston-based music journalist, highlights the hybridity in SPM's art: "SPM is a uniquely Houston character, a Tejano raised in the black ghetto of South Park, a hustling Hispanic whose vivid raps about dead-end street life, smuggling weed from the Valley, and an uplifted raza blended gritty black funk with borderlands Spanglish slang."[114] In many ways, Houston's "black ghettos" like South Park have served as foundations from which a generation or two of Latino/a youths have made sense of the world around them.

The SPM-led Latino/a rap revolution in Houston provided opportunities for new black artists as well as black-brown artistic fusions. Rasheed is an African American rap artist who arrived in Houston from Philadelphia and yet found it hard to build his career as an artist there because he was not from the South. Since he lived in the same neighborhood, South Park, as SPM, he soon became a follower and especially was attracted to SPM's underdog status as a Latino rapper trying to crack the southern hip-hop market. Rasheed recalls, "Once I started hanging out with SPM, I started seeing the way people would treat him as a Latin rapper . . . By me seeing how people would treat him and underestimate him, it was just like the way people would treat the slaves back in the day. That made me down for the cause. That made me motivated to get down."[115]

To accentuate the commonality he felt with Houston-area Latinos/as, Rasheed joined with Houston-based Latino rapper Low-G, and they released the album *Wetblack* in 2002.[116] Low-G, the son of Honduran immigrants, and Rasheed, an African American, chose the album title as a play on "black" and "wetback," slang for "illegal alien." Rather than viewing the plights of Latinos/as as subsumable through blackness, *Wetblack* symbolizes a hybrid subjectivity formed out of the experience of black and Latino/a lives that have been pushed together, the imaginations of two racialized groups compressed by their shared histories of injustice to the extent that they become one subjectivity.

The album cover for *Wetblack* more clearly symbolizes this mutation. It depicts Low-G and Rasheed standing back to back on a platform surrounded by masses of suffering blacks and Latinos/as in an open field. It appears as if the rappers have summoned this crowd to announce a new path to their salvation. Their shirtless poses suggest warrior chiefs emancipated from bondage whose alliance represents the last hope for populations facing systemic obliteration.

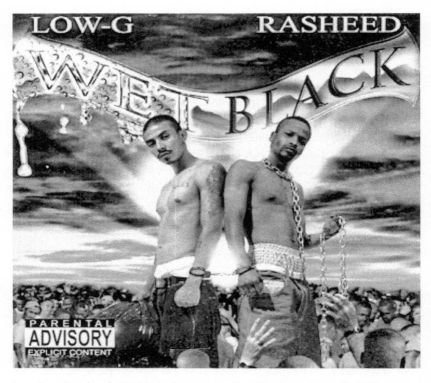

Low-G and Rasheed, *Wetblack* album cover. Shut 'Em Down Records, 2002.

Their baggy jeans, hair, and tattooed bodies tell us they are also quintessential ghetto soldiers who have been popularized by gangsta-rap culture.

In the image, Low-G's left wrist is bound to Rasheed's right by handcuffs, suggesting that the two men are fugitives of the Texas penal system and on the run from state agents in search of their due freedom. This link symbolizes the variant modalities of expendability that blacks and Latinos/as have endured throughout their histories in places like the Houston area. In their visual allegory, the handcuffs they have donned suggest that the two have no choice but to work together. Their bound arms must function as one, making them a formidable two-headed, three-armed foe—that is, only if they choose to work together. Choosing otherwise would only make both of them easier to oppress.

The CD cover finally implies that the two groups have trodden different historical paths. Rasheed holds a thick steel chain that hangs around his neck to represent the history and impact of slavery on the Gulf South and beyond. This history is much deeper and more pervasive than what is represented by his Latino band mate. Low G holds a large plastic bag that is dripping wet, signifying the much more recent plight of undocumented immigrants fleeing disastrous conditions wrought by neoliberalism in Latin America to search for new lives in large cities like Houston in the global North. Low-G's prop symbolizes the despair of many Latinos/as who arrive in the United States literally naked after they have navigated the waters of the Rio Grande with their clothes and personal belongings floating beside them in plastic bags. As they flee rampant poverty and political corruption, they arrive in places like Houston neighborhoods only to find another type of despair, one with which their black neighbors have been struggling for generations.

The term *mayatero* has been used by Latinos/as in other parts of the United States to criticize people like Low-G for their allegiance to people like Rasheed. *Mayatero* is a derivative of *mayate*, a Spanish-language equivalent of the term "nigger." The term literally translates as "one who performs niggerness." It is also widely held to mean "nigger lover." If one types the word *mayatero* into an Internet search engine, what he or she will often discover is a list of references to Houston-area Latinos/as being made by Latinos/as from the Southwest. The Latino/a culture and politics forum at Brownpride.com has a series of threads dedicated to disassociating Houston-area Latinos/as from a discussion of Latino/a politics at large because they are, in essence, too black and too allied to black culture and political causes.

In one thread, appropriately titled "How Do You Feel about Mayateros?" a respondent from Long Beach, California, wrote that Houston's Latinos/as "act like that cuz they don't know anything about their own culture." A respondent from Houston replied, "It's a different culture over here. If you grew up here, you'd be acting that way too."[117] A Latino who works in Houston's rap music industry told music journalist Lomax that he has been called a "naco" by his own family members who live in South Texas due to his southern accent, his fashion choices, and the distinctively Houston-style rap music he listens to. "Naco," he explains, is short for "a nigger taco."[118]

Houston-area Latinos/as thus boast about their ties to blackness and their pride in southern roots. They even suggest that by comparison, Latinos/as in places like Southern California are constrained by the influences of Chicano/a cultural nationalism originating in the 1960s and too easily buy into stereotypes of "cholo" or "low-riding" culture without realizing just how profoundly influenced they have been by blackness. This blindness, they argue, is exacerbated by the popularity of Chicano prison-gang culture in California as it has been popularized by Hollywood movies. In the Lomax article, Chingo Bling certainly glosses over the diversity of Latino/a culture in that region and even admitted that Latinos/as in the Bay Area of northern California were also criticized by Latinos/as from Southern California for being *mayateros*: "We go about it a different way than Californians. Out there, the rappers use a lot of different symbols: the Aztec calendar, their style of tattoos. They look at us like we wanna be black, and we look at them and say, man, them fools are straight outta movies."[119]

This division appears in the language and dialect of Houston-area Latinos/as, Chingo Bling said. He argued that many of them do not speak proper English or Spanish but rather a regional patois that he calls "wetbonics," for "wetback" with "ebonics." This dialect filters northern Mexican slang through southern black slang and is the product of Mexican immigrants learning to speak English by mimicking African Americans, the English speakers in closest proximity to them as neighbors, classmates, and coworkers in Houston-area neighborhoods.

Wetbonics is thus seen as a linguistic survival tactic because it helps Latinos/as shed the stigma of being a perpetual immigrant or outsider. They become insiders, albeit differentially, by performing a linguistically hybrid articulation of blackness. In a reference to his own father's experience in migrating to the Houston area from Mexico, Chingo Bling raps on the song "They Can't Deport Us All": "He crossed with a trampoline, not with a passport. The accent will get his ass caught . . . Learned English from the black folks."[120] In this instance the assimilation of immigrants is not associated with whiteness but linked to blackness as an adaptive strategy for becoming American. From his vantage point, these fusions and demographic shifts have destabilized white privilege in the South to the benefit of both blacks and Latinos/as. Chingo Bling rants about this in a tune titled "Reppin' da Soufside": "We takin' ova the south. So go and take down your confederate flag!"

Beyond language, Chingo Bling draws other distinctions between Houston and Southern California Latinos/as: "In California, the strife is real bad. I don't know if it's a cultural thing, but in Texas, we just blend better."[121] He explains in his best wetbonics accent that "we just mo' playa" as a way to suggest that Houston-area Latinos/as are able to adapt to the world around them in dynamic ways rather then getting bogged down in resentment stemming from ethnic rivalries of old.

Another Houston-based Latino rapper, H-Town Slim, draws further distinctions between the Gulf South and Southern California as he comments about the ways cultural nationalism discourages Latinos/as from building tighter bonds with blacks: "Out there, it's all about la raza and Brown pride. But here, where is the line between black and Mexican neighborhoods? We share our cultures."[122]

One of the more controversial ways Chingo Bling and other Houston-area Latinos/as envision their more fluid relation to blackness is through their use of the term "nigga" as a self- and peer reference. While there is indeed much controversy about the history of the word "nigger" and its sociolinguistic cousin "nigga" within black communities,[123] debates over the use of the terms by Latinos/as and other nonblack ethnic groups offer an intriguing lens through which to view relations between blacks and Latinos/as. Civil rights organizations have openly criticized Latino/a musicians from New York and Los Angeles for explicitly using the word "nigga" in their songs. However, their use of the word pales in comparison to the lyrics that have emerged from Houston-area Latino/a rappers—and generally without any controversy. Ben Westhof notes in the *Houston Press* that "Hispanic Houston rappers use 'nigga' without blinking."[124]

Houston-based music journalist Rolando Rodriguez describes Lucky Luciano, another well-known Latino rap artist from Houston, as "a 28-year-old hip-hop hybrid of Houston's black urban influence, 90s Southern rap funk and the type of entrepreneurial spirit that lives in Latino newcomers who go from dish-washer to Mexican restaurant chain-owner."[125] He continues:

> Lucky personifies the cultural evolution of thousands of Hispanic youth and adults entering their thirties who arrived in Houston in the early '80s, and whose assimilation into Americana took a sharp, unexpected turn. When their families migrated to Houston from South Texas, or perhaps a small Mexican village, they didn't know . . . that black urban culture would define their children's upbringing, whether they liked it or not. But it did, by blending with brown.[126]

The blends Rodriguez describes speak to the historical development of the region, its racial formation, and conditions such as the racial state of expendability that have served as a catalyst to emulsify black and Latino/a subjectivities.

From prominent black artist Gil Scott-Heron describing Houston-area Latinos/as as "new niggers" to the fusion of blacks and Latinos/as into an ethnically compound racial category by hip-hop culture and young Latinos/as becoming "niggas" or "nigger tacos," these examples suggest distinctive connections between black and Latino/a lives in the Houston area. The connections have often resulted in the formation of transethnic racial subjectivities that a comparative ethnic studies lens helps us comprehend.

To place them in a broader context beyond the Gulf South, those subjectivities also challenge us to consider how more intense transnational realities commonly associated with globalization and neoliberalism are influencing the politics of race in local U.S. spaces. Since the 1970s, civil wars in Latin America and neoliberal free-trade policies like the North American Free Trade Agreement (NAFTA) and the Dominican Republic–Central American Free Trade Agreement (DR-CAFTA) have been cited as important reasons for a drastic increase in immigrants from Latin America to the United States. Immigrants have poured into U.S. cities seeking better means of economic survival, and their arrival has contributed greatly to the Latino/a population boom. Low-G, Lucky Luciano, and Chingo Bling all became political actors in Houston as a result of these structural realities, as did Ron Hamilton, Rude-Boi, and Psycho. Low-G came to the United States in 1988 after his father was killed in El Salvador's civil war and his family was caught up in disorder in Honduras.[127] As he was transplanted to Houston's South Park neighborhood, Low-G said he adapted to his new environs by "becoming black" and linking his plight with those of his African American friends and neighbors. Chingo Bling's parents immigrated to Houston in the 1980s; like Low-G's, his subjectivity was profoundly influenced by black peers. Building on Mignolo's concept of "border gnosis,"[128] the global designs of transnational migrations have collided with the racial formation of Houston to produce hybrid forms of racial knowledge. Terms like "wetblack" are privileged examples of knowledge produced in the wake of those collisions. They suggest that the meaning and influence of black history are being remixed within Latino/a subjectivities in ways that complicate the understanding of racial politics at the dawn of a new millennium.

CHAPTER FOUR

RODNEY KING EN ESPAÑOL: BAYTOWN'S ACTIVIST AWAKENING

IN THIS CHAPTER I ARGUE THAT BAYTOWN'S war on gangs in the 1990s exacerbated the expendability of working-class black and Latino/a communities there and contributed to the death of Luis Alfonso Torres in 2002. Torres, as described earlier, was a forty-five-year-old Mexican immigrant who lost his life while in custody of Baytown police officers. His death and the activist awakening it spawned among Baytown's black and Latino/a communities symbolize three phenomena that have been central to this book's design. The first is the browning of the region, the boom of the Latino/a population over recent decades primarily from immigration from Mexico. As they have grown in number, Latinos/as have increasingly been perceived as a threat to the racial status quo in the region, as evident in the deaths of Jose Campos Torres in 1978 and Pedro Oregon in 1998. Luis Alfonso Torres joined that list of cases that have galvanized Latino/a resistance and forced conversations regarding the social meaning of race to further exceed a black-white binary.

The second phenomenon this chapter highlights is the racial state of expendability, as it demonstrates how blacks and Latinos/as have been routinely subjected to a certain kind of state-sanctioned terror over time and most commonly as each group has been experiencing a population boom. The third phenomenon is foundational blackness, or the role that African American history plays in structuring acts of antiracism in the Gulf South, the Torres case being yet another example.

A FATHER, NOT A GANGSTER

The main impetus for my claims regarding the effects of Baytown's war on gangs in the 1990s on the Torres case of 2002 derives from a statement by the ACLU of Texas to the Houston-area press soon after Torres died. The statement reads, "Luis Torres wasn't a 'blood' or a 'crip.' He didn't carry guns or have any drugs. He was simply a father and now he is not."[1] This statement suggests that Torres was killed unjustly and as a result of tensions between police officers and gang members in places like Baytown that caused Baytown to be perceived in the media as a gang-ridden community. The ACLU's statement, however, also implicitly normalizes the killing of persons who may be considered gangsters by law enforcement agents. I do not presume that this was the ACLU's intention. But it does deserve attention as an example of how discourse produces and enhances expendability.

A biographical sketch of Torres helps illuminate how this discursive transformation the ACLU is proposing, his apparent evolution from immigrant worker or "father" to dangerous gangster in the eyes of law enforcement agents, unfolded. His biography also puts a human face on the effects of neoliberalism in Latin America and its relation to both the Latino/a population boom of the late twentieth and early twenty-first centuries and the kinds of civil and human rights challenges the Latino/a population currently faces.

Torres was one of ten children of a farming family from a rural community near Michoacan, Mexico. He entered the United States as an "illegal immigrant" in the 1970s to work picking fruit and vegetables in various locales of the U.S. Southwest. Torres made his way to Baytown in the early 1980s to seek work in its booming oil-refinery industry. He developed skills at sheet metal installation and pipe insulation and secured work from various subcontractors in Houston-area refineries.[2] Those employers enabled Torres to secure a work visa to enter and exit the United States at will throughout the 1980s and 1990s.[3] His skills were in demand in Baytown's and Houston's neoliberal industrial economy.

In January 2002 Torres was visiting with family and friends in Baytown for the holidays. He and his son had planned to leave on January 19 for a job installing sheet metal at a construction site in Kansas City, Missouri. Torres and his son were at this point migrant contract workers who traveled throughout the United States as mandated by the needs of construction firms that recruited and hired them. Torres decided to stay longer in Baytown because he felt ill. His son left Baytown for Kansas City without him and mistakenly took Torres's hypertension medication with him in his luggage. Without his medication, Torres became ill, and family members took him to a nearby hospital emergency room for treatment. Torres received the proper medication at the hospital and was eager to join his son in Kansas City so they could begin work.[4]

Once back at his brother's residence, however, Torres reportedly continued to feel dizzy, and family members called the paramedics out of fear that he was having a heart attack. Torres refused treatment by the paramedics, saying he merely needed to take a walk to clear his mind and soothe his nerves. Worried about his brother's health, Jose Torres then placed a 911 emergency call for an ambulance. The tape and transcript of that phone call reveal Jose stating in broken English, "He (Luis) is acting really bad . . . He don't feel right." Jose told police officers that "weapons were unnecessary because he was unarmed and ill," to which police responded by saying "not to worry about it. It was their problem now, that they would take care of it and go find him."[5]

At some time between that conversation and the moment an ambulance crew reached Torres on the street, normative discourses regarding threat, illegality, and criminality created an alternate reality. Upon being approached by the paramedics, Torres fled. Presumably he was annoyed that his medical condition was being blown out of proportion, and he did not want to be hospitalized because it would further delay his trip to Kansas City. In response to that, the paramedics reported to police that Torres was armed, dangerous, and apparently intoxicated.[6] Their report stated, "We seem to have an Hispanic male here with a pistol . . . (unintelligible) gotten away from a psychiatric facility . . . going southbound toward east Honeycutt towards Alexander . . . heavy set Hispanic male with no shirt and it looks like he had a gun in his hand." According to the Torres family attorney, Michael Solar, this report characterized Torres as "a mental patient with a gun" and a person any law enforcement agent should be deeply concerned about. According to his family, the only object that Torres carried with him that evening was his wallet. Furthermore, as explained by Solar, Torres "had no history of violence. He and his family are well regarded, very nice farm people . . . He's never been a psychiatric patient in his life . . . This illness [hypertension] was something new that his family had never observed before."[7]

This marked an important moment leading to Torres's demise. It is quite indicative of how police brutality often unfolds and how the racial state of expendability manifests in discourse. Here you have a man in poor health and for whom family members are concerned transformed into an intoxicated or hallucinating man of color who is stalking innocent citizens on the streets of Baytown with no shirt on and a pistol in his hand. This, moreover, is not a mere matter of opinion but is the official discourse and state record being exchanged between medical and police staff. It begs the question of what evidence they drew from to paint this horrific and dangerous depiction of Torres. They had no idea whether the man was drunk or hallucinating. Torres did not threaten or attack anyone. He was not carrying anything in his hand, much less a pistol or even anything "shiny" as was initially reported. But somehow each of these characteristics was ascribed to him in a way that was not so much as even questioned by any of the authorities involved. Normative discourses associated with and authenticated within the colonial dynamics of the region put the gun in Torres's hand. Baytown's history of segregation and racial violence, and especially the recent tensions stirred by its war on gangs, helped transform him into a deranged and possibly deadly killer.

As Torres's encounter with police proceeded that evening, his expendability and inaccessibility to justice became quite clear. Once the paramedics issued their inaccurate report to police, officers sought and found Torres within a matter of minutes. When the officers approached him, one of them asked him to put his hands on the hood of the patrol car while they searched him for weapons and interrogated him. The officer spoke in English; Torres, who spoke only Spanish, misinterpreted the requests and took two slow steps away from the vehicle. Within seconds, the officers threw Torres to the ground, sprayed him in the face repeatedly with pepper spray, and proceeded to beat and choke him until he lay motionless. They then handcuffed Torres as he lay facedown on the pavement. Upon seeing that Torres was motionless and apparently not breathing, the officers called the paramedics. When Torres arrived at Baycoast Hospital's emergency room he was already dead. Doctors there officially pronounced him so at 1:10 a.m. on January 20, 2002.[8]

Baytown's interim police chief, Byron Jones, was quick to address any suspicion of wrongdoing or aggression by his officers. Jones had just been appointed interim chief by retiring chief Schaffer, the person responsible for Baytown's Operation Valdez. When first questioned by a local journalist whether the arresting officers committed any breach of protocol, Jones responded, "There were no errors at all . . . The officers worked within the established guidelines and policies. They were still trying to find out if he was the individual in the earlier call. Mr. Torres was trying to walk off."[9] Jones said, "I don't think there was excessive force used or any intentional acts." City Clerk Gary Smith reinforced Jones's opinion by stating to local media that the interim chief's initial review of the case "led him to conclude that the officers acted accordingly." Baytown Mayor Pete Alfaro supported Jones's statements by describing Torres's death an "unfortunate accident."[10]

After reviewing postmortem photographs of Torres's badly bruised and swollen head, face, and neck, the Torres family grew suspicious that much more took place than his being pepper-sprayed for stepping away from police officers. Luis Torres's brother Jose told local journalists, "I'd like to find out about his problems, make sure if he died by himself or if they caused any problems."[11] Jose and other relatives hired attorney Solar to investigate the case and file a lawsuit. Roughly one month after Torres met his fate, Solar delivered a letter to Baytown's city clerk, city manager, and mayor that read, in part:

We've formally served the city with our notice of intention to bring a claim against the city for the acts or omissions of all culpable parties. . . . What we do know is that there is a very different reporting of the facts by the family and the police department as it relates to the circumstances preceding Mr. Torres' death . . . The police department has talked about pepper spray being used. We have post-mortem photographs suggesting that something more than pepper spray was used.[12]

Baytown city officials were initially dismissive about the case and made it seem to be a matter of inconvenience and a waste of public funds. City clerk Smith responded to the Torres family suit by saying, "We never welcome a lawsuit because of the expense involved in defending the city."[13]

As more information about the Torres case was gathered and made available, the Torres family's suspicions proved to be quite valid. Like all police departments in Harris County, Baytown's Police Department is under the jurisdiction of the Harris County District Attorney's Office in Houston. All "in custody" deaths are investigated by the Harris County medical examiner. That office conducted an autopsy or cause-of-death study and report for the Torres case and released its findings on February 22, 2002. The report ruled that Torres died as a result of "homicide caused by repeated blunt force trauma and mechanical asphyxiation."[14] This means far more than a quick douse of pepper spray was implemented against Torres and in ways that refute Chief Jones's initial claims. The report concluded that Torres endured severe bruising of his neck and trachea and repeated blows to the head, causing brain hemorrhages:

Blunt impact trauma to the subscalp, wrists, back and neck . . . hemorrhages in the interior portion of the left frontal lobe of the brain and on the interior of the left temporal lobe and evidence of mechanical asphyxia with mechanical compression based on hemorrhages in the eyes, soft tissue hemorrhages of the neck muscles and hemorrhages within the trachea.[15]

Torres's hypertension could not have caused these types of injuries, nor could any psychological condition he acquired that day. In defense of her office's report and perhaps in anticipation of how local law enforcement authorities might attempt to nullify it, Dr. Joyce Carter, Harris County's chief medical examiner, told local journalists, "This is not an accidental ruling. It is our medical opinion that someone is responsible for another person's death."[16] Carter added details about Torres's injuries. Regarding the issue of mechanical asphyxiation, she said, "That means more than just blocking his nose and mouth . . . In this case, it could have happened when piling onto someone's chest, preventing it from going up and down. There were also some bruises to the neck and some injury to the airways." Carter said evidence of asphyxiation included "hemorrhages of the neck muscles and trachea and in Torres' eyes; his forehead exhibited cuts, bruises, abrasions, and swelling; and his eyes were blackened and swollen shut."[17]

The medical examiner's office released photos of Torres's gruesomely bruised head, face, and upper torso.[18] The photos provided further evidence of the level of brutality that determined his fate. Attorney Solar said of the evidence, "I think, first and foremost, it paints a very different picture from that offered by the Baytown Police Department the day of Mr. Torres' death . . . Whenever you have as many blows to the head as I saw in the postmortem photos, it could hardly be considered an accident."[19] The medical examiner's report also ruled that Torres did not have a trace of hallucinogenic drugs or alcohol in his body, refuting police reports that Torres was delusional after an eight-day drinking binge. Police said the family initially reported that information to them, but the family has vehemently denied this and the reports by paramedics to police officers that Torres was intoxicated.

Even in the face of clear, scientific evidence, Baytown's police chief, mayor, and city manager stubbornly claimed that officers Bert Dillow, Micah Aldred, and Rodney Evans did not breach legal protocol and acted as they were trained to proceed. After reviewing the cause-of-death report and a videotape of the incident, Chief Jones said at a press conference, "I don't feel there was any unjustified force used."[20] Jones said only pepper spray was used against Torres: "There was a night stick there, but it wasn't used." He said there were still "unknown factors" about the case.[21] Chief Jones's only acknowledgment of potential injustice was in placing all three officers on paid administrative leave after the autopsy results were released. This action suggests that despite his strong claims otherwise, he realized that the video and postmortem medical evidence did not corroborate what he had been claiming to local media. The press conference marks the first moment Chief Jones acknowledged the video evidence and began to avoid its release to local media. By law, video evidence taken from police patrol cars is public information and should be made immediately available to the public at large. Federal mandates have attached such importance to this protocol that the U.S. Justice Department has granted more than $20 million to help local departments buy cameras.

The lack of cooperation from Baytown officials pushed Solar to seek federal aid in investigating the Torres case:

> Suffice it to say that we will be contacting the FBI and other police agencies who may have an interest in this matter . . . I believe that the evidence is

going to point to an overreaction on the part of the authorities in this instance . . . Rest assured that we're going to take all actions available under the law to obtain justice not only for Mr. Torres but for his widow and children that he left behind.[22]

The potential involvement of federal authorities seemed to have a quick influence on Chief Jones and other local officials. The day after the press conference, special agent Bob Doguim of the Federal Bureau of Investigation announced that the FBI was launching a preliminary investigation of the Torres case and the Baytown Police Department.[23]

Baytown officials' hesitation in acknowledging and releasing the video evidence suggests that they realized its content did not corroborate their public statements. City spokesman Gary Smith told local media that although Baytown officials realized they are forbidden to withhold public information, they were still willing to do so until after consulting with Texas Attorney General John Cornyn: "Anything that's on a 911 tape has its own statute and is public record."[24] The *Houston Chronicle* and *Baytown Sun* petitioned under the Freedom of Information Act to have the videotape released within days after Torres's death. They did so with a clear recognition that the Baytown Police Department was violating the law by withholding information from the public.[25] Their FOIA petitions were ignored, which stirred more suspicion of a cover-up, as an editorial in the *Baytown Sun* noted: "The delay clearly impeded the public's right to know what happened that night. At the same time, and as one local journalist acknowledged, it allowed rumor and innuendo to flourish."[26]

Nearly two months after Torres died, the Baytown Police Department released the video for public viewing. Baytown's police chief, city attorney, and city manager justified the delay by saying releasing it earlier would "interfere with the detection, investigation or prosecution of crime."[27] That statement seems illogical, as it is unclear how the public viewing the video would deter an investigation. Just hours after Baytown's civic officials issued an official request to block the videotape's release, Attorney General Cornyn's office ruled that it should be released immediately and in a way that complied with federal law. A letter signed by State Senator Mario Gallegos Jr. of Houston on February 27, 2002, and sent to Cornyn urged the attorney general to order the videotape's release and to expedite the order. Regarding the delay Solar said, "The Baytown Police Department's release of the film is clearly a result of a concerted effort from citizens and elected officials putting pressure on the police department."[28] As soon as the Texas Attorney General's Office denied Baytown officials' request to withhold it, Chief Jones quickly changed his opinion on the videotape. Rather than being something that would interfere, Jones said, "We don't feel that anything in our investigation, the district attorney's office investigation, or the FBI's investigation, would be compromised by the release of this tape."[29]

The events surrounding the stalled release of the videotape can be compared to the Smith lynching case in Baytown in 1917. As described earlier, after Smith was lynched and his body mutilated and burned for a supposed crime of sexual aggression toward a white woman that he most likely did not commit, one of the first actions of Baytown residents and civic officials was to destroy telegraph lines that connected Baytown to media outlets and law enforcement agencies in Houston and the state. The mob seized and destroyed the camera of a local photographer who recorded the incident. The logic in this strategy was that they wanted the Smith case to remain a local affair that pertained to local history and tradition and would be dealt with by local authorities. Once information regarding the Smith case reached authorities and journalists in the Greater Houston area, Baytown became the site of much critical scrutiny by county and state authorities. Eighty-five years later, the Torres case was dealt with in a similar way.

Even after they were mandated to release the video to the public, Baytown officials sought other ways to delay it. Prior to its release to the media, the videotape of the Torres incident was screened at police headquarters to a small group of people identified as Latino/a community leaders. It is unclear what interim chief Jones and city manager Mercer intended to accomplish by doing this. But the screening was most likely meant to influence what was being perceived in a way that might allow for those "leaders" to quell any unrest in the Latino/a community in particular. This maneuver seemed to be an implicit acknowledgment of injustice toward Latinos/as historically. Before showing the video, Jones informed the viewers that they were about to see an example of officers using "standard procedure" to subdue Luis Torres after he failed to comply with their requests. One of those present, Eva Benavides, recalled, "He tried to prepare us so we expected something routine." Benavides is an intriguing character in the story of Baytown's activist awakening. She had been a member of Baytown City Council, the first Latino or Latina to hold that position and only the second woman of color. During an oral history interview I did with her, she cited her father as an inspiration for community involvement and mutual aid. She said she left electoral politics due to her frustrations with racial intimidation and patriarchy from Baytown's white-male power structure.[30]

The video of the incident illustrated a level of brutality that was not only questionable but that Benavides and others found reprehensible. Benavides said, "For them to tell us right then and there that it appeared the officers used proper procedures, I looked at them and said 'You got to be kidding.' They ganged up on this man. I don't know what tape you're seeing, but the tape I'm seeing shows this man beat to death."[31] Benavides said the tape was so horrific that it affected her physiologically and psychologically: "I was sick for a couple of days. It made me ill and I just could not believe the police department, that this is the way things are done."[32] Her disbelief and disgust led her to write a letter to the editor of the *Baytown Sun*:

> Baytown has a history of police abuse and it still seems to exist. The hypocrisy of the police department allows them to treat people like criminals without giving them due process of the law first. The law is there to protect everyone not just the police officers. If the Baytown police department feels that they are bashed then this could be because more and more critics are coming forward with their stories.[33]

Other emerging Latino/a leaders concurred with her. They too were bothered by Jones's attempt to shape their opinions beforehand by claiming that Torres's demise was the result of "proper procedure." Ruben De Hoyos left the meeting with Jones telling local media that he was "deeply concerned." De Hoyos offered other interesting commentary to a journalist from the *Texas Observer* magazine: "Back in my era, the police wouldn't talk to you except by beating you . . . They would put you in the patrol car and use the baton right away and nothing was ever done."[34] Fred Aguilar, who attended the private screening, offered more extensive comments: "When I saw it, I felt that very unnecessary force was used . . . If that's proper police procedure, then I'm very concerned."[35] De Hoyos and Aguilar were recognized as civic leaders due to their volunteer work in Baytown's Latino/a communities, largely on behalf of Latino/a youths and small businesses.

The Baytown Police Department continued to defend the innocence of its officers. Jones commented about the video to journalists: "It just looks like they're trying to wrestle a guy that's stiffened up, and hit his torso four times for pain compliance. Another time, Torres is on top of an officer and holding his leg, and you can't see anything but the officer, and he may be hitting (Torres') face. But, that's about it."[36] Jones was implying that Torres was an aggressor even to the extent that he claims that Torres somehow pinned one of the officers under him and was in command of that officer's leg. Jones made this claim while also saying these moments were not visible on the videotape, although the video chronicled the entire encounter.

As outrage over the privately screened video spread from the opinions of those who witnessed it, police officials began to take other steps toward blunting any link between the Torres case and Baytown's troubled history. Soon after screening the video before the private audience, Jones took steps to influence how the public at large would view the video once it was released to all media outlets. Anticipating that Baytown's history of racial violence would be connected to Torres's death, he attempted to preemptively negate that link. Before any cries of racism were voiced in the media or by residents of the community, he stated, "Anyone who sees the video and listens to the audio will see that racism is not involved. The officers are polite and call him Mr. Torres. There are no racial remarks or epithets."[37] His comment suggests that race could only come into play in Torres's treatment if the officers had used racial epithets and had been impolite. It also suggests that the severe beating and choking that Torres endured, after he was spared from racial epithets, can in no way be acts of racially motivated aggression. According to this logic, racism would only be a part of the Torres case if police officers had been screaming something like "Die, Mexican, die" or "I hate Latinos" or "white power" as they beat the life out of Torres.

A lawyer for one of the officers attempted an even bolder method for depoliticizing race: "Anyone who tries to depict the officers as being racially motivated is wrong. Officer Dillow is married to a Mexican national who is seven months pregnant with his child."[38] The attorney went on to explain that Officer Dillow's wife and her Mexican family were "outraged by the way some are trying to present these officers." Like Jones's comment about the officers' politeness in not vocalizing racial insults, this comment by Dillow's attorney further confuses an understanding of how racial power functions. It suggests that by impregnating a woman of color, in this case a Latina who happens to also be an immigrant from Mexico, the potentially racist beliefs of a white man can be erased. The logic in this strategy is that had this officer not been married to and/or impregnated a Mexican immigrant, he might have harbored preconditioned stereotypes or fears about Torres, also a Mexican immigrant. The lack of a Mexican sexual partner or breeding partner for the officer could then have led to his using extra and unnecessary force to arrest Torres, albeit unwarrantedly. This logic seems even more absurd considering that a police officer need not even be white in order for a racially motivated act of police brutality to take place. Again, attorneys and city officials were attempting to distance the Torres case from any sign of racism prior to any antiracist critiques being voiced.

Once the video was released to local media outlets and aired repeatedly on the news of Houston's major television stations, outrage about the Torres case gained momentum. The video provided clear and gruesome evidence of the brutal beating he endured. It showed Torres screaming "Don't kill me!" in broken English while the officers swept Torres's legs from underneath him, threw him violently to the ground, beat him repeatedly on the head and face with their fists, choked him, and piled onto his back until he lay facedown on the pavement, motionless, and breathless. Once he was immobilized, the officers talked among themselves rather casually and even jokingly about their scuffle with Torres as Jimi Hendrix's song "Are You Experienced?" blared from the radio of one of their patrol cars.

After viewing the video, journalist Jake Bernstein of *Texas Monthly* described the irony of the Hendrix tune in deeper detail:

We will never know if Luis Alfonso Torres heard these lyrics as they poured out of Baytown Police Officer Bert Dillow's open squad car about half past midnight on Sunday January 20. We cannot ask him. Seven minutes later, Torres was dead, lying on the street, his hands cuffed behind his back, the left side of his head turning purple from the beating he had just received from three of Baytown's finest . . . Their victim makes the sound of a wounded animal fighting for his life. It's a hoarse and guttural cry, a noise whose origin is deep inside the body.[39]

George L. Kirkham, an expert criminologist who was hired by the Torres family attorney, reviewed the autopsy report and the videotape and concluded that the police officers clearly used excessive force. He said the "leg sweep" they used to knock Torres to the ground before beating and choking him was unnecessary because they knew Torres was not armed and was posing no threat to them.[40] The Mexican consulate in Houston also became involved with the case. Mexican Consul General Enrique Buj said, "We are respectful of the judicial system of the United States and its law enforcement officers. But we are not utterly fools, and know sometimes there are acts of excessive force against Hispanics simply because they are Hispanics."[41]

To emphasize the shared struggles of blacks and Latinos/as against police violence, I cannot help but draw a connection between Consul General Buj's comment and one aired by Malcolm X decades earlier. When asked about police brutality in the United States, he said, "Let us remember that we're not brutalized because we're Baptist, we're not brutalized because we're Methodists, we're not brutalized because we're Muslims, we're not brutalized because we're Catholics, we're brutalized because we are blacks in America."[42]

The first moment of organized protest surrounding the Torres case took place in the Magnolia Park neighborhood about ten miles west of Baytown near downtown Houston. Magnolia Park is also near Segundo Barrio, the

Third Ward, Denver Harbor, and the Fifth Ward and is one of the older barrios in the Houston area. By the late twentieth century, Segundo Barrio and Magnolia Park were widely regarded as a center of Latino/a culture and politics. On March 3, 2002, the Houston chapter of LULAC organized a meeting and candlelight vigil there on behalf of the Torres family at the Teatro Bilingue community performing arts center, which often served as a venue for Latino/a political dialogues.

LULAC leaders said the Torres case was clearly comparable to the cases of Pedro Oregon in 1998 and Jose Campos Torres in 1977 and called attention to the growing anti-Latino/a nature of the Houston area's racial hierarchy. LULAC's district director, Mary Ramos, made reference to the Joe Torres case of the late 1970s: "We don't want another riot to start because of what happened to this man [Luis Torres] here."[43] The event was attended by about sixty people, including a contingent of around ten Latinos/as from Baytown. Ruben De Hoyos spoke at the event and said, "We in the Hispanic community of Baytown are deeply concerned and highly critical of the actions of the Baytown Police Department . . . We have viewed the videotape and we have found that the events that led up to the death of Mr. Torres showed clearly that the police used excessive force."[44]

The video of the Torres incident was then screened before the audience at Teatro Bilingue, and many wept or covered their eyes as Torres was being choked and beaten to death while he struggled to scream for the officers to relent. The stage upon which the video was screened was adorned with numerous posters, some reading "Homicide is murder! Bring the cops to justice!" and "Luis Torres did not deserve to die." One poster featured postmortem photographs of Torres and read, "Is this resisting arrest, or police brutality?" Another member of Baytown's Latino/a community, Mercedes Rentería, told reporters, "I'm very concerned about the way the whole situation was handled . . . What crime did this man commit? Is it against the law to walk down the street?"[45] Stipulations of Baytown's Operation Valdez declared that occupying certain public spaces was, in fact, illegal. Luis Torres was killed in a location deemed a hot spot by Baytown Police Department officials in 1992.[46]

The LULAC event marked a moment when LULAC spokesman Johnny Mata evolved into a key figure in the Torres case. At the event he aired his frustration over the Torres case and called the police actions "brutal and unnecessary."[47] He said, "The Latino community is horrified . . . These acts must be carefully examined . . . If they are deemed to be criminal, justice demands that they be prosecuted to the fullest extent of the law."[48] As yet another example of the rampant nature of anti-Latino/a police terror in the Houston area, one woman drove to the event from the northern suburb of Katy to show her support but also to gather more information about a fate that she felt befell her brother just months earlier. Criselda Aldape said her brother also died while in custody of local law enforcement agents, and yet there was never any explanation or investigation for what exactly killed him. Similar to what was being proposed to Torres's family in Baytown, law enforcement officials asked her to think of her brother's death as an unsolvable mystery. Watching the video of Torres's murder raised her suspicion, as she commented to the media, "It makes me wonder how my brother went down."[49]

The LULAC event was the first through which the solidarity of black activists and residents was aired about the Torres case. Yolanda Smith, executive director of the Houston chapter of the NAACP, attended the Torres vigil at Teatro Bilingue and said, "This is not just a civil rights issue; it is a human rights issue . . . This was not an accident. We need the entire city of Houston to be upset about this death."[50] In an expression of black solidarity with Latinos/as at the Teatro Bilingue meeting, Kufi Taharka, chairman of the Houston-based National Black United Front, charged that not much had changed in the Houston area since the police killing of Jose Campos Torres in 1977. On behalf of the black and Latino/a populations of the region, he proclaimed, "This system is based upon white supremacy."[51]

Soon after the event at Teatro Bilingue, Baytown's Latino/a community leaders announced that they were planning a demonstration in Baytown. At a press conference to announce their intentions, De Hoyos said their purpose "would be twofold, in honor of the memory of Mr. Torres and to show that the community is involved and concerned and outraged."[52] The event took place on March 9, 2002, in central Baytown, with a march down Market Street, a major thoroughfare, and a rally at Bicentennial Park, a historical gathering point for Baytown festivals and other community events as well as the site of a memorial to World War II veterans of the region. About 150 people took part in the march, most of them black or Latino/a. The march was the first in a series of important events to come.

After the march, black activists and residents from Baytown and elsewhere in the Houston area began to organize demonstrations on behalf of Torres, through which some of the first and more resounding critiques of white supremacy and racism were aired in the public at large. The involvement of black political leaders and antiracist speakers carried the spirit of protest to new heights, a surge that I argue was the result of the discursive condition I have called foundational blackness. One day after the LULAC event, minister Quanell X and members of the New Black Panther Party based in Houston conducted a much more volatile rally at the doorstep of the Baytown Police Department headquarters. The New Black Panther Party is a self-described black-supremacist organization formed by former members of the Nation of Islam who were ousted for being too militant. Houston's Khalid Muhammad was the founder of the organization, and upon his mysterious death in 2001 his protégé, Quanell X, became the national spokesman for the New Black Panther Party.[53]

Beginning in the 1990s Quanell X was becoming a known presence in Houston's political scene. Hailing from the same neighborhood that produced the Geto Boys' Scarface and South Park Mexican (SPM), X had a few appearances in rap videos recorded in Houston, such as the Geto Boys' "City under Siege." He was an important voice behind smaller protest rallies held on behalf of Latino/a victims and was an essential part of the Justice for Pedro Oregon Coalition in the late 1990s. In 2002 Quanell X dispatched members of his organization to the march and prayer vigil in Baytown, where they announced that they would be holding another event the following day.[54]

At the second event, Quanell X pushed Baytown's activist awakening to a new height and sought to inspire local blacks and Latinos/as. One of his first statements at that event was "We will not tolerate cops that kill innocent people. What happened to Mr. Torres was murder, and not an accident."[55] He then warned Baytown police officials that they must change their "racist ways." He proclaimed, "We are saying to the Baytown Police Department . . . Change or Die!" An African American resident of Baytown who was in attendance found X's presence encouraging: "Until we get this situation resolved, we're going to always have problems in Baytown."[56] Mercedes Rentería, a Baytown Latino community leader, was asked whether the NBPP represented the best interests of Baytown's Latino/a residents and responded: "It's good to see minorities stick together and seek for justice in this Torres case. We need all the help we can get."[57]

Support for the NBPP's presence was surely not the consensus, as Quanell X's involvement in the Torres case polarized relationships between whites and nonwhites. White Baytown residents attended the NBPP rally to counter-protest.[58] A white man, the son of a well-known funeral director in the community, stormed to the front of the rally and took the microphone to declare his support for the Baytown Police Department and his love for Baytown. Ed Christianson of the Harris County Deputies Organization told local media he attended the event because "this city has one of the finest police departments." He addressed connections being made between the Torres case and the widely seen beating of Rodney King by Los Angeles police in 1991: "This is not the Rodney King case. The officers did everything by the book." Two white women in attendance communicated their support for the Baytown officers by holding up large signs that read, "Baytown Police Are Innocent!" One of the sign bearers told a reporter, "I'm just here to support the BPD. They were just doing their jobs. They're risking their lives to protect us!"[59]

Some whites in attendance, however, sympathized with the New Black Panthers and others protesting Torres's death. They said the aggression of white counterdemonstrators was proof that Baytown was rife with racial hostility and that it had generally failed to address one of the city's most serious problems. One of the sympathetic whites, a Baytown native in his twenties, delivered a courageous and impressive critique of racism in his hometown, emphasizing that Baytown had neglected its history of violent segregation for far too long. His father accompanied him for support, wearing a T-shirt expressing his opposition to racial bigotry.[60]

Black residents of Baytown seemed to be inspired by what was going on. On March 16, 2002, a group of McNair residents used the Torres case and the impetus to announce to the media that they would be hosting a community event to address white supremacy and to serve as a forum for all people of color in Baytown to discuss organizing strategies. The event's planner, Trixie Washington, was a lifelong resident of McNair and recognized as a leader among its African American residents. She commented on the event and Baytown's need to address its tumultuous history of racial strife:

> I see prejudice and racism every day and it needs to be brought out and clinched. It's unfortunate that someone had to die to bring about these problems. There needs to be behavioral changes so that people can better understand each other. This day has been brought together to formally apply to record the moans of tax paying citizens of our city. Our objective is to make those cries duly noted publicly and civilly.[61]

The highlight of the event was a keynote lecture by Robert Coleman, a local black minister and head of an organization called Real Urban Ministries. He said the spirit of protest and interminority solidarity stirred by the Torres case "shows something is not right. With something like this, it's an affront to the entire community. We need black, Hispanic, and white leaders to all rally together. The leaders here today are doing what other leaders who have been here longer should have done." Baytown's activist awakening was unfolding.

Washington's event was not as well attended as she hoped it would be. Nonetheless, she and others there said they felt encouraged about its effects. The day after the event, she said, "We didn't want to just meet. We wanted to accomplish something. We talked about opening an NAACP chapter in Baytown or some group that people can go to when there is a problem."[62] A few days after Washington's forum in McNair, the Baytown Police Department released another version of the Torres video that had been enhanced by the FBI. The enhanced video proved to heighten opposing opinions about whether Torres was a victim of police brutality. Greg Cagle, an attorney for the Texas Municipal Police Association, said, "The people that I have talked to and that have seen both copies think that the enhanced version showed a little more clearly that Mr. Torres was resisting the officers."[63] Considering that there was literally no evidence of resistance on the previous version, Cagle himself did not seem all too convinced about his own claim, to the extent that he could only state that his sources told him it was "a little more" convincing. A little more than nothing is still rather unconvincing.

Pro-Torres opinions agreed that the enhanced video provided "a lot more" evidence of police misconduct. In it, images of Torres aggressively subduing one of the officers as originally claimed by the interim police chief were still not at all visible. In response to the enhanced video Torres family attorney Solar said, "It's clearer now than it was before that Mr. Torres was never the aggressor . . . It is very clear to anyone that watches the tape that this man is pleading for his life."[64] Fred Aguilar said, "I saw more. It does clearly show the blows and I did not see any resistance from Torres at all. I saw him brought down." Mata, Houston's LULAC leader, was equally convinced about the new evidence. He said the enhanced video further refuted claims that Torres was drunk and out of control: "This was not a man out of control. The whole thing was badly handled and the results of the autopsy report are very compelling in showing that excessive force was used. I find it appalling that a tragedy occurred."[65] The certainty and conviction that characterized Solar's, Aguilar's, and Mata's comments present a strong contrast to those of Cagle, who said he was told the enhanced video showed just a little more evidence to support police officers' claims that they were merely doing their jobs.

Police officials continued to make blunders that made them appear even more suspect of an attempted cover-up. Three months after Torres's death, interim chief Jones announced that he was placing a fourth officer on administrative leave due to his role in the Torres case. That officer apparently was the last on the scene, and the video evidence revealed that he arrived with enough time to wrest his knee into Torres's back to help force him face-first into the asphalt. Without the enhanced video, the police chief apparently had no way of knowing that a fourth officer was involved. When asked by reporters why he had not addressed the fourth officer sooner, Jones replied, "No one ever asked." By this he implied that he did not report a fourth officer's involvement because journalists had not asked him something they would not have known to ask. The statement only added to the growing tension.[66]

At this point, Jones began to allege that activists were far more responsible for racial tensions in Baytown than were he or any other civic officials: "It seems that there are a few individuals who have attempted to garner attention of the media in an effort to promote their own agendas. As a result of their efforts, they stand poised to divide a community, the results of which can only be detrimental."[67] Jones's suggestions that Baytown was an undivided community prior to its activist awakening are completely absurd considering its history. In one of the oddest moments of the city's public relations campaign, Jones attempted to gain sympathy for the police officers involved in the Torres case. He said the fourth officer "is taking it hard. He's the youngest. The others are scared, too. Not knowing what the grand jury will do, if they're going to lose their jobs or go to jail or get sued and lose their house. Imagine being in their place, living with uncertainty from day to day."[68] That uncertainty, I argue, is a defining element of black and Latino/a subjectivity in that community and from every day to every other day. The history of violence, exploitation, and segregation in the community speaks for itself.

The Harris County District Attorney's Office is in charge of conducting investigations regarding police misconduct within municipal law enforcement agencies such as Baytown's. These cases are judged by a grand jury that is selected by the district attorney and take place at the Harris County courthouse in downtown Houston. The Torres case was scheduled to be presented to a grand jury in Houston on April 25, 2002.

As the day approached when a Harris County grand jury would convey its findings in the Torres case, many prepared for the worst. LULAC organized a forum at the Carlos Garcia Theatre in Houston. At the forum Mata asserted, "History has shown us that a vigorous prosecution of police officers in Harris County has been non-existent."[69] The forum marked a moment when local scholars began to contribute to the discourse. Professor Michael Olivas of the University of Houston law school said, "This is a textbook example of abuse of police power. This is an abject failure of public institutions."[70] He said Torres "was characterized (by police) as a crazy, drunken Mexican."[71] A representative from the Mexican consulate in Houston attended the forum, where he announced, "My government is very concerned about the treatment that our citizens receive from the Baytown Police Department."[72]

As anxieties continued to build in anticipation of the grand jury's findings, Quanell X used them as an opportunity to strengthen the resolve of the pro-Torres camp in Baytown. In a second event held at Baytown's Bicentennial Park, he announced, "If they don't indict these officers for murder, I will hold a march against the Baytown Police Department . . . The people will indict them!"[73] In response to claims made by Jones and other city officials that he was exploiting the Torres case for publicity purposes, Quanell X said, "I do not hate police. I hate corruption. I only came to educate my brothers and sisters." He added that he viewed Baytown's police officials as "cowardly and weak," and he challenged them:

I am not here for a publicity stunt. I am here to stand up for the residents. Justice is what the people deserve. If you slay one more black, one more Hispanic in this city, I guarantee you will see a revolution![74]

The second NBPP rally is especially significant in that it was the moment X began to more explicitly address the supposed contradiction in what its founders considered a black-supremacist organization defending the rights of a Mexican immigrant. It was at this rally that X announced the formation of the Brown Panthers, a subchapter of his NBPP: "You need a strong Hispanic organization. If blacks and Hispanics work together, we can become the new police department!"[75]

A black attendee said Quanell X's contribution "was a positive message that needs to be sent out."[76] Another said, "Rights need to be made known to the public. The public should be aware of what's going on in our community."[77] An African American expressed a sense of liberation because of the NBPP presence: "I love this! This is what we need out here. We have too many problems out here." Yet another black attendee commented, "They should do it more often out here."[78]

On May 3, 2002, the Harris County District Attorney's Office issued a press release stating that after analyzing all the evidence presented and considering charges of manslaughter, murder, or criminal negligent homicide, the grand jury members decided to "no-bill" the four police officers responsible for Torres's death. The ruling legally deemed that Torres's death was a mystery, despite the video that shows him being slain and despite autopsy evidence that verifies his death as a homicide. With all that evidence, the grand jury could not come up with an answer to why Torres lost his life.[79]

Baytown's new activists expressed disappointment and outrage at the grand jury's ruling. A visibly saddened De Hoyos seemed at a loss for words during a press conference. His only statement was "My reaction right now is one of anger and disappointment."[80] Mata of LULAC said, "This sends a clear message that it's open season to kill Mexicans, Hispanics, African Americans, and other minorities because you are not going to get punished!"[81] Michael Solar, the Torres family attorney, went further: "I could only be disappointed if I had any expectation that the Harris County District Attorney had the will to obtain an indictment of a police officer under these circumstances. The District Attorney's office has demonstrated that it will try children as adults but it has never gained the appetite for prosecuting its own."[82] Solar said the Torres family felt "betrayed and bewildered" by the ruling. "But they are not surprised," he explained. "I had prepared them for it, because never in the history of Harris County has a police officer been indicted for killing a Mexican."[83]

Solar issued a comment comparing the Torres case of 2002 to the Jose Campos Torres case of 1977. To underscore their commonalities he stated that although nearly two decades separated their deaths, "little has changed between Joe Torres and Luis Torres."[84] A few hours after Solar's comments were issued at his press conference, Enrique Buj, the consul general of Mexico in Houston, held a press conference at which he announced that the grand jury's ruling was "a manifestation of the persisting pattern of abuses and police violence, and perhaps, even discrimination that adversely affects Mexican residents in Houston."[85]

Baytown's police and city officials saw no inconsistency or flaw in the ruling. Interim chief Jones and mayor Alfaro held a press conference at Baytown City Hall in which they expressed gratitude for the district attorney's ruling. Jones said, "The Baytown Police Department has repeatedly confirmed its confidence in the criminal justice system. We respect the decision of the grand jury."[86]

Baytown Mayor Pete Alfaro sounded a bit more diplomatic and recognized that federal authorities still could override the district attorney's decision: "We will continue to provide them with any and all information that we have. Our community regrets this unfortunate incident."[87] Considering the history of the Torres case, the mayor could have been referring to the grand jury's ruling as unfortunate as much as he was saying so about Torres's death. Don Smyth, the governmental affairs bureau chief for the district attorney's office, explained the ruling by stating, "There was a full inquiry. The jurors were thoughtful and deliberate before no-billing these officers . . . They could not find that anything intentional, reckless or criminally negligent was done."[88] Attorneys for the exonerated officers justified the ruling in a way that posited them as victims along with Torres. Cagle, for the Texas Municipal Police Association, said, "The officers are glad to be cleared of any wrongdoing, but are remorseful. They feel bad that Mr. Torres died . . . It's something that they sleep with every night. But they did exactly as they were trained and they did nothing criminally wrong. The video verified this."[89]

Baytown's new activists continued their struggle although the grand jury's ruling clearly dampened their spirits. On May 4, 2002, they held their second candlelight prayer vigil at Bicentennial Park, this time at the concrete memorial erected to honor those who died in World War II. Only eight people were in attendance in addition to journalists from most Houston-area newspapers and television stations. At the vigil De Hoyos, a decorated veteran of World War II, posed questions about America's promise of democracy and egalitarianism. The septuagenarian seemed deeply troubled as he posed a question to God about "how America could allow for a police state to exist."[90] While pointing to the memorial commemorating fallen servicemen, he commented quite powerfully about the commitment of World War II veterans of color fight for civil rights: "Today it seems like they died unnecessarily." Others in attendance did not appear as solemn and instead vocalized an increased sense of outrage. Eva Benavides said the ruling was "an insult to our community." Carmen Torres said, "If there had not been evidence on the videotape, this would have gone nowhere. The least we can get from this is the truth."[91]

A week after the district attorney announced that he would no-bill the officers who killed Luis Torres, an event to recognize the twenty-fifth anniversary of the slaying of Joe Campos Torres was being organized. Janie Torres was only ten years old when the body of her brother Jose was found floating in Buffalo Bayou on Mother's Day 1977. As in the Luis Torres case twenty-five years later, the Harris County District Attorney's Office ruled to no-bill the officers involved in her brother's death despite clear and compelling evidence of their misconduct and brutality. As with the Pedro Oregon case of 1998, the family of Jose Campos Torres lent its support to activism on behalf of the Luis Torres case in 2002. At the anniversary event, Janie Torres commented: "I am very (angry) because nothing has been done . . . I don't want him to just have been murdered and we do nothing. I don't want him to be forgotten as if he were nobody. He was someone."[92] As she spoke, Ms. Torres drew even stronger comparisons between her brother Joe and Luis Torres:

> Twenty-five years later, he's still missed. Twenty-five years later, we still have another "wetback" that's been murdered. Come on. Where are the changes?! If we've had one after him, I don't see where the progress is. Am I blind?
> I just don't see it. I understand the police have a job to do and it's a tough job. It's also tough just being a citizen. If you move wrong, you might get shot down. What is it going to take? This is very, very pathetic. Are we supposed to close our eyes to this? This is so sad. In my lifetime, I hope I can see a change come about where the police don't shoot first and ask questions later.[93]

Immediately after the district attorney's announcement, a not-for-profit organization of attorneys calling themselves Corpus Justice organized an event at Houston's Family Law Center to discuss the Torres case and strategize about a new plan to protest the district attorney's decision. The meeting was attended by a number of local activist groups and scholars from local universities. During an open-microphone session at the event, Robert Buzzanco, a history professor at the University of Houston, asked the question "How can we call this a democracy if we can't oversee the people that protect us? This is a case where police kill people on tape!" Marty Butler Head, the president of Corpus Justice, used the event to announce an action: "What we are about today is calling for citizens to go to the Texas legislature to allow civilian oversight boards. I want civilian oversight with guts to be able to present to the grand jury. There is police truth, a district attorney truth, and citizen truth."[94]

Activism continued to build in communities within Houston's urban core. On May 8, 2002, LULAC held another event at Teatro Bilingue in Magnolia Park to sustain the efforts to seek justice for Torres at the state or federal level. The event was attended by an aide to U.S. Congresswoman Sheila Jackson Lee (D-Houston). As a member of the congressional Black Caucus, Lee was an outspoken advocate of antiracist causes as they pertain to African Americans in particular. She along with Congresswoman Maxine Waters from Los Angeles used her position to advance the civil rights of Latinos/as and to critique border militarization and other anti-immigrant policies that affect Latino/a immigrants. Throughout the Torres ordeal, Lee remained informed about the investigation from Washington and used the LULAC event to strengthen black-Latino/a political coalitions in Houston and beyond. At that meeting, her spokesman Larry Green announced, "We look forward to working with LULAC and other leaders to devise an action plan."[95] There were other expressions of interminority solidarity at the event. Masrur Javed Kahn, president of the Pakistan Association of Greater Houston, attended and offered his support for Latinos/as, blacks, and all others who experienced state-sanctioned violence in Houston and elsewhere: "I'm here today with a message of condolences for the Torres family. . . . Justice has to be equal and blind for everybody."[96]

The LULAC event attracted the attention of activists from other parts of the United States. King Downing, an attorney from New York City and head of the ACLU's racial-profiling initiative, traveled to Houston to learn more about the Torres case and offer his services. At a press conference he noted the widespread news about the Torres case: "Everybody is paying attention to this case all over the country . . . We want to see justice in this case."[97]

Baytown activists gained momentum when they decided to form a grassroots organization. On June 7, 2002, a group of black and Latino/a residents met that included Ruben De Hoyos, Eva Benavides, Hilda Martinez, Fred Aguilar, Marga Hernandez, Charles Mixon, and Henry Carr. Raquel Aguilar,

Ricky Brownfield, K. Mitchell, and Susan Rosales joined the group days later. They named the organization the United Concerned Citizens of Baytown and Henry Carr as its president. In naming Carr, they acknowledged his influence in the community as the head pastor at one of Baytown's oldest and largest African American churches, the Blessed Hope Church of God in Christ, in the historic Oak Addition neighborhood. The naming of a black minister as the leader of the UCBB is a reflection of what I have been referring to as foundational blackness, a discursive condition that grants African American history a hegemonic influence over antiracist causes in the Gulf South.

At the press conference held to announce the new organization, the group issued this statement: "We the members of the United Concerned Citizens of Baytown have just started the process of addressing issues that a large segment of the Baytown community are concerned with. We are optimistic that this effort will come to a satisfactory conclusion for both sides."[98] In making this statement, the UCCB allowed for the ambiguity of their activist dedication to continue. For example, why would they be concerned about the satisfaction of the other side of the Torres struggle, especially when that side had done so much to impede justice and spoil harmonious relations among residents of color and officials? De Hoyos explained that the UCCB was not only a response to the Torres case, considering that the initial plans for the organization were discussed in 1997 after the police killing of sixteen-year-old Juan Carlos Espinosa in Old Baytown.[99]

On June 26, 1997, three police officers raided the home of a Mexican immigrant family in Old Baytown while in pursuit of an alleged auto theft suspect.[100] One of the police officers shot and killed Juan Carlos Espinosa. Ironically, Espinosa was the son of the same man who had phoned in the missing-vehicle report. Juan Carlos had frustrated his parents by taking their van joyriding without their permission. The father phoned police about his son's joyriding in an effort to teach him a lesson. While police were in pursuit, Espinosa was returning the vehicle to the family home. Fearing the officers and not fully aware of what was taking place, Espinosa parked the vehicle on the street and quickly ran inside his family's home.

The officers pursued Espinosa into the attic of the family's home, where they found him hiding under a bed. Seconds later an officer shot the scared teen in the face at point-blank range while Espinosa was pleading with the officers, "Leave me alone. Just leave me alone," according to the Espinosa family's attorney. They did not leave him alone, and instead Espinosa died instantly from the gunshot wounds. Espinosa's cousin would later tell a journalist, "It was just a simple report, no reason to shoot the damn kid . . . There was no reason to kill him in front of his dad . . . They killed him, cold-blooded murder."[101] After an internal affairs investigation, a routine procedure in which the police investigate themselves for potential wrongdoing or misconduct, police officials found that the officer who shot Espinosa followed proper protocol and that the shooting was accidental. Regardless of whether the officer intended to discharge his weapon, the aggression he displayed offers an indication of how law enforcement policies are practiced in neighborhoods like those where Torres and Espinosa were slain.

Another case involving use of a family vehicle unfolded a decade later involving a twenty-three-year-old black resident of Bellaire, an older suburb of Houston. In January 2008 Robert Tolan and a friend had taken his family's vehicle to a nearby fast-food restaurant. Upon returning to his family's home, Tolan was confronted by a police officer with weapon drawn and falsely accusing him of auto theft. In fear for their lives, Tolan and his friend did as they were told and lay on their ground with their hands behind their heads. As Tolan's mother exited the home to investigate the commotion, the arresting officer was belligerent toward her as well, angering Tolan. At one point the officer violently shoved the woman against a brick wall. In response to that shove, Tolan raised his head to question the police officer's unnecessary aggression toward his mother. This slight movement and intervention provoked the officer to fire several shots toward Tolan, one striking him in the torso. Tolan survived despite being badly wounded. The bullet that struck him remains lodged in his liver. His friend escaped injury. The Tolan case of 2008 represents a slightly different form of racial profiling than what transpired in the Espinosa case of 1997. Espinosa lived in a working-class community with a majority Latino/a population and a few black families. That community was also identified as crime- and gang-ridden, stigmas that encouraged the aggression that sealed his fate.

The Tolan case, however, transpired in one of Houston's "whiter" suburbs. Tolan was not an immigrant from Latin America, as was Torres, nor was he the working-class son of an immigrant from Latin America, as was Espinosa. The Tolan family was rather well off compared to many black and Latino/a families in the United States. Tolan's father, Bobby Tolan Sr., was a former professional baseball player and a successful businessman.[102] Bearing that in mind, Bellaire represents a community of the kind that David Theo Goldberg has described as a "no nigger zone," a place where the presence of blacks has been rendered abnormal and/or illogical to the extent that signifies an always already suspicion of criminality.[103] The Tolan family's attorney told reporters, "There's no doubt in my mind that if these had been two white kids, they never would have been shot."[104] A Tolan family member agreed: "An officer sees two black youngsters get out in a white neighborhood and he approaches them. I don't understand it. I'm upset about it."[105] On May 11, 2010, a jury acquitted the police sergeant who shot Tolan.[106]

The plight of the Espinosa family in Baytown was indeed tragic to many people of color there, and it sparked a new sense of solidarity and outrage among residents in the community. As details of the incident spread, a large group of frustrated black and Latino/a neighbors gathered outside the Espinosa home to voice their outrage and frustration. They promptly identified Espinosa as but the latest victim of police terror without knowing the details regarding his killing. They did not seem to care much about the details surrounding the events of Espinosa's death. All they needed to know was that he was a young person of color killed inside his own home by Baytown police in a neighborhood where aggressive policing was quite the norm to know that he was a victim of injustice. Fearing a riot, the police called for additional officers to help disperse the crowd. While a riot never ensued, this was still an important moment in Baytown's history of racial politics for what it symbolized. Each was rendered expendable by memories and discourses of racial difference.

Memories of the Espinosa case loomed large as the Torres case of 2002 unfolded. There was a direct connection between the two, as the UCCB seemed poised to accentuate a growing sense of solidarity that had been developing between blacks and Latinos/as in Baytown. In their first press statement, the UCCB contended, "We will not stand by and condone the taking of a life without cause. This is not a Hispanic only issue, it is a community-wide issue, and we will strive to bring all segments of the community together in our efforts."[107] Fred Aguilar commented on the transethnic alliance: "We hope to work together to find some way to make sure that this doesn't happen again. I think that we're going in the right direction." At the UCCB press conference Reverend Carr, the UCCB leader, was called upon to speak and offered these initial comments: "I was very disturbed with what happened. If those guidelines result in the death of a person, then someone needs to go back and look at procedures and come up with a better effort."[108] UCCB member Hilda Martinez spoke from her experience:

> I know what I've experienced personally and what I have heard from friends and acquaintances. There are stories many people have to tell, but they are just too afraid to speak up. With this group, I hope we can educate and empower the community and have them report things and feel good about it.[109]

Eva Benavides demonstrated a similar resolve. Regarding the district attorney's ruling she said, "Just because they were 'no-billed' and found in compliance with police department procedure doesn't mean they did not commit an offense. It doesn't mean they did not overstep their boundaries."[110] Martinez and Benavides were among the most vocal members of the UCCB. During an oral history interview with me, Martinez cited the struggles and courage of her own family as a reason she tried to involve herself in community politics. She cited her responsibilities as a mother as well; hearing stories of how her own son felt racially profiled and harassed by police officers on a few occasions was more than enough to push her to get involved in community activism. UCCB member Marga Hernandez also became concerned with the condition of police brutality after her son was brutalized by police officers just a year prior.[111]

On June 8, 2002, the Corpus Justice nonprofit group of civil rights attorneys and Civilians Down, a national support group for family and friends of people who died in police custody, organized a public forum at the Montrose library in Houston. They screened a documentary film they produced titled *Police State 2000* as a way to place the Torres case within a broader national and international context. This was also an effort to remind Baytown residents that they were not alone and that a strategy of local isolation and cooperation would only hinder their critiques and ability to fight for justice. During an open discussion about the Torres case following the film, Arlene Kelly of Civilians Down said, "If those officers did not violate policy . . . then what's wrong with police policy? If they can kill an innocent man like that, then we know there's something wrong."[112] After viewing the Torres video, Ray Hill, producer and host of *The Prison Show*, a talk show focused on the criminal justice system in Texas that aired weekly on Houston's KPFT radio, told the audience, "We just sat here and saw police officers attack." A member of Corpus Justice replied, "We've let police get away with this kind of stuff. It's our own fault."[113]

While activists in other areas around Houston maintained their protests against police brutality at large, the UCCB members began to turn their attention toward removing interim chief Jones from his position. Despite the turmoil of the Torres case, Jones was still the top candidate to become Baytown's new police chief. After conducting what they called an open search and fielding applications, Baytown's mayor and city manager decided to move forward with nominating Jones as police chief; the Baytown City Council was to vote in favor of or against his promotion. Once again, this was despite the glaring and serious blunders he made during the Torres case, including withholding crucial information about an officer involved in Torres's murder and justifying it as "no one ever asked." The logic in this explanation is that someone must ask the chief of police if one of his officers was involved in the killing of a criminal suspect, and otherwise the chief had the right to occlude or conceal such information.

Public hearings regarding Jones's nomination began on June 14, 2002, at a city council meeting held at Baytown's Civic Center near Old Baytown. Members of the UCCB attended to protest. Jones's nomination was interpreted as a figurative slap in the face to them considering that its timing made it seem he was being promoted for his handling of the Torres case. If anything, evidence of Jones's deficiencies should have removed him from a short list of candidates. But that was not the case.

Reverend Henry Carr spoke before the council with direct reference to the Torres case: "We urge elected officials to table the vote until we can find a chief who is truly qualified. We want someone who is accountable, accessible, has professionalism, and a respect for human life. We are prepared to launch a new civil rights movement."[114] Carr urged city officials to have courage to break from tradition and embrace a more progressive and nonprovincial perspective: "We are a city motivated by fear." Once Jones's nomination was officially brought to a vote, UCCB member Hilda Martinez interjected a critique regarding the lack of diversity in the pool of candidates, all white men, being considered for Baytown's new police chief: "Excuse me, is this the best we can do? Why are there no females, no African American men, Latinos, or Asian Americans?"[115]

Jones was not without his supporters, especially among white men who were either current or former colleagues. A retired police officer and former colleague of Jones told the council, "I don't know anyone who has more integrity than Byron Jones. I can stand up and say he does the right thing even when (the facts) hurt."[116] The chaplain of the Baytown Police Department and an employee of Jones spoke on his behalf by saying in a manner that insulted the intelligence of UCCB members, "I know his (Jones') heart. The recent tragedy has taken a toll on our community. I think a lot of people here do not understand due process from a legal standpoint." Two city councilmen expressed visible and demonstrative anger toward the UCCB members and emotional support for Jones. After comments from 9 of the 160 people who asked to speak before the council, Councilmen Calvin Mundinger and Don Murray proposed that the nomination be brought to a vote. Murray was especially distraught about the opposition to Jones. Regarding the UCCB's decision to illustrate the Torres autopsy photos, he commented, "To broadcast this kind of filth to this community is not needed. These are not images you would show to children. We can talk above the table. This (pointing to one of the photos) is below the table."[117]

Councilman Scott Sheley said he did not want to vote on Jones's promotion until the FBI and other federal authorities had completed their investigations of the Torres case. But the only clear-cut opposition to Jones's nomination came from the city council's only member of color, Mercedes Rentería. He was an active participant in the protests in support of the Torres family, so it was of little surprise to anyone that he would not support Jones. In a ten-minute speech he attempted to point out the broader stakes of Jones's nomination beyond racial politics. In part he said,

> This is not a black or Hispanic thing, this is a public safety issue. My stance was that somebody died here. When his (Jones') supporters stand up and say he is the best and because they have known him for 30 years that's fine. But, this is what I learned about the man. I have some serious considerations about this man. I'm sorry, but honestly maybe we didn't work hard enough (in selecting the next chief).[118]

Rentería's intervention and Sheley's desire to consider the FBI investigation's findings were enough to delay the vote until the next scheduled city council meeting, on June 27, 2002. Following the meeting at the Civic Center, Rentería told reporters he felt the delay was only prolonging the inevitable:

> I think (council's) wanting to put him in no matter what. What I want is to explore the options with council and the mayor to find out what recourse we have with the situation. I want to whole process to start again with our new city manager to do it. I also want to wait because the FBI report has not come back yet. We need to have somebody who can deal with the diverse community.[119]

In anticipation that Rentería's premonition would prove accurate, the UCCB once again turned to social protest to voice concerns. Only this time, the coalition allowed Houston-based activists to help organize and coordinate the next event. In a press conference to announce what they anticipated to be their largest and most volatile event, Fred Aguilar said, "The rally is to protest the reinstatement of the Baytown police officers involved in the Luis Torres case. We're hoping to get about 300 people out there."[120] Houston LULAC leader Johnny Mata anticipated an event of unprecedented magnitude and impact, considering that a coalition of local and national civil rights organizations were joining forces with the UCCB in the local battle for justice: "By bringing persons of religious and community groups together, I think there's awareness that something was wrong, it needs to be acknowledged by the public officials of Baytown. We want to make sure that we seek to bring justice to this community."[121]

Aguilar and Mata announced that the event would also be used to address what they perceived would be the inevitable yet unjust promotion of Jones to police chief. Mata commented on Jones's mishandling of the Torres case as evidence of his lack of leadership: "It appears that he [Jones] felt he needed to get a jump-start to say that there's no wrongdoing before the investigation was complete."[122] When asked about Jones's possible promotion, Aguilar responded, "That's what a lot of people are protesting, the fact that Byron Jones was selected to become our chief from way back. I don't think the city really considered anybody else along the line."[123]

It is interesting to note that on the same day LULAC and the UCCB held their press conference regarding their planned rally, the Juneteenth Appreciation Dinner and awards ceremony was taking place in north Baytown at the J. D. Walker Community Center in McNair. This event was being held to honor residents who had donated the most time and services toward McNair's annual Juneteenth celebration, an event that had taken place in their community since the early twentieth century. Sheila Baker, the director of the J. D. Walker Center, explained, "The people awarded tonight were part of the original organization of the community. They did an outstanding job of pulling the community together and keeping it together."[124] One of the honorees that evening was James Fretty, a McNair resident who was recognized for his contributions as president of the McNair Civic Association as well as for his work with the Houston Police Department. Fretty was one of the first three officers hired to work in the Harris County detention system for decades prior to the Baytown Police Department being integrated. From his position, he was also active in addressing and organizing against police corruption in Houston as he joined seventeen other black law enforcement agents in a march on Houston's City Hall against discrimination in the 1970s.[125] That these actions took place outside of Baytown bears witness to the city's history of isolation and intensified segregation as residents of color in Baytown turned their attention toward insulating themselves within segregated communities as a way of coping with Baytown's racial tensions. This was true even to the extent that a Baytown resident was engaging in protest outside of Baytown yet while in Baytown was exhausting most of his time and energy toward self-help and mutual aid in his home community.

Baytown's activist awakening of 2002 marked a historical shift in many ways as the moment when social protest became not only possible but also somewhat effective. In acceptance of his honor, Fretty humbly commented, "I'm very happy to receive this award and I hope everything I've done has been beneficial to everyone and I'll continue to work until I'm no longer able to."[126] Other honorees at the Juneteenth awards dinner were Eunice Fretty and Roy McZeal for being two of the oldest members of the McNair community and Sherman Gray Jr. for his civic leadership and volunteerism. Joe Tex was honored posthumously for performing at numerous Juneteenth celebrations, and Carmen Wilson was recognized for her excellence as a local educator. McNair resident Jimmy Norris, who emceed the event, said each of the honorees should be commended for the tremendous sacrifices they made in the face of often outright racial hostility and injustice. Through their contributions, he said, "they stepped away from oppression and depression. . . . These people have suffered many days and sleepless nights."[127]

Two days after the Juneteenth commemoration in McNair, the joint LULAC- and UCCB-sponsored rally took place in Baytown's Bicentennial Park. Members of the ACLU, AFL-CIO, New Black Panther Party, LULAC, La Resistencia, Black United Front, and Corpus Justice represented their organizations and led area residents in various chants. While the collective outrage and memories of Baytown and other Houston-area residents of all ethnicities served as the shaft of the spear being thrust against white supremacy, blackness was indeed the hardened tip of that spear, providing the most penetrating critiques and challenges to the powers that be. Quanell X urged Baytown's black and Latino/a residents to "organize and overrun" Baytown's governmental institutions, especially its police department: "The police will never be respected until they realize that the community is not a servant to the police but that the police are servants to the community."[128]

Many in attendance at the rally carried posters asking and answering, "¿Cómo se dice Rodney King en español? How do you say Rodney King in Spanish? Luis Alfonso Torres!" The posters were issued by the Houston chapter of the ACLU, and Baytown's first-time activists used the slogan as their rallying cry. The slogan was particularly compelling in that it drew comparisons between Torres and the 1991 Rodney King case in Los Angeles. Both incidents were recorded on film. Both involved the excessive force of police officers. In both cases, police officers were exonerated for obviously violating their sworn duties as state agents. The main differences between the Torres and King cases were that Torres did not violate any laws, died from his ordeal, and was a Latino, while King was black. The ACLU included its own description of the link between the King and Torres cases with text it placed on the posters:

> Two things separate Luis Torres from Rodney King. First, not one of the four Baytown cops who beat him was ever charged with a crime. Second,

Luis Torres was choked, pepper sprayed, handcuffed, and beaten by four cops. Within eight minutes of being detained he stopped breathing. The cops claimed they did it "by-the-book." They later admitted there is no written policy on the use of force for the City of Baytown. The coroner ruled it "homicide." No one is in jail; one man is dead. Eleven years after Rodney King, what have we learned?[129]

Beyond the ACLU's use of the term, "Rodney King en español" was appropriated by Latinos/as in Baytown as an example of the discursive condition I have referred to as foundational blackness. To restate that concept for clarity, memories and symbols of anti-black racism and black anti-racism function as a base from which Latinos/as wage resistance against white supremacy and within a social climate that often reduces racial politics to a condition pertinent to black-white relations alone. By linking the Torres case to the King case, therefore, Latinos/as in Baytown and Houston were critiquing and building upon the black-white binary in their calls for justice. They were, on the one hand, demonstrating how cases like that of Luis Torres are often rendered invisible or less significant because they involve victims who are not black and/or, more specifically, are not African American. On the other hand, they are demonstrating how by linking themselves to the black side of

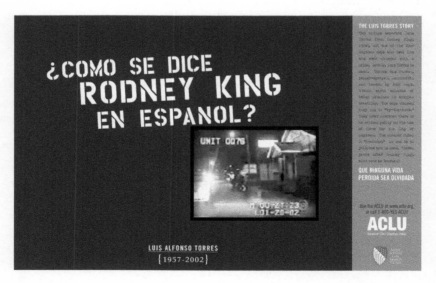

ACLU poster comparing the 2002 Luis Torres case in Baytown to the 1991 Rodney King case in Los Angeles. Courtesy of the American Civil Liberties Union.

ACLU poster in 2002 naming Latinos killed by law enforcement officers in the Houston area beginning with Jose Campos Torres in 1978. Two victims, Juan Carlos Espinosa and Luis Torres, were killed by Baytown police. Courtesy of the American Civil Liberties Union.

the black-white binary they can broadcast their message and raise more critical awareness about anti-Latino/a racism to a broader audience. Images and memories of anti-black racism and black antiracism beyond Baytown functioned as a conduit that discursively and emotionally tethered the Torres case to the well-publicized King case and the antiracist fury of the L.A. rebellion it produced. As Torres's body was laid next to King's in that metaphor, the streams of blood from their bodies flowed together into a larger stream that was more alarming. It was through that stream that Torres's plight entered a more comprehensive or recognizable awareness regarding civil and human rights.

In retrospect, the joint UCCB-LULAC rally failed to reach the magnitude and impact that its organizers expected. About 200 people attended, falling 100 short of what they anticipated. Organizers blamed the low turnout on what they called "police intimidation." Members of the ACLU expressed the most concern about this possibility, as it violates some of the more important liberties the ACLU defends, especially the right to organize and protest publicly. Annette Lamoreaux of the ACLU raised the question of intimidation at an ACLU press conference in Houston after the event: "We understand that many people from Baytown were afraid to show up because of fear of retaliation by the Baytown Police Department."[130] Houston LULAC leaders agreed with the ACLU and contacted marshals from the U.S. Justice Department to investigate police intimidation toward activists in Baytown.

Ironically, the LULAC national convention was being held in Houston in 2002 during the same early-summer period when Baytown's activist awakening was peaking. Mata used the occasion of the LULAC convention to raise awareness of the Torres case and to expose Baytown's hostile racial climate before a national and international audience. On the next-to-last day of the convention Mata submitted a resolution to be reviewed and voted on by LULAC's members nationally. It passed with overwhelming support. The final phrases of the proclamation read: "Now therefore, be it resolved, that LULAC proclaim the city of Baytown, Texas as 'one of the most unfriendly and feared cities in Texas toward minorities.'"[131]

In an interview with journalists, Mata explained his motivations for submitting and getting the resolution passed. "This action is rarely done," he said, yet the resolution had to be passed considering the blatant injustice he witnessed during his involvement with the Torres case. Mata went on to say that it is not his fault that Baytown is being publicized in such a harsh light to the nation; it is the fault of Baytown's civic leaders and police officials: "It's not a good picture of Baytown in regards to what the police officers did. There's a lot of good people in the city. The police department and what has occurred—their attitude is like it's no big deal. That's what has angered a lot of people."[132] Mata explained that the resolution was not only the result of the Torres case. Once becoming involved with the case and more familiar with Baytown, he realized that far more deep, underlying tensions showed Baytown's troubled past: "All these developments came out, more people started expressing fear, and more people are talking about incidents they have encountered themselves."[133]

By this point in the story, the response of Baytown city officials should be easy to predict. When asked by journalists for his opinions about LULAC's resolution, City Councilman Don Murray commented that it was the result of nothing more than emotionally hysterical and misguided residents of color who did not seem to understand the utopic conditions under which they live: "I think the resolution is badly misguided. It's based upon comments and inputs from a vocal minority of the minorities who are talking to LULAC and leading them astray."[134] Murray's city council colleague Calvin Mundinger supported this claim and laid more blame on LULAC itself for inciting protest among those who would be otherwise docile residents of color: "It never ceases to amaze me what any national organization will stoop to further their own cause through media sensationalism. I would hope that the men and women of our Baytown Police Department will be able to work through this egregious attack on our police department."[135] City Councilman Coleman Godwin went so far as to say that he and his son being ticketed by police officers during separate occasions was evidence enough that Baytown was a colorblind community: "I've been given a ticket. My son has been stopped at three in the morning by officers just wanting to check him out. I don't look at that as being unfriendly, I look at that as them doing their job."[136]

MORAL WITNESSES AND MOTHER 'HOODS

MY GOAL IN THIS CONCLUSION IS TWOFOLD. First, I aim to justify Baytown's activist awakening as an example of black-Latino/a solidarity but also as a critique of postracial discourse and its effects. The awakening demonstrates that communities in the Gulf South, like communities across the South and Southwest, are just beginning to experience the amalgamation of structural and psychosocial characteristics that social-movements theorist Aldon Morris has described as creating an indigenous base for effective antiracist activism to be waged.[1] The civil rights struggle is then ongoing. It did not end in 1968. Indigenous bases now are more commonly multiracial, often constituted by coalitions of blacks and Latinos/as, which further highlights the kinds of hybrid subjectivities I have argued are the result of demographic shifts and other dynamics of the late twentieth and early twenty-first centuries.

My second objective in this chapter is to highlight gender dynamics in expressions of black-Latino/a solidarity as well as in contemporary movements to combat police brutality. Baytown's activist awakening was like many contemporary initiatives opposing police brutality across the United States in being largely inspired by the leadership and courage of women of color to speak truth to power, to rise to the defense of men of color who have been victimized, and to show how cases of police brutality are the product of much more extensive social processes and historical patterns that have contributed to structuring lives and subjectivities in their home neighborhoods. To underscore the importance of Latinas and black women in building coalitions I offer an autobiographical narrative of how the Torres case influenced gender dynamics within my own family in Baytown and consequently the reasons and ways I have written this book.

THE POLITICS OF BLOOD MEMORY

In the wake of Baytown's activist awakening, the *Baytown Sun* ran an editorial by its editor and publisher, Wanda Garner Cash, about the Torres case and its effects in which she stated, "We are loathe to believe this was a racial crime. Baytown is not the kind of community that will tolerate that label or that reality."[2] Soon thereafter, Baytown's mayor proclaimed a similar position. When asked if the Torres case reflected lingering racial tensions in Baytown, he responded, "Maybe in some quarters it has. But, the majority of the people recognize what has happened and are willing to work together and move forward . . . Our community knows who we are! We have worked together for many, many years and we're going to continue to work together as one."[3] City Councilman Don Murray contributed to the discourse, too: "I think that certain members of the minority community of Baytown [have] motivations I really don't understand. I can personally attest by comments I've gotten from members of the minority races in Baytown, that it is not supported by the majority of minority members of our community."[4]

The mayor, city councilman, and newspaper editor/publisher implicitly aimed to isolate and demonize those who protested Torres's death. Their words were intended to marginalize the protesters and castigate them as irrational, emotionally volatile, ignorant, and the source of racial division in an otherwise race-neutral community. Condemnations like theirs are a basic component of the postracial paradox writ large, a condition wrought by popular perceptions that the civil rights movement of the mid-twentieth century cured the United States of racial tensions. Antiracist critics in this context often are accused of reverse discrimination.

Condemnations of antiracist activists are also often accompanied by the phrase "playing the race card," a term born of a presupposition and attached conventional wisdom that relations of power in a modern, liberal, capitalist state are a card game of sorts with a uniform set of rules that allow for fair competition and equal chances for each player to win. To extend the metaphor, every player (citizen) in this social game has been dealt the same number of cards from a deck that has been arranged randomly and distributed (liberalism) by a dealer (the state) who has no preference as to who wins (universality, colorblindness). When deployed as a critique of contemporary antiracist protests, the term "playing the race card" then implies a form of cheating and a violation of the game's fundamental set of rules because it involves playing a card that history (namely, the civil rights movement) has removed from the dealer's deck and that therefore is outside the logic of liberal fair play, or meritocracy.

A critical attention to the history of communities like Baytown from the perspective of its black and Latino/a residents suggests that the dealer is crooked and the deck is stacked. Western modernity is flawed; its promises of universality are undermined by what Ferreira da Silva describes as raciality, a form of modern knowledge that is fundamental to the designs and mainte-nance of law enforcement apparatuses, especially within settler-colonial for-mations like the United States.[5] Baytown demonstrates that the deck has been and continues to be loaded with race cards and that many people have been denied a seat at the table, much less the ability to win a hand or two.

The kinds of proclamations offered by Baytown's mayor, newspaper pub-lisher, and city councilman attempt to render the legacy of inequality in-visible. Theirs are typical pronouncements of colorblindness grounded by what I identify as two key tropes of historical memory: distortion and quaran-tine. I borrow the trope of distortion from Howard Zinn to suggest a method through which acts of injustice in the past are simply ignored, or they are manipulated to convey a different moral or ethical stance than what actually motivated them.[6] The relationship between Ross Sterling and the Ku Klux Klan, for example, can be ignored or distorted to preserve his image as one of Baytown's founding fathers and a man who is worthy of public institutions being named in his honor.

The quarantine trope is a bit more complex. It is a kind of historical mem-ory that considers all historical periods to have a beginning and an end mo-ment, transpiring in a rigid, linear, teleological trajectory toward universality. Consequently, when a moral or ethical crisis is recognized as part of a histori-cal period, the crisis is quarantined from having any connection to relations of power in the present. The crisis is quarantined as part of a different, previ-ous moment in time that has been improved upon. Because of quarantine, the most hegemonic trope informing postracial proclamations, there is then no continuum between the ethical standards or normative discourses that moti-vated acts of injustice in the past and the ethical standards and normative dis-courses that structure life in the present. Sterling's relationship to the KKK can be quarantined as a mere sign of his time, a relationship that chose him rather than his choosing it and that thus should not tarnish his contributions to the community.

Either Baytown's mayor, publisher, and city councilman were completely ignorant of the history of the community that they represented or they explic-itly were distorting or quarantining its history so as to proclaim Baytown a postracial space and not "one of the most unfriendly and feared cities in Texas toward minorities," as LULAC proclaimed after a Harris County grand jury exonerated the officers who beat and choked Luis Torres to death. To the three civic leaders, the blood spilled from Luis Torres was but a puddle, let by accident, and could be sanitized quickly through the decisive actions of elected officials. By contrast, the hundreds of working- and middle-class black and Latino/a residents who protested Torres's death knew that his blood was not so easily sanitized and not spilled on unbloodied soil. Instead, their subjectivities informed them that his was only the freshest in a stream of blood that had been flowing for decades and had never dried. It was a history of violence unresolved and memories that in 2002 bound blacks and Latinos/as into a united front and a political collective.

Enough of Torres's blood was spilled to push an already swollen river beyond its banks to flood political discourse in a cataclysmic fashion. The flood of emotions the Torres case elicited pushed much of Baytown's black and Latino/a residents to cry out against racism like never before and in a way that represented a strong dedication to black-Latino/a solidarity, a collective opposition to expendability.

The blood metaphor I have invoked to describe Baytown's activist awakening is inspired by novelist Assia Djebar's "attempt at autobiography" as a liberated Arab woman living in France after Algerian independence.[7] She acknowledges that historical events have unfolded that have, to some, quarantined settler colonialism as a historical condition, as something that has been left behind. Her own memories and subjectivity, however, disrupt and perforate this quarantine. They, like the memories and subjectivities of all displaced Algerians, remain attuned to a colonial architecture of power that has retained expendability albeit under the discursive disguise of liberation or the postcolonial condition. She comments in her retrospective narrative from the present position of liberation: "Wounds are reopened, veins weep, one's own blood flows and that of others, which has never dried."[8]

Those who rose to Torres's defense in 2002 represent moral witnesses, persons who counter postracial proclamations through art, performance, and activism that make the invisible visible. The moral witness, argues Bhabha, conducts "barbaric transmissions" in how he or she envisions and illuminates a continuum of barbarisms past and present.[9] The words and actions of moral witnesses like the Geto Boys, the New Black Panther Party, and Baytown's UCCB create discomfort in how they unsettle white privilege. They sting rather than soothe; they help heal rather than numb social wounds. "History tells us never again," Bhabha explains, "while memory tells us again, and again, and again."[10] Moral witnesses do not create racial divisions. They, and their memories, are the product of them.

YO MAMA'S A RACIST

Robin D. G. Kelley's *Yo Mama's DisFUNKtional! Fighting the Culture Wars in Urban America* (1998) is seminal in how it has countered the increasingly pathological and condemning discourse regarding urban communities of color, resulting from distortion and quarantine, the hegemony of colorblindness. As the opinions of elected officials and social scientists routinely and increasingly highlight the ethics and culture of what they term "minority" populations as the source of their continued depravity, Kelley has sought to reverse the gaze and narrative. Speaking from the perspective of the subaltern, as a moral witness himself, Kelley enacted a barbaric transmission, demonstrating how it was indeed the ethics and culture of elites that continued to be the source of chaos, violence, and crime in the postracial and post–civil rights inner city.

The title of Kelley's book is a play on the "dozens" tradition common among urban working-class communities of color, a game children play to legitimate themselves as worthy of respect, as intelligent, quick-witted, and emotionally mature and thus not affected by their peers' degrading comments about them even in moments when those peers ridicule their very mothers. In Baytown we often referred to this game as "crackin'"; if you could not take the heat and think quickly enough to sound off in witty replies to your peers, then you only set yourself up for more ridicule and marginalization within your 'hood.

Inspired by how Kelley flipped the script of post–civil rights tropes of black pathology and chaos, I have intended this book as my effort to crack back at those elites in my hometown who aimed to condemn and criminalize its moral witnesses of 2002. The motivation for writing it is as political as it is personal. The elites who were describing Baytown as a racial utopia were crackin' on my mama, quite literally, and they chose the wrong mama to crack on.

The connections to my family are more explicit, as a troubled history in Baytown served as a reason we all acted as moral witnesses in response to the Torres case. My older sister was employed as a clerk at the hospital emergency room where Luis Torres was taken on the night of his death in 2002. She was one of the first people to hear police officers report that they were unsure what happened to Torres and their suggestions that Torres had likely succumbed to a heart attack, an overdose of narcotics, or alcohol poisoning. The swarm of police officers at her workplace and the tense atmosphere, however, raised her suspicion about police brutality.

It was not that moment, however, that was the primary cause of her suspicion. By her early thirties, she had become quite wary of police brutality and especially during the police department's war on gangs in the 1990s. She and I were teenagers at the time, caught often on the wrong end of this war, as were most of our peers. Few among us, though, were gangsters or criminals of any sort. In most cases, we were simply the wrong types of people, young blacks or Latinos/as, in the wrong places, neighborhoods profiled as being riddled with black and Latino/a gangs and crime, at the wrong time, an era when the police had literally declared war against such persons in such places. A facial scar, the result of a gang-busting cop's baton and unwarranted aggression during one of their routine neighborhood raids, is my daily reminder of the terror we faced during those years.

This corporeal reminder stemmed from an incident I find to be particularly emblematic of the time and gives some indication of the social setting Luis Torres would enter and never exit over a decade later. On a weekday afternoon in the fall of 1991, a friend and I (he, a darker-brown African American, and I, a darker-brown Latino) were tossing a football in the street when an unmarked police car rounded a corner at a high rate of speed, jumped a curb onto the sidewalk, and came to a screeching halt just inches away from us. Two out-of-uniform police officers stormed out of their vehicle with their firearms drawn as they forced us to the ground and placed the barrels of their weapons to the backs of our heads. They repeatedly insisted that we confess our gang affiliation and surrender whatever weapons and drugs we were carrying, although we had neither. They delivered hard kicks to our backs and jabs with rifle butts to our heads and abdomens while they dared us to resist or attempt to flee. My friend got the worst of it, suffering a strong kick to the jaw that altered his ability to talk for weeks thereafter. I recall one officer telling us, "Please make a move . . . I need some excitement today and I want to shoot a few rats." My face in the dirt and a gun to my head, I thought about my life and the possibility that it might end; a ridiculous death it would be. History had apparently transformed me from human to vermin.

I knew his anger was not elicited by the way I threw or caught a football, and I doubted that it stemmed from the way I dressed, since I wore only basketball shorts and shoes that day. I certainly was not a model teenage citizen, but other than an occasional fistfight in the 'hood and a few acts of vandalism, I was a law-abiding citizen. Like Luis Torres, I was no gangster. I was simply enjoying a recreational activity in a space where leisure and recreation had apparently been criminalized for certain types of people.

My sister was the person I most often turned to for support in moments of crisis. She had a fierce sense of leadership in a house full of rowdy little brothers and a unique way of comforting and empowering people when they felt expendable. As a boy, tears of outrage and frustration would well up in my eyes as I would stand before her with fists clenched yet not knowing what or whom to punch out of the frustrations I encountered on the streets of Baytown. She would often respond by saying, "Shut up. You're not gonna do anything" or "That's nothing to cry about!" and "Man up!" while she also cursed police officers and white folks in general as a way to help me become numb to conditions that at that time seemed rather permanent to us. We were like most of our neighbors of color in that we kept our protests "in house" so as to help us survive without exacerbating already tough living conditions. These moments of cussing, crying, and being told as a young boy to "man up" by a young girl were often all I needed to get by.

To make matters worse, our father nearly died in 1997 after a violent encounter with police officers who were attempting to detain him on suspicion of public intoxication near our home in Old Baytown. There was not much detail in the police reports of this incident, only that my father was intoxicated, fled from the officers, and then resisted arrest. Eyewitness reports from neighbors, however, recorded it as a brutal act of aggression toward my father that traumatized them and that they intervened in to halt.

Regardless of whether it was actually brutal in this way, memories of life in Baytown made this assessment seem truer for many of us. My father's case was very similar to the Torres case five years later and just a few blocks away. Both were middle-aged Latinos whom officers claimed to be intoxicated and described to be acting aggressively toward the police while refusing to comply with their demands. Both were pursued in neighborhoods that had originally been segregated for blacks and Latinos/as, that had been profiled as populated with black and Latino/a criminals, and that were routinely targeted for zero-tolerance policing. The primary difference between my father's and Torres's cases was that my father survived his, thanks to the intervention of our neighbors and friends who pleaded with the officers to relent. After days of hospitalization, during two of which he lay in a coma clinging to life with a fractured skull, my father was incarcerated at the Harris County jail in downtown Houston. He was there for a few years, and for most of that time I was in graduate school being taught how to talk and write about the social significance of race, about matters with which I was already and traumatically quite familiar. The guilt I felt for being so far away from my family as they endured crises was only eased by my faith in ethnic studies scholarship, that the training I was receiving would allow me to be a moral witness one day through the words I would write on behalf of people like my father, Luis Torres, and Smith.

My sister was part of a group of residents who gathered outside the home of a local teenager, Juan Carlos Espinosa, in 1997 in Old Baytown after he was shot in the face by a Baytown police officer while hiding under a bed in his family's home. It was a moment the Baytown Police Department classified as a freak accident and Espinosa's family and friends recall as a murder. My sister remembers the moment of following Espinosa's death as one when the collective outrage of black and Latino/a neighbors almost spilled over into an act of social protest. Or, as she said, "It felt like people were ready to riot then. Everyone was seriously pissed off. Something was about to happen." Nothing happened, though.

Something did happen in 2002. Memories of these kinds of events were the reason my sister suspected police brutality in the Torres case and was actually the first person who attempted to intervene on Torres's behalf. Not long after Torres was brought into the hospital, she phoned me to express her growing concern and outrage. I recall her saying, "It looks like the cops took another brother out. I'm so tired of this. What do we do?"

My sister had reached a point where she was no longer numbed by expendability. Her transformation reflects Anne Anlin Cheng's recent ruminations on "melancholia" as a common characteristic of the subjectivities of people of color in the United States.[11] Cheng borrows from Freud's concept of melancholia to describe a "melancholy of race" as a "defensive numbness" to conditions of systemic and pervasive inequality. This racial melancholy is a component of psychological survival but is not a permanent or debilitating condition. It is an evolutionary stage of moving toward a more defiant and oppositional racial consciousness manifest in acts of resistance.

Corey Robin offers an interesting take on this condition in his discussion of the social origins of "political fear" and its distinction from "personal fear." The latter, he argues, is a product of intimate personal experience and subsequent memories that shape one's psyche, personality, and demeanor in unique and often detrimental ways.[12] By contrast, Robin shows that when public conditions afford the opportunity for interpersonal dialogue to take place, personal fears are often transformed into political fear, a collective consciousness that stems from experiences that are not unique to individuals but are understood as specific to social groups and the processes and histories that produce them. A political fear was then manifest within Baytown's activist awakening, transforming melancholia into resistance.

When my sister asked me "What do we do?" about Luis Torres's death, I responded by saying, "Nothing. For now, at least." I was, perhaps, still melancholic or defensively numb, not wary of the building political fear that was bubbling in Baytown's streets. Granted, it was quite early in the morning on the West Coast when she called, and I was just out of bed. Nonetheless, I did not hesitate in my opinion. It was clear to me. I had been involved in all sorts of antiracist and social justice campaigns by that point in my life, and this was a reason for my sister's phone call to me; she was attempting to draw upon my experience and expertise. In fact, I left Baytown in search of the tools and knowledge to become a better activist after becoming frustrated by my role in Baytown's Gang Activity Prevention initiative, a program I felt was undermined by state surveillance and control and lacked a more critical attention to race and expendability. Upon leaving Baytown on this journey, I was an activist parasite of sorts, denumbing myself as a sojourner, tapping into and benefiting from the political fear of other communities, learning to resist and organizing against injustice in communities within which I was but a newcomer. And yet here I was in January 2002, discouraging my sister from that same kind of activism in our own hometown, the place I fled, a place I was still defensively numb to.

To my credit, my discouragement was also an act of profound love for her, a sheer concern for her safety. Memories of the evil sneers and taunts of police officers; of the times I felt the blows of their fists, boots, and batons; of the times I wondered whether they would actually shoot and kill me or my peers just for being who we were and in the places where we socialized; of being described as a rat by 5-0; of my father clinging to life in a hospital bed with his head busted open; of our high school band playing "Dixie" at our Friday-night football games; and of the Confederate flags that once adorned the hallways of the public schools I attended—all these memories flashed before my eyes. At that moment I could not identify with my sister's urgency to "do something."

My sister was not at all impressed by my desire to protect her. I recall her saying something like "What good is all that protest stuff you do if you can't help do it for your own people?" I am glad she ignored my momentary discouragement. At the time, I was actually struggling to find a topic for research that I felt I could write about with serious conviction. She ended that search for me, and this book is the result.

Despite my intended intervention, my sister volunteered to speak at the first protest event at Baytown's Bicentennial Park during the late spring of 2002. She spoke alongside Quanell X and his New Black Panther Party contingent. Standing next to the NBPP regiments dressed in their all-black paramilitary attire and representatives of La Resistencia, a local organization formed to address immigrant rights and combat police brutality, my brown and blood sister delivered a scathing critique of the Baytown Police Department that incited the crowd. My mother was there too, applauding and holding signs demanding "Justicia!" Mom joined my sister, niece, and nephew at that march and played an active role in much of the organizing efforts that produced the UCCB. Many of the UCCB's founding members were lifelong

Mayor: Stay calm
More than 100 protest death of Luis Torres

Front-page coverage in the March 10, 2002, *Baytown Sun* of protests surrounding Luis Torres's death. Pictured are the author's mother, sister, and niece. Courtesy of the *Baytown Sun*.

friends of hers, people she met in the 1970s upon moving to Baytown with my dad and their young daughter.

A photograph of my sister, mother, and niece participating in the march that day and carrying protest banners and posters was splashed across the front page of the *Baytown Sun* the following day, depicting them as leaders of Baytown's activist awakening. Above their image was a quote from Baytown's mayor stating, "Stay calm," explicitly suggesting that people like my mom and sister were acting irrationally, protesting for nothing, or creating racial divisions. My response to that mediated imagery and quote and to whoever is responsible for it, is: Yo mama needs to stay calm.

HOMELAND DEFENSE

To conclude, I offer a critique of myself to facilitate a more critical dialogue about gender. I sense that there was something patriarchal about the way I discouraged my sister and mother from moral witnessing in their hometown. This may or may not be true actually. My feminist friends will tell me that it is true, and my macho friends will tell me that I was just keeping it real by trying to protect my mom and sister. Both sides are correct in some way. I surely was not suggesting, as the mayor and newspaper publisher implied, that my mother and sister were acting irrationally. Instead, I was seriously concerned about their safety.

My father contributed toward discouraging the women in our home. He was outraged like they were about Torres's death yet also concerned about their safety. Real threats of intimidation were felt by Baytown's moral witnesses, my mom and sister included, and recognized by civil rights organizations from across the region. My father's motivations varied slightly from mine. He was freshly out of jail and did not want anything to do with those he called *la pinche jura*. As my mother marched he remained in her car with his favorite pocket knife and a small baseball bat, ready to protect her if needed. For my part, I longed to be back in Baytown to lead the charge. That is, at least, what I told people back home on my mobile phone. Many, for example, assumed that I would be the perfect leader for Quanell X's new Brown Panthers. I never went home, however, to lead anything. I stayed in California to think and write about Baytown and its history, a different kind of moral witnessing.

Granted, both my mother and sister had discouraged me from activism before. My mother still does, concerned for my safety, primarily. So I am perhaps being a bit hard on myself by critiquing myself as guilty of patriarchy. But it is useful to offer a self-critique within this context. While I have paid critical attention to gender and sexual dynamics within the spaces I have examined, this book has still generally privileged examples of subjectivity that derive from black and Latino males, a significant shortcoming that is deserving of critique. My discouragement of the women in my family from protesting could easily be linked to a much more pervasive history of men marginalizing women within antiracist movements, a maneuver produced by the presupposition that activism is a role for men and women should play a complementary role. I certainly hope I was and am above this presupposition, as the script was flipped in 2002 when I played a complementary role to my mom's and sister's activism.

Heteropatriarchy is something I have lectured and campaigned against for decades now. But that is the tricky thing about privilege—signs of it slip by us more easily when we have it. Thus, as much as I understood the ways expendability and other conditions had shaped my own subjectivity, as much as I have worked to facilitate critical dialogues about gender and sexuality within ethnic studies and community activist circles, as much as I have been inspired by and mentored by queer and women-of-color feminists and activists, it has always been imperative for me to pay a critical attention to how my own privileges as a heterosexual man of color grant me an unearned capacity to further marginalize women in my private life, even those whom I declare to love and care about the most. I am a work in progress, as we all are. We are all blinded by some form of privilege, and the amount of time we spend thinking about and explaining how we are not is often the clearest evidence of just how much privilege we are trying to conceal. Exposing our deficiencies, making ourselves vulnerable to critique, is an important characteristic of any moral witness. We must crave critique in order to progress.

For better or worse, these are lessons I have learned primarily from the contributions of women-of-color feminist scholars, those who have aimed to recuperate the neglected histories of women within antiracist movements. As I began to think critically about my mother's and sister's heroism under those conditions, I began to better notice that Baytown was no aberration. Women of color have been leaders of protests against police brutality across the United States, and this is despite the ways this condition generally victimizes men of color. There is something telling about those dynamics. Women of color are certainly not immune from conditions like police brutality. They are often victimized by it in addition to other kinds of state-sanctioned violence from which all men are generally immune.

Nonetheless, women of color have been at the forefront of protests against this condition and quite often in defense of men or boys in their families or communities who have been victimized. Women like Trixie Washington, my mother and sister, Eva Benavides, Hilda Martinez, Janie and Sandra Torres, Carmen Torres, and Marga Hernandez were particularly outspoken as moral witnesses against police brutality in the Torres case. None were related to Luis Torres, but many were motivated by their concern for their own husbands, brothers, and sons.

Hilda Martinez and Marga Hernandez were founding members of Baytown's UCCB. In an intimate conversation with them and Arthur Martinez, Hilda's husband, at the Martinez home in north Baytown in 2003, Hilda and Marga informed me that much of their rationale for getting involved with the Torres case was that they worried about their own sons being racially profiled and expendable. The connection between mothers and sons became more vivid when Ms. Martinez stepped out of the room as I chatted with Hernandez and returned with a photo of her son and me playing together at the age of four at a festival at Our Lady of Guadalupe Catholic Church in Old Baytown. She handed the photo to me, and we sat there in a moment of silence. I interpreted her gesture as an act of support for me, a symbol that she had my back like a mother and wanted me to bear moral witness by writing this book. I am forever grateful for her and her husband's leadership in our community. They have been a real inspiration.

Like my father, Arthur Martinez strategically played a complementary role to his wife's moral witnessing across Baytown. He stepped in and out of the dining-interview room offering a few comments to accentuate his wife's words and Marga's. Throughout the organizing campaign on behalf of Luis Torres, Mr. Martinez helped his wife strategize and coordinate much of the activity of the UCCB. He also opted, however, for a complementary rather than leadership role; he played a role that he explained to me as a guardian or "body guard" primarily invested in protecting his wife, an outspoken UCCB leader, during public events.

Marga Hernandez was similarly vocal about the significance of her mother-hood as a motivating factor for becoming a moral witness. She cited an incident in which her teenage son was wounded by police officers after they had falsely profiled him for a crime and were taking him into custody. She took photographs of his wounds and cites them as her daily reminder of why she has chosen to become a moral witness in her community.

Baytown's women-of-color activist leaders reflect the dynamics of movements against police brutality across the United States. In many examples, the motherhood of those women activists was made even more explicit. Women of color were often at the front lines of the activism, with men of color either absent or in the background. In some cases, women of color have made it a point to acknowledge their motherhood in naming their initiatives, as with Mothers Organized Against Police Terror, in Oakland, California, and Mothers Against Police Brutality, in New York City. The latter group has been featured in a documentary film about police brutality titled *Every Mother's Son* that chronicles the activities of black women, Latinas, and white women who have lost sons to police brutality.[13] The most famous of the mothers featured in that film are Kadiatou Diallo, the mother of Amadou Diallo, and Iris Baez, the mother of Anthony Baez. Each son's death was a high-profile case in New York City during the 1990s.

The film *Justifiable Homicide: A Mother's Relentless Battle for Justice* chronicles the struggle of Margarita Rosario to seek justice on behalf of her son and nephew, two Latinos unjustly slain by police officers in New York City. Rosario formed the organization Parents Against Police Brutality and has been joined by Juanita Young, an African American woman whose son Malcolm Ferguson was slain by police officers under similar conditions in 2000. Young and Rosario have made it a point to accentuate their roles as mothers of victims as a method of galvanizing black-Latino/a solidarity.[14]

During an interview about her struggle for justice published in the activist newspaper *Revolutionary Worker*, Margarita Rosario explained how she has been able to overcome fear and become a moral witness on behalf of all mothers who have lost sons to police terror:

I know what happened to my son was wrong because I raised that child, and I know what my son was about. . . . I am willing to do anything to stand up for his rights. And that's the way people should feel also. They should stand up for what they believe is right, not for what they believe is going to secure them. If they believe what the cops are doing is wrong, then get up there and fight. Don't be afraid. You cannot be afraid because this is what they want you to do. They want you to be afraid. We've been afraid for so many years, for centuries, and we haven't stood up to these people. I think that has to stop. That blue wall of silence, we have to bring that down completely. . . . My son is gone but I still have a younger son here who's 14 years old. So I have to fight for him too. And for other kids that are growing up . . . I'm doing it for them too. It's for the future kids that we're concerned about.[15]

Rosario's activism continues the legacy of activists like Ida B. Wells in the continuum between lynching and police brutality. Her role as a mother is also similar to the influence of Mamie Till on the civil rights movement of the 1950s. Like my mother and Hilda Martinez and Marga Hernandez, Rosario, Young, and Mamie Till stretched and redefined the trope of motherhood or domestic caretaker beyond the walls of their private spaces to include their communities or neighborhoods, positioning them as apt and capable defenders of their 'hoods as symbolic mothers of the racially oppressed. This strategy has been central to building civil rights and racial power struggles in U.S. history and yet has been routinely neglected within social movements' historiography.[16]

Fifteen years after the Till case, Coretta Scott King delivered a letter to Mexican American civil rights leader César Chávez while he was incarcerated for his pro-union activism in California. Speaking as a widow and mother, she offered a compelling call for black-Latino/a solidarity:

Those who control the billion-dollar economy have said Blacks and Chicanos do not have the right to decent life or to human dignity. They must live on the crumbs from the table groaning with food . . . Black people and Brown people are herded at the bottom and told to be quiet and to wait for slow change. But change has never come to us in waiting . . . We are not enemies of the nation, but we are treated as if we were conquered and enslaved. We have fed and clothed the nation by our sweat and toil. But our share in its goods is the share of prisoners.[17]

This message of solidarity was written and delivered not two years after Mrs. King's husband was slain. Memories of his martyrdom give a moral weight and urgency to that performance of solidarity. Subsequently the image and words of the civil rights martyr's wife, the mother of his children, and the symbolic mother of the civil rights movement infused the Latino/a civil rights cause with a collective memory of black suffering, survival, and triumph. That fusion helped raise a more critical awareness about Chicanos/as, granting them a more critical space within debates regarding civil rights at the time.

INTRODUCTION

1. In Juan Carlos Llorca, "West Texas WWII Vet to Get Posthumous Purple Heart," *Huffington Post*, December 6, 2012.

2. Gloria Anzaldúa, *Borderlands/La Frontera: The New Mestiza*, 3d edition (San Francisco: Spinster/Aunt Lute, 2007).

3. Saidiya Hartman, *Lose Your Mother: A Journey along the Atlantic Slave Route* (New York: Farrar, Straus, and Giroux, 2008).

4. Clyde Woods, *Development Arrested: Race, Power, and the Blues in the Mississippi Delta* (New York: Verso, 1998).

5. On blackness as performance see John L. Jackson Jr., *Harlemworld: Doing Race and Class in Contemporary Black America* (Chicago: University of Chicago Press, 2003); E. Patrick Johnson, *Appropriating Blackness: Performance and the Politics of Authenticity* (Durham, NC: Duke University Press, 2003); D. Soyini Madison, *Critical Ethnography: Method, Ethics, and Performance* (Thousand Oaks, CA: Sage, 2005).

6. Barnor Hesse, "Racialized Modernity: An Analytics of White Mythologies," *Racial and Ethnic Studies* 30 (2007): 643–663; Denise Ferreira da Silva, *Towards a Global Idea of Race* (Minneapolis: University of Minnesota Press, 2007); David Theo Goldberg, *The Racial State* (London: Blackwell, 2000).

7. Michel Foucault, *Psychiatric Power: Lectures at the Collège de France, 1973–1974*, ed. Jacques Lagrange (London: Palgrave, 2006); Antonio Gramsci, *Selections from the Prison Notebooks of Antonio Gramsci*, ed. Q. Hoare and G. Novell-Smith (New York: International, 1971); Louis Althusser, "Ideology and Ideological State Apparatuses," in *Lenin and Philosophy*, ed. Ben Brewster, 127–186 (London: NewLeft Books, 1971).

8. Kelly Oliver, *The Colonization of Psychic Space: A Psychoanalytic Social Theory of Oppression* (Minneapolis: University of Minnesota Press, 2004).

9. Ibid., xv.

10. Doug Sanders, *Arrival City: How the Largest Migration in Human History Is Reshaping Our World* (New York: Pantheon Books, 2011).

11. David Harvey, *The Condition of Postmodernity: An Enquiry into the Origins of Cultural Change* (New York: Blackwell, 1990).

12. David Slater, *Geopolitics and the Post-Colonial: Rethinking North-South Relations* (London: Wiley-Blackwell, 2004).

13. Stephen L. Klineberg, "The Changing Face of Houston: Tracking the Economic and Demographic Transformations through 29 Years of Houston Surveys" (Houston: Kinder Institute of Urban Research, Rice University, 2010).

14. Michael Omi and Howard Winant, *Racial Formation in the United States: From the 1960s to the 1980s* (New York: Routledge and Kegan Paul, 1986).

15. On cross-racial influences see Vijay Prashad, *Everybody Was Kung Fu Fighting: Afro-Asian Connections and the Myth of Cultural Purity* (Boston: Beacon Press, 2002); Heike Raphael-Hernandez and Shannon Steen, eds., *AfroAsian Encounters: Culture, History, Politics* (New York: New York University Press, 2006); Nitasha Sharma, *Hip Hop Desis, South Asians, Blackness, and Global Race Consciousness* (Durham, NC: Duke University Press, 2010).

16. Avery F. Gordon, *Ghostly Matters: Haunting and the Sociological Imagination* (Minneapolis: University of Minnesota Press, 2008).

17. Homi K. Bhabha, *The Location of Culture* (New York: Routledge, 1994).

18. Ibid., 66.

19. Stuart Hall, "New Ethnicities," in *"Race," Culture, and Difference*, ed. James Donald and Ali Rattansi (London: Sage, 1992), 252–259. See also Paul Gilroy, "British Cultural Studies and the Pitfalls of Identity," in *Cultural Studies and Communications*, ed. J. Curran, D. Morley, and V. Walkerdine, 34–49 (London: Arnold, 1996); Bhabha, *Location of Culture*; Néstor García Canclini, *Hybrid Cultures* (Minneapolis: University of Minnesota Press, 1990); Anzaldúa, *Borderlands/La Frontera*; Walter Mignolo, *Local Histories/Global Designs: Coloniality, Subaltern Knowledges, and Border Thinking* (Princeton, NJ: Princeton University Press, 2000).

20. Stuart Hall, "Who Needs 'Identity'?" in *Questions of Cultural Identity*, ed. Stuart Hall and P. du Gay (London: Sage, 1996), 1.

21. Edward W. Said, *Culture and Imperialism* (New York: Random House, 1993), 336.

22. Manuela Ribeiro Sanches, introduction to *Europe in Black and White: Immigration, Race, and Identity in the "Old Continent,"* ed. Manuela Ribeiro Sanches, Fernando Clara, João Ferreira Duarte, and Leonor Pires Martins (Chicago: University of Chicago Press, 2010), 8.

23. Nelson Maldonado Torres, *Against War: Views from the Underside of Modernity* (Durham, NC: Duke University Press, 2008); Emma Pérez, *The Decolonial Imaginary: Writing Chicanas into History* (Bloomington: Indiana University Press, 1999); Bhabha, *Location of Culture*; Mignolo, *Local Histories/Global Designs*.

24. Michel Foucault, *The History of Sexuality*, vol. 1: *An Introduction*, trans. Robert Hurley (New York: Pantheon Books, 1976); Michel Foucault, *Society Must Be Defended: Lectures at the Collège de France, 1975–1976* (New York: Picador, 2003).

25. Michael Hardt, "Militant Life," *New Left Review* 2, no. 64 (2010): 151–160.

26. Lisa Blackman et al., "Creating Subjectivities," *Subjectivity* 22 (2008): 1–27.

27. Giorgio Agamben, *State of Exception* (Chicago: University of Chicago Press, 2005); Jacques Derrida, "Force of Law: The Mythical Foundation of Authority," in *Violence and Its Alternatives*, ed. Manfred B. Steger and Nancy S. Lind (New York: St. Martin's Press, 1999); Michel Foucault, *Security, Territory, Population* (New York: Palgrave Macmillan, 2007); Michel Foucault, *The Birth of Biopolitics* (New York: Palgrave Macmillan, 2008); Henry A. Giroux, *Against the New Authoritarianism: Politics after Abu-Ghraib* (Winnipeg, Canada: Arbeiter Ring, 2005); Bart Simon, "The Return of Panopticism: Supervision, Subjection, and the New Surveillance," *Surveillance and Society* 3, no. 1 (2005): 1–20.

28. Claudio Colaguori, "Symbolic Violence and the Violation of Human Rights: Continuing the Sociological Critique of Domination," *International Journal of Criminology and Sociological Theory* 3, no. 2 (2010): 380–400; Paul Gilroy, "Paul Gilroy Speaks on the Riots, August 2011, Tottenham, North London," blog post, *Dream of Safety*, August 16, 2011.

29. Ferreira da Silva, *Towards a Global Idea of Race*; Hesse, "Racialized Modernity."

30. Carlos Muñoz, *Youth Identity and Power: The Chicano Movement* (New York: Verso, 1989); Rodolfo Acuña, *Occupied America: The Chicano Struggle for Liberation* (New York: Harper and Row, 1972); Stokeley Carmichael and Charles Hamilton, *Black Power: The Politics of Liberation in America* (New York: Random House, 1967); Harold Cruse, *The Crisis of the Negro Intellectual* (New York: Morrow, 1967); John H. Bracey Jr., August Meier, and Elliott Rudwick, eds., *Black Nationalism in America* (Indianapolis: Bobbs Merrill, 1970); William H. Chafe, *Civilities and Civil Rights: Greensboro, North Carolina, and the Black*

Struggle for Freedom (New York: Oxford University Press, 1981); Clayborne Carson, *In Struggle: SNCC and the Black Awakening of the 1960s* (Cambridge, MA: Harvard University Press, 1981).

31. Anzaldúa, *Borderlands/La Frontera*; Patricia Hill Collins, "Learning from the Outsider Within: The Sociological Significance of Black Feminist Thought," *Social Problems* 33 (1986): 514–532; Darlene Clark Hine, *Black Women in White: Racial Conflict and Cooperation in the Nursing Profession, 1890–1950* (Bloomington: Indiana University Press, 1989); Vicki L. Ruiz, *Cannery Women, Cannery Lives: Mexican Women, Unionization, and the California Food Processing Industry* (Albuquerque: University of New Mexico Press, 1987).

32. David G. Gutiérrez, *Walls and Mirrors: Mexican Americans, Mexican Immigrants, and the Politics of Ethnicity* (Berkeley: University of California Press, 1995).

33. There are indeed some exceptions. Gilroy, for example, argues that black musical forms like hip-hop have been essential to the shaping of black subjectivities not only across the black diaspora but also across youth culture at large; Gilroy, "British Cultural Studies."

34. Sharon Holland, *Raising the Dead: Readings of Death and (Black) Subjectivity* (Durham, NC: Duke University Press, 2002), 2.

35. Ramon A. Gutierrez, "Ethnic Studies: Its Evolution in American Colleges and Universities," in *Multiculturalism: A Critical Reader*, ed. David Theo Goldberg, 157–167 (London: Blackwell, 1994). See also Yen Le Espiritu, "Disciplines Unbound: Notes on Sociology and Ethnic Studies," *Contemporary Sociology* 28 (1999): 510–514. Model comparative works include Leland T. Saito, *Race and Politics: Asian Americans, Latinos, and Whites in a Los Angeles Suburb* (Champaign: University of Illinois Press, 1998); Nayan Shah, *Contagious Divides: Epidemics and Race in San Francisco's Chinatown* (Berkeley: University of California Press, 2001); Natalia Molina, *Fit to Be Citizens? Public Health and Race in Los Angeles, 1879–1939* (Berkeley: University of California Press, 2006); Tomás Almaguer, *Racial Fault Lines: The Historical Origins of White Supremacy in California* (Berkeley: University of California Press, 1994); Claire Jean Kim, *Bitter Fruit: The Politics of Black-Korean Conflict in New York City* (New Haven, CT: Yale University Press, 2000).

36. Stuart Hall, David Morley, and Kuan-Hsing Chen, *Stuart Hall: Critical Dialogues in Cultural Studies* (London: Routledge, 1996), 443.

37. Barnor Hesse deserves credit for the phrasing "delink," as I recall him making a version of this statement at a symposium in which he and I participated.

38. Muneer Ahmad, "Homeland Insecurities: Racial Violence the Day after September 11" *Social Text* 72 (2002): 101–115. See also Maldonado Torres, *Against War*, 252.

39. Good examples of this more comparative, transethnic, and transnational approach are George Mariscal, *Brown-Eyed Children of the Sun: Lessons from the Chicano Movement, 1965–1975* (Albuquerque: University of New Mexico Press, 2005); Lorena Oropeza, *¡Raza Sí! ¡Guerra No! Chicano Protest and Patriotism during the Viet Nam War Era* (Berkeley: University of California Press, 2006); Laura Pulido, *Black, Brown, Yellow, and Left: Radical Activism in Los Angeles* (Berkeley: University of California Press, 2006); Cynthia Young, *Soul Power: Culture, Radicalism, and the Making of the U.S. Third World Left* (Durham, NC: Duke University Press, 2006); Luis Alvarez, *The Power of the Zoot: Youth Culture and Resistance during World War II* (Berkeley: University of California Press, 2008).

40. Jesús Ruiz Mantilla, "Más 'speak spanish' que en España," (Madrid) *El País*, June 10, 2008.

41. Ruben Castaneda, "LA Job Fight: A Bitter Struggle or an Alliance?" *California Tomorrow*, Winter 1989, 7; Richard R. Delgado and Jean Stefancic, eds., *The Latina/o Con-*

dition: A Critical Reader (New York: New York University Press, 1998); Paula D. McClain, "The Changing Dynamics of Urban Politics: Black and Hispanic Municipal Employment— Is There Competition?" *Journal of Politics* 55 (1993): 399–414; Tatcho Mindiola Jr., Yolanda Flores Niemann, and Nestor Rodriguez, *Black-Brown Relations and Stereotypes* (Austin: University of Texas Press, 2002); Melvin L. Oliver and James H. Johnson Jr., "Inter-Ethnic Conflict in an Urban Ghetto: The Case of Blacks and Latina/os in Los Angeles," *Research in Social Movements, Conflicts, Coalitions, and Change* 6 (1984): 57–94. See also Bill Piatt, "Origins of Black/Brown Conflict," in *The Latina/o Condition: A Critical Reader*, ed. Richard R. Delgado and Jean Stefancic (New York: New York University Press, 1998), 457–465; Nicolas C. Vaca, *The Presumed Alliance: The Unspoken Conflict between Latinos and Blacks and What It Means for America* (New York: HarperCollins, 2004).

42. Leo A. Despres, ed., *Ethnicity and Resource Competition in Plural Societies* (The Hague: Mouton, 1975).

43. For a survey of urban inequality and racial stratification in the United States see Douglas S. Massey, *Categorically Unequal: The American Stratification System* (New York: Russell Sage Foundation, 2007). On political representation see John D. Griffin and Brian Newman, *Minority Report: Evaluating Political Equality in America* (Chicago: University of Chicago Press, 2008). For discussions on environmental pollution and racial inequality see Melissa Checker, *Polluted Promises: Environmental Racism and the Search for Justice in a Southern Town* (New York: New York University Press, 2005); and David Pellow, *Garbage Wars: The Struggle for Environmental Justice in Chicago* (Cambridge, MA: MIT Press, 2004). On the criminal justice system see Bruce Western, *Punishment and Inequality in America* (New York: Russell Sage Foundation, 2007).

44. W. E. B. Du Bois, *The Souls of Black Folk* (Boston: Dover, 1903), 3.

45. Stephen Gregory, *Black Corona: Race and the Politics of Place in an Urban Community* (Princeton, NJ: Princeton University Press, 1999) 5.

46. Julia Preston, "In Big Shift, Latino Vote Was Heavily for Obama," *New York Times*, November 6, 2008. See also Andres Ramirez, "Latinos Vote in 2008: Analysis of U.S. Presidential Exit Polls," *NDN*, http://ndn.org/essay/latinos-vote-2008.

47. Earl Ofari Hutchinson, "Discrimination, Not Illegal Immigration, Fuels Black Job Crisis," *New America Media*, April 24, 2006; Devah Pager, *Marked: Race, Crime, and Finding Work in an Era of Mass Incarceration* (Chicago: University of Chicago Press, 2007).

48. Ibid.

49. George Borjas, Jeffrey Grogger, and Gordon H. Hanson, "Immigration and African American Employment Opportunities: The Response of Wages, Employment, and Incarceration to Labor Supply Shock," NBER Working Paper 12518, National Bureau of Economic Research (NBER), September 2006.

50. Tanya K. Hernandez, "Roots of Anger: Longtime Prejudices, Not Economic Rivalry, Fuel Latino-Black Tensions," op-ed, *Los Angeles Times*, January 7, 2007.

51. In Andrew Murr, "Feds Take on Latino Gang Accused of Targeting Blacks," *Newsweek*, October 24, 2007.

52. On Fox News (from Associated Press), "Black-Hispanic Gang Rivalries Plague Los Angeles," August 12, 2006.

53. In Tarso Luís Ramos, "Who Gains from Framing Gang Attacks in LA as 'Ethnic Cleansing'?" *Color Lines*, News Report, *New America Media*, June 5, 2007.

54. Kim, *Bitter Fruit*.

55. Maldonado Torres, *Against War*, xiii.

CHAPTER 1

1. Mary Louise Pratt, "Art of the Contact Zone," in *Profession 91* (New York: MLA, 1991), 33–40.

2. Thomas A. Gugliemo, "Fighting for Caucasian Rights: Mexicans, Mexican Americans, and the Transnational Struggle for Civil Rights in World War II Texas," *Journal of American History* 92 (March 2006): 1212–1237; Ian Haney-López, "White Latinos," *Harvard Latino Law Review* 6 (2003): 1; Neil Foley, "Becoming Hispanic: Mexican Americans and the Faustian Pact with Whiteness," in *Reflexiones 1997: New Directions in Mexican American Studies*, ed. Neil Foley (Austin: Center for Mexican American Studies, University of Texas, 1998), 53, 63–64; Neil Foley, "Over the Rainbow: *Hernandez v. Texas, Brown v. Board of Education,* and *Black v. Brown,*" *Chicano-Latino Law Review* 25 (2005): 139, 140; Brian Behnken, *Fighting Their Own Battles: Mexican Americans, African Americans, and the Struggle for Civil Rights in Texas* (Chapel Hill: University of North Carolina Press, 2011).

3. Neil Foley, *Quest for Equality: The Failed Promise of Black-Brown Solidarity* (Cambridge, MA: Harvard University Press, 2010); Nicolás C. Vaca, *The Presumed Alliance: The Unspoken Conflict between Latinos and Blacks and What It Means for America* (New York: HarperCollins, 2004); Behnken, *Fighting Their Own Battles*; Mindiola, Flores Niemann, and Rodriguez, *Black-Brown Relations*.

4. Foley, *Quest for Equality.*

5. Behnken, *Fighting Their Own Battles.*

6. Ibid. To his credit, Behnken does highlight examples of racial power activism that exceeded this reformist approach. However, he still privileges civil rights activism and the reformist civil rights movement as the central organizing theme in his analysis.

7. Dipesh Chakrabarty, "Belatedness as Possibility: Subaltern Histories, Once More," in *The Indian Postcolonial: A Critical Reader*, ed. Elleke Boehmer and Rosinka Chaudhuri, 163–176 (London: Routledge, 2011).

8. Gayatri Spivak, "Can the Subaltern Speak?" in *Marxism and the Interpretation of Culture*, ed. Cary Nelson and Lawrence Grossberg, 271–313 (Chicago: University of Illinois Press, 1988).

9. Robin D. G. Kelley, *Freedom Dreams: The Black Radical Imagination* (Boston: Beacon Press, 2002), ix.

10. Laurence Cox and Colin Barker, "'What Have the Romans Ever Done for Us?' Activist and Academic Forms of Movement Theorizing," in *Proceedings of the Eighth International Conference on Alternative Futures and Popular Protest* (Manchester, England: Manchester Metropolitan University, 2002), 1.

11. Ralph Ellison, *Shadow and Act* (New York: Vintage, 1964), 123.

12. Cox and Barker, "'What Have the Romans Ever Done for Us?'"

13. George Mariscal, *Brown-Eyed Children of the Sun: Lessons from the Chicano Movement, 1965–1975* (Albuquerque: University of New Mexico Press, 2005). Cynthia Young, *Soul Power: Culture, Radicalism, and the Making of a U.S. Third World Left* (Durham, NC: Duke University Press, 2006). Laura Pulido, *Black, Brown, Yellow, and Left: Radical Activism in Los Angeles* (Berkeley: University of California Press, 2006). Luis Alvarez, *The Power of the Zoot: Youth Culture and Resistance During World War II* (Durham, NC: Duke University Press, 2009).

14. Jacques Derrida, "Différance," trans. Alan Bass, in *Margins of Philosophy* (Chicago: University of Chicago Press, 1982).

15. Jacques Derrida, "Force of Law: The Mystical Foundation of Authority," in *Decon-

struction and the Possibility of Justice, ed. Drucilla Cornell, Michel Rosenfeld, and David Gray Carlson (New York: Routledge, 1992), 27.

16. Peter Fitzpatrick, *The Myth of Modern Law* (London: Blackwell, 1992).

17. Glenn Coulthard, "Subjects of Empire: Indigenous Peoples and the 'Politics of Recognition in Canada,'" *Contemporary Political Theory* 6, no. 4 (2007): 449.

18. Derrida, "Force of Law," 27.

19. Jakobi E. Williams, "Racial Coalition Politics in Chicago: A Case Study of Fred Hampton, the Illinois Black Panther Party, and the Origin of the Original Rainbow Coalition" (Ph.D. Diss., University of California, Los Angeles, 2008). See Also, Antonio R. López, "In the Spirit of Liberation: Race, Governmentality, and the De-Colonial Politics of the Original Rainbow Coalition of Chicago. (Ph.D. Diss., University of Texas at El Paso, 2012).

20. Jeffrey Haas, *The Assassination of Fred Hampton: How the Chicago Police and the FBI Murdered a Black Panther* (Chicago: Chicago Review Press, 2010).

21. Fred Hampton, "Power Anywhere There's People," Chicago, ca. 1970, Black Panther Party, Political Pamphlets, P201234, Special Collections, Northwestern University, Evanston, IL.

22. Luis Alvarez and Daniel Widener, "Brown-Eyed Soul: Popular Music and Cultural Politics in Los Angeles," in *The Struggle in Black and Brown: African American and Mexican American Relations During the Civil Rights Era*, ed. Brian Behnken, 211–236 (Lincoln: University of Nebraska Press, 2011).

23. Benjamin Heber Johnson, *Revolution in Texas: How a Forgotten Rebellion and Its Bloody Suppression Turned Mexicans into Americans* (New Haven, CT: Yale University Press, 2005).

24. Luis J. Rodriguez, "Why We Need a Deeper Dialogue on Black-Brown Relations," *Huffington Post*, August 31, 2011.

25. Martha Menchaca, *Recovering History, Constructing Race: The Indian, Black, and White Roots of Mexican Americans* (Austin: University of Texas Press, 2001).

26. David Dorado Romo, *Ringside Seat to a Revolution: An Underground Cultural History of El Paso and Juarez, 1893–1923* (El Paso, TX: Cinco Puntos Press, 2005), 208.

27. Langston Hughes and Arne Botemps, *Boy on the Border* (El Paso, TX: Sweet Earth Flying Press, 2009).

28. Antonio Gramsci, *Prison Notebooks*, vol. 2 (New York: Columbia University Press, 1998).

29. Laurence Cox and Caitriona Mullan, "Social Movements Never Died: Community Politics and the Social Economy in the Irish Republic," in *International Sociological Association and British Sociological Association Special Movements Conference*, Manchester, England, November 2001.

30. Ibid. See also Laurence Cox, "Gramsci, Movements, and Method: The Politics of Activist Research," in *Fourth International Conference on Alternative Futures and Popular Protest*, ed. Colin Barker and Mike Tyldesley (Manchester, England: Manchester Metropolitan University, 1998).

31. Hesse, "Racialized Modernity."

32. Ferreira da Silva, *Towards a Global Idea of Race*.

33. Denise Ferreira da Silva, "No-Bodies: Law, Raciality, and Violence," *Griffith Law Review* 18, no. 2 (2009): 213.

34. Denise Ferreira da Silva, "Toward a Critique of the Socio-Logos of Justice: The

Analytics of Raciality and the Production of Universality," *Social Identities* 7, no. 3 (2001): 421–454.

35. Andrea Smith, "Indigeneity, Settler Colonialism, White Supremacy," *Global Dialogue* 12, no. 2, *Race and Racisms* (Summer/Autumn 2010): N.p.

36. Walter Benjamin, "Critique of Violence," in *Walter Benjamin: Selected Writings*, vol. 1: *1913–1926*, ed. Marcus Bullock and Michael Jennings, trans. Edmund Jephcott (Cambridge, MA: Belknap, Harvard University Press, 2004), 277–300; Frantz Fanon, *The Wretched of the Earth* (New York: Grove Press, 1963), 53–54.

37. Patrick Wolfe, "Settler Colonialism and the Elimination of the Native," *Journal of Genocide Research* 8, no. 4 (2006): 388.

38. Richard Slotkin, *Regeneration through Violence: The Mythology of the American Frontier, 1600–1860* (Norman: University of Oklahoma Press, 2000).

39. Ken Gonzales-Day, *Lynching in the West: 1850–1935* (Durham, NC: Duke University Press, 2006). See also William D. Carrigan and Clive Webb, "The Lynching of Persons of Mexican Origin or Descent in the United States, 1848 to 1928," *Journal of Social History* 37, no. 2 (2003): 411–438.

40. Human Rights Watch, *Shielded from Justice: Police Brutality and Accountability in the United States*, June 1998, http://www.hrw.org/legacy/reports98/police/index.htm; United Nations, Committee on the Elimination of Racial Discrimination, "In the Shadows of the War on Terror: Persistent Police Brutality and the Abuse of People of Color in the United States," U.S. Second and Third Periodic Report to the Committee on the Elimination of Racial Discrimination (New York: United Nations, December 2007); National Lawyers Guild, Anthony Baez Foundation, and October 22nd Coalition, *Stolen Lives: Killed by Law Enforcement* (New York: October 22nd Coalition, 1999); Malcolm Holmes and Brad Smith, "Race, Threat, and Police Brutality: A Social Psychological Perspective," paper presented at the annual meeting of the American Society of Criminology (ASC), Los Angeles, November 1, 2006.

41. Neil Foley, *The White Scourge: Mexicans, Blacks, and Poor Whites in Texas Cotton Culture* (Berkeley: University of California Press, 1997).

42. Cary D. Wintz, "Blacks," in *The Ethnic Groups of Houston*, ed. Fred R. von der Mehden (Houston: Rice University Studies, 1984), 12.

43. Caroline Levander, "Sutton Griggs and the Borderlands of Empire," *American Literary History* 22, no. 1 (2010):57–84.

44. Robert D. Bullard, *Invisible Houston: The Black Experience in Boom and Bust* (College Station: Texas A&M University Press, 1987); Rick Mitchell, "A Little-Known Fact: Houston Is the Blues Capital," *Houston Chronicle*, September 30, 2007; Roger Wood and James Fraher, *Texas Zydeco* (Austin: University of Texas Press, 2006).

45. Roger Wood and James Fraher, *Down in Houston: Bayou City Blues* (Austin: University of Texas Press, 2003). See also Wood and Fraher, *Texas Zydeco*.

46. Arthur F. Raper, *Preface to Peasantry* (Chapel Hill: University of North Carolina Press, 1936).

47. Samuel C. Hyde Jr., *Sunbelt Revolution: The Historical Progression of the Civil Rights Struggle in the Gulf South, 1866–2000* (Gainesville: University Press of Florida, 2003), 1.

48. Howard Beeth and Cary D. Wintz, eds., *Black Dixie: Afro-Texan History and Culture in Houston* (College Station: Texas A&M University Press, 1992).

49. Beeth and Wintz, *Black Dixie*; Bullard, *Invisible Houston*.

50. Arnoldo De León, *Ethnicity in the Sunbelt: Mexican Americans in Houston* (College

Station: Texas A&M University Press, 2001); Guadalupe San Miguel Jr., *Brown, Not White: School Integration and the Chicano Movement in Houston* (College Station: Texas A&M University Press, 2005); Robert Treviño, *The Church in the Barrio: Mexican American Ethno-Catholicism in Houston* (Chapel Hill: University of North Carolina Press, 2006).

51. *Texas Observer*, "Justice in Jasper," September 17, 1999; CNN, "3 Whites Indicted in Dragging Death of Black Man in Texas," July 6, 1998; Sam Howe Verhovek, "One Man's Arrival in Town Exposes a Racial Fault Line," *New York Times*, February 27, 1993; Wade Goodwyn, "Beating Charges Split La. Town along Racial Lines," *All Things Considered*, National Public Radio, July 30, 2007; Andy Gallacher, "Huge Rally in Small-Town Louisiana," BBC News, September 21, 2007; Maria Newman, "Jena, La.," *New York Times*, September 24, 2007.

52. Chingo Bling, *They Can't Deport Us All* (Asylum Records, 2007).

53. La Monica Everett-Haynes, "Latino Students Recruited by Black Colleges," *Houston Chronicle*, October 15, 2004.

54. Gil Scott-Heron, "Jose Campos Torres," *The Mind of Gil Scott-Heron: A Collection of Poetry and Music* (TVT Records, 1978).

55. D. Soyini Madison, "Critical Ethnography As Street Performance: Reflections of Home, Race, Murder, and Justice," in *The Sage Handbook of Qualitative Research*, ed. N. K. Denzin and Y. S. Lincoln (Thousand Oaks, CA: Sage, 2005), 540.

56. Richard Iton, *In Search of the Black Fantastic: Politics and Popular Culture in the Post–Civil Rights Era* (New York: Oxford University Press, 2008). See also Paul Gilroy, "British Cultural Studies," 34–49.

57. Kim, *Bitter Fruit*.

58. Gugliemo, "Fighting for Caucasian Rights." See also Foley, "Becoming Hispanic" and "Over the Rainbow," and Haney-López, "White Latinos."

59. De León, *Ethnicity in the Sunbelt*; San Miguel, *Brown, Not White*.

60. David Montejano, *Quixote's Soldiers: A Local History of the Chicano Movement: 1966–1981* (Austin: University of Texas Press, 2010).

61. Ibid. Also see Oropeza, *¡Raza Sí!* See also Gustavo Cano, "Orale! Politics: Mobilization of Mexican Immigrants in Chicago and Houston," in *Inside Urban Politics: Voices from America's Cities and Suburbs*, ed. Dick Simpson, 38–50 (New York: Pearson Longman, 2004).

62. Stuart Hall, "Gramsci's Relevance to the Study of Race and Ethnicity," *Journal of Communication Inquiry* 10 (1986): 5–27.

63. Eduardo Bonilla-Silva, "From Bi-Racial to Tri-Racial: Towards a New System of Racial Stratification in the USA," *Ethnic and Racial Studies* 27 (2004): 931–950; George A. Yancey, *Who Is White? Latinos, Asians, and the New Black/Nonblack Divide* (Boulder, CO: Lynne Rienner, 2003).

64. René Francisco Poitevin, "David Roediger's *Working Toward Whiteness*," review, *Solidarity: A Socialist, Feminist, Anti-Racist Organization* (November–December 2006): N.p. http://www.solidarity-us.org/node/184.

65. Eileen O'Brien, *The Racial Middle: Latinos and Asian Americans Living Beyond the Racial Divide* (New York: New York University Press, 2008).

66. Arlene Dávila, *Latino Spin: Public Image and the Whitewashing of Race* (New York City: New York University Press, 2008), 7–8.

67. Hesse, "Racialized Modernity," 645.

68. Laura Guthman, "More Latinos Identify as Native Americans, Census Shows," CNN, September 30, 2011.

69. Hesse, "Racialized Modernity," 646.

70. Lawrence Wright, "One Drop of Blood," *New Yorker*, July 24, 1994.

71. George J. Sanchez, "Y tu que: Latino History in the New Millennium," in *Latinos: Remaking America*, ed. Marcelo Suarez and Mariela M. Paez (Berkeley: University of California Press, 2002), 50–51.

72. David Roediger, *Working toward Whiteness: How America's Immigrants Became White* (New York: Basic Books, 2005).

73. De León, *Ethnicity in the Sunbelt*; Reginald Horsman, *Race and Manifest Destiny: The Origins of American Racial Anglo-Saxonism* (Cambridge, MA: Harvard University Press, 1981).

74. Ibid.

75. U.S. Senate, "Illegal Immigration: Border-Crossing Deaths Have Doubled since 1995. Border Patrol's Efforts to Prevent Death Have Not Been Fully Evaluated," S. Rpt. GAO-06-770 (Washington, DC: Government Accountability Office, 2006). See also John D. Márquez, "Latinos as the 'Living Dead': Raciality, Expendability, and Border Militarization," *Latino Studies* 10, no. 4 (2012): 474.

76. Mexican American Legal Defense Fund, "Hate Crimes against Latinos at Record Levels," press release, October 28, 2008.

77. Maureen Costello, "Alabama's Immigration Law: The New Jim Crow," *Huffington Post*, June 15, 2011; Talib Kweli, "Papers Please," song and interview, *Smoking Section*, May 18, 2010, http://smokingsection.uproxx.com/.

78. Lekan Oguntoyinbo, "Alabama's New Immigration Law Evokes 'Fugitive Slave Act,'" op-ed, *Birmingham News*, June 19, 2011.

79. Alex Caballero, "Alabama Plans to Bring Back Slavery for Latinos," *The Guardian*, October 12, 2011.

80. Samuel Huntington, "The Hispanic Challenge," *Foreign Policy*, March 1, 2004.

81. Luke Reidenbach and Christian Waller, "The State of Minorities in 2010," press release, Center for American Progress, January 15, 2010.

82. Foley, *Quest for Equality*, 18–19. For a discussion of Mexican Americans' educational access prior to *Brown v. Board of Education* see Ian Haney-López, "Race and Color-blindness after Hernandez and Brown," *Chicano-Latino Law Review* 25 (2005): 61–76.

83. Poitevin, "David Roediger's *Working toward Whiteness*."

84. Ibid., n.p.

85. John D. Márquez, "Nations Re-Bound: Race and Biopolitics at EU and US Borders," in *Europe in Black and White: Immigration, Race, and Identity in the "Old Continent*,*"* ed. Manuela Ribeiro Sanches, Fernando Clara, João Ferreira Duarte, and Leonor Pires Martins (London/Chicago: Intellect Books/University of Chicago Press, 2010).

86. Bonilla-Silva, "From Bi-Racial to Tri-Racial," 936.

87. Michael A. Hughes and Bradley R. Hertel, "The Significance of Color Remains: A Study of Life Chances, Mate Selection, and Ethnic Consciousness among Black Americans," *Social Forces* 68, no. 4 (1990): 1105–1120; Nancy Krieger, Steven Sidney, and Eugenie Coakley, "Racial Discrimination and Skin Color in the CARDIA Study: Implications for Public Health Research," *American Journal of Public Health* 88, no. 9 (September 1998): 1308–1313.

88. Juan Flores, *From Bomba to Hip-Hop: Puerto Rican Culture and Latino Identity* (New York City: Columbia University Press, 2000).

89. Greg Tate, *Everything but the Burden: What White People Are Taking from Black Culture* (New York: Random House, 2003).

90. Toni Morrison, "On the Backs of Blacks," *Time*, December 2, 1993.

CHAPTER 2

1. Pierre Bourdieu and Loic Wacquant, *An Invitation to Reflexive Sociology* (Chicago: University of Chicago Press, 1992); J. B. Thompson, "Symbolic Violence: Language and Power in the Sociology of Pierre Bourdieu," in *Studies in the Theory of Ideology* (Cambridge, England: Polity Press, 1984); Loic Wacquant, "Pierre Bourdieu," in *Key Sociological Thinkers*, ed. Rob Stone, 261–276 (London: Palgrave Macmillan, 2007).

2. Colaguori, "Symbolic Violence," 396.

3. Richard Slotkin, *Regeneration through Violence: The Mythology of the American Frontier, 1600–1860* (Norman: University of Oklahoma Press, 2000); Richard Slotkin, *Gunfighter Nation: The Myth of the Frontier in Twentieth-Century America* (Norman: University of Oklahoma Press, 1998); Marita Sturtken, *Tangled Memories: The Vietnam War, the AIDS Epidemic, and the Politics of Remembering* (Berkeley: University of California Press, 1997).

4. David J. Weber, *The Spanish Frontier in North America* (New Haven, CT: Yale University Press, 1994).

5. Randolph B. Campbell, *An Empire for Slavery: The Peculiar Institution in Texas, 1821–1865* (Baton Rouge: Louisiana State University Press, 1989).

6. Jesus de la Teja, *San Antonio de Bexar: A Community on New Spain's Northern Frontier* (Albuquerque: University of New Mexico Press, 1996). See also David A. Williams, *Bricks without Straw: A Comprehensive History of African Americans in Texas* (Austin: University of Texas Press, 1997), 6.

7. Williams, *Bricks without Straw*, 6.

8. Alwyn Barr, *Black Texans: A History of African Americans in Texas, 1528–1995* (Norman: University of Oklahoma Press, 1996), 15.

9. Ben Vinson, *Bearing Arms for His Majesty: The Free-Colored Militia in Colonial Mexico* (Stanford, CA: Stanford University Press, 2004). See also Gerald Horne, *Black and Brown: African Americans and the Mexican Revolution, 1910–1920* (New York: New York University Press, 2005).

10. Barr, *Black Texans*, 15. See also Herbert Aptheker, *American Negro Slave Revolts* (New York: International, 1943).

11. Kenneth W. Wheeler, *To Wear a City's Crown: The Beginnings of Urban Growth in Texas, 1836–1865* (Cambridge, MA: Harvard University Press, 1968), 14. See also Works Progress Administration (WPA), Texas, *Houston: A History and Guide* (Austin: Anson Jones Press, Harris County Historical Society, 1942), Houston Public Library; David G. McComb, *Houston: A History* (Austin: University of Texas Press, 1969).

12. Barr, *Black Texans*, 9, 17.

13. Ibid., 17.

14. Harris County, TX, 1850 Census, #496, U.S. Census Agricultural Schedules, Harris and Liberty Counties, Harris County Deed Records, m 283, N 11, 226, X 593.

15. Barr, *Black Texans*, 24.

16. Ibid., 31.

17. Horsman, *Race and Manifest Destiny*, 230.

18. Arnoldo De León, *They Called Them Greasers: Anglo Attitudes Towards Mexicans in Texas: 1826–1836* (Austin: University of Texas Press, 1986), 11.

19. Menchaca, *Recovering History*.

20. Baytown Historical Society, "Bayland Guards Historical Marker Dedication, September 18, 2010," pamphlet, Baytown History Museum.

21. Baytown Historical Society, "Confederate Naval Works of Goose Creek: Historical Marker Dedication, March 19, 2008," pamphlet, Baytown History Museum.

22. In WPA, *Houston*, 79.

23. Don E. Carlton and Thomas E. Kreneck, "Houston Back Where We Started," pamphlet (Houston: De Menil, 1979), 7.

24. Bullard, *Invisible Houston*, 15. See also Wheeler, *To Wear a City's Crown*.

25. Bullard, *Invisible Houston*, 21; Carlton and Kreneck, "Houston Back Where We Started," 6.

26. Black Educational Access Committee of Lee College (BEAC), "Black History Facts in Baytown," pamphlet (Baytown: BEAC, 1997), 21, Baytown History Museum and copy donated to author by BEAC member Ray Wilson.

27. Henson, *History of Baytown*, 93; Michelle M. Mears, "African-American Settlement Patterns in Austin, Texas, 1865–1928," master's thesis, Baylor University, 2001; Ronald D. Traylor, "Harrison Barrett: A Freedman in Post-Civil War Texas," master's thesis, University of Houston, 1999; Thad Sitton and James H. Conrad, *Freedom Colonies: Independent Black Texans in the Time of Jim Crow* (Austin: University of Texas Press, 2005).

28. Allyson Gonzalez, "People Have Not Forgotten This Day," *Baytown Sun*, June 20, 2002.

29. Harris County, TX, 1860 Census, Harris County, Population and Slave Schedules; 1870, 1880, and 1900 Censuses, Harris and Chambers Counties; Henson, *History of Baytown*, 40–41, 44, 59.

30. Henson, *History of Baytown*, 61.

31. Louise Wood, *Lynching as Spectacle* (Chapel Hill: University of North Carolina Press, 2009).

32. De León, *Ethnicity in the Sunbelt*.

33. Ibid., 6. See also Henrietta Larson and Kenneth Wiggins Porter, *History of Humble Oil and Refining Company: A Study in Industrial Growth* (New York: Harper and Brothers, 1959), 5; Joe R. Feagin, *Free Enterprise City: Houston in Political and Economic Perspective* (Newark, NJ: Rutgers University Press, 1988).

34. De León, *Ethnicity in the Sunbelt*, 12.

35. San Miguel, *Brown, Not White*, 8.

36. Carrigan and Webb, "Lynching of Persons of Mexican Origin."

37. De León, *Ethnicity in the Sunbelt*, 12–14.

38. Ibid., 13. See also Benjamin Heber Johnson, *Revolution in Texas: How a Forgotten Rebellion and Its Bloody Suppression Turned Mexicans into Americans* (New Haven, CT: Yale University Press, 2005).

39. Robert V. Haynes, *A Night of Violence: The Houston Riot of 1917* (Baton Rouge: Louisiana State University Press, 1976), 17.

40. Edgar A. Schuler, "The Houston Race Riot, 1917," *Journal of Negro History* 29, no. 3 (July 1944): 300–338.

41. Ibid.

42. Hazel Haynesworth Young, interview by Elma Barrera, October 5, 2007, Houston, Oral History Project, Houston Metropolitan Research Center, Houston Public Library.

43. Ibid.

44. *Houston Daily Post*, letter, August 13, 1917.

45. *Houston Daily Post*, letter, August 15, 1917.

46. J. W. Carroll, "Oral History Conversation with J. W. Carroll," interview by William J. McNeil, September 29, 1976, Local History Archives, Sterling Municipal Library, Baytown.

47. Ibid.

48. Olga Miller Haenel, "A Social History of Baytown, Texas, 1912–1956," master's thesis, University of Texas, Austin, 1958, 1–2. See also Nicholas Reigleman, "Baytown's Adolescence: The Early Years," in *From Humble Beginnings: Exxon Baytown Seventy-Fifth Anniversary, 1920–1995*, 26–27 (Baytown: Exxon, 1995), Baytown History Museum; Walter J. Rundell, *Early Texas Oil: A Photographic History, 1866–1936* (College Station: Texas A&M University Press, 1977), 119.

49. "Goose Creek," *Cedar Bayou Weekly* 1, no. 4 (October 7, 1915). 7. The *Cedar Bayou Weekly* is compiled in *Miscellaneous Issues of Barthea Bulletin, 1914–1915*, ed. Louis Can Meldert, July 19, 1919, Local History Archives, Sterling Municipal Library, Baytown.

50. Rundell, *Early Texas Oil*, 119–120; Henson, *History of Baytown*, 79–80.

51. Feagin, *Free Enterprise City*, 66.

52. Haenel, "Social History," 4; *Baytown, Highlands, and La Porte City Directory, 1952–53* (Columbus, OH: 1952); *Baytown Sun*, September 21, 1953; January 19, 1969; February 27, 1983. *Humble Bee*, July 28, 1938; April 6, 1939, 10–11.

53. Woods, *Development Arrested*.

54. *Houston Chronicle*, "Negro Assailant of Mrs. Cowart Is Lynched by Mob of Goose Creek Oilmen," September 21, 1917, Houston Public Library.

55. Ibid.

56. Garrett R. Herring, "Oral History Conversation with Garrett Herring," interviews by Sara Swafford, February 7 and 14, 1980, Local History Archives, Sterling Municipal Library, Baytown.

57. G. R. Herring, interview by Olga Haenel, July 9, 1956, Local History Archives, Sterling Municipal Library, Baytown.

58. Henson, *History of Baytown*.

59. In Central and South Texas, Mexicanos were the main targets of lynch mobs and others who used violence. See De León, *They Called Them Greasers*; Mike Kingston, *A Concise History of Texas* (Houston: Taylor Trade, 1991).

60. D. W. Griffith, prod., and Christy Chabanne, dir., *Martyrs of the Alamo* (Delta Studios, 1915).

61. Ibid., scene 15.

62. Larson and Porter, *History of Humble Oil*, 66–67; Michael Botson, "We're Sticking by Our Union: The Battle for Baytown, 1942–1943," *Houston History* 8, no. 7 (2011): 9.

63. Henson, *History of Baytown*, 93–95.

64. Larson and Porter, *History of Humble Oil*, 69; Haenel, "Social History," 23.

65. Larson and Porter, *History of Humble Oil*, 69–71.

66. Henson, *History of Baytown*, 93–95.

67. Ibid., 96; Feagin, *Free Enterprise City*, 26; Marilyn McAdams Sibley, *The Port of Houston: A History* (Austin: University of Texas Press, 1968), 150.

68. Henson, *History of Baytown*, 96; Larson and Porter, *History of Humble Oil*, 73–74.

69. Ruben De Hoyos, interviews by the author, May 22, 2002, and August 26, 2003, Baytown; De León, *Ethnicity in the Sunbelt*, 10; Hispanic Educational Access Committee of Lee College (HEAC), "Cinco de Mayo Celebration," pamphlet (Baytown, 1998), HEAC Archives, Baytown History Museum; Henson, *History of Baytown*, 96.

70. Larson and Porter, *History of Humble Oil*, 69–71; Haenel, "Social History," 45.

71. Ibid.

72. Nicholas Reigleman, "Baytown's Adolescence," 25.

73. Haenel, "Social History," 31–41; Michael Ray Wilson and Ray Wilson, interview by the author, August 27, 2003, Baytown.

74. ExxonMobil, "ExxonMobil Baytown: A Ninety-Year Legacy" (Baytown: Exxon-Mobil, 2010), 13, Local History Archives, Sterling Municipal Library, Baytown, and Baytown History Museum.

75. ExxonMobil, "50-Year Anniversary of Baytown, 1998: A Proud Heritage" (Baytown: ExxonMobil Baytown, 1998), Baytown History Museum; HEAC, "Cinco de Mayo Celebration"; De Hoyos, interview, 2002.

76. HEAC, "Cinco de Mayo Celebration"; ExxonMobil, "ExxonMobil Baytown."

77. Ibid.

78. *Baytown Directory*, 1952; BEAC, "Black History Facts."

79. *Baytown Directory*, 1952, 171–172. See also ExxonMobil, "50-Year Anniversary of Baytown."

80. Ibid.

81. De Hoyos, interview, 2003.

82. Ibid.

83. Hilda Martinez, interview by the author, August 27, 2003, Baytown.

84. Larson and Porter, *History of Humble Oil*; Henson, *History of Baytown*, 96.

85. Omar Dyer in "The Ku Klux Klan in Baytown: An Interview with W. O. Tidmon, Omar Dyer, and Jimmy Carroll," interview by Betsy Webber and Bill McNeil, August 13, 1976, Baytown, Local History Archives, Sterling Municipal Library, Baytown.

86. Casey Greene, "Guardians against Change: The Ku Klux Klan in Houston and Harris County, 1920–1925" (University of Houston Center for Public History), *Houston History* 8, no. 1, *Confronting Jim Crow* (Fall 2010): 3.

87. Ibid.

88. Kenneth T. Jackson, *The Ku Klux Klan in the City, 1915–1930*, Urban Life in America Series (New York: Oxford University Press, 1967), 239.

89. Greene, "Guardians against Change," 4.

90. Ibid.

91. Tidmon in "Ku Klux Klan in Baytown," interview.

92. Carroll, "Oral History Conversation," interview by McNeil.

93. Henry Cathriner, interview by Olga Haenel, July 10, 1956, Local History Archives, Sterling Municipal Library, Baytown.

94. Bess Shannon, interviews by Olga Haenel, July 11, 12, and 16, 1956, Local History Archives, Sterling Municipal Library, Baytown.

95. Chris Myers, interview by Olga Haenel, July 22, 1956, Local History Archives, Sterling Municipal Library, Baytown.

96. Dyer in "Ku Klux Klan in Baytown," interview; *Colonel Mayfield's Weekly*, "Goose Creek Klansmen Visit Revival," July 15, 1922, Texas Room, Houston Metropolitan Research Center, Houston Public Library.

97. Henson, *History of Baytown*, 102; Susan Blankenship, "Oil and Morals: The Ku Klux Klan in Goose Creek," in *Baytown Vignettes* (Baytown: Lee College, 1995), Local History Archives, Sterling Municipal Library, Baytown.

98. Greene, "Guardians against Change," 4.

99. M. Ardella Grant, interview by Olga Haenel, July 1, 1957, Local History Archives, Sterling Municipal Library, Baytown.

100. Henson, *History of Baytown*, 102; Blankenship, "Oil and Morals," 83; Haenel, "Social History," 32–37.

101. Grant, interview by Haenel.

102. Ibid.

103. Dyer in "Ku Klux Klan in Baytown," interview.

104. Blankenship, "Oil and Morals," 47.

105. Ibid., 87.

106. *Houston Press*, "Here's More about Jailed Men," June 28, 1923.

107. Blankenship, "Oil and Morals," 87.

108. Grant, interview.

109. Feagin, *Free Enterprise City*, 74.

110. J. W. Carroll, "Oral History Conversation with J. W. Carroll," interview by Martha Mayo, February 25, 1986, Local History Archives, Sterling Municipal Library, Baytown.

111. BEAC, "Black History Facts."

112. *Humble Bee*, November 2, 1949.

113. Botson, "We're Sticking by Our Union," 13.

114. *Humble Bee*, July 2, 1928.

115. *Goose Creek Gasser*, "Juneteen Has Inspired Many Colored Boys to Slip from Righteous Bondage," July 3, 1931; BEAC, "Black History Facts."

116. BEAC, "Black History Facts."

117. Ray Wilson, interview.

118. "Historical and Biographical Baytown, Texas, 1952," *Baytown City Directory*, ed. Chester P. Rogers (Baytown: Page Interstate Company), 6, Local History Archives, Sterling Municipal Library, Baytown.

119. Allyson Gonzalez, "Memories Run Deep for Old Carver School," *Baytown Sun*, June 21, 2002.

120. Ibid.

121. Ibid.

122. Ibid.

123. ExxonMobil, "50-Year Anniversary of Baytown."

124. Ibid.

125. Virginia Moreno, "Oral History Conversation with Virginia Moreno," interview by Myra Hornberger, April 17, 1980, Local History Archives, Sterling Municipal Library, Baytown.

126. Ibid.

127. Hispanic Educational Access Committee of Lee College (HEAC), "Cinco de Mayo Celebration," pamphlet, Baytown, 1998, HEAC Archives, Baytown History Museum.

128. Ibid.

129. Mindiola, Flores Niemann, and Rodriguez, *Black-Brown Relations*.

130. HEAC, "Cinco de Mayo Celebration."

131. D. J. Brewer, "Humble's Impact on World War II," in *From Humble Beginnings:*

Exxon Baytown Seventy-Fifth Anniversary, 1920-1995, 41-42 (Baytown: Exxon Baytown Public Relations Office, 1995), Baytown History Museum and Local History Archives, Sterling Municipal Library.

132. Ibid. See also ExxonMobil, "ExxonMobil Baytown," 18.

133. Larson and Porter, *History of Humble Oil*, 570.

134. *Humble Bee*, "Humble Company Needs Men and Women at Baytown Refinery," April 1944, 14-15.

135. Donna Bonin, "Baytown's Rosie the Riveter," in *From Humble Beginnings: Exxon Baytown Seventy-Fifth Anniversary, 1920-1995* (Baytown: Exxon Baytown Public Relations Office, 1995), Baytown History Museum and Local History Archives, Sterling Municipal Library, Baytown; Sherna B. Gluck, *Rosie the Riveter Revisited: Women, the War, and Social Change* (Boston: Twayne, 1987).

136. Botson, "We're Sticking by Our Union."

137. Ibid., 12.

138. Ibid.

139. National Labor Relations Board (NLRB), Case File 4936, Labor Board Exhibit 8; NLRB, Case File 5945, Employees Federation, Bulletins 11 and 63, Records of the NLRB, National Archives and Records Administration, College Park, MD.

140. Botson, "We're Sticking by Our Union," 13.

141. In Emilio Zamora, *Claiming Rights and Righting Wrongs in Texas: Mexican Workers and Job Politics During World War II* (College Station: Texas A&M University Press, 2009), 166-167.

142. Ibid.

143. Ralph Fusco, "World War II's Effects on Consolidation," in *Baytown Vignettes* (Baytown: Lee College, 1995), 139, Local History Archives, Sterling Municipal Library.

144. ExxonMobil, "ExxonMobil Baytown," 20.

145. Haenel, "Social History," 115-117.

146. *Baytown Sun*, February 19, 1984; BEAC, "Black History Facts."

147. Ibid. See also Botson, "We're Sticking by Our Union."

148. Edward Escobar, *Race, Police, and the Making of a Political Identity: Mexican Americans and the Los Angeles Police Department, 1900-1945* (Berkeley: University of California Press, 1999), 11; Neil Websdale, *Policing the Poor: From Slave Plantation to Public Housing* (New York: Northeastern University Press, 2001).

149. Robin D.G. Kelley, *Race Rebels* (New York: Free Press, 1994), 84.

150. De Hoyos, interview, 2003.

151. In Michael P. Mihalik, *Baytown Police Department: 50 Years, 1948-1998* (Baytown: Baytown Historical Society, 1998), 8, Local History Archives, Sterling Municipal Library, Baytown.

CHAPTER 3

1. Jon Maranica, "Seeping out of Houston, Slowly," *New York Times*, June 4, 2010.

2. Cyrus Bina, *The Economics of the Oil Crisis* (New York: St. Martin's Press, 1985); Michael Economides and Ronald Oligney, *The Color of Oil* (Katy, TX: Round Oak, 2000); Feagin, *Free Enterprise City*; Robert Mabro, ed., *The 1986 Oil Price Crisis: Economic Effects and Policy Responses. Proceedings of the Eighth Oxford Energy Seminar* (New York: Oxford University Press, 1988); Joseph Nocera, ed., *Bidness: The Booms and Busts of the Texas Economy*

(Austin: Texas Monthly Press, 1986); Gary Anderson, "Whither Houston," *Houston Post*, December 5, 1983; Eugene Carlson, "Would You Believe Houston as a New–Business Hot Spot?" *Wall Street Journal*, December 2, 1986; James H. DeNike, "Energy Shortage Boost to Economy in This Area," *Houston Chronicle*, January 16, 1980; Cleveland Grammer, "Houston Recovery Foreseen, but Not in '86," *Houston Post*, January 24, 1986; Leslie Kaufman, "Feeling the Pinch on Luxury Leather," *New York Times*, March 29, 2001; Terry Kliewer, "Houston May Again Become a 'Boom Town,' Economic Consultant Says," *Houston Post*, August 12, 1983; George Lardner and Lois Romano, "Bush Name Helps Fuel Oil Dealings," *Houston Post*, July 30, 1999; Ray B. Nesbit, "Petrochemicals Future Strong, Houston to Share Growth," *Houston Chronicle*, January 16, 1980; Kenneth Schnitzer, "Houston Is Better Off than Most Believe," *Houston Post*, June 27, 1984; Leslie Sowers, "A Bruised and Confused City Fights Back," *Houston Chronicle*, July 14, 1985; Leslie Sowers, "Diversified City Economy Called Cure," *Houston Chronicle*, July 23, 1986; *Houston Post*, "Houston to Continue to Offer Business Growth, Experts Say," January 15, 1982; *Houston Business Journal*, "Low Oil Prices, Oversupply of Space Could Slow Growth," January 14, 1985; Immanuel Wallerstein, "The Global Picture, 1945–90," in *The Age of Transition: Trajectory of the World System: 1945–2025*, ed. Terence E. Hopkins and Immanuel Wallerstein (London: Zed Books, 1996).

3. Feagin, *Free Enterprise City*, 73.

4. Ibid, 74.

5. U.S. Census Bureau, Census 1970, 1980; Stephen L. Klineberg, *Houston's Economic and Demographic Transformations: Findings from the Expanded Survey of Houston's Ethnic Communities* (Houston: Kinder Institute for Urban Research, Rice University, 2002).

6. Ray Vu, "Constructing a Southern Vietnamese Community and Identity in Houston" (University of Houston), *Houston Review* 3, no. 1 (2006): 27–31, 63–66; *New York Times*, "Houston Becoming Burgeoning Vietnamese Society," June 2, 1980.

7. David Kaplan, "Vietnam Refugees, a True Success Story," *Houston Chronicle*, April 29, 2005.

8. U.S. District Court, S. D. Texas, Houston Division, *Vietnamese Fishermen's Association, et al., Plaintiffs, v. The Knights of the Ku Klux Klan, et al., Defendants*. Civ. A. No. H-81-895, July 15, 1981.

9. Ron Hamilton, interview by the author, June 22, 2009, Baytown.

10. Ibid.

11. Louis Chude-Sokei, "Redefining 'Black': Obama's Candidacy Spotlights the Divide between Native Black Culture and African Immigrants," *Los Angeles Times*, February 18, 2007.

12. Ibid. For more on Caribbean black identity in the United States, see Reul Rogers, *Afro-Caribbean Immigrants and the Politics of Incorporation: Ethnicity, Exception, or Exit* (New York: Cambridge University Press, 2006).

13. Hamilton, interview.

14. Rude-Boi, interview by the author, June 24, 2009, Baytown.

15. Netra Charles, interview by the author, July 16, 2009, Baytown.

16. Ibid.

17. Hamilton, interview.

18. Mihalik, *Baytown Police Department: 50 Years*.

19. Dwight Watson, *Race and the Houston Police Department* (College Station: Texas A&M University Press, 2005), 111.

20. In Tuala Williams, "Forty Years Later: The Legend of Carl Hampton," *African American News and Issues*, July 12, 2010.

21. Travis Morales, "Echoes of the Moody Park Rebellion," *Revolutionary Worker*, no. 960 (June 7, 1998).

22. Martin Waldron, "Houston Police Man Accused of Burnings," *New York Times*, March 7, 1973.

23. Houston Civilian Complaints Forum, transcript, May 13, 1978, Houston Metropolitan Research Center, Houston Public Library.

24. (Reverend) William Lawson, interview by Veronica Perry, August 12, 1974, Oral History Project, Houston Metropolitan Research Center, Houston Public Library.

25. Tom Curtis, "Support Your Local Police (or Else)," *Texas Monthly*, September 1977, 83–88.

26. Ibid., 86.

27. Ibid., 88.

28. Daniel Bustamante, interview by Megan Schneider, April 30, 2008, Oral History Project, Houston Metropolitan Research Center, Houston Public Library.

29. De León, *Ethnicity in the Sunbelt*.

30. Bustamante, interview.

31. Watson, *Race and the Houston Police Department*, 112–115.

32. In Curtis, "Support Your Local Police (or Else)," 83.

33. Vance Muse, *Don't Buy a Car Made on Monday: An Arbitrary Encyclopedia of Things to Be Afraid Of* (New York: Times Books, 1979), 59. See also Watson, *Race and the Houston Police Department*, 111.

34. De León, *Ethnicity in the Sunbelt*.

35. Morales, "Echoes."

36. Bustamante, interview.

37. Bullard, *Invisible Houston*, 121.

38. Guadalupe San Miguel Jr., *Brown, Not White: School Integration and the Chicano Movement in Houston* (College Station: Texas A&M University Press, 2005).

39. Lawson, interview.

40. Ibid.

41. Thomas Wright, "Who Fingered Carl Hampton?" *Sepia Magazine*, November, 1970, 13; T. Williams, "Forty Years Later"; J. R. Gonzales, "The Death of Carl Hampton," *Bayou City History—A Blog about Houston's Past, Houston Chronicle*, July 26, 2010.

42. Behnken, *Fighting Their Own Battles*, 130.

43. *Dallas Morning News*, "Priest Urges Latin-Negro Axis," August 13, 1967.

44. Treviño, *Church in the Barrio*, 197–199. See also Behnken, *Fighting Their Own Battles*, 102.

45. Howard Jefferson, interview by David Goldstein, May 15, 2008, Oral History Project, Houston Metropolitan Research Center, Houston Public Library.

46. Ibid.

47. Marc Campos, interview by Megan Schneider, April 18, 2008, Oral History Project, Houston Metropolitan Research Center, Houston Public Library.

48. Ibid.

49. Feagin, *Free Enterprise City*, 75; Georgia Redonet, "The Impact of World Events on the Petroleum Industry of Houston, Texas, in the 1970s and 1980s," Honors Program paper, University of Houston, 1999.

50. Robin D.G. Kelley, *Yo Mama's DisFUNKtional! Fighting the Culture Wars in Urban America* (Boston: Beacon Press, 1998), 47.

51. Christian Parenti, *Lockdown America: Police and Prisons in the Age of Crisis* (New York: Verso, 1999).

52. Ibid., 49. Also see Websdale, *Policing the Poor*.

53. *Baytown Sun*, "Criminal Gangs in Our Neighborhoods," editorial, October 27, 1993; State of Texas, Title 11, Organized Crime, Chapter 71, Organized Crime, §71.02, Engaging in Organized Criminal Activity, Texas Constitution and Statutes.

54. In Cindy Horswell, "Gangs in Baytown, Parallels on Opposite Turf," *Houston Chronicle*, May 19, 1991.

55. Carlton Stowers, *Hard Lessons: True Story of Life in a Street Gang* (Dallas: Community Justice Foundation of Texas, 1994).

56. John D. Márquez, "The Black Mohicans: Representations of Everyday Violence in Postracial Urban America," *American Quarterly* 64, no. 3 (2012): 625–651.

57. Fanon, *Wretched of the Earth*, 54.

58. CNN, "Where Are the Jobs? Look to Baytown, Texas," May 20, 2011. See also Jeanie Kever, "It's School, or Hard Knocks, in Baytown," *Houston Chronicle*, October 30, 2011.

59. Frankie Hildenbrand, interview by the author, November 20, 2001, Baytown.

60. Ibid.

61. City of Baytown, crime statistics, September 13, 2010, http://www.baytown.org /public/police/statistics/default.htm, accessed October 30, 2010.

62. Cindy Horswell, "Baytown Turf War Takes Toll in Blood," *Houston Chronicle*, January 11, 1987.

63. *Houston Chronicle*, "Can't Tolerate Street Gangs," editorial, January 13, 1987.

64. Ken Fountain, "Suspects Sought in Pine Street Slaying," *Baytown Sun*, April 4, 2006.

65. Ken Fountain, "Murder Charges Filed in Pine Street Slaying," *Baytown Sun*, April 21, 2006; Ken Fountain, "Murder Suspect Arrested in Highlands," *Baytown Sun*, April 27, 2006.

66. In Horswell, "Gangs in Baytown."

67. Ibid.

68. In Kari Griffin, "Killer Gets 25 Years," *Baytown Sun*, July 22, 2008.

69. In Jane Howard Lee, "Three Years Later, Sister Still Wants Answers," *Baytown Sun*, April 1, 2009.

70. Cindy Horswell, "Bridging a Big GAP," *Houston Chronicle*, October 18, 1992.

71. Cindy Horswell, "Rehearing Sought in Baytown Death," *Houston Chronicle*, April 10, 1991; Roma Khanna and Lise Olsen, "A Chronicle Special Report: Few Police Punished in Shootings," *Houston Chronicle*, July 26, 2004.

72. In Horswell, "Rehearing Sought in Baytown Death."

73. Robert Soro, "Houston Police Face Civil Rights Probe," *Washington Post*, November 11, 1998; Steve McVicker, "Dead, Dead, Dead: The Police Killings of Pedro Oregon, Ida Lee Delaney, and Byron Gillum," *Houston Press*, May 6, 1999, 1–2.

74. McVicker, "Dead, Dead, Dead."

75. Justice for Pedro Oregon Coalition (JPOC), press release, February 1999, obtained by author at JPOC demonstration.

76. In Tim Fleck, "The More Things Change," *Houston Press*, October 29, 1998, 2.

77. KRS-1, "Black Cop," *Return of the Boom Bap* (Jive Records, 1993); N.W.A., "Fuck tha Police," *Straight Outta Compton* (Ruthless Records, 1988); Geto Boys, "Crooked Officer," *Till Death Do Us Part* (Rap-A-Lot Records, 1993).

78. Alan Green, interview by the author, July 3, 2009, Washington, DC.

79. Ibid.

80. American Institute of Architects, Regional/Urban Design Assistance Team (R/UDAT), Programs and Initiatives, "Baytown Report, 1990," Local History Archives, Sterling Municipal Library, Baytown; a copy was donated to the author from personal archives of a member of the Baytown 2000 vision planning team.

81. In Cindy Horswell, "Baytown Going to War against Gangs," *Houston Chronicle*, September 20, 1992.

82. State of Texas, Title 11, Chapter 71, §71.02.

83. Horswell, "Baytown Going to War against Gangs."

84. U.S. Department of Justice, Racketeer Influenced and Corrupt Organizations Act (RICO), Title IX of the Organized Crime Control Act of 1970, Pub. L. No. 91–452, 84 Stat. 941, codified at 18 U.S.C. Ch. 96, §§1961–1968.

85. Charles Mills, *The Racial Contract* (Ithaca, NY: Cornell University Press, 1997), 41–43.

86. In Horswell, "Baytown Going to War against Gangs."

87. Homero Rangel, interview by the author, August 25, 2009, Baytown.

88. In Cindy Horswell, "'We Are Living in the Most Violent Society in the World,'" *Houston Chronicle*, October 2, 1991.

89. Capone, interview by the author, August 24, 2009, Baytown.

90. City of Baytown, "Crime Stats Presentation," vol. 4, http://www.baytown.org/news /releases/crime-stats.htm, accessed October 28, 2010.

91. "Vic," interview by the author, February 18, 2008, Baytown.

92. "Big Mike," interview by the author, February 21, 2004, Baytown.

93. Horswell, "Baytown Turf War."

94. In Howard Campbell, *Drug War Zone: Dispatches from the U.S.-Mexico Border* (Austin: University of Texas Press, 2009).

95. Ibid., 116.

96. Ibid., 126.

97. Ibid., 116.

98. Hall, "New Ethnicities."

99. Jeff Chang, *Can't Stop, Won't Stop: A History of the Hip-hop Generation* (New York: St. Martin's Press, 2005); Sharma, *Hip-Hop Desis*.

100. Geto Boys, "City under Siege," *The Geto Boys* (Rap-A-Lot Records, 1989), distributed by Warner Brothers Records in 1990.

101. Sasha Frere-Jones, "A Place in the Sun: Houston Hip-Hop Takes Over," *New Yorker*, November 14, 2005.

102. Mitchell, "A Little-Known Fact."

103. Ibid.

104. Ibid.

105. *Spinner Magazine*, "Worst Band Feuds No. 3: Joe Tex vs. James Brown," September 14, 2003.

106. Texas State Historical Association (TSHA), "Arrington, Joseph Jr. [Joe Tex]," *Handbook of Texas Online*.

107. Ibid.

108. Frere-Jones, "Place in the Sun."

109. Ibid.

110. Mitchell, "Little-Known Fact."

111. John Nova Lomax, "South Park Monster," *Houston Press*, June 6, 2002.

112. Ibid.

113. South Park Mexican (SPM), "SPM and Bun B at the Dopehouse," interview, originally posted at djscrewlagacy.com, accessed on YouTube, August 18, 2012.

114. Lomax, "South Park Monster."

115. In Rolando Rodriguez, "Alfonso Cook Is Rasheed, the 'Texas Chainsaw,'" *Houston Press*, January 29, 2010.

116. Low-G and Rasheed, *Wetblack* (Shut 'Em Down Records, 2002).

117. Brown Pride Forum, http://boards.brownpride.com/showthread.php/do-feel-mayateros-72372.html, accessed January 3, 2008.

118. In John Nova Lomax, "Hip-Hop Tejas: Latinos Take on Rap Music and Make It Their Own," *Houston Press*, December 4, 1995.

119. Ibid.

120. Chingo Bling, "They Can't Deport Us All," *They Can't Deport Us All* (Asylum Records, 2007).

121. In Lomax, "Hip-Hop Tejas."

122. Ibid.

123. Randall Kennedy, *Nigger: The Strange Career of a Troublesome Word* (New York: Vintage, 2003).

124. Ben Westhoff, "Not Your Father's N-Word," *Houston Press*, April 3, 2008.

125. Rolando Rodriguez, "Lucky Luciano: Boss of Houston's Latin Rap Family," *Houston Press*, December 3, 2000.

126. Ibid.

127. Rolando Rodriguez, "Low-G: From ESL Mockery to Historic Spanish Hip-Hop," *Houston Press*, January 27, 2010.

128. Mignolo, *Local Histories/Global Designs*.

CHAPTER 4

1. American Civil Liberties Union (ACLU), "The Luis Torres Story" posters, 2002, http://www.aclu.org/FilesPDFs/aclu%20torres%20finals%20v3.pdf; ACLU, "¿Cómo se dice Rodney King en español? Posters Promote Reform, Commemorate Texas Victim of Police Brutality," press statement, October 15, 2002.

2. Robert Crowe, "Torres Aftermath Leaves Deep Wounds in Baytown," *Houston Chronicle*, June 13, 2002. See also League of United Latin American Citizens (LULAC), Resolution, June 29, 2002, http://www.lulac.net/advocacy/resolutions/2002/22.html.

3. Crowe, "Torres Aftermath"; Matthew Cook, "FBI Investigating Death of Luis Torres," *Baytown Sun*, February 26, 2002.

4. Ibid.

5. Cindy Horswell and Edward Hegstrom, "Baytown Chief Backs Officers in Fatal Fight," *Houston Chronicle*, February 23, 2002.

6. Ibid.

7. Cindy Horswell, "Man Fled Hospital before Death," *Houston Chronicle*, February 27, 2002.

8. Matthew Cook, "Man Dies in Police Custody after Pepper Spray," *Baytown Sun*, January 21, 2002.

9. Ibid.

10. Ibid.

11. Matthew Cook, "Family of Man Who Died in Police Custody to Sue City," *Baytown Sun*, February 21, 2002.

12. Ibid.

13. Ibid.

14. Harris County, TX, Medical Examiner's Office, "Cause of Death Report, Luis Alfonso Torres," February 22, 2002, Houston.

15. Ibid.

16. Horswell and Hegstrom, "Baytown Chief Backs Officers."

17. Ibid.

18. Ibid.

19. Ibid.

20. In Matthew Cook, "Torres Death Called a 'Homicide,'" *Baytown Sun*, February 22, 2002.

21. Ibid.

22. Ibid.

23. Cook, "FBI Investigating Death."

24. Ibid.

25. Matthew Cook, "City to Release Tape of Torres Arrest Today," *Baytown Sun*, March 1, 2002.

26. David Bloom, "The Torres Videotape," editorial, *Baytown Sun*, March 3, 2002.

27. *Baytown Sun*, "City Releases Tape of Torres Arrest," March 1, 2002.

28. In Cook, "City to Release Tape."

29. Ibid.

30. Eva Benavides, interview by the author, August 29, 2003, Baytown.

31. In Crowe, "Torres Aftermath."

32. Ibid.

33. Eva Benavides, letter, *Baytown Sun*, June 15, 2002.

34. In Jake Bernstein, "Video of a Police Killing Produces Shockwaves in Baytown, Texas," *Texas Observer*, March 29, 2002.

35. In Matthew Cook, "March on Market Street to Honor Torres," *Baytown Sun*, March 8, 2002.

36. In Horswell and Hegstrom, "Baytown Chief Backs Officers."

37. In David Bloom, "Torres Case Challenges City Public Relations," *Baytown Sun*, March 31, 2002.

38. In Cindy Horswell, "Officers Cleared in Death," *Houston Chronicle*, May 3, 2002.

39. Bernstein, "Video of a Police Killing."

40. In Horswell, "Officers Cleared in Death."

41. In Cindy Horswell, "Police to Release Video of Torres," *Houston Chronicle*, March 1, 2002.

42. In Orlando Bagwell, dir., *Make it Plain*, documentary film, 1965.

43. In Horswell and Hegstrom, "Baytown Chief Backs Officers."

44. In Matthew Cook, "Hispanic Community Rallies in Support," *Baytown Sun*, March 4, 2002.

45. Ibid.

46. Ibid.

47. Ibid.

48. Ibid.

49. Ibid.

50. Ibid.

51. Eric Berger, "Justice Sought after Man Dies in Custody," *Houston Chronicle*, March 4, 2002.

52. Cook, "March on Market Street."

53. Chris Vogel, "Quanell X: The Houston Activist Says He's Dumped the Hate," *Houston Press*, January 14, 2009.

54. Matthew Cook, "Quanell X Leads Rally on Steps of Baytown PD," *Baytown Sun*, March 11, 2002.

55. Ibid.

56. Ibid.

57. Ibid.

58. Ibid.

59. Ibid.

60. Dennis Robbins, interview with the author, March 16, 2002, Baytown.

61. In Jonathan Cooper, "McNair Rally Brings Racism to the Forefront," *Baytown Sun*, March 16, 2002.

62. In Jonathan Cooper, "Residents Rally for Civil Rights Group in Baytown," *Baytown Sun*, March 18, 2002.

63. In Matthew Cook, "Enhanced Video of Torres Reinforces Opinions," *Baytown Sun*, March 23, 2002.

64. Ibid.

65. Ibid.

66. Wanda Garner Cash, "The Latest Misstep," editorial, *Baytown Sun*, March 27, 2002.

67. Matthew Cook, "Jones Clarifies 'Misinformation' in Case," *Baytown Sun*, March 27, 2002.

68. In David Bloom, "Torres Case."

69. In Matthew Cook, "Torres Case Heads to Grand Jury," *Baytown Sun*, April 24, 2002.

70. Ibid.

71. In Kristen Mack, "Death in Baytown Struggle Called Abuse of Police Power," *Houston Chronicle*, April 24, 2002.

72. In Cook, "Torres Case Heads to Grand Jury."

73. In Matthew Cook, "Quanell X Leads 2nd Baytown Rally," *Baytown Sun*, April 29, 2002.

74. Ibid.

75. Ibid.

76. Ibid.

77. Ibid.

78. Ibid.

79. Matthew Cook, "Grand Jury Declines to Indict Baytown Cops," *Baytown Sun*, May 3, 2002; Cindy Horswell, "Officers Cleared in Death," *Houston Chronicle*, May 3, 2002.

80. In Cook, "Grand Jury Declines to Indict Baytown Cops."

81. Ibid.

82. Ibid.

83. Ibid.

84. In Horswell, "Officers Cleared in Death."

85. In Kristen Mack, "Court Ruling Sparks Outrage," *Houston Chronicle*, May 3, 2002.

86. In Cook, "Grand Jury Declines to Indict Baytown Cops."

87. Ibid.

88. In Mack, "Court Ruling Sparks Outrage,"

89. In Horswell, "Officers Cleared in Death."

90. *Baytown Sun*, "Vocal Group Demands Justice in Torres Case," May 4, 2002.

91. Ibid.

92. In Matthew Cook, "Houston Activists Planning Response to Torres Ruling," *Baytown Sun*, May 10, 2002.

93. In Lisa Teachey, "25 Years Later, Distrust Remains," *Houston Chronicle*, May 6, 2002.

94. In Lia Martin, "Activists Speak out against Grand Jury," *Baytown Sun*, May 9, 2002.

95. In Cook, "Houston Activists Planning Response."

96. Ibid.

97. Ibid.

98. Matthew Cook, "Citizens Hope to Bridge Gap with Police," *Baytown Sun*, June 8, 2002; Crowe, "Torres Aftermath."

99. Cook, "Citizens Hope to Bridge Gap."

100. T. J. Milling, "Baytown Police Say Teen Shooting Was Accident," *Houston Chronicle*, June 28, 1997.

101. T. J. Milling, "Tension Mounts over Shooting," *Houston Chronicle*, June 27, 1997.

102. James C. McKinley Jr., "Texas Officer Acquitted in Shooting," *New York Times*, May 11, 2010.

103. David Theo Goldberg, "The New Segregation," *Race and Society* 1 (1998): 15–32.

104. In Mike Tolson and Linday Wise, "Family: Bellaire Officer Shot Man Because He's Black," *Houston Chronicle*, January 1, 2009.

105. Ibid.

106. James C. McKinley Jr., "In Houston, 2 Cases Raise Tough Racial Questions," *New York Times*, May 14, 2010.

107. In Crowe, "Torres Aftermath."

108. Ibid.

109. Ibid.

110. Ibid.

111. Hilda Martinez, interview by the author, August 27, 2003, Baytown; Marga Hernandez, interview by the author, August 30, 2003, Baytown.

112. In Matthew Cook, "Activists Suggest State Help in Torres Case," *Baytown Sun*, June 9, 2002.

113. Ibid.

114. In Allyson Gonzalez, "Jones: 'We'll Just Have to Work Harder,'" *Baytown Sun*, June 14, 2002.

115. Ibid.

116. Ibid.

117. Ibid.

118. Ibid.

119. In Allyson Gonzalez, "Decision Needs to Be Made on Police Chief," *Baytown Sun*, June 16, 2002.

120. In Matthew Cook, "'We Seek to Bring Justice to This Community,'" *Baytown Sun*, June 21, 2002.

121. Ibid.

122. Ibid.

123. Ibid.

124. In Austin Kinghorn, "McNair Honors Outstanding Residents," *Baytown Sun*, June 21, 2002.

125. Ibid.

126. Ibid.

127. Ibid.

128. In Austin Kinghorn, "Protesters at Third Baytown Rally," *Baytown Sun*, June 24, 2002.

129. ACLU, "¿Cómo se dice Rodney King en español?" posters.

130. In Kinghorn, "Protesters at Third Baytown Rally."

131. LULAC, Resolution.

132. In Matthew Cook, "LULAC Delegates Want Resolution," *Baytown Sun*, June 27, 2002.

133. Ibid.

134. Ibid.

135. Ibid.

136. Allyson Gonzalez, "LULAC Approves Resolution Degrading Baytown," *Baytown Sun*, June 30, 2002.

CONCLUSION

1. Aldon Morris, *The Origins of the Civil Rights Movement* (New York: Free Press, 1984).

2. Wanda Garner Cash, "Baytown's Response," editorial, *Baytown Sun*, March 16, 2002.

3. In Cook, "LULAC Delegates Want Resolution."

4. Ibid.

5. Ferreira da Silva, "No-Bodies."

6. Howard Zinn, *A People's History of the United States: 1492–Present* (New York: Harper Perennial, 2003), 8–9.

7. Assia Djebar, *Fantasia: An Algerian Cavalcade* (New York: Heinemann, 1993).

8. Ibid., 156.

9. Homi K. Bhabha, "The Aesthetics of Barbaric Transmission," video, public lecture at (World) Art? Art History and Global Practice Conference, Northwestern University, Evanston, IL, May 23, 2008.

10. Ibid.

11. Anne Anlin Cheng, *The Melancholy of Race: Psychoanalysis, Assimilation, and Hidden Grief* (New York: Oxford University Press, 2001).

12. Corey Robin, *Fear: The History of a Political Idea* (New York: Oxford University Press, 2004).

13. Kelly Anderson, Tami Gold, and Erik Moe, *Every Mother's Son*, documentary film (New York: AndersonGold Films, 2004).

14. *Revolution*, "Jury Awards Millions to Family of Malcolm Ferguson: The Struggle Is Far from Over," July 17, 2007, http://revcom.us/a/092/juanita-young-en.html; Neil McFadden, "New York Pays Settlement to Families of Two Men Shot by Police in 1995," *New York Times*, March 20, 2009.

15. *Revolutionary Worker*, "Margarita Rosario: Fighting to Break the Blue Wall," interview, http://revcom.us/a/firstvol/rosa.htm.

16. For works that foreground the significance of mothers to activism, see Mary S. Pardo, *Mexican American Women Activists* (Philadelphia: Temple University Press, 1998); Anellise Orleck, *Storming Caesar's Palace: How Black Mothers Fought Their Own War on Poverty* (Boston: Beacon Press, 2006); Elsa Barkley Brown, "Womanist Consciousness: Maggie Lena Walker and the Independent Order of Saint Luke," *Signs* 14 (1989): 610–633; Elaine Brown, *A Taste of Power: A Black Woman's Story* (New York: Anchor Books, 1993); Pulido, *Black, Brown, Yellow, and Left*, 180–213; Aldaljiza Sosa-Ridell, "Chicanas and El Movimiento," *Aztlan* 5 (1974): 155–166; Kimberly Springer, *Living for the Revolution: Black Feminist Organizations, 1968–1980* (Durham, NC: Duke University Press); Chandra Talpade Mohanty, *Feminism without Borders: Decolonizing Theory, Practicing Solidarity* (Durham, NC: Duke University Press, 2005).

17. Coretta Scott King, "Coretta King Visits with Cesar Chavez in Jail: Asks Blacks to Boycott Lettuce," letter, December 19, 1970, box 21, folder 458, Beinecke Rare Book and Manuscript Library, Yale University, New Haven, CT.

Note: For readers' convenience, the bibliography is divided into primary and secondary sources. The Primary Sources section is subdivided into Archives, Musical Recordings and Films, and Oral Histories. The undivided Secondary Sources section includes published works, dissertations and theses, and lectures.

PRIMARY SOURCES

ARCHIVES

American Institute of Architects, Regional/Urban Design Assistance Team (R/UDAT). Programs and Initiatives. "Baytown Report, 1990." Local History Archives, Sterling Municipal Library, Baytown.

Baytown, City of. Crime statistics, September 13, 2010. http://www.baytown.org/public /police/statistics/default.htm. Accessed October 30, 2010.

———. "Crime Stats Presentation," vol. 4. http://www.baytown.org/news/releases/crime -stats.htm. Accessed October 28, 2010.

Baytown City Directory, 1929–1952, 1960, 1970. Title varies. Local History Archives, Sterling Municipal Library, Baytown.

Baytown Historical Society. "Bayland Guards Historical Marker Dedication, September 18, 2010." Pamphlet. Baytown History Museum.

———. "Confederate Naval Works of Goose Creek: Historical Marker Dedication, March 19, 2008." Pamphlet. Baytown History Museum.

Baytown Vignettes. Baytown: Lee College, 1995. Local History Archives, Sterling Municipal Library.

Black Alliance for Just Immigration. "Working in Coalition." Pamphlet. http://blackalliance .org/main/?q=node/23.

Black Educational Access Committee of Lee College (BEAC). "Black History Facts in Baytown." Pamphlet. Baytown: BEAC, 1997. Baytown History Museum.

Blankenship, Susan. "Oil and Morals: The Ku Klux Klan in Goose Creek." In *Baytown Vignettes*. Baytown: Lee College, 1995. Local History Archives, Sterling Municipal Library.

Bonin, Donna. "Baytown's Rosie the Riveter." In *From Humble Beginnings: Exxon Baytown Seventy-Fifth Anniversary, 1920–1995*. Baytown: Exxon Baytown Public Relations Office, 1995. Baytown History Museum and Sterling Municipal Library, Baytown.

Brewer, D. J. "Humble's Impact on World War II." In *From Humble Beginnings: Exxon Baytown Seventy-Fifth Anniversary, 1920–1995*. Baytown: Exxon Baytown Public Relations Office, 1995. Baytown History Museum and Local History Archives, Sterling Municipal Library, Baytown.

Cedar Bayou Weekly. 1915. Local History Archives, Sterling Municipal Library, Baytown.

Colonel Mayfield's Weekly. Texas Room, Houston Metropolitan Research Center, Houston Public Library.

Exxon. *From Humble Beginnings: Exxon Baytown Seventy-Fifth Anniversary, 1920–1995*. Baytown: Exxon Baytown Public Relations Office, 1995. Baytown History Museum and Sterling Municipal Library, Baytown.

ExxonMobil. "50-Year Anniversary of Baytown, 1998: A Proud Heritage." Baytown: ExxonMobil, 1998. Local History Archives, Sterling Municipal Library, Baytown.

———. "ExxonMobil Baytown: A Ninety-Year Legacy." Baytown: ExxonMobil, 2010. Baytown History Museum and Local History Archives, Sterling Municipal Library, Baytown.

———. *From Humble Beginnings: Exxon Baytown Seventy-Fifth Anniversary, 1920–1995.* Baytown: Exxon Baytown Public Relations Office, 1995. Baytown History Museum and Local History Archives, Sterling Municipal Library, Baytown.

Epperson, Jean La Delle. "William Scott." Monograph, 1989. Local History Archives, Sterling Municipal Library, Baytown.

Fusco, Ralph. "World War II's Effects on Consolidation." In *Baytown Vignettes*. Baytown: Lee College, 1995. Local History Archives, Sterling Municipal Library.

Goose Creek Gasser. 1921. Local History Archives, Sterling Municipal Library, Baytown.

Goose Creek Mirror. 1930. Local History Archives, Sterling Municipal Library, Baytown.

Goose Creek News Tribune. 1933. Local History Archives, Sterling Municipal Library, Baytown.

Goose Creek Semi-Weekly Tribune. 1926–1927. Local History Archives, Sterling Municipal Library, Baytown.

Hampton, Fred. "Power Anywhere There's People." Chicago, ca. 1970. Black Panther Party, Political Pamphlets, P201234, Special Collections, Northwestern University, Evanston, IL.

Harris County, TX. 1850 Census, Harris County, #496, U.S. Census Agricultural Schedules, Harris and Liberty Counties. Harris County Deed Records, m 283, N 11, 226, X 593. Houston Public Library.

———. 1850–1920 Censuses. Harris, Liberty, and Chambers Counties, TX. Houston Public Library.

———. 1860 Census. Harris County, Population and Slave Schedules. Houston Public Library.

———. 1870, 1880, and 1900 Censuses. Harris and Chambers Counties.

———. 1880–2000 Censuses. Houston Public Library.

———. Medical Examiner's Office. "Cause of Death Report, Luis Alfonso Torres." Houston, February 22, 2002.

Henson, Margaret Swett. *The History of Baytown.* Baytown: Baytown Historical Society, 1986. Baytown History Museum and Local History Archives, Sterling Municipal Library, Baytown.

Hispanic Educational Access Committee of Lee College (HEAC). "Cinco de Mayo Celebration." Pamphlet. Baytown, 1998. HEAC Archives, Baytown History Museum.

Houston Chronicle. "Negro Assailant of Mrs. Cowart Is Lynched by Mob of Goose Creek Oilmen." September 21, 1917. Houston Public Library.

Houston Civilian Complaints Forum. Transcript, May 13, 1978. Houston Metropolitan Research Center, Houston Public Library.

Humble Bee. Humble Oil Company newsletter. Local History Archives, Sterling Municipal Library, Baytown.

Jones, I. M. "Deacon." "Historical Sites and Markers." Local History Archives, Sterling Municipal Library, Baytown.

Justice for Pedro Oregon Committee (JPOC). Press release. February 1999. Copy in author's possession.

King, Coretta Scott. "Coretta King Visits with Cesar Chavez in Jail: Asks Blacks to Boycott Lettuce." Letter, December 19, 1970. Box 21, folder 458. Beinecke Rare Book and Manuscript Library, Yale University, New Haven, CT.

League of United Latin American Citizens (LULAC). Resolution. June 29, 2002. http://www.lulac.net/advocacy/resolutions/2002/22.html.

Meldert, Louis Can, ed. *Miscellaneous Issues of Barthea Bulletin, 1914–1915*. July 19, 1919. Local History Archives, Sterling Municipal Library, Baytown.

Mihalik, Michael P. *Baytown Police Department: 50 Years, 1948–1998*. Baytown Historical Society, 1998. Local History Archives, Sterling Municipal Library, Baytown.

National Labor Relations Board (NLRB). Bulletins. Records of the NLRB, National Archives and Records Administration, College Park, MD.

Reigleman, Nicholas. "Baytown's Adolescence: The Early Years." In *From Humble Beginnings: Exxon Baytown Seventy-Fifth Anniversary, 1920–1995*, 26–27. Baytown: Exxon, 1995. Baytown History Museum.

Texas, State of. Title 11, Organized Crime. Chapter 71, Organized Crime. §71.02, Engaging in Organized Criminal Activity. Texas Constitution and Statutes.

Tri-Weekly Telegraph. Houston Public Library.

Webber, Betsy. "Law and Order under Hood and Robe." Baytown: Baytown Historical Society, 1976. Baytown History Museum and Local History Archives, Sterling Municipal Library, Baytown.

Works Progress Administration (WPA), Texas. *Houston: A History and Guide*. Austin: Anson Jones Press, Harris County Historical Society, 1942. Houston Public Library.

MUSICAL RECORDINGS AND FILMS

Ace, Buddy. *The Duke Recordings*. Duke, 2005.

Anderson, Kelly, Tami Gold, and Erik Moe. *Every Mother's Son*. Documentary film. New York: AndersonGold Films, 2004.

Bagwell, Orlando, dir. *Make It Plain*. Documentary film. 1965.

College Boyz. *Radio Fusion Radio*. Virgin, 1992.

Chamillionaire, *The Sound of Revenge*. Universal, 2005.

Chingo Bling. *They Can't Deport Us All*. Asylum Records, 2007.

Geto Boys. *Da Good Da Bad and Da Ugly*. Rap-A-Lot Records, 1998.

———. *The Geto Boys*. Rap-A-Lot Records, 1989.

———. *Resurrection*. Rap-A-Lot Records, 1996.

———. *Till Death Do Us Part*. Rap-A-Lot Records, 1993.

Griffith, D. W., prod., and Christy Chabanne, dir. *Martyrs of the Alamo*. Film. Delta Studios, 1915.

KRS-1. *Return of the Boom Bap*. Jive Records, 1993.

Kweli, Talib. "Papers Please" song and interview. *Smoking Section*, May 18, 2010. http://smokingsection.uproxx.com/.

Low-G and Rasheed. *Wetblack*. Shut 'Em Down Records, 2002.

N.W.A. *Straight Outta Compton*. Los Angeles: Ruthless Records, 1988.

Scott-Heron, Gil. *The Mind of Gil Scott-Heron: A Collection of Poetry and Music*. TVT Records, 1978.

South Park Mexican (SPM). *Hillwood*. Dope House Records, 1995.

————. *Hustle Town*. Dope House Records, 1998.
————. *When Devils Strike*. Dope House Records, 2006.
Tex, Joe. *The Best of Joe Tex*. Dial/Atlantic, 1967.
————. *Hold on to What You've Got*. Dial/Atlantic, 1965.
————. *I've Got to Do a Little Better*. Dial/Atlantic, 1966.
————. *The Love You Save*. Dial/Atlantic, 1966.
————. *The New Boss*. Dial/Atlantic, 1965.
————. *Show Me*. Dial/Atlantic, 1966.
————. *Soul Country*. Dial/Atlantic, 1968.

ORAL HISTORIES

Benavides, Eva. Interview by the author, August 29, 2003, Baytown.
Big Mike (alias). Interview by the author, February 21, 2004, Baytown.
Bustamante, Daniel. Interview by Megan Schneider, April 30, 2008. Oral History Project, Houston Metropolitan Research Center, Houston Public Library.
Campos, Marc. Interview by Megan Schneider, April 18, 2008. Oral History Project, Houston Metropolitan Research Center, Houston Public Library.
Capone (alias). Interview by the author, August 24, 2009, Baytown.
Carroll, J. W. "Oral History Conversation with J. W. Carroll." Interview by Martha Mayo, February 25, 1986. Local History Archives, Sterling Municipal Library, Baytown.
————. "Oral History Conversation with J. W. Carroll." Interview by William J. McNeil, September 29, 1976. Local History Archives, Sterling Municipal Library, Baytown.
Cathriner, Henry. Interview by Olga Haenel, July 10, 1956. Local History Archives, Sterling Municipal Library, Baytown.
Charles, Netra. Interview by the author, July 16, 2009, Baytown.
De Hoyos, Ruben. Interviews by the author, May 22, 2002, and August 26, 2003, Baytown.
Grant, M. Ardella. Interview by Olga Haenel, July 1, 1957. Local History Archives, Sterling Municipal Library, Baytown.
Green, Alan. Interview by the author, July 3, 2009, Washington, DC.
Hamilton, Ron. Interview by the author, June 22, 2009, Baytown.
Hernandez, Marga. Interview by the author, August 30, 2003, Baytown.
Herring, G. R. Interview by Olga Haenel, July 9, 1956, Local History Archives, Sterling Municipal Library, Baytown.
Herring, Garrett R. "Oral History Conversation with Garrett Herring." Interviews by Sara Swafford, February 7 and 14, 1980. Local History Archives, Sterling Municipal Library, Baytown.
Hildenbrand, Frankie. Interview by the author, November 20, 2001, Baytown.
Jefferson, Howard. Interview by David Goldstein, May 15, 2008. Oral History Project, Houston Metropolitan Research Center, Houston Public Library.
Lawson, (Reverend) William. Interview by Veronica Perry, August 12, 1974. Oral History Project, Houston Metropolitan Research Center, Houston Public Library.
Martinez, Arthur. Interview by the author, August 27, 2003, Baytown.
Martinez, Hilda. Interview by the author, August 27, 2003, Baytown.
Moreno, Virginia. "Oral History Conversation with Virginia Moreno." Interview by Myra Hornberger, April 17, 1980. Local History Archives, Sterling Municipal Library, Baytown.

Myers, Chris. Interview by Olga Haenel, July 22, 1956. Local History Archives, Sterling Municipal Library, Baytown.

Rangel, Homero. Interview by the author, August 25, 2009, Baytown.

Rivere, Virgie. "Oral History Conversation with Virgie Rivere." N.d. Local History Archives, Sterling Municipal Library, Baytown.

Rude-Boi (alias). Interview by the author, June 24, 2009, Baytown.

Shannon, Bess. Interviews by Olga Haenel, July 11, 12, and 16, 1956. Local History Archives, Sterling Municipal Library, Baytown.

Silva, Lorraine. "Oral History Conversation with Lorraine Silva." Interview by Ann Ruland, November 28, 1976. Local History Archives, Sterling Municipal Library, Baytown.

Tidmon, W. O. "Oral History Conversation with W. O. Tidmon." August 11, 1976. Local History Archives, Sterling Municipal Library, Baytown.

Tidmon, W. O., Omar Dyer, and Jimmy Carroll. "The Ku Klux Klan in Baytown: An Interview with W. O. Tidmon, Omar Dyer, and Jimmy Carroll." Interview by Betsy Webber and Bill McNeil, August 13, 1976, Baytown. Local History Archives, Sterling Municipal Library, Baytown.

Vic (alias). Interview by the author, February 18, 2008, Baytown.

Wilson, Michael Ray. Interview by the author, August 27, 2003, Baytown.

Wilson, Ray. Interview by the author, August 27, 2003, Baytown.

Young, Charles. "Oral History Conversation with Charles Young." August 31, 1988. Local History Archives, Sterling Municipal Library, Baytown.

Young, Hazel Haynesworth. Interview by Elma Barrera, October 5, 2007. Oral History Project, Houston Metropolitan Research Center, Houston Public Library.

SECONDARY SOURCES

Ackerman, Todd. "LULAC Wants Probe into Death." *Houston Chronicle*, June 30, 2002.

Acuña, Rodolfo. *Occupied America: The Chicano Struggle for Liberation*. New York: Harper and Row, 1972.

Ahmad, Muneer. "Homeland Insecurities: Racial Violence the Day after September 11." *Social Text* 72 (2002): 101–115.

Almaguer, Tomás. *Racial Fault Lines: The Historical Origins of White Supremacy in California*. Berkeley: University of California Press, 1994.

Althusser, Louis. "Ideology and Ideological State Apparatuses." In *Lenin and Philosophy*, ed. Ben Brewster, 127–186. London: NewLeft Books, 1971.

Alvarez, Luis. *The Power of the Zoot: Youth Culture and Resistance during World War II*. Berkeley: University of California Press, 2008.

Alvarez, Luis, and Daniel Widener. "Brown-Eyed Soul: Popular Music and Cultural Politics in Los Angeles." In *The Struggle in Black and Brown: African American and Mexican American Relations during the Civil Rights Era*, ed. Brian Behnken, 211–236. Lincoln: University of Nebraska Press, 2011.

American Civil Liberties Union (ACLU). "¿Cómo se dice Rodney King en español? Posters Promote Reform, Commemorate Texas Victim of Police Brutality." Press statement, October 15, 2002.

———. *Driving while Black*. See David A. Harris.

———. "The Luis Torres Story" posters. 2002. http://www.aclu.org/FilesPDFs/aclu%20 torres%20finals%20v3.pdf.

Amnesty International. *Rights for All: Amnesty International's Campaign on the United States of America*. New York: Amnesty International, 2000.

Anderson, Gary. 1983. "Whither Houston." *Houston Post*, December 5.

Anderson, Talmadge. "Comparative Experience Factors among Black, Asian, and Hispanic Americans: Coalition or Conflicts?" *Journal of Black Politics* 23, no. 1 (September 1992): 27–38.

Anti-Defamation League. "New Black Panther Party for Self-Defense." http://www.adl.org.

Anzaldúa, Gloria. *Borderlands/La Frontera: The New Mestiza*. 3d edition. San Francisco: Spinster/Aunt Lute, 2007.

Aptheker, Herbert. *American Negro Slave Revolts*. New York: International, 1943.

Ashenfelter, David, and Joe Swickard. "Detroit Cops Are Deadliest in U.S." *Detroit Free Press*, May 15, 2000.

Associated Press. "Baytown Police Say Teen Shooting Was Accident." June 28, 1997.

Barr, Alwyn. *Black Texans: A History of African Americans in Texas, 1528–1995*. Norman: University of Oklahoma Press, 1996.

Baytown Sun. "Criminal Gangs in Our Neighborhoods." Editorial, October 27, 1993.

———. "Vocal Group Demands Justice in Torres Case." May 4, 2002.

Beeth, Howard, and Cary D. Wintz, eds. *Black Dixie: Afro-Texan History and Culture in Houston*. College Station: Texas A&M University Press, 1992.

Behnken, Brian. *Fighting Their Own Battles: Mexican Americans, African Americans, and the Struggle for Civil Rights in Texas*. Chapel Hill: University of North Carolina Press, 2011.

Benavides, Eva. Letter. *Baytown Sun*, June 15, 2002.

Bender, Steven W. *Greasers and Gringos: Latinos, Law, and the American Imagination*. New York: New York University Press, 2004.

Bendixen and Associates, New Media Organization. "Deep Divisions, Shared Destiny: A Poll of African Americans, Hispanics, and Asian Americans on Race Relations." December 12, 2007. http://www.bendixenandassociates.com/studies2007.html. Accessed September 17, 2009.

Benjamin, Walter. *Walter Benjamin: Selected Writings*. Vol. 1: *1913–1926*. Ed. Marcus Bullock and Michael Jennings, trans. Edmund Jephcott. Cambridge, MA: Belknap, Harvard University Press, 2004.

Berger, Eric. "Justice Sought after Man Dies in Custody." *Houston Chronicle*, March 4, 2002.

Bernstein, Jake. "Video of a Police Killing Produces Shockwaves in Baytown, Texas." *Texas Observer*, March 29, 2002. http://www.texasobserver.org/showArticle.asp?ArticleID=597. Accessed April 4, 2002.

Bhabha, Homi K. "The Aesthetics of Barbaric Transmission." Public lecture at (World) Art? Art History and Global Practice Conference, Northwestern University, Evanston, IL, May 23, 2008.

———. *The Location of Culture*. New York: Routledge, 1994.

Bina, Cyrus. *The Economics of the Oil Crisis*. New York: St. Martin's Press, 1985.

Blackman, Lisa, John Cromby, Derek Hook, Dimitris Papadopoulos, and Valerie Walkerdine. "Creating Subjectivities," *Subjectivity* 22 (2008): 1–27.

Bloom, David. "Torres Case Challenges City Public Relations." *Baytown Sun*, March 31, 2002.

———. "The Torres Videotape." Editorial. *Baytown Sun*, March 3, 2002.

Borjas, George, Jeffrey Grogger, and Gordon H. Hanson. "Immigration and African American Employment Opportunities: The Response of Wages, Employment, and Incarceration to Labor Supply Shock." NBER Working Paper 12518. Washington, DC: National Bureau of Economic Research (NBER), September 2006.

Botson, Michael. "We're Sticking by Our Union: The Battle for Baytown, 1942–1943. *Houston History* 8, no. 7 (2011): 8–14.

Bourdieu, Pierre, and Loic Wacquant. *An Invitation to Reflexive Sociology*. Chicago: University of Chicago Press, 1992.

Bracey John H. Jr., August Meier, and Elliott Rudwick, eds. *Black Nationalism in America*. Indianapolis, IN: Bobbs Merrill, 1970.

Brown, Elaine. *A Taste of Power: A Black Woman's Story*. New York: Anchor Books, 1993.

Brown, Elsa Barkley. "Womanist Consciousness: Maggie Lena Walker and the Independent Order of Saint Luke." *Signs* 14 (1989): 610–633.

Bullard, Robert D. *Dumping in Dixie: Race, Class, and Environmental Inequality*. New York: Westview Press, 1988.

———. *Invisible Houston: The Black Experience in Boom and Bust*. College Station: Texas A&M University Press, 1987.

Caballero, Alex. "Alabama Plans to Bring Back Slavery for Latinos." *The Guardian*, October 12, 2011.

Campbell, Howard. *Drug War Zone: Dispatches from the U.S.-Mexico Border*. Austin: University of Texas Press, 2009.

Campbell, Randolph B. *An Empire for Slavery: The Peculiar Institution in Texas, 1821–1865*. Baton Rouge: Louisiana State University Press, 1989.

Canclini, Néstor García. *Hybrid Cultures*. Minneapolis: University of Minnesota Press, 1990.

Cano, Gustavo. "Orale! Politics: Mobilization of Mexican Immigrants in Chicago and Houston." In *Inside Urban Politics: Voices from America's Cities and Suburbs*, ed. Dick Simpson, 38–50. New York: Pearson Longman, 2004.

Carlson, Eugene. "Would You Believe Houston as a New–Business Hot Spot?" *Wall Street Journal*, December 2, 1986.

Carlton, Don E., and Thomas E. Kreneck. "Houston Back Where We Started." Pamphlet. Houston: De Menil, 1979.

Carmichael, Stokely, and Charles Hamilton. *Black Power: The Politics of Liberation in America*. Random House: New York, 1967.

Carrigan, William D., and Clive Webb. "The Lynching of Persons of Mexican Origin or Descent in the United States, 1848 to 1928." *Journal of Social History* 37, no. 2 (2003): 411–438.

Carson, Clayborne. *In Struggle: SNCC and the Black Awakening of the 1960s*. Cambridge, MA: Harvard University Press, 1981.

Cash, Wanda Garner. "Baytown's Response." Editorial. *Baytown Sun*, March 16, 2002.

———. "The Latest Misstep." Editorial. *Baytown Sun*, March 27, 2002.

Castaneda, Ruben. "LA Job Fight: A Bitter Struggle or an Alliance?" *California Tomorrow*, Winter 1989, 7.

Chafe, William H. *Civilities and Civil Rights: Greensboro, North Carolina, and the Black Struggle for Freedom*. New York: Oxford University Press, 1981.

Chakrabarty, Dipesh. "Belatedness as Possibility: Subaltern Histories, Once More." In *The Indian Postcolonial: A Critical Reader*, ed. Elleke Boehmer and Rosinka Chaudhuri, 163–176. London: Routledge, 2011.

Chang, Jeff. *Can't Stop, Won't Stop: A History of the Hip-Hop Generation.* New York: St. Martin's Press, 2005.

Checker, Melissa. *Polluted Promises: Environmental Racism and the Search for Justice in a Southern Town.* New York: New York University Press, 2005.

Cheng, Anne Anlin. *The Melancholy of Race: Psychoanalysis, Assimilation, and Hidden Grief.* New York: Oxford University Press, 2001.

Chude-Sokei, Louis. "Redefining 'Black': Obama's Candidacy Spotlights the Divide between Native Black Culture and African Immigrants." *Los Angeles Times,* February 18, 2007.

CNN. "3 Whites Indicted in Dragging Death of Black Man in Texas." July 6, 1998.

———. "Where Are the Jobs? Look to Baytown, Texas." Blog post, May 20, 2011.

Colaguori, Claudio. "Symbolic Violence and the Violation of Human Rights: Continuing the Sociological Critique of Domination." *International Journal of Criminology and Sociological Theory* 3, no. 2 (2010): 380–400.

Collins, Patricia Hill. "Learning from the Outsider Within: The Sociological Significance of Black Feminist Thought." *Social Problems* 33 (1986): 514–532.

Cook, Matthew. "Activists Suggest State Help in Torres Case." *Baytown Sun,* June 9, 2002.

———. "Citizens Hope to Bridge Gap with Police." *Baytown Sun,* June 8, 2002.

———. "City to Release Tape of Torres Arrest Today." *Baytown Sun,* March 1, 2002.

———. "Enhanced Video of Torres Reinforces Opinions." *Baytown Sun,* March 23, 2002.

———. "Family of Man Who Died in Police Custody to Sue City," *Baytown Sun,* February 21, 2002.

———. "FBI Investigating Death of Luis Torres." *Baytown Sun,* February 26, 2002.

———. "Grand Jury Declines to Indict Baytown Cops." *Baytown Sun,* May 3, 2002.

———. "Hispanic Community Rallies in Support." *Baytown Sun,* March 4, 2002.

———. "Houston Activists Planning Response to Torres Ruling." *Baytown Sun,* May 10, 2002.

———. "Jones Clarifies 'Misinformation' in Case." *Baytown Sun,* March 27, 2002.

———. "LULAC Delegates Want Resolution." *Baytown Sun,* June 27, 2002.

———. "Man Dies in Police Custody after Pepper Spray." *Baytown Sun,* January 21, 2002.

———. "March on Market Street to Honor Torres." *Baytown Sun,* March 8, 2002.

———. "Quanell X Leads 2nd Baytown Rally." *Baytown Sun,* April 29, 2002.

———. "Quanell X Leads Rally on Steps of Baytown PD." *Baytown Sun,* March 11, 2002.

———. "Torres Case Heads to Grand Jury." *Baytown Sun,* April 24, 2002.

———. "Torres Death Called a 'Homicide.'" *Baytown Sun,* February 22, 2002.

———. "'We Seek to Bring Justice to This Community.'" *Baytown Sun,* June 21, 2002.

Cooper, Jonathan. "McNair Rally Brings Racism to the Forefront." *Baytown Sun,* March 16, 2002.

———. "Residents Rally for Civil Rights Group in Baytown." *Baytown Sun,* March 18, 2002.

Costello, Maureen. "Alabama's Immigration Law: The New Jim Crow." *Huffington Post,* June 15, 2011.

Coulthard, Glenn. "Subjects of Empire: Indigenous Peoples and the 'Politics of Recognition in Canada.'" *Contemporary Political Theory* 6, no. 4 (2007): 437–460.

Cox, Laurence. "Gramsci, Movements, and Method: The Politics of Activist Research." In *Fourth International Conference on Alternative Futures and Popular Protest,* ed. Colin

Barker and Mike Tyldesley. Manchester, England: Manchester Metropolitan University, 1998.

Cox, Laurence, and Colin Barker. "'What Have the Romans Ever Done for Us?' Activist and Academic Forms of Movement Theorizing." In *Proceedings of the Eighth International Conference on Alternative Futures and Popular Protest*, ed. Colin Barker and Mike Tyldesley. Manchester, England: Manchester Metropolitan University, 2002.

Cox, Laurence, and Caitriona Mullan. "Social Movements Never Died: Community Politics and the Social Economy in the Irish Republic." In *International Sociological Association and British Sociological Association Special Movements Conference*, Manchester, England, November 2001.

Crowe, Robert. "Torres Aftermath Leaves Deep Wounds in Baytown." *Houston Chronicle*, June 13, 2002.

———. "Torres Case Heads to Grand Jury." *Baytown Sun*. Thursday, April 24.

Cruse, Harold. *The Crisis of the Negro Intellectual*. New York: Morrow, 1967.

Dallas Morning News. "Priest Urges Latin-Negro Axis." August 13, 1967.

Daniels, Anne R. "Baytown during the Depression, 1929–1933." Master's thesis, Lamar University. Beaumont, TX, 1981.

Davidson, Chandler. *Bi-Racial Politics: Conflict and Coalition in the Metropolitan South*. Baton Rouge: Louisiana State University Press, 1982.

Dávila, Arlene. *Latino Spin: Public Image and the Whitewashing of Race*. New York City: New York University Press, 2008.

de la Teja, Jesus. *San Antonio de Bexar: A Community on New Spain's Northern Frontier*. Albuquerque: University of New Mexico Press, 1996.

De León, Arnoldo. *Ethnicity in the Sunbelt: Mexican Americans in Houston*. College Station: Texas A&M University Press, 2001.

———. *They Called Them Greasers: Anglo Attitudes Towards Mexicans in Texas: 1826–1836*. Austin: University of Texas Press, 1986.

Delgado, Richard R., and Jean Stefancic, eds. *The Latina/o Condition: A Critical Reader*. New York: New York University Press, 1998.

DeNike, James H. "Energy Shortage Boost to Economy in This Area." *Houston Chronicle*, January 16, 1980.

Derrida, Jacques. "Force of Law: The Mystical Foundation of Authority." In *Deconstruction and the Possibility of Justice*, ed. Drucilla Cornell, Michel Rosenfeld, and David Gray Carlson, 3–67. New York: Routledge, 1992.

———. *Margins of Philosophy*. Trans. Alan Bass. Chicago: University of Chicago Press, 1982.

Despres, Leo E., ed. *Ethnicity and Resource Competition in Plural Societies*. The Hague: Mouton, 1975.

Djebar, Assia. *Fantasia: An Algerian Cavalcade*. New York: Heinemann, 1993.

Du Bois, W. E. B. *The Souls of Black Folk*. Boston: Dover, 1903.

Dyer, James, Arnold Vedlitz, and Stephen Worchel. "Social Distance among Racial and Ethnic Groups in Texas: Some Demographic Correlates." *Social Science Quarterly* 70, no. 3 (September 1989): 607–616.

Economides, Michael, and Ronald Oligney. *The Color of Oil*. Katy, TX: Round Oak, 2000.

Edmondson, J. R. *The Alamo Story—From History to Current Conflicts*. Plano, TX: Republic of Texas Press, 2000.

Ellison, Ralph. *Shadow and Act*. New York: Vintage, 1964.

Escobar, Edward. *Race, Police, and the Making of a Political Identity: Mexican Americans and the Los Angeles Police Department, 1900–1945*. Berkeley: University of California Press, 1999.

Espiritu, Yen Le. "Disciplines Unbound: Notes on Sociology and Ethnic Studies." *Contemporary Sociology* 28 (1999): 510–514.

Everett-Haynes, La Monica. "Latino Students Recruited by Black Colleges." *Houston Chronicle*, October 15, 2004.

Fanon, Frantz. *Black Skin, White Masks*. New York: Grove Press, 1952.

———. *The Wretched of the Earth*. New York: Grove Press, 1963.

Feagin, Joe R. *Free Enterprise City: Houston in Political and Economic Perspective*. New Brunswick, NJ: Rutgers University Press, 1988.

Ferreira da Silva, Denise. "No-Bodies: Law, Raciality, and Violence." *Griffith Law Review* 18, no. 2 (2009): 212–236.

———. "Towards a Critique of the Socio-Logos of Justice: The Analytics of Raciality and the Production of University." *Social Identities* 7, no. 3 (2001): 421–454.

———. *Towards a Global Idea of Race*. Minneapolis: University of Minnesota Press, 2007.

Fisher, Ian. "In Striving Section of the Bronx, the Races Mix but Don't Mingle." *New York Times*, January 2, 1993.

Fitzpatrick, Peter. *The Myth of Modern Law*. London: Blackwell, 1992.

Flores, Juan. *From Bomba to Hip-Hop: Puerto Rican Culture and Latino Identity*. New York City: Columbia University Press, 2000.

Foley, Neil. "Becoming Hispanic: Mexican Americans and the Faustian Pact with Whiteness." In *Reflexiones 1997: New Directions in Mexican American Studies*, ed. Neil Foley, 53–69. Austin: Center for Mexican American Studies, University of Texas, 1998.

———. "Over the Rainbow: *Hernandez v. Texas*, *Brown v. Board of Education*, and *Black v. Brown*." *Chicano-Latino Law Review* 25 (2005): 139–152.

———. *Quest for Equality: The Failed Promise of Black-Brown Solidarity*. Cambridge, MA: Harvard University Press, 2010.

———. *The White Scourge: Mexicans, Blacks, and Poor Whites in Texas Cotton Culture*. Berkeley: University of California Press, 1997.

Foucault, Michel. *The History of Sexuality*. Vol. 1: *An Introduction*. Trans. Robert Hurley. New York: Pantheon Books, 1976.

———. *Psychiatric Power: Lectures at the Collège de France, 1973–1974*, ed. Jacques Lagrange. London: Palgrave, 2006.

———. *Society Must Be Defended: Lectures at the Collège de France, 1975–1976*. New York: Picador, 2003.

Fountain, Ken. "Murder Charges Filed in Pine Street Slaying." *Baytown Sun*, April 21, 2006.

———. "Murder Suspect Arrested in Highlands." *Baytown Sun*, April 27, 2006.

———. "Suspects Sought in Pine Street Slaying." *Baytown Sun*, April 4, 2006.

Fox News (from Associated Press). "Black-Hispanic Gang Rivalries Plague Los Angeles." August 12, 2006.

Frere-Jones, Sasha. "A Place in the Sun: Houston Hip-Hop Takes Over." *New Yorker*, November 14, 2005.

Gallacher, Andy. "Huge Rally in Small-Town Louisiana." BBC News, September 21, 2007.

Gilroy, Paul. "British Cultural Studies and the Pitfalls of Identity." In *Cultural Studies and Communications*, ed. J. Curran, D. Morley, and V. Walkerdine, 34–49. London: Arnold, 1996.

———. "Paul Gilroy Speaks on the Riots, August 2011, Tottenham, North London." Blog post. *Dream of Safety*, August 16, 2011.

Giroux, Henry A. *Against the New Authoritarianism: Politics after Abu-Ghraib.* Winnipeg, Canada: Arbeiter Ring, 2005.

Gluck, Sherna B. *Rosie the Riveter Revisited: Women, the War, and Social Change.* Boston: Twayne, 1987.

Goldberg, David Theo. "The New Segregation." *Race and Society* 1 (1998): 15–32.

———. *The Racial State.* London: Blackwell, 2000.

Gonzales-Day, Ken. *Lynching in the West: 1850–1935.* Durham, NC: Duke University Press, 2006.

Gonzalez, Allyson. "Decision Needs to Be Made on Police Chief." *Baytown Sun*, June 16, 2002.

———. "Jones: 'We'll Just Have To Work Harder.'" *Baytown Sun*, June 14, 2002.

———. "LULAC Approves Resolution Degrading Baytown." *Baytown Sun*, June 30, 2002.

———. "Memories Run Deep for Old Carver School." *Baytown Sun*, June 21, 2002.

———. "People Have Not Forgotten This Day," *Baytown Sun*, June 20, 2002.

Goodwyn, Wade. "Beating Charges Split La. Town along Racial Lines." *All Things Considered*, National Public Radio, July 30, 2007.

Gordon, Avery F. *Ghostly Matters: Haunting and the Sociological Imagination.* Minneapolis: University of Minnesota Press, 2008.

Grammer, Cleveland. "Houston Recovery Foreseen, but Not in '86." *Houston Post*, January 24, 1986.

Gramsci, Antonio. *Prison Notebooks*, vol. 2. New York: Columbia University Press, 1998.

———. *Selections from the Prison Notebooks of Antonio Gramsci.* Ed. Q. Hoare and G. Novell-Smith. New York: International, 1971.

Greene, Casey. "Guardians against Change: The Ku Klux Klan in Houston and Harris County, 1920–1925." (University of Houston Center for Public History) *Houston History* 8, no. 1, *Confronting Jim Crow* (Fall 2010): 1–5.

Gregory, Stephen. *Black Corona: Race and the Politics of Place in an Urban Community.* Princeton, NJ: Princeton University Press, 1999.

Griffin, John D., and Brian Newman. *Minority Report: Evaluating Political Equality in America.* Chicago: University of Chicago Press, 2008.

Griffin, Kari. "Killer Gets 25 Years." *Baytown Sun*, July 22, 2008.

Gugliemo, Thomas A. "Fighting for Caucasian Rights: Mexicans, Mexican Americans, and the Transnational Struggle for Civil Rights in World War II Texas." *Journal of American History* 92 (March 2006): 1212–1237.

Guthman, Laura. "More Latinos Identify as Native Americans, Census Shows." CNN, September 30, 2011.

Gutiérrez, David G. *Walls and Mirrors: Mexican Americans, Mexican Immigrants, and the Politics of Ethnicity.* Berkeley: University of California Press, 1995.

Gutierrez, Ramon A. "Ethnic Studies: Its Evolution in American Colleges and Universities." In *Multiculturalism: A Critical Reader*, ed. David Theo Goldberg, 157–167. London: Blackwell, 1994.

Haas, Jeffrey. *The Assassination of Fred Hampton: How the Chicago Police and the FBI Murdered a Black Panther.* Chicago: Chicago Review Press, 2010.

Haenel, Olga Miller. "A Social History of Baytown, Texas, 1912–1956." Master's thesis, University of Texas, Austin, 1958.

Hall, Stuart. "Gramsci's Relevance to the Study of Race and Ethnicity." *Journal of Communication Inquiry* 10 (1986): 5–27.

———. "New Ethnicities." In *Race," Culture, and Difference*, ed. James Donald and Ali Rattansi, 252–259. London: Sage, 1992.

———. "Who Needs 'Identity'?" In *Questions of Cultural Identity*, ed. Stuart Hall and P. du Gay, 1–17. London: Sage, 1996.

Hall, Stuart, David Morley, and Kuan-Hsing Chen. *Stuart Hall: Critical Dialogues in Cultural Studies*. London: Routledge, 1996.

Haney-López, Ian. "Race and Colorblindness after Hernandez and Brown." *Chicano-Latino Law Review* 25 (2005): 61–76.

———. "White Latinos." *Harvard Latino Law Review* 6 (2003): 1.

Hardt, Michael. "Militant Life." *New Left Review* 2, no. 64 (2010): 151–160.

Harris, David A. *Driving while Black: Racial Profiling on Our Nation's Highways*. ACLU special report, June 1999. http://www.aclu.org/racial-justice/driving-while-black-racial -profiling-our-nations-highways.

Hartman, Saidiya. *Lose Your Mother: A Journey along the Atlantic Slave Route*. New York: Farrar, Straus, and Giroux, 2008.

Harvey, David. *The Condition of Postmodernity: An Enquiry into the Origins of Cultural Change*. New York: Blackwell, 1990.

Haynes, Robert V. *A Night of Violence: The Houston Riot of 1917*. Baton Rouge: Louisiana State University Press, 1976.

Hernandez, Michael V. "Bridging Gibraltar: Latina/os as Agents of Reconciliation in Relations between Black and White America." *La Raza Law Journal* 11, no. 2 (1999–2000): 99–111.

Hernandez, Tanya K. "Roots of Anger: Longtime Prejudices, Not Economic Rivalry, Fuel Latino-Black Tensions." Op-ed. *Los Angeles Times*, January 7, 2007.

Hesse, Barnor. "Racialized Modernity: An Analytics of White Mythologies." *Racial and Ethnic Studies* 30 (2007): 643–663.

Hine, Darlene Clark. *Black Women in White: Racial Conflict and Cooperation in the Nursing Profession, 1890–1950*. Bloomington: Indiana University Press, 1989.

Holland, Sharon. *Raising the Dead: Readings of Death and (Black) Subjectivity*. Durham, NC: Duke University Press, 2002.

Holmes, Malcolm, and Brad Smith. "Race, Threat, and Police Brutality: A Social Psychological Perspective." Paper presented at the annual meeting of the American Society of Criminology (ASC), Los Angeles, November 1, 2006.

Hopkins, Terence E., and Immanuel Wallerstein, eds. *The Age of Transition: Trajectory of the World System: 1945–2025*. London: Zed Books, 1996.

Horne, Gerald. *Black and Brown: African Americans and the Mexican Revolution, 1910–1920*. New York: New York University Press, 2005.

Horsman, Reginald. *Race and Manifest Destiny: Origins of American Racial Anglo-Saxonism*. Cambridge, MA: Harvard University Press, 1981.

Horswell, Cindy. "Baytown Going to War against Gangs," *Houston Chronicle*, September 20, 1992.

———. "Baytown Turf War Takes Toll in Blood." *Houston Chronicle*, January 11, 1987.

———. "Bridging a Big GAP." *Houston Chronicle*, October 18, 1992.

———. "Gangs in Baytown, Parallels on Opposite Turf." *Houston Chronicle*, May 19, 1991.

———. "Man Fled Hospital before Death." *Houston Chronicle*, February 27, 2002.

———. "Officers Cleared in Death." *Houston Chronicle*, May 3, 2002.

———. "Police to Release Video of Torres." *Houston Chronicle*, March 1, 2002.

———. "Rehearing Sought in Baytown Death." *Houston Chronicle*, April 10, 1991.

———. "'We Are Living in the Most Violent Society in the World.'" *Houston Chronicle*, October 2, 1991.

Horswell, Cindy, and Edward Hegstrom. "Baytown Chief Backs Officers In Fatal Fight." *Houston Chronicle*, February 23, 2002.

Houston Business Journal. "Low Oil Prices, Oversupply of Space Could Slow Growth." January 14, 1985.

Houston Chronicle. "Can't Tolerate Street Gangs." Editorial, January 13, 1987.

———. "Police Scrutiny, Baytown 'Homicide' Case Cannot Be Ignored." Editorial, April 12, 2002.

Houston Post. "Houston to Continue to Offer Business Growth, Experts Say." January 15, 1982.

Hughes, Langston, and Arne Botemps, *Boy on the Border.* El Paso, TX: Sweet Earth Flying Press, 2009.

Hughes, Michael A., and Bradley R. Hertel. "The Significance of Color Remains: A Study of Life Chances, Mate Selection, and Ethnic Consciousness among Black Americans." *Social Forces* 68, no. 4 (1990): 1105–1120.

Human Rights Watch. *Shielded from Justice: Police Brutality and Accountability in the United States.* June 1998. http://www.hrw.org/legacy/reports98/police/index.htm.

Huntington, Samuel. "The Hispanic Challenge." *Foreign Policy*, March 1, 2004.

Hutchinson, Earl Ofari. "The Black-Latino Blame Game: Finger-Pointing between the Two Minorities Is Not Going to Help Either Group." Op-ed. *Los Angeles Times*, November 25, 2007.

———. "Discrimination, Not Illegal Immigration, Fuels Black Job Crisis." *New America Media*, April 24, 2006.

Hyde, Samuel C. Jr. *Sunbelt Revolution: The Historical Progression of the Civil Rights Struggle in the Gulf South, 1866–2000.* Gainesville: University Press of Florida, 2003.

Iton, Richard J. *In Search of the Black Fantastic: Politics and Popular Culture in the Post-Civil Rights Era.* New York: Oxford University Press, 2008.

Jackson, Byran A., and Preston, Michael B., eds. *Racial and Ethnic Politics in California.* Berkeley: IGS Press, Institute of Governmental Studies, University of California, Berkeley, 1991.

Jackson, John L. Jr. *Harlemworld: Doing Race and Class in Contemporary Black America.* Chicago: University Of Chicago Press, 2003.

Jackson, Kenneth T. *The Ku Klux Klan in the City, 1915–1930.* Urban Life in America Series. New York: Oxford University Press, 1967.

Jimenez, Felix. "Dangerous Liaisons." *Hispanic*, April 1991, 13–18.

Johnson, Benjamin Heber. *Revolution in Texas: How a Forgotten Rebellion and Its Bloody Suppression Turned Mexicans into Americans* (New Haven, CT: Yale University Press, 2005.

Johnson, E. Patrick. *Appropriating Blackness: Performance and the Politics of Authenticity.* Durham, NC: Duke University Press, 2003.

———. *Sweet Tea: Black Gay Men of the South.* Chapel Hill: University of North Carolina Press, 2008.

Kaplan, David. "Vietnam Refugees, a True Success Story." *Houston Chronicle*, April 29, 2005.

Kaufman, Leslie. "Feeling the Pinch on Luxury Leather." *New York Times*, March 29, 2001.

Kelley, Robin D.G. *Freedom Dreams: The Black Radical Imagination*. Boston: Beacon Press, 2002.

———. *Race Rebels*. New York: Free Press, 1994.

———. *Yo Mama's DisFUNKtional! Fighting the Culture Wars in Urban America*. Boston: Beacon Press, 1998.

Kennedy, Randall. *Nigger: The Strange Career of a Troublesome Word*. New York: Vintage, 2003.

Kever, Jeanie. "It's School, or Hard Knocks, in Baytown." *Houston Chronicle*, October 30, 2011.

Khanna, Roma, and Lise Olsen, "A Chronicle Special Report: Few Police Punished in Shootings." *Houston Chronicle*, July 26, 2004.

Kim, Claire Jean. *Bitter Fruit: The Politics of Black-Korean Conflict in New York City*. New Haven, CT: Yale University Press, 2000.

Kinghorn, Austin. "McNair Honors Outstanding Residents." *Baytown Sun*, June 21, 2002.

———. "Protesters at Third Baytown Rally." *Baytown Sun*, June 24, 2002.

Kingston, Mike. *A Concise History of Texas*. Houston: Taylor Trade, 1991.

Kliewer, Terry. "Houston May Again Become a 'Boom Town,' Economic Consultant Says." *Houston Post*, August 12, 1983.

Klineberg, Stephen L. "The Changing Face of Houston: Tracking the Economic and Demographic Transformations through 29 Years of Houston Surveys." Houston: Kinder Institute of Urban Research, Rice University, 2010.

———. *Houston's Economic and Demographic Transformations: Findings from the Expanded Survey of Houston's Ethnic Communities*. Houston: Kinder Institute for Urban Research, Rice University, 2002.

Krieger, Nancy, Steven Sidney, and Eugenie Coakley. "Racial Discrimination and Skin Color in the CARDIA Study: Implications for Public Health Research." *American Journal of Public Health* 88, no. 9 (September 1998): 1308–1313.

Lardner, George, and Lois Romano. "Bush Name Helps Fuel Oil Dealings." *Houston Post*, July 30, 1999.

Larson, Henrietta, and Kenneth Wiggins Porter. *History of Humble Oil and Refining Company: A Study in Industrial Growth*. New York: Harper and Brothers, 1959.

Lawrence, Aten. *Indians of the Upper Texas Coast*. New York: Academic Press, 1983.

Lee, Jane Howard. "Three Years Later, Sister Still Wants Answers." *Baytown Sun*, April 1, 2009.

Levander. Caroline. "Sutton Griggs and the Borderlands of Empire." *American Literary History* 22, no. 1 (2010): 57–84.

Llorca, Juan Carlos. "West Texas WWII Vet to Get Posthumous Purple Heart." *Huffington Post*, December 6, 2012.

Lomax, John Nova. "Hip-Hop Tejas: Latinos Take on Rap Music and Make It Their Own." *Houston Press*, December 4, 1995.

———. "South Park Monster." *Houston Press*, June 6, 2002.

López, Antonio R. "In the Spirit of Liberation: Race, Governmentality, and the De-Colonial Politics of the Original Rainbow Coalition of Chicago." PhD diss., University of Texas at El Paso, 2012.

Mabro, Robert, ed. *The 1986 Oil Price Crisis: Economic Effects and Policy Responses. Proceedings of the Eighth Oxford Energy Seminar*. New York: Oxford University Press, 1988.

Mack, Kristen. "Court Ruling Sparks Outrage." *Houston Chronicle*, May 3, 2002.

———. "Death in Baytown Struggle Called Abuse of Police Power." *Houston Chronicle*, April 24, 2002.

Madison, D. Soyini. "Critical Ethnography as Street Performance: Reflections of Home, Race, Murder, and Justice." In *The Sage Handbook of Qualitative Research*, ed. Norman K. Denzin and Yvonna S. Lincoln, 537–546. Thousand Oaks, CA: Sage, 2005.

———. *Critical Ethnography: Method, Ethics, and Performance*. Thousand Oaks, CA: Sage, 2005.

Maldonado Torres, Nelson. *Against War: Views from the Underside of Modernity*. Durham, NC: Duke University Press, 2008.

Maranica, Jon. "Seeping out of Houston, Slowly." *New York Times*, June 4, 2010.

Mariscal, George. *Brown-Eyed Children of the Sun: Lessons from the Chicano Movement, 1965–1975*. Albuquerque: University of New Mexico Press, 2005.

Márquez, John D. "The Black Mohicans: Representations of Everyday Violence in Postracial Urban America." *American Quarterly* 64, no. 3 (2012): 625–651.

———. "Latinos as the 'Living Dead': Raciality, Expendability, and Border Militarization." *Latino Studies* 10, no. 4 (2012): 473–498.

———. "Nations Re-Bound: Race and Biopolitics at EU and US Borders." In *Europe in Black and White: Immigration, Race, and Identity in the "Old Continent,"* ed. Manuela Ribeiro Sanches, Fernando Clara, João Ferreira Duarte, and Leonor Pires Martins. London/Chicago: Intellect Books/University of Chicago Press, 2010.

Martel, James. "Waiting for Justice: Benjamin and Derrida on Sovereignty and Immanence." *Republics of Letters: A Journal for the Study of Knowledge, Politics, and the Arts* 2, no. 2 (June 1, 2011): N.p. http://rofl.stanford.edu/node/92.

Martin, Lia. "Activists Speak out against Grand Jury." *Baytown Sun*, May 9, 2002.

Massey, Douglas S. *Categorically Unequal: The American Stratification System*. New York: Russell Sage Foundation, 2007.

McClain, Paula D. "The Changing Dynamics of Urban Politics: Black and Hispanic Municipal Employment—Is There Competition?" *Journal of Politics* 55 (1993): 399–414.

McComb, David G. *Houston: A History*. Austin: University of Texas Press, 1969.

McFadden, Neil. "New York Pays Settlement to Families of Two Men Shot by Police in 1995." *New York Times*, March 20, 2009.

McKinley James C. Jr. "In Houston, 2 Cases Raise Tough Racial Questions." *New York Times*, May 14, 2010.

———. "Texas Officer Acquitted in Shooting." *New York Times*, May 11, 2010.

McVicker, Steve. "Dead, Dead, Dead: The Police Killings of Pedro Oregon, Ida Lee Delaney, and Byron Gillum." *Houston Press*, May 6, 1999.

Mears, Michelle M. "African-American Settlement Patterns in Austin, Texas, 1865–1928." Master's thesis, Baylor University, 2001.

Menchaca, Martha. *Recovering History, Constructing Race: The Indian, Black, and White Roots of Mexican Americans*. Austin: University of Texas Press, 2001.

Mexican-American Legal Defense Fund. "Hate Crimes against Latinos at Record Levels." Press release, October 28, 2008.

Mignolo, Walter. *Local Histories/Global Designs: Coloniality, Subaltern Knowledges, and Border Thinking*. Princeton, NJ: Princeton University Press, 2000.

Miles, Tiya. *Ties That Bind: The Story of an Afro-Cherokee Family in Slavery and Freedom*. Berkeley: University of California Press, 2005.

Milling, T. J. "Baytown Police Say Teen Shooting Was Accident." *Houston Chronicle*, June 28, 1997.

———. "Tension Mounts over Shooting." *Houston Chronicle*, June 27, 1997.

Mills, Charles. *The Racial Contract*. Ithaca, NY: Cornell University Press, 1997.

Mindiola, Tatcho Jr., Yolanda Flores Niemann, and Nestor Rodriguez. *Black-Brown Relations and Stereotypes*. Austin: University of Texas Press, 2002.

Mitchell, Rick. "A Little-Known Fact: Houston Is the Blues Capital." *Houston Chronicle*, September 30, 2007.

Mohanty, Chandra Talpade. *Feminism without Borders: Decolonizing Theory, Practicing Solidarity*. Durham, NC: Duke University Press, 2005.

Molina, Natalia. *Fit to Be Citizens? Public Health and Race in Los Angeles, 1879–1939*. Berkeley: University of California Press, 2006.

Montejano, David. *Quixote's Soldiers: A Local History of the Chicano Movement: 1966–1981*. Austin: University of Texas Press, 2010.

Morales, Travis. "Echoes of the Moody Park Rebellion." *Revolutionary Worker* #960, June 7, 1998, 1–2.

Morris, Aldon. *The Origins of the Civil Rights Movement*. New York: Free Press, 1984.

Morrison, Toni. "On the Backs of Blacks." *Time*, December 2, 1993.

Muñoz, Carlos. *Youth Identity and Power: The Chicano Movement*. New York: Verso, 1989.

Murr, Andrew. "Feds Take on Latino Gang Accused of Targeting Blacks." *Newsweek*, October 24, 2007.

Muse, Vance. *Don't Buy a Car Made on Monday: An Arbitrary Encyclopedia of Things to Be Afraid Of*. New York: Times Books, 1979.

National Advisory Commission on Civil Disorders. *Report of the National Advisory Commission on Civil Disorders*. New York: E. P. Dutton, 1968.

National Lawyers Guild, Anthony Baez Foundation, and October 22nd Coalition to Stop Police Brutality in New York City. *Stolen Lives: Killed by Law Enforcement*. New York: October 22nd Coalition, 1999.

Nesbit, Ray B. "Petrochemicals Future Strong, Houston to Share Growth." *Houston Chronicle*, January 16, 1980.

New York Times. "Houston Becoming Burgeoning Vietnamese Society." June 2, 1980.

———. "Masked Men Flog Woman and Caller." January 14, 1923.

Newman, Maria. "Jena, La." *New York Times*, September 24, 2007.

Nocera, Joseph, ed. *Bidness: The Booms and Busts of the Texas Economy*. Austin: Texas Monthly Press, 1986.

O'Brien, Eileen. *The Racial Middle: Latinos and Asian Americans Living beyond the Racial Divide*. New York: New York University Press, 2008.

Oguntoyinbo, Lekan. "Alabama's New Immigration Law Evokes 'Fugitive Slave Act.'" Op-ed. *Birmingham News*, June 19, 2011.

Oliver, Kelly. *The Colonization of Psychic Space: A Psychoanalytic Social Theory of Oppression*. Minneapolis: University of Minnesota Press, 2004.

Oliver, Melvin L., and James H. Johnson Jr. "Inter-Ethnic Conflict in an Urban Ghetto: The Case of Blacks and Latina/os in Los Angeles." *Research in Social Movements, Conflicts, Coalitions, and Change* 6 (1984): 57–94.

Omi, Michael, and Howard Winant. *Racial Formation in the United States: From the 1960s to the 1980s*. New York: Routledge and Kegan Paul, 1986.

Orleck, Anellise. *Storming Caesar's Palace: How Black Mothers Fought Their Own War on Poverty*. Boston: Beacon Press, 2006.

Oropeza, Lorena. *¡Raza Sí! ¡Guerra No! Chicano Protest and Patriotism during the Viet Nam War Era*. Berkeley: University of California Press, 2006.

Orton, Wanda. "Lee and Carver Were in Different Worlds." *Baytown Sun*, March 25, 2002.

Pager, Devah. *Marked: Race, Crime, and Finding Work in an Era of Mass Incarceration*. Chicago: University of Chicago Press, 2007.

Pardo, Mary S. *Mexican American Women Activists*. Philadelphia: Temple University Press, 1998.

Parenti, Christian. *Lockdown America: Police and Prisons in the Age of Crisis*. New York: Verso, 1999.

Pellow, David. *Garbage Wars: The Struggle for Environmental Justice in Chicago*. Cambridge, MA: MIT Press, 2004.

Pérez, Emma. *The Decolonial Imaginary: Writing Chicanas into History*. Bloomington: Indiana University Press, 1999.

Perkinson, Robert. *Texas Tough: The Rise of America's Prison Empire*. New York: Metropolitan Books, 2010.

Pew Hispanic Center. *Statistical Portrait of Hispanics in the United States, 2006*. January 23, 2008.

Piatt, Bill. "Origins of Black/Brown Conflict." In *The Latina/o Condition: A Critical Reader*, ed. Richard R. Delgado and Jean Stefancic, 457–465. New York: New York University Press, 1998.

Poitevin, René Francisco. "David Roediger's *Working Toward Whiteness*." Review. *Solidarity: A Socialist, Feminist, Anti-Racist Organization* (November–December 2006): N.p. http://www.solidarity-us.org/node/184.

Prashad, Vijay. *Everybody Was Kung Fu Fighting: Afro-Asian Connections and the Myth of Cultural Purity*. Boston: Beacon Press, 2002.

Pratt, Mary Louise. "Art of the Contact Zone." In *Profession 91*, 33–40. New York: MLA, 1991.

Preston, Julia. "In Big Shift, Latino Vote Was Heavily for Obama." *New York Times*, November 6, 2008.

Pulido, Laura. *Black, Brown, Yellow, and Left: Radical Activism in Los Angeles*. Berkeley: University of California Press, 2006.

Ramirez, Andres. "Latinos Vote in 2008: Analysis of U.S. Presidential Exit Polls." *NDN*, 2008. http://ndn.org/essay/latinos-vote-2008.

Ramos, Tarso Luís. "L.A. Story." *Color Lines: The National News Magazine on Race and Politics*, no. 39 (May 29, 2007): N.p.

———. "Who Gains from Framing Gang Attacks in LA as 'Ethnic Cleansing'?" *Color Lines*, News Report, *New America Media*, June 5, 2007.

Raper, Arthur F. *Preface to Peasantry*. Chapel Hill: University of North Carolina Press, 1936.

Raphael-Hernandez, Heike, and Shannon Steen, eds. *AfroAsian Encounters: Culture, History, Politics*. New York: New York University Press, 2006.

Redonet, Georgia. "The Impact of World Events on the Petroleum Industry of Houston, Texas, in the 1970s and 1980s." Honors Program paper, University of Houston, 1999.

Reidenbach, Luke, and Christian Waller. "The State of Minorities in 2010." Center for American Progress. Press release, January 15, 2010.

Reno, Jamie. "Black-Brown Divide." *Daily Beast*, January 25, 2008.

Revolution. "Jury Awards Millions to Family of Malcolm Ferguson: The Struggle Is Far from Over." July 17, 2007. http://revcom.us/a/092/juanita-young-en.html.

Revolutionary Worker. "Margarita Rosario: Fighting to Break the Blue Wall." Interview. http://revcom.us/a/firstvol/rosa.htm.

Ribeiro Sanches, Manuela. Introduction to *Europe in Black and White: Immigration, Race, and Identity in the "Old Continent,"* ed. Manuela Ribeiro Sanches, Fernando Clara, João Ferreira Duarte, and Leonor Pires Martins. Chicago: University of Chicago Press, 2010.

Robin, Corey. *Fear: The History of a Political Idea*. New York: Oxford University Press, 2004.

Rodriguez, Luis J. "Why We Need a Deeper Dialogue on Black-Brown Relations." *Huffington Post*, August 31, 2011.

Rodriguez, Rolando. "Alfonso Cook Is Rasheed, the 'Texas Chainsaw.'" *Houston Press*, January 29, 2010.

———. "Low-G: From ESL Mockery to Historic Spanish Hip-Hop." *Houston Press*, January 27, 2010.

———. "Lucky Luciano: Boss of Houston's Latin Rap Family." *Houston Press*, December 3, 2000.

Rogers, Reul. *Afro-Caribbean Immigrants and the Politics of Incorporation: Ethnicity, Exception, or Exit*. New York: Cambridge University Press, 2006.

Romo, David Dorado. *Ringside Seat to a Revolution: An Underground Cultural History of El Paso and Juarez, 1893–1923*. El Paso, TX: Cinco Puntos Press, 2005.

Ruiz, Vicki L. *Cannery Women, Cannery Lives: Mexican Women, Unionization, and the California Food Processing Industry*. Albuquerque: University of New Mexico Press, 1987.

Ruiz Mantilla, Jesús. "Más 'speak spanish' que en España." (Madrid) *El País*, June 10, 2008.

Rundell, Walter J. *Early Texas Oil: A Photographic History, 1866–1936*. College Station: Texas A&M University Press, 1977.

Said, Edward W. *Culture and Imperialism*. New York: Random House, 1993.

Saito, Leland T. *Race and Politics: Asian Americans, Latinos, and Whites in a Los Angeles Suburb*. Champaign: University of Illinois Press, 1998.

Sanchez, George J. "Y tu que: Latino History in the New Millennium," in *Latinos: Remaking America*, ed. Marcelo Suarez and Mariela M. Paez, 45–58. Berkeley: University of California Press, 2002.

Sanders, Doug. *Arrival City: How the Largest Migration in Human History Is Reshaping Our World*. New York: Pantheon Books, 2011.

San Miguel, Guadalupe Jr. *Brown, Not White: School Integration and the Chicano Movement in Houston*. College Station: Texas A&M University Press, 2005.

Schnitzer, Kenneth. "Houston Is Better Off than Most Believe." *Houston Post*, June 27, 1984.

Schuler, Edgar A. "The Houston Race Riot, 1917." *Journal of Negro History* 29, no. 3 (July 1944): 300–338.

Shah, Nayan. *Contagious Divides: Epidemics and Race in San Francisco's Chinatown*. Berkeley: University of California Press, 2001.

Sharma, Nitasha. *Hip Hop Desis, South Asians, Blackness, and Global Race Consciousness*. Durham, NC: Duke University Press, 2010.

Sibley, Marilyn McAdams. *The Port of Houston: A History*. Austin: University of Texas Press, 1968.

Silverthorne, Elizabeth. *Ashbel Smith of Texas: Pioneer, Statesman, 1805–1886*. College Station: Texas A&M University Press, 1982.

Simon, Bart. "The Return of Panopticism: Supervision, Subjection, and the New Surveillance." *Surveillance and Society* 3, no. 1 (2005): 1–20.

Sitton, Thad, and James H. Conrad. *Freedom Colonies: Independent Black Texans in the Time of Jim Crow*. Austin: University of Texas Press, 2005.

Slater, David. *Geopolitics and the Post-Colonial: Rethinking North-South Relations*. London: Wiley-Blackwell, 2004.

Slotkin, Richard. *Gunfighter Nation: The Myth of the Frontier in Twentieth-Century America*. Norman: University of Oklahoma Press, 1998.

———. *Regeneration through Violence: The Mythology of the American Frontier, 1600–1860*. Norman: University of Oklahoma Press, 2000.

Smith, Andrea. *Conquest: Sexual Violence and American Indian Genocide*. New York: South End Press, 2005.

———. "Indigeneity, Settler Colonialism, White Supremacy." *Global Dialogue* 12, no. 2, *Race and Racisms* (Summer/Autumn 2010): N.p.

Soro, Robert. "Houston Police Face Civil Rights Probe." *Washington Post*, November 11, 1998.

Sosa-Ridell, Aldaljiza. "Chicanas and El Movimiento." *Aztlan* 5 (1974): 155–166.

South Park Mexican (SPM). "SPM and Bun B at the Dopehouse." Interview. Originally posted at djscrewlagacy.com. Accessed on YouTube, August 18, 2012.

Southern Poverty Law Center. "Hate Map. Active U.S. Hate Groups." http://www.splcenter.org/intel/map/hate.jsp.

———. "The New Black Panther Party Is Unlike Its Namesake of the 1960s." *Intelligence Report*, no. 100 (Fall 2000): N.p.

Sowers, Leslie. "A Bruised and Confused City Fights Back." *Houston Chronicle*, July 14, 1985.

———. "Diversified City Economy Called Cure." *Houston Chronicle*, July 23, 1986.

Spinner Magazine. "Worst Band Feuds No. 3: Joe Tex vs. James Brown." September 14, 2003.

Spivak, Gayatri. "Can the Subaltern Speak?" In *Marxism and the Interpretation of Culture*, ed. Cary Nelson and Lawrence Grossberg, 271–313. Chicago: University of Illinois Press, 1988.

Springer, Kimberly. *Living for the Revolution: Black Feminist Organizations, 1968–1980*. Durham, NC: Duke University Press.

Stowers, Carlton. *Hard Lessons: True Story of Life in a Street Gang*. Dallas: Community Justice Foundation of Texas, 1994.

Sturtken, Marita. *Tangled Memories: The Vietnam War, the AIDS Epidemic, and the Politics of Remembering*. Berkeley: University of California Press, 1997.

Swarns, Rachel. "Growing Unease for Some Blacks on Immigration." *New York Times*. May 4, 2006.

Tate, Greg. *Everything but the Burden: What White People Are Taking from Black Culture*. New York: Random House, 2003.

Teachey, Lisa. "25 Years Later, Distrust Remains." *Houston Chronicle*, May 6, 2002.

Texas Observer. "Justice in Jasper," September 17, 1999.

Thompson, J. B. "Symbolic Violence: Language and Power in the Sociology of Pierre Bourdieu." In *Studies in the Theory of Ideology*. Cambridge, England: Polity Press, 1984.

Tolson, Mike, and Linday Wise. "Family: Bellaire Officer Shot Man Because He's Black." *Houston Chronicle*, January 1, 2009.

Traylor, Ronald D. "Harrison Barrett: A Freedman in Post–Civil War Texas." Master's thesis, University of Houston, 1999.

Treviño, Robert R. *The Church in the Barrio: Mexican American Ethno-Catholicism in Houston*. Chapel Hill: University of North Carolina Press, 2006.

United Nations, Committee on the Elimination of Racial Discrimination. "In the Shadows of the War on Terror: Persistent Police Brutality and the Abuse of People of Color in the United States." U.S. Second and Third Periodic Report to the Committee on the Elimination of Racial Discrimination. New York: United Nations, December 2007.

U.S. Census Bureau. Censuses 1970, 1980. In Archives section above see also Harris County, TX.

U.S. Department of Justice. Racketeer Influenced and Corrupt Organizations Act (RICO), Title IX of the Organized Crime Control Act of 1970, Pub. L. No. 91–452, 84 Stat. 941, codified at 18 U.S.C. Ch. 96, §§1961–1968.

U.S. Department of Justice, Federal Bureau of Prisons. "Prison Statistics." 2003. http:// www.ojp.usdoj.gov/bjs/prisons.htm.

U.S. District Court, S. D. Texas, Houston Division. *Vietnamese Fishermen's Association, et al., Plaintiffs, v. The Knights of the Ku Klux Klan, et al., Defendants*. Civ. A. No. H-81–895. July 15, 1981.

U.S. Senate. "Illegal Immigration: Border-Crossing Deaths Have Doubled since 1995. Border Patrol's Efforts to Prevent Death Have Not Been Fully Evaluated," S. Rpt. GAO-06-770. Washington, DC: Government Accountability Office, 2006.

Vaca, Nicolas C. *The Presumed Alliance: The Unspoken Conflict between Latinos and Blacks and What It Means for America*. New York: HarperCollins, 2004.

Verhovek, Sam Howe. "One Man's Arrival in Town Exposes a Racial Fault Line." *New York Times*, February 27, 1993.

Vinson, Ben. *Bearing Arms for His Majesty: The Free-Colored Militia in Colonial Mexico*. Stanford, CA: Stanford University Press, 2004.

Vogel, Chris. "Quanell X: The Houston Activist Says He's Dumped the Hate." *Houston Press*, January 14, 2009.

Vu, Ray. "Constructing a Southern Vietnamese Community and Identity in Houston" (University of Houston). *Houston Review* 3, no. 1 (2006): 27–31, 63–66.

Wacquant, Loic. "Pierre Bourdieu." In *Key Sociological Thinkers*, ed. Rob Stone, 261–276. London: Palgrave Macmillan, 2007.

Waldron, Martin. "Houston Police Man Accused of Burnings." *New York Times*, March 7, 1973.

Wallerstein, Immanuel. "The Global Picture, 1945–90." In *The Age of Transition: Trajectory of the World System: 1945–2025*, ed. Terence E. Hopkins and Immanuel Wallerstein. London: Zed Books, 1996.

Washington Post. "Fatal Shootings by Police 1990–2000." 2001. http://www.washingtonpost .com/wp-srv/metro/specials/pgshoot/shootstats.htm.

Watson, Dwight. *Race and the Houston Police Department*. College Station: Texas A&M University Press, 2005.

Weber, David J. *The Spanish Frontier in North America*. New Haven, CT: Yale University Press, 1994.

Websdale, Neil. *Policing the Poor: From Slave Plantation to Public Housing*. New York: Northeastern University Press, 2001.

West, Cornel, Jorge Klor de Alva, and Earl Shorris. 1996. "Our Next Race Question: The Uneasiness between Blacks and Latina/os." *Harper's Magazine*, April 1996, 55–63.

Western, Bruce. *Punishment and Inequality in America*. New York: Russell Sage Foundation, 2007.

Westhoff, Ben. "Not Your Father's N-Word." *Houston Press*, April 3, 2008.

Wheeler, Kenneth W. *To Wear a City's Crown: The Beginnings of Urban Growth in Texas, 1836–1865*. Cambridge, MA: Harvard University Press, 1968.

Wickham, DeWayne. "Immigrants A Scapegoat For Blacks' Unemployment." *USA Today*, August 27, 2007.

Williams, David A. *Bricks without Straw: A Comprehensive History of African Americans in Texas*. Austin: University of Texas Press, 1997.

Williams, Jakobi E. "Racial Coalition Politics in Chicago: A Case Study of Fred Hampton, the Illinois Black Panther Party, and the Origin of the Original Rainbow Coalition." PhD diss., University of California, Los Angeles, 2008.

Wintz, Cary D. "Blacks." In *The Ethnic Groups of Houston*, ed. Fred R. von der Mehden, 9–40. Houston: Rice University Studies, 1984.

Wolfe, Patrick. "Settler Colonialism and the Elimination of the Native." *Journal of Genocide Research* 8, no. 4 (2006): 387–409.

Wood, Louise. *Lynching as Spectacle*. Chapel Hill: University of North Carolina Press, 2009.

Wood, Roger, and James Fraher. *Down in Houston: Bayou City Blues*. Austin: University of Texas Press, 2003.

———. *Texas Zydeco*. Austin: University of Texas Press, 2006.

Woods, Clyde. *Development Arrested: Race, Power, and the Blues in the Mississippi Delta*. New York: Verso, 1998.

Wright, Lawrence. "One Drop of Blood." *New Yorker*, July 24, 1994.

Yancey, George A. *Who Is White? Latinos, Asians, and the New Black/Nonblack Divide*. Boulder, CO: Lynne Rienner, 2003.

Young, Cynthia. *Soul Power: Culture, Radicalism, and the Making of the U.S. Third World Left*. Durham, NC: Duke University Press, 2006.

Zamora, Emilio. *Claiming Rights and Righting Wrongs in Texas: Mexican Workers and Job Politics During World War II*. College Station: Texas A&M University Press, 2009.

Zinn, Howard. *A People's History of the United States: 1492–Present*. New York: Harper Perennial, 2003.

Page numbers shown in **bold** indicate illustrations.

Lightning Source UK Ltd.
Milton Keynes UK
UKHW010322230620
365308UK00017B/114